N CRIMINOLOGY

Social Structure Approaches

Social Disorganization

1920s-1930s **Park & Burgess** Social ecology, social pathology, concentric zones (Chicago School)

1929 **Shaw & McKay** Cultural transmission (Chicago School)

1987 **Rodney Stark** Theory of deviant neighborhoods

Culture Conflict

1927 **Frederic Thrasher** Gangs and gang typologies

1938 **Thorsten Sellin** Conduct norms, primary conflict, secondary conflict

1955 **Albert Cohen** Gangs, reaction formation

1957 **Sykes & Matza** Techniques of neutralization

1958 **Walter B. Miller** Focal concerns

1960s **Cloward & Ohlin** Illegitimate opportunity structure, delinquent subcultures

1967 **Ferracuti & Wolfgang** Violent subcultures

Strain Theory

1938 **Robert Merton** Anomie, conformity, innovation, ritualism, retreatism, rebellion

1982 **Blau & Blau** Relative deprivation, frustration, distributive justice

1992 **Robert Agnew** General Strain Theory

1994 **Messner & Rosenfeld** American Dream

Social Process Theories

Social Learning Theory

1939 **Edwin Sutherland** Differential association

Social Control Theory

1950s **Walter Reckless** Containment theory, inner and outer containment

1969 **Travis Hirschi** Social bond and self control: attachment, commitment, belief, involvement

1970s **Howard Kaplan** Self degradation

1990 **Hirschi & Gottfredson** Social bonds and self control

1995 **Charles Tittle** Control-balance, control surplus, control deficit

Labeling Theory

1951 **Edwin Lemert** Primary deviance, secondary deviance

1963 **Howard Becker** Outsiders, moral enterprise

Social Conflict Theories

1848 **Karl Marx** The Communist Manifesto

1916 **Willem Bonger** Class struggle

1938 **Thorsten Sellin** Culture conflict

Radical Criminology

1958 **George Vold** Political conflict between groups, conflict is normal

1959 **Ralf Dahrendorf** conflict is normal, destructive change

1969 **Austin Turk** Social order= pattern of conflict, laws serve to control

1970s **William Chambliss** Power gaps, crime reduces surplus labor

1974 **Richard Quinney** Contradictions of capitalism, socialist principles

Feminist Criminology

1975 **Adler & Simon** Gender socialization

1977 **Carol Smart** Gender bias in criminology

1988 **Daly & Chesney-Lind** Androcentricity, crime may not be normal

1989 **John Hagan** Power-control theory

Peacemaking Criminology

1986 **Pepinsky & Quinney** Restorative justice, participatory justice

1989 **Lozoff & Braswell** New Age principles

Convict Criminology

2001 **John Irwin, K.C. Carceral, Thomas J. Bernard** Insights from convicted offenders

CRIMINOLOGY

a brief introduction

POLICE
54018
11 23 63

Frank Schmalleger

Distinguished Professor Emeritus,
The University of North Carolina at Pembroke

Prentice Hall

Boston Columbus Indianapolis New York San Francisco Upper Saddle River
Amsterdam Cape Town Dubai London Madrid Milan Munich Paris Montreal Toronto
Delhi Mexico City Sao Paulo Sydney Hong Kong Seoul Singapore Taipei Tokyo

DEDICATION

Editor in Chief: Vernon R. Anthony
Acquisitions Editor: Eric Krassow
Associate Editor: Elisa Rogers
Editorial Assistant: Lynda Cramer
Director of Marketing: David Gesell
Senior Marketing Manager:
    Adam Kloza
Senior Marketing Coordinator:
    Alicia Wozniak
Marketing Assistant: Les Roberts
Senior Managing Editor:
    JoEllen Gohr
Project Manager: Steve Robb
Senior Operations Supervisor:
    Pat Tonneman
Operations Specialist: Deidra M. Skahill
Creative Director: Design Development
    Services, John Christiana
Art Director: Mary Siener
Text Designer: Mary Siener
Cover Designer: Elina Frumerman Design

For
Ava and
Malia

Cover Photo: NARA/President John F. Kennedy
    Assassination Records Collection
Manager, Rights and Permissions:
    Zina Arabia
    Manager, Visual Research:
    Beth Brenzel
    *Manager, Cover Visual Research &
    Permissions:* Karen Sanatar
    Photo Researcher: Jerry Marshall,
    Truitt & Marshall AV
Image Permission Coordinator: Cynthia
    Vincenti
Media Editor: Michelle Churma
Media Project Manager: Karen Bretz
Full-Service Project Management:
    GEX Publishing Services
Composition: GEX Publishing Services
Printer/Binder: Quebecor World Color/Versailles
Cover Printer: Lehigh-Phoenix
    Color/Hagerstown
Text Font: Versailles Light

Credits and acknowledgments borrowed from other sources and reproduced, with permission, in this textbook appear or on page 319.

Library of Congress Cataloging-in-Publication Data
Schmalleger, Frank.
 Criminology : a brief introduction / Frank Schmalleger.
    p. cm.
 Includes bibliographical references and index.
 ISBN-13: 978-0-13-234069-4 (pbk. : alk. paper)
 ISBN-10: 0-13-234069-0 (pbk. : alk. paper) 1. Criminology. I. Title.
 HV6025.S344 2011
 364--dc22

                    2009040083

10 9 8 7 6 5 4 3 2 1

Prentice Hall
is an imprint of

www.pearsonhighered.com

ISBN 10: 0-13-234106-9
ISBN 13: 978-0-13-234106-6

Brief Contents

Contents

Each main topic is typically presented as a two-page spread, providing all the necessary, related information about a particular topic in one spot. This modular format compartmentalizes the information, making it easy to navigate and easy to teach and learn the topics in a flexible sequence.

The book exhibits a balance between text, photos, and figures to present the information in both a text format and a visual format.

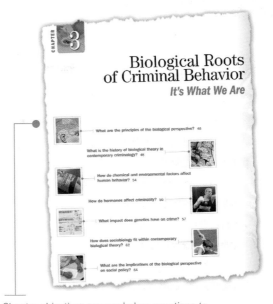

Chapter objectives are worded as questions to pique interest, focus attention on the topics to be discussed, and access any prior knowledge readers may have about the topics.

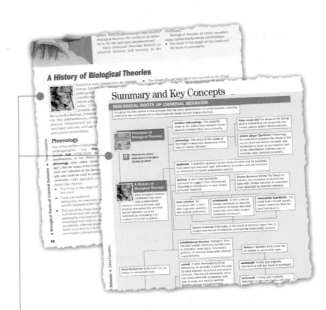

Each objective has an associated icon that also appears in the related chapter section and in the end-of-chapter material. The icon is a navigational tool, making it easy to locate explanations of or find review material for a particular topic, and is also a visual key to aid memory and retention of information related to the topic.

Some say that communism's rise and later fail in Eastern Europe means that only capitalism can provide a stable economic basis for society. Do you agree?

Socialist societies, Chambliss claims, should reflect much lower crime rates than capitalist societies because a "less intense class struggle should reduce the forces leading to and the functions of crime."

Key ideas are highlighted in blue throughout the text for easy identification of the most important concepts.

The Evolution of Radical-Critical Criminology

Some say that market societies, or those based on free enterprise, are especially likely to have high levels of violent crime. Why?

Four of the most interesting emerging theories are those of peacemaking, feminist, convict, and postmodern criminology.

Photo captions are presented as questions for reflection and discussion.

Potential buyers examine a semi-automatic handgun at a gun show. What's your position on gun control?

Multicultural and diverse societies, like the United States, find it difficult to achieve shared consensus. Here, even minor matters may spawn complex debates over the issues.

Important quotes pulled from the text reflect the central ideas in the chapter.

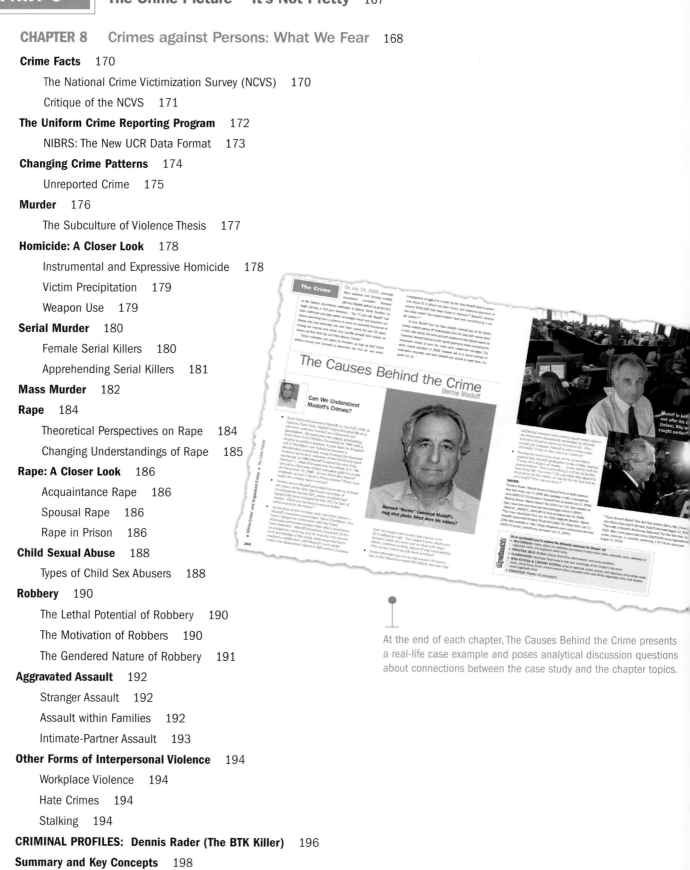

At the end of each chapter, The Causes Behind the Crime presents a real-life case example and poses analytical discussion questions about connections between the case study and the chapter topics.

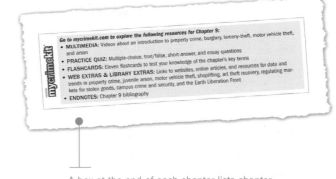

A box at the end of each chapter lists chapter-specific resources and study tools available on the MyCrimeKit website that support the chapter material (www.mycrimekit.com).

The chapter summary displays the chapter's key information as a chart with images and critical-thinking review questions embedded throughout. This visual format is designed to be a helpful study and review tool.

Preface

In crafting this textbook, I—along with the very capable people at Pearson Education—set out to provide an easy-to-use resource that would teach students about the exciting field of criminology using the learning skills that many already possess.

In recognition of the visual orientation of today's learners, we sought to achieve a comprehensive integration of graphic art with the concepts and ideas of criminology. Consequently, *Criminology: A Brief Introduction* is intensely visual. Its layout and design invite readers to explore its pages, while powerfully illustrating the critical concepts that are central to the field of criminology today. As you explore this text, the lavish use of color photographs, figures, charts, and line art will become apparent. Our intent is to visually attract readers to the subject matter of criminology, making for ease of learning. The elaborate use of visuals aids recognizes the power of graphics and the relevance of visual-based learning for today's students. In keeping with the theme of visually enhanced learning, every chapter's teaching objectives, along with its summary and key concept section, use "thumbnail" photographs that are correlated with chapter headings, allowing readers to build intuitively clear mental links among important concepts, and to remember easily what has been discussed.

Since its early days as a social science discipline, criminology has been characterized by a challenging vocabulary and elaborate theoretical perspectives that can be difficult to comprehend. Hence, our second goal was to move beyond the confusing terminology found in other criminology texts in order to provide students with straightforward explanations of criminology's important concepts and most fascinating schools of thought.

In *Criminology: A Brief Introduction*, content is made readily accessible through the use of plain language and common-sense definitions of key term. Case studies, in every chapter, illustrate the principles discussed and provide true-to-life stories of real criminal offenders. When we talk about white-collar crime, for example, the story of Bernie Madoff illustrates concepts in the area, and thought-provoking questions within the case study provide students with the opportunity to apply what they've learned. Similarly, the case study found in the chapter on globalization and terrorism explores the background and motivations of Mohammed Atta, the 9/11 hijacker who led the attacks on the World Trade Center.

By making the study of criminology both relevant and easily approachable, it is my belief that *Criminology: A Brief Introduction* provides today's students with coverage of this important field in a way that is both understandable and interesting. If you use this book, I'd like to hear from you, and you may write to me at the e-mail address below.

Frank Schmalleger, Ph.D.
Distinguished Professor Emeritus
The University of North Carolina at Pembroke
schmall@cjtoday.net

Criminology: A Brief Introduction is intensely visual. Its layout and design invite readers to explore its pages, while powerfully illustrating the critical concepts that are central to the field of criminology today.

TO THE INSTRUCTOR

A number of significant features in *Criminology: A Brief Introduction* are specifically designed to help instructors communicate the important concepts in the field of criminology to their students. They include the following:

- **Learning objectives at the start of each chapter** that are coordinated with the major headings within the chapter and also to the visual summaries at the end of the chapter
- **Highlighted text throughout the book** that makes important ideas stand out
- **Boldfaced key terms and key names** that are linked to end-of-chapter summaries
- **Circled pull-quotes** throughout the book that emphasize each chapter's central features
- **Thought-provoking questions** that are superimposed on the book's photographs and visuals

An instructor's manual with test bank, PowerPoint presentations, and computerized test bank also accompanies the text. Of special interest to instructors is a media correlation chart found in the instructor's manual, which shows the media pieces (PowerPoint slides and MyCrimeKit media, Web Extras, and Library Extras) that correspond with each heading in the text, and can be used to teach the topics under each heading.

To access supplementary materials online, instructors need to request an instructor access code. Go to **www.pearsonhighered.com**, click the **Instructor Resource Center** link, and then click **Request IRC access** for an instructor access code. Within 48 hours after registering you will receive a confirming e-mail including an instructor access code. Once you have received your code, go the site and log on for full instructions on downloading the materials you wish to use.

TO THE STUDENT

No learning tool today would be complete without the integration of the vast resources available on the Internet. To that end, *Criminology: A Brief Introduction* comes with its own website, **www.mycrimekit.com**. Of special interest to students, the site includes the following:

- **Multimedia** in the form of videos, simulations, and review sessions to provide interactive ways for readers to build upon their knowledge of the chapter topics
- **Practice quizzes** designed to help readers grasp the critical concepts of each chapter
- **Flashcards** highlighting the key ideas and important names in each chapter
- **Web Extras** providing virtual visits to sites of special relevance to the study of criminology
- **Library Extras** linking to selected documents of interest to those studying criminology
- **Criminology Blogspace** providing links to blogs of special relevance to the field of criminology
- **E-mail discussion list** allowing students and professors to interact with one another, and with others using *Criminology: A Brief Introduction* wherever they may be

To access these resources, visit **www.mycrimekit.com** and click on the cover of your textbook.

Another resource, **Criminology Interactive**, is a specially enhanced multimedia feature related to the concepts and theoretical perspectives under discussion. This extensive online media resource explores crime theories and types of criminal offenses in a fully interactive 3-D environment. Its game-like look and feel helps students have fun while learning about criminology. To access Criminology Interactive, **visit www.pearsonhighered.com/crimi**. A note on the opening page of select chapters in the book directs readers to the section of Criminology Interactive that supports the chapter.

Acknowledgments

A book like *Criminology: A Brief Introduction* draws upon the talents and resources of many people and is the end result of much previous effort. This text could not have been written without the groundwork laid by previous criminologists, academics, and researchers; hence, a hearty thank you is due everyone who has contributed to the development of the field of criminology throughout the years, and especially to those theorists, authors, and social commentators who are cited in this book. Without their work, the field would be that much poorer. I would like to thank, as well, all the adopters—professors and students alike—of my previous textbooks, for they have given me the encouragement and fostered the steadfastness required to write *Criminology: A Brief Introduction.*

The Prentice Hall team members, whom I have come to know so well and who have worked so professionally with

me on this and other projects, deserve a special thanks. The team includes Alicia Wozniak, JoEllen Gohr, David Gesell, Adam Kloza, Eric Krassow, Tim Peyton, Steve Robb, Elisa Rogers, Lynda Cramer, Santos Shih, Deidra Skahill, and Pat Tonneman. My thanks also to cover and interior designer Mary Siener and photo researcher Jerry Marshall, whose efforts have helped make *Criminology: A Brief Introduction* both attractive and visually appealing.

My friends and professional colleagues Ellen Cohn, Florida International University; Cassandra Renzi, Keiser University; the late Debra Kelley, Virginia's Longwood University; and Karel Kurst-Swanger, Oswego State University, helped in many ways. I am especially thankful to Ellen Cohn for the quality products she has created and for her exceptional ability to build intuitively upon concepts in the text.

Thanks, too, to development editor Tracey Dils and to Kelly Morrison and the folks at GEX Publishing Services for their insight and vision in keeping the development of this text on track.

This book has benefited greatly from the quick availability of information and other resources through online services and in various locations on the World Wide Web. I am grateful to the many information providers who, although they are too numerous to list, have helped establish such useful resources.

Manuscript reviewers who have contributed to the development of *Criminology: A Brief Introduction* include Wendie Johnna Albert, Keiser University; Tiffiney Y. Barfield-Cottledge, University of North Texas–Dallas; Kathryn A. Branch, University of Tampa; Lisa A. Kort-Butler, University of Nebraska–Lincoln; Michael J. Leiber, Virginia Commonwealth University; Samantha L. Lewis, Miami Dade College; Mark A. Noe, Keiser University; Cassandra L. Renzi, Keiser University; and Patricia Y. Warren, Florida State University.

Finally, but by no means least, I am indebted to a small but very special group of contemporary criminologists who have laid the foundation for our discipline's presence on the Internet. Among them are Cecil Greek at Florida State University, whose online lecture notes (**www.criminology .fsu.edu/crimtheory**) are massively informative; Tom O'Connor of Austin Peay State University, whose Megalinks in Criminal Justice (**http://www.apsu.edu/oconnort**) provide an amazingly comprehensive resource; Matthew Robinson at Appalachian State University, whose Crime Theory Links (**www.appstate.edu/~robinsnmb/theorylinks.htm**) allow visitors to vote on what they think are the causes of crime; Bruce Hoffman, whose Crime Theory site (**http://crimetheory.com**) at the University of Washington offers many great insights into the field; and Regina Schekall, volunteer Webmaster for the Santa Clara Police Department. All of these excellent resources are mentioned throughout this book—and it is to these modern-day visionaries that *Criminology: A Brief Introduction* owes much of its technological depth.

About the Author

Frank Schmalleger, Ph.D., is professor emeritus at the University of North Carolina at Pembroke, where he also was recognized as Distinguished Professor. Dr. Schmalleger holds degrees from the University of Notre Dame and The Ohio State University, having earned both a master's (1970) and a doctorate in sociology (1974) from The Ohio State University with a special emphasis in criminology. From 1976 to 1994, he taught criminal justice courses at the University of North Carolina at Pembroke. For the last 16 of those years, he chaired the university's Department of Sociology, Social Work, and Criminal Justice. As an adjunct professor with Webster University in St. Louis, Missouri, Schmalleger helped develop the university's graduate program in security administration and loss prevention. He taught courses in that curriculum for more than a decade. Schmalleger has also taught in the New School for Social Research's online graduate program, helping build the world's first electronic classrooms in support of distance learning through computer telecommunications. An avid Web user and site builder, Schmalleger is also the creator of award-winning World Wide Web sites, including the Prentice Hall Cybrary (available at **MyCrimeKit.com**).

Frank Schmalleger is the author of numerous articles and many books, including the widely used *Criminal Justice Today: An Introductory Text for the 21st Century* (Pearson, 2011), now in an 11th edition; *Juvenile Delinquency* (with Clemmens Bartollas; Pearson, 2011), *Criminal Justice: A Brief Introduction,* 8th edition (Pearson, 2010); *Criminal Law Today,* 4th edition (with Daniel Hall and John Dolatowski; Pearson, 2011); *Crime and the Justice System in America: An Encyclopedia* (Greenwood Publishing Group, 1997); *Trial of the Century: People of the State of California vs. Orenthal James Simpson* (Prentice Hall, 1996); *Career Paths: A Guide to Jobs in Federal Law Enforcement* (Regents/Prentice Hall, 1994); *Computers in Criminal Justice* (Wyndham Hall Press, 1991); *Criminal Justice Ethics* (Greenwood Press, 1991); *Finding Criminal Justice in the Library* (Wyndham Hall Press, 1991); *Ethics in Criminal Justice* (Wyndham Hall Press, 1990); *A History of Corrections* (Foundations Press of Notre Dame, 1983); and *The Social Basis of Criminal Justice* (University Press of America, 1981). Schmalleger is also founding editor of the journal *Criminal Justice Studies* (formerly *The Justice Professional*).

Schmalleger's philosophy of both teaching and writing can be summed up in these words: "In order to communicate knowledge we must first catch, then hold, a person's interest—whether a student, colleague, or policymaker. Our writing, our speaking, and our teaching must be relevant to the problems facing people today, and they must—in some way—help solve those problems."

PART 1

Criminology Explained
—The Evil Men (and Women) Do

"Society secretly wants crime, needs crime, and gains definite satisfactions from the present mishandling of it! We condemn crime; we punish offenders for it; but we need it. The crime and punishment ritual is part of our lives!"

What Is Criminology?
Understanding Crime and Criminals

What is crime and what is deviance? 4

How does the consensus perspective
differ from the pluralist perspective? 6

What do criminologists do? 7

What is criminology? 10

How does criminology cooperate with other disciplines
to solve crimes? 12

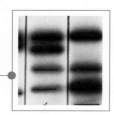

How does criminological theorizing impact the
making of laws and social policy? 14

"If you wish to make a big difference in crime, you must make
fundamental changes in society."
—James Q. Wilson

"I hate this 'crime doesn't pay' stuff. Crime in the United States is perhaps one of the biggest businesses in the world today."
—Peter Kirk, professor of criminalistics, University of California

A FASCINATION WITH CRIME AND CRIMINALS

According to social commentators, **people are simultaneously attracted to and repulsed by crime**—especially gruesome crimes involving extreme personal violence. The popularity of today's TV crime shows, Hollywood-produced crime movies, true-crime books and magazines, and websites devoted exclusively to the coverage of crime supports that observation. The CBS TV megahit *CSI: Miami*, for example, is entering its eighth season. With 50 million regular viewers in more than 55 countries, it's currently the most popular television show in the world.[2] But *CSI* programming extends well beyond its Miami-based series, and the *CSI* franchise, which now includes shows featuring New York City, Las Vegas, and other locales, is available to a global audience of nearly 2 billion viewers in 200 countries around the globe.[3] The popularity of prime-time television crime shows is not limited to *CSI*, as other widely followed series demonstrate. Included here are shows like *Criminal Minds* (CBS), *Without a Trace* (CBS), *Numb3rs* (CBS), *The Unit* (CBS), *The Unusuals* (ABC), *The*

What Is Crime?

As the word implies, *criminology* is clearly concerned with some aspect of crime. As we begin our discussion of criminology, let's consider just what the term *crime* means. Like anything else, crime can be defined several ways. For our purposes, **crime** is *human conduct that violates the criminal laws of a state, the federal government, or a local jurisdiction that has the power to make and enforce the laws.* We prefer this definition because **without a law defining a particular form of behavior, there is no crime, no matter how deviant or socially repugnant the behavior in question may be.**

Crime is human conduct that violates the criminal law.[4] Edwin Sutherland, regarded by many as a founding figure in American criminology, said that crime's "essential characteristic . . . is that it is behavior which is prohibited by the State as an injury to the State and against which the State may react . . . by punishment."[5] This is a legalistic perspective, and it recognizes that **laws are social products. The legalistic approach to crime assumes that powerful individuals who are in a position to politically influence lawmaking strategies can impose their preferred definitions of criminal behavior on lawbreakers.** By making their own laws, powerful but immoral individuals might therefore escape the label "criminal," and may also escape punishment for wrongdoings they have committed. Although democratic societies like that of the United States seem immune from legislative process abuse, history demonstrates otherwise. Consequently, crime is socially relative, in the sense that it is created by legislative activity. Without a law defining it, there can be no crime. Hence, as social scientists are fond of saying, "crime is whatever a society says it is." Later in this book we will focus on the process of *criminalization*, which is used to **criminalize** some forms of behavior—or make them illegal.

Crime and Deviance

In line with sociological thought, many crimes are seen as deviant or abnormal forms of behavior. The definition of **deviant behavior** that we will use in this book is as follows: Deviant behavior is human activity that violates social norms. Some activities, not condemned by **statute**, are nonetheless regarded as "bad behavior." Sufficiently "bad behavior" calls out for a societal response, echoing, "That ought to be a crime!" or "There should be a law against that!"

Abnormality, deviance, and crime are concepts that do not always easily mesh. Some forms of deviance are not violations of the criminal law, and the reverse is equally true (see Figure 1–1). Deviant styles of dress, for example, are not restricted by criminal law unless they violate decency statutes by virtue of lack of clothing. Laws are generally subject to interpretation, and may be modified as social norms evolve. In 2008, for example, a Palm Beach County (Florida) judge struck down a law banning baggy pants, calling the measure unconstitutional. The judge agreed with a public defender representing a teenager arrested for exposing his underwear by wearing pants that sagged.

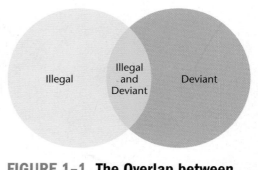

FIGURE 1–1 The Overlap between Deviance and Crime

Sopranos (in reruns on HBO), *The District* (CBS), *The Shield* (FX), *The Wire* (HBO), *Cold Case* (CBS), *NCIS* (CBS), *Prison Break* (Fox), and *Law and Order* (NBC)—along with the *Law and Order* spin-offs, *Law and Order: Criminal Intent* and *Law and Order: Special Victims' Unit*. American TV viewers are hungry for crime-related entertainment and have a fascination with criminal motivation and detective work.

Some crimes cry out for explanation. **One thing that fascinates people about crime—especially violent crime—is that it is inexplicable. While it's true that some crimes are especially difficult to understand, our natural tendency is to seek out some reason for the unreasonable. We search for explanations for the seemingly unexplainable.** How can, for example, the behavior of child killers be understood, anticipated, and even prevented? Why don't terrorists acknowledge the emotional and personal suffering they inflict? Why do some robbers kill, utterly disregarding human life?

Toward this end, people wonder about spectacular crimes, and "everyday" crimes like burglary, drug use, assault, vandalism, and computer intrusion need explaining. Why do people fight? Does it matter to a robber that he may face prison time? How can people sacrifice love, money, careers, and even their lives for access to illegal drugs? What motivates terrorists to give up their own lives to take others? Why do gifted techno-savvy teens and preteens hack seemingly secure sites on the Internet? While this text may not answer every question, it examines the causative factors in effect when a crime is committed, and encourages an appreciation of the challenges of crafting effective crime control policy.

The attorney argued that the law was unacceptable because it restricted styles of dress and empowered "the fashion police."[6]

However, some types of behavior, although neither deviant nor abnormal, are still against the law. Although speeding on interstate highways in some circumstances is considered the *nòrm* and not deviant, it is still illegal. Complicating matters further still, certain behaviors are illegal in some jurisdictions, but not in others. Commercialized gambling (slot machines and games of chance) are against the law in most parts of the United States, although they are legitimized in Nevada, some Native American reservations, cruise ships operating outside of U.S. territorial waters, and on some Mississippi riverboats. Even state governments seeking to enhance revenues allow gambling through state lotteries—which now operate in 38 states—although online gambling is forbidden in an effort to protect states' lottery revenues. Similarly, prostitution, almost uniformly illegal in the United States, is legal in Nevada if it occurs within licensed brothels that meet state licensing and health requirements.

Sagging pants. A fashion statement, a deviant act, or a law violation?

5

What Should Be Criminal?

By now, you have probably realized that the question "What is crime?" differs from the question "What should be criminal?" Everyone would agree that murder, rape, burglary, and theft, are illegal activities, but, there is far less agreement about the legal status of controlled substance abuse, abortion and "abortion pills" (RU-486 or Mifeprex), gambling, and "deviant" forms of consensual adult sexual behavior. State legislatures, along with the general public, have debated the pros and cons of same-sex marriages and certain forms of biomedical research (specifically human cloning and stem cell research).

Certainly, the question "What should be criminal?" can be answered in many different ways. The social and intellectual processes addressing this question can be found in two contrasting points of view: (1) the consensus perspective and (2) the pluralist perspective. The **consensus perspective** holds that laws should be enacted to criminalize given forms of behavior when members of society agree that such laws are necessary. The consensus perspective is most applicable to homogeneous societies with shared values, norms, and belief systems. Multicultural and diverse societies, like the United States, find it difficult to achieve shared consensus. Here, even minor matters may spawn complex

A drug deal goes down. Should drugs be legalized?

Prostitutes solicit a "John." Could you support legalized prostitution if it were subject to strict regulation?

Potential buyers examine a semi-automatic handgun at a gun show. What's your position on gun control?

debates over the issues. For example, a Chicago municipal ordinance banned giving wine to a dog, and provided that anyone who did so could be arrested and jailed.[7] While the ordinance seemed reasonable when enacted, (after all, dogs sometimes need to be shielded from their owners' indiscretions), others viewed the law as silly and unnecessary. The ordinance pitted wine connoisseurs against collectors, growers, and sellers; as well as some animal rights activists against animal protectionists and some city council members. Those favoring repeal of the ordinance argued that it was old-fashioned and reflected badly on an acceptable consumer product that is a staple of certain ethnic diets. Eventually, the ordinance was repealed, and the hubbub it had inspired ended. The debate, however, shows the inherent difficulties in

Multicultural and diverse societies, like the United States, find it difficult to achieve shared consensus. Here, even minor matters may spawn complex debates over the issues.

achieving a consensus over minor matters in our complex society.

In line with the pluralist view of crime, the **pluralist perspective** recognizes the importance of diversity in our society. It states that behaviors are typically criminalized through a political process, only after debate over the appropriate course of action. The political process creates legislation and may involve additional appellate court action to interpret the laws passed by the legislature. After the Virginia Tech University shootings in 2007, for example, state and federal legislatures reexamined gun laws to determine if new laws would keep guns out of the hands of potential mass killers. With our society's diversity of perspectives, agreement was not easy to reach—and gun control proponents won out, at least temporarily.

What Do Criminologists Do?

A typical dictionary definition of a **criminologist** is "one who studies crime, criminals, and criminal behavior."[8] Occasionally, the term *criminologist* describes almost anyone working in the criminal justice field, regardless of formal training. Today, the growing tendency is to reserve applying the term *criminologist* to academics, researchers, and policy analysts with advanced degrees who study crime, trends, and analyze societal reactions to crime. In respect to this designation, we describe highly skilled investigators, crime laboratory technicians, fingerprint experts, crime scene photographers, ballistics experts, and others who work to solve particular crimes as criminalists. A **criminalist** is "a specialist in the collection and examination of the physical evidence of crime."[9] By contrast, police officers, corrections professionals, probation and parole officers, judges, district attorneys, criminal defense attorneys, and others who do the day-to-day work of the criminal justice system are best referred to as criminal justice professionals.

Academic criminologists and research criminologists generally hold doctoral degrees (Ph.D.) in criminology or criminal justice from accredited universities. Some criminologists hold degrees in related fields like sociology and political science, specializing in the study and control of crime and deviance. Most Ph.D. criminologists teach either criminology or criminology-related subjects in institutions of higher learning, including universities and two- and four-year colleges. Nearly all criminology professors are involved in research or writing projects, thereby advancing criminological knowledge and expertise. Some Ph.D. criminologists are strictly researchers and work for federal agencies like the National Institute of Justice (NIJ), the Bureau of Justice Statistics (BJS), and the National Criminal Justice Reference Service (NCJRS), or for private (albeit often government-funded) organizations such as RAND and the Search Group, Inc.

With a master's or bachelor's degree in the field of criminology, criminologists often find easy entrance into police investigative or support work, probation and parole agencies, court-support activities, and correctional (prison) venues. Criminologists also work for government agencies developing effective social policies intended to deter or combat crime.

Additionally, private security offers individuals interested in criminology and criminal justice other career options. Twice as many law enforcement personnel are employed by private security agencies than public law enforcement agencies, and the gap is widening. Many upper- and mid-level private managers at private security firms hold criminology or criminal justice degrees.

Training in criminology offers many career alternatives (see Table 1–1). Some people trained in criminology or criminal justice decide to attend law school, while others become teachers or even private investigators. Many criminologists provide civic organizations (such as victims' assistance and justice advocacy groups) with their expertise, work for politicians and legislative bodies, or appear on talk shows debating social policies designed to "fight" crime. Some criminologists even write books like this one!

A criminalist is a specialist in the collection and examination of the physical evidence of crime. Given a choice, would you rather work in the field or in a lab?

TABLE 1–1

What Do Criminologists Do?

The term criminologist *refers to credentialed individuals holding advanced degrees in the field and studying crime, criminal behavior, and crime trends. The word* criminalist *describes people who collect and examine the physical evidence associated with specific crimes. Others working in the criminal justice system are called* criminal justice professionals.

The activities of criminologists include but are not limited to the following:

Data gathering and analysis	Public service
Crime pattern analysis and trend identification	
Theory construction	Scholarly presentations and publications
Hypothesis testing	Education and training
Social policy creation	Threat assessment and risk analysis
Public advocacy	Service as an expert witness at trial or in other court proceedings

Jobs in the field of criminalistics include but are not limited to the following:

Forensics examiner	Crime scene photographer and investigator
Crime laboratory technician	Polygraph operator
Ballistics expert	Fingerprint examiner

Jobs in the field of criminal justice include but are not limited to the following:

Law enforcement officer	Judge
Probation or parole officer	Defense attorney
Correctional officer	Prosecutor
Prison program director	Jailer
Computer crime investigator	Private security officer
Juvenile justice worker	Victims' advocate

A police training class. What's the difference between a police officer and a criminologist? Might there be some people who are both?

What Is Criminology?

This book describes various criminological theories and explains the most popular ones in detail. Let's start by defining the term *criminology*.

Theorists believe that the word *criminology* was coined in 1889[10] by a Frenchman, Paul Topinard, to describe the study of criminal body types within the field of anthropology.[11]

Numerous definitions of *criminology* are found in literature today with varying interpretations. One straightforward definition comes from a linguistic analysis of the word *criminology*, which literally means "the study of criminal accusations"—or put simply, "the study of crime."

Edwin H. Sutherland, referred to as the "dean of American criminology," offered definitions of the field emphasizing its importance as a discipline of study.[12] Sutherland's textbook, first published in 1924, set the stage for much of American criminology. By 1974, in the final printing of that text, Sutherland's original definition of *criminology* was restated as follows: "Criminology. . . includes the processes of making laws, of breaking laws, and of reacting toward the breaking of laws."[13]

For our purposes, we will use a definition that brings together the works of previous writers and recognizes the increasingly professional status of the criminological enterprise. Throughout this book, then, we view **criminology** as *an interdisciplinary profession built on the scientific study of crime and criminal behavior, including their manifestations, causes, legal aspects, and control.* As this definition indicates, criminology includes consideration of possible solutions to the problem of crime. This text (in later chapters) describes treatment strategies and social policy initiatives that grew out of existing theoretical explanations for crime.

Our definition of *criminology* shows that it is more than a field of study or a collection of theories; it is also a profession.[14] More than a decade ago, experts recognized the importance of controlling crime through the prevention, rehabilitation, and deterrence of repeat offences. In this way, our society ensures that the criminal justice system reflects the high aspiration we have as a society of "justice for all," which is characterized by the principal goals that motivate the work of the field of criminology.[15]

Notably, criminology also contributes to the discipline of **criminal justice**, which emphasizes application of criminal

A mixed group of shooters at an outdoor firing range. What's the difference between criminology and criminal justice?

law and the study of the components of the justice system, especially the police, courts, and correctional systems. As one author stated, "Criminology gives prominence to questions about the *causes of criminality*, while the *control of lawbreaking* is at the heart of criminal justice."[16]

Theoretical Criminology

Theoretical criminology, considered a subfield of general criminology, is the type of criminology usually studied in colleges and universities. Theoretical criminology, instead of simply describing crime and its occurrence, offers explanations for criminal behavior. As Edwin Sutherland said, "The problem in criminology is to explain the criminality of behavior. . . . However, an explanation of criminal behavior should be a specific part of [a] general theory of behavior and its task should be to differentiate criminal from non-criminal behavior."[17]

Criminologists have developed many theories to explain and understand crime. A *theory*, ideally, is made of clearly stated propositions suggesting relationships, often causal, between events and occurrences being studied. An old Roman theory, for example, believed insanity was caused by lunar influences and followed its cycles—hence the term lunacy.

Theories provide us with explanatory power, aiding our understanding of the phenomenon under study. A **general theory** of crime is one that attempts to explain most forms of criminal conduct through a single, overarching approach. Unfortunately, as prominent scholars observe, "Theories in criminology tend to be unclear and lacking in justifiable generality."[18] When we consider all criminal behaviors—from murder, to drug use, to white-collar and computer crime—who would imagine that one theory could explain them all? Still, many past theoretical approaches to crime causation were **unicausal**, posing a single identifiable source for all serious deviant and criminal behavior.

An **integrated theory** does not necessarily explain all criminality, but is distinguished because it merges concepts drawn from different sources. As noted criminologist Gregg Barak states, "An integrative criminology . . . seeks to bring together the diverse bodies of knowledge that represent the full array of disciplines that study crime."[19] This is why integrated theories provide potentially wider explanatory power than narrower formulations.

Both theoretical integration and the ability to apply criminological theories to a wide variety of law-violating behavior are appealing concepts. Even far more limited attempts at criminological theorizing, however, often face daunting challenges. As criminologist Don C. Gibbons notes, "criminologists have not managed to articulate a large collection of relatively formalized arguments in a general or integrated form."[20] Many social scientists insist that to be considered theories, explanations must consist of sets of clearly stated, logically interrelated, and measurable propositions. The fact that only a few of the theories described in this book rise above the level of organized conjecture—and those offer only limited applicability to other settings, and have rarely been integrated—is one of the greatest challenges facing criminology today. So, although we will use the word *theory* in describing the many explanations for crime covered by this book, the word will only loosely apply to many of the theories that we will discuss.

Edwin Sutherland, whom many regard as the most important criminologist of the twentieth century. How did Sutherland define crime?

A theory clearly explains the causal relationship between events. Offer your own theory of why people speed.

11

The Social Context of Crime

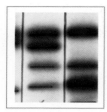

Crime does not occur in a vacuum. For this reason, we say that criminal activity is diversely created and variously interpreted—meaning that different people will have various interpretations regarding the who, what, when, where, and why of crime. We recognize in this book that **crime is not an isolated individual activity, but really a social event.**

Every crime has a unique set of causes, consequences, and participants. Crime affects some people more than others, even impacting those who are not direct participants in the act itself—offenders, victims, police officers, witnesses, and so on. In general, crime provokes reactions from the individuals it victimizes. These reactions flow from concerned groups of citizens, to the criminal justice system, and sometimes to society as a whole. This can manifest itself in the creation of new social policy, or laws. Reactions to crime, from the everyday to the precedent-setting, may color the course of punishment for future criminal events.[21]

Like other social events, crime is fundamentally a social construction.[22] However, agreeing that crime is a social construction doesn't lessen the impact of victimization experienced by people affected by crime. Nor does this statement trivialize the significance of crime prevention efforts or the activities of members of the criminal justice system. Crime has a measurable cost to individual victims and to society as a whole. Although a given instance of criminal behavior may have many causes, it may also carry with it many different kinds of meanings. There may be one meaning for offenders, another (generally quite different) for victims, and still another for agents of the criminal justice system. In view of this fact, social interest groups (victims' advocates, prisoner "rights" advocates, and gun control organizations) all interpret lawbreaking behavior from their own unique point of view. Then each arrives at different conclusions regarding resolving the so-called problems inherent in crime.

For these reasons, criminologists apply the concept of **social relativity** to the study of criminality.[23] Social relativity means that social events are interpreted differently according to the cultural experiences and personal interests of the initiator, the observer, or the recipient of that behavior. This is why **crime has a different meaning to the offender, the criminologist studying it, the police officer investigating it, and the victim experiencing it firsthand** (Figure 1–2).

Criminology's Interdisciplinary Nature

Academically, criminology is presently considered primarily a social scientific discipline. Nonetheless, contemporary criminologists recognize that their field is interdisciplinary—drawing on other disciplines to provide an integrated approach to crime in contemporary society and advancing solutions to the social problems crime creates. Here, anthropology (cultural anthropology or ethnology), biology, sociology, political science, psychology, psychiatry, economics, ethology (the study of character), medicine, law, philosophy, ethics, and numerous other fields all have something to offer the student of criminology. Other disciplines providing the tools to measure results are found in statistics, computer science, and other forms of scientific and data analysis (see Figure 1–3).

Many contemporary criminologists operate primarily from a sociological perspective. A large number of today's theoretical explanations of criminal behavior are routinely presented in the language of social science, and emerge within the framework of sociological theory.

Some disagree with people who claim that the sociological perspective should be elevated in importance in today's criminological enterprise. Those who agree with the primacy of sociology emphasize the fact that the study of crime is a social phenomenon. Central to any study of crime, they say, is the social context of the criminal event, because it brings victims and criminals together.[24] Moreover, much of contemporary criminology rests on a tradition of social scientific investigation into the nature of crime and criminal behavior,

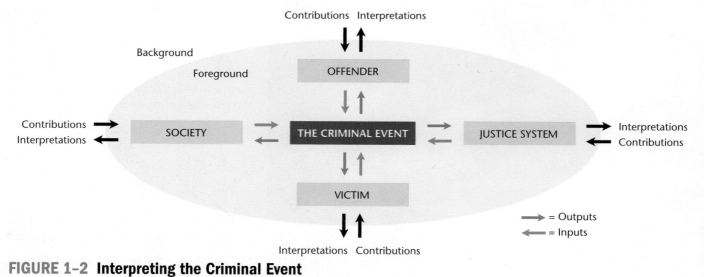

FIGURE 1–2 Interpreting the Criminal Event

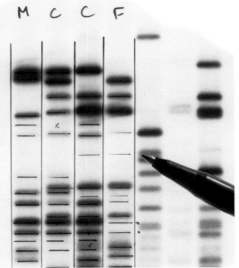

DNA banding. What does it mean to say that criminology is interdisciplinary?

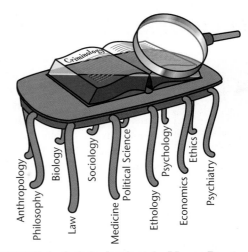

FIGURE 1–3 Criminology's Many Roots

Anthropology · Philosophy · Biology · Law · Sociology · Medicine · Political Science · Ethology · Psychology · Economics · Ethics · Psychiatry

as rooted in European and American sociological thought and traditions well over 200 years old.[25]

One of sociology's problems is its apparent reluctance to accept the significance of findings from research gathered in other fields. It traditionally has a frequent inability to integrate such findings into existing sociological understandings of crime. Another problem has been its seeming inability to demonstrate conclusively an effective means of controlling violent and other forms of crime. Diana Fishbein, professor of criminology at the University of Baltimore, says, "Sociological factors play a role. But they have not been able to explain why one person becomes violent and another doesn't."[26]

While sociological theories continue to develop, new and emerging perspectives ask to be recognized. The role of biology in explaining criminal tendencies, for example, appears to be gaining strength as investigations into the mapping of human DNA continue. One expert puts it this way: "the future development of causal theory is dependent upon our movement toward integrated theories that involve biological, social, and cultural dimensions. Our failure to achieve much in the way of understanding the causal sequences of crime is in part a reflection of our slowness in moving toward multidisciplinary, integrated theoretical structures. . . . Fortunately in the last 20 years, this

has begun to change. Today we see under way substantial research efforts that are based upon models of explanation that far exceed the traditional sociological approaches."[27]

In line with current thought, **it is highly likely sociological perspectives will continue to dominate the field of criminology for some time to come.** This dominance plays out because crime—regardless of the causative nuances identified in its development—occurs within the context of a social world. For this reason, the primary significance of crime and criminal behavior is fundamentally social in nature, and only effective social policy will effectively curb criminal activity.

A purse snatching in progress. Is it easier to explain crime, or to prevent it? How do the two go hand-in-hand?

Criminology and Social Policy

More important than criminological theorizing are social policies based on research findings. Some policy implications, those relating to the physical environment for example, are agreed on by most scholars, who determine that they are easy to implement. One example is installing brighter lighting in crime-prone areas to stop criminal activity.[28]

Other policy innovations, especially those calling for cultural or social changes, can be too difficult to implement, even when there is strong support for their likely success. In 2007, for example, an editorial in the highly-regarded British magazine, *New Scientist*, asked "why are we so reluctant to accept that on-screen violence is bad for us?"[29] The article, entitled "In Denial," noted that "by the time the average U.S. schoolchild leaves elementary school, he or she will have witnessed more than 8,000 murders and 100,000 other acts of violence on television." For children who play computer games and watch cable TV, the numbers will be far higher. Scientific studies show the obvious detrimental effects of media violence, according to the article, "yet every time a study claims to have found a link between aggression, violence, educational, or behavioral problems and TV programs or computer games, there are cries of incredulity. . . ."

A number of professional groups—including the American Medical Association, the American Academy of Pediatrics, the American Psychological Association, and the American Academy of Child and Adolescent Psychiatry—agree that violence in television, music, video games, and movies leads to increased levels of violent behavior among children.[30] A joint statement issued by those organizations says that the effects of violence in the media "are measurable and long-lasting." The groups reached the conclusion "based on over 30 years of research . . .

New Mexico Governor Bill Richardson signing a bill that makes anyone who exposes a child to methamphetamine subject to child abuse charges. How do crime control policies come to be enacted into law?

that viewing entertainment violence can lead to increases in aggressive attitudes, values and behaviors, particularly in children." Moreover, "prolonged viewing of media violence can lead to emotional desensitization toward violence in real life." Similarly, some years ago the Federal Trade Commission (FTC) issued a report[31] on teenage violence that concluded that "Hollywood aggressively markets violent movies, music and electronic games to children even when they have been labeled as appropriate only for adults."[32]

Even after these results, however, policy makers are reluctant to slow the production of violent media. For this reason, violence on TV and in

Playing a video game. Do today's media desensitize children to crime and violence?

Government policies fashioned by elected representatives set the tone for crime control efforts. What kinds of policies would you like to see enacted?

video games is still prominent in the United States. *New Scientist* says media vendors dissuade "any criticism of a multibillion-dollar business" where they would lose profits resulting from any policies aimed at crime reduction.[33]

Professional criminologists understand the necessity of linking sound **social policy** to the objective findings of well-conducted criminological research. A meeting of the American Society of Criminology (ASC), for example, focused on the need to forge just such a link. At the meeting, ASC president Alfred Blumstein of Carnegie Mellon University told criminologists gathered there that the mission of the ASC is to generate data useful in fighting crime and aiding public officials to utilize that data intelligently and efficiently. Blumstein added that he supports changing the way people think about the problems inherent in crime, because so little is known about the causes, and new insights can be "extremely revealing."

Social Policy and Public Crime Concerns

Despite American crime rates steadily declining for more than a decade beginning in the mid-1990s, concern over national security, crime, and terrorism remains pervasive in the United

> Fear of violence and concern over personal safety are once again moving to the forefront of national issues.

States. About 25 years ago, crime was the number one concern of Americans voicing opinions in public polls. Since then, concern over crime has been replaced by economic worries over job loss and personal finances. After national news coverage of seemingly random violence, however, including widely publicized shootings, cult-based violence, gang-related drive-by shootings, terrorist attacks, and highly visible inner-city crime, fear of violence and concern over personal safety are once again moving to the forefront of national issues.

A recent Gallup poll found that 67% of respondents believed that crime in the United States is more prevalent than it was a year earlier, and 49% rated the problem of crime in the United States as "extremely serious" or "very serious." While some issues, such as immigration, racial integration, and wars, have come and gone from the list of concerns identified by pollsters, crime, education, and the economy appear to be enduring worries.[34]

Even though crime rates have declined, concern over crime remains an important determinant of public policy. Here, political agendas promising to lower crime rates or to keep them low can be quite successful for candidates or incumbents promoting them in an environment where concern over crime remains high.[35]

---

mycrimekit

Go to mycrimekit.com to explore the following resources for Chapter 1:

- **MULTIMEDIA:** Interactive review about the roles of criminologists and a simulation about theories of criminology.
- **PRACTICE QUIZ:** Multiple-choice, true/false, short-answer, and essay questions.
- **FLASHCARDS:** Fifteen flashcards to test your knowledge of the chapter's key terms.
- **WEB EXTRAS & LIBRARY EXTRAS:** Links to websites, online articles, and resources introducing the study of criminology and providing foundational information.

Summary and Key Concepts

Criminology is the scientific study of crime and criminal behavior. As a field of study, criminology has a long and diverse history. Until recently, however, few explanations for crime were actually tested by the scientific community, and social policies meant to control crime were often implemented without empirical justification.

What Is Crime?

Crime is human conduct that violates the criminal law. Without a law defining a particular form of behavior, there is no crime, no matter how deviant or socially repugnant the behavior in question may be.

crime Human conduct that violates the criminal laws of a state, the federal government, or a local jurisdiction that has the power to make and enforce the laws.

criminalize To make an act illegal.

Edwin Sutherland Often referred to as the father of American Criminology, Sutherland saw crime as a social product. The laws that define what is criminal, he said, are made by people–particularly those who are in positions to influence lawmaking strategies.

Q: *What is crime? Who determines what is criminal and what is not? How are such determinations made?*

Crime and Deviance

Many crimes are deviant or abnormal forms of behavior. Not all deviance, however, is criminal, and some crimes are not seen as deviant by those who commit them, or even by significant segments of the population.

deviant behavior Human activity that violates social norms.

statute A formal written enactment of a legislative body.

Q: *What is deviance? What kinds of human behavior might be deviant, but not criminal? What things might be criminal, but not necessarily regarded as deviant?*

Q: *Should all deviance be criminal?*

What Should Be Criminal?

The question "What is crime?" differs from the question "What should be criminal?" While it is easy to agree that certain behaviors, like murder, should be criminal, it is not so easy to agree on other forms of behaviors–especially those that seem to involve willing participants.

consensus perspective A viewpoint that holds that laws should be enacted to criminalize given forms of behavior when members of society agree that such laws are necessary.

pluralist perspective A viewpoint that recognizes the importance of diversity in our society and says that behaviors are typically criminalized through a political process.

Q: *How does the consensus perspective differ from the pluralist perspective? Which would be most effective in establishing a clear set of criminal laws?*

What Do Criminologists Do?

Criminologists are credentialed individuals holding advanced degrees in the field and studying crime, criminal behavior, and crime trends. The word *criminalist* describes people who collect and examine the physical evidence associated with specific crimes. Others working in the criminal justice system are called criminal justice professionals.

criminologist A person trained in the field of criminology who studies crime, criminals, and criminal behavior.

criminalist A specialist in the collection and examination of the physical evidence of crime.

What are the duties of a criminologist? How do they differ from those of criminalists? Of police officers?

What Is Criminology?

Criminology is the scientific study of crime and criminal behavior. While some crimes are especially difficult to understand, our natural tendency is to seek out explanations for such behavior, and we look to criminology for answers about how to prevent crime.

criminology The scientific study of crime and criminal behavior, including their manifestations, causes, legal aspects, and control.

criminal justice The scientific study of crime, criminal law, the criminal justice system, police, courts, and correctional systems.

general theory A theory that attempts to explain most forms of criminal conduct through a single, overarching approach.

unicausal Of or having one cause. Theories posing one source for all that they attempt to explain.

integrated theory An explanatory perspective that merges concepts drawn from different sources.

What is criminology? What do criminologists study?

How does criminology cooperate with other disciplines to solve crimes?

Give an example of a unicausal theory of crime. Can you think of one explanation that encompasses the behavior of diverse offenders such as those who deal in drugs or participate in prostitution?

The Social Context of Crime?

Crime is not an isolated individual activity, but is a social event. Every crime has a unique set of causes, consequences, and participants. Consequently, different people will have various interpretations regarding the who, what, when, where, and why of crime.

social relativity The notion that social events are interpreted differently according to the cultural experiences and personal interests of the initiator, the observer, or recipient of that behavior.

Q: *Explain how the concept of social relativity applies to a hate crime.*

Q: *What does it mean to say that "crime is fundamentally a social construction"?*

Criminology and Social Policy

social policy A government initiative, person, or plan intended to address problems in society.

Q: *Explain the difference between social policy and statutory law. Can a statute determine or influence social policy, or is it the other way around?*

PART 2

Crime Causation
What We Do and Why We Do It

Men have always loved to fight. If they didn't love to fight, they wouldn't be men."
—General George S. Patton, Jr.[1]

"If you wish to make a big difference in crime, you must make fundamental changes in society."

—James Q. Wilson[2]

Classical and Neoclassical Criminology
Choice and Consequences

What are the roots of classical criminology? 22

How did neoclassical criminology develop and what were some of its components? 26

How did neoclassicism view punishment as a deterrent to crime? 32

What are the arguments for and against the death penalty? 34

What are the policy implications of the classical school? 38

"Nature has placed mankind under the governance of two sovereign masters, pain and pleasure."
—*Jeremy Bentham*

"People make choices, but they cannot choose the choices available to them. Nor can they be sure what chain of events will follow from their choices, including choices made by others."
—*Marcus Felson*

PRINCIPLES OF CLASSICAL AND NEOCLASSICAL CRIMINOLOGY

In the eighteenth century, a social and intellectual movement known as the Enlightenment swept through Europe. **The Enlightment was based on the idea that rational thought, and the application of reasoned scientific principles, would liberate humankind from superstitious and unfounded beliefs. This enlightened thinking would change the way members of Western society understood their world.**

The Enlightenment was a powerful intellectual initiative that fueled the fires of social change. It eventually lead to the French and American Revolutions and provided many of the intellectual foundations of the U.S. Constitution and the French Declaration of the Rights of Man and of the Citizen. It also inspired other social movements and freed innovative thinkers from old conventional thoughts. Because of this, superstitions—such as the belief that evil spirits caused people to violate the law—were widely discarded. Men and women began to think, for the first time, for themselves, and started excercising freedom of choice in their beliefs. Following the Enlightenment, supernatural explanations for human behavior were largely abandoned. This is important because, at least in Europe, free will and

A formal gathering in the late-1700s. What was the Enlightenment?

The Roots of Classical Criminology

Classical criminology developed out of the writings of a number of influential thinkers. Especially important were the ideas developed by Cesare Beccaria and Jeremy Bentham.

Cesare Beccaria (1738–1794): Punishment as Deterrence

Cesare Beccaria (Cesare Bonesana, who held the title "Marchese di Beccaria") was born in Milan, Italy. He was the eldest of four children, was trained at Catholic schools, and earned a doctor of laws degree at 20 years old.

In 1764, Beccaria published his *Essay on Crimes and Punishments*. Beccaria's purpose in penning the book was not to set forth a theory of crime, but to communicate his observations on the laws and justice system of his time. In the *Essay*, Beccaria distilled the notion of the social contract into the idea that "laws are the conditions under which independent and isolated men united to form a society."[3] More importantly, his writings contained a philosophy of punishment. Beccaria claimed that although most criminals are punished based on an assessment of their criminal intent, they should be punished instead based on the degree of injury they cause. **The purpose of punishment, Beccaria said, should be deterrence rather than retribution, and punishment should be imposed to prevent offenders from committing additional crimes.** Beccaria saw punishment as a tool to an end, not an end in itself, and crime prevention was more important to him than revenge.

To help prevent crimes, Beccaria argued, trial and punishment should both be swift, and once punishment is decreed it should be certain. In his words, "The more promptly and the more closely punishment follows upon the commission of a crime, the more just and useful it will be." Punishment that is imposed immediately following crime commission, claimed Beccaria, is connected with the wrongfulness of the offense, both in the mind of the offender and in the minds of others who might see the punishment imposed. Others would thereby learn of the consequences of being involved in criminal activity, and it would act as a deterrent for would-be offenders.

Beccaria concluded that punishment should be only severe enough to outweigh the personal benefits derived from committing crimes. Any additional punishment, he argued, would be superfluous. Beccaria's concluding words on punishment are telling. "In order," he said, "for punishment not to be, in every instance, an act of violence of one or of many against a private citizen, it must be essentially public, prompt, necessary, the least possible in the given circumstances, proportionate to the crimes, [and] dictated by the laws."

Beccaria condemned the torture of suspects, a practice still used in the eighteenth century, saying that it was a device that ensured that weak suspects would incriminate themselves, while strong ones would be found innocent. Torture, he argued, was also unjust by punishing individuals before determining their guilt in a court of law. In Beccaria's words, "No man can be called guilty before a judge has sentenced him, nor can society deprive him of public protection before it has been decided that he has in fact violated the conditions under which such protection was accorded him. What right is it then, if not simply that of might, which empowers a judge to inflict punishment on a citizen while doubt still remains as to his guilt or innocence?"

Beccaria's ideas were widely recognized as progressive by his contemporaries. His principles were incorporated into the French penal code of 1791 and significantly influenced the justice-related activities of European leaders like Catherine the Great of Russia, Frederick the Great

rational thought became the link binding all significant human activity. In summary, the Enlightenment inspired the reexamination of existing doctrines of human behavior from the viewpoint of rational thought.

Within criminology, the Enlightenment led to the development of the **Classical School** of criminological thought. Crime and deviance, previously explained by referencing mythological influences and spiritual shortcomings, came to be understood as products of the exercise of free will. People controlled their own lives, and **crime was explained as moral wrongdoing fueled by personal choice.** For this reason, the Classical School of criminology became the first modern approach to making sense of crime and criminal behavior.

The eight key elements of classical and current-day neoclassical criminology are as follows:

1. Human beings are fundamentally rational, and most human behavior results from free will coupled with rational choice.

2. Pain and pleasure are the two central determining factors of human behavior.

3. Punishment serves to deter law violators and as an example to others who might contemplate violating the law.

4. The principles of right and wrong are inherent in our nature and cannot be denied.

5. Society exists to provide benefits to individuals that they would not receive living in isolation.

6. When people band together for the protection offered by society, they forfeit some of their personal freedoms in order to enjoy the benefits of living amongst others cooperatively.

7. Certain key rights of the individual are necessary for the enjoyment of life, and governments that restrict and prohibit the excerise of those rights should be disbanded.

8. Crime lessens the quality of the contractual bond that exists between individuals and their society. Therefore, criminal acts can not be tolerated by any members if everyone wants to receive the most benefit from living in a cooperative society.

of Prussia, and Emperor Joseph II of Austria. Evidence suggests that Beccaria's *Essay* influenced framers of the U.S. Constitution, and some scholars claim that the first ten amendments to the Constitution, known as the Bill of Rights, might not have existed were it not for Beccaria's emphasis on the rights of individuals in the face of state power. **Perhaps more than anyone else, Beccaria is responsible for the contemporary belief that criminals have control over their behavior, that they choose to commit crimes, and that they can be deterred by the threat of certain punishment.**

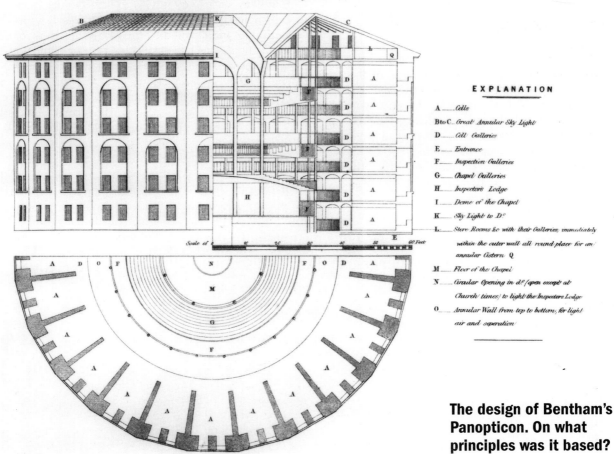

The design of Bentham's Panopticon. On what principles was it based?

Jeremy Bentham (1748–1832): The Pain versus Pleasure Balance

Jeremy Bentham, another founding personality of the Classical School, wrote in his *Introduction to the Principles of Morals and Legislation* (1789) that "nature has placed mankind under the governance of two sovereign masters, pain and pleasure."[4] To reduce crime or, as Bentham put it, "to prevent the happening of mischief," the pain associated with crime commission must outweigh the pleasure to be derived from criminal activity. Bentham's claim rested upon his belief, spawned by Enlightenment thought, that human beings are fundamentally rational and that criminals will weigh the resulting pain of punishment against any pleasures derived from crime commission.

Bentham advocated neither extreme nor cruel punishment—only punishment sufficiently distasteful to the offender, so that the discomfort experienced would outweigh the benefits gained from committing crimes. Generally, Bentham argued, the more serious the offense, the more reward it holds for its perpetrator, and therefore the more weighty the resulting punishment. "Pain and pleasure," said Bentham, "are the instruments the legislator has to work with" in controlling antisocial and criminal behavior.

Bentham's approach has been termed **hedonistic calculus** or <u>utilit</u>arianism because of its emphasis on the worth any action holds for an individual undertaking it. As Bentham stated, "By the principle of utility is meant that principle which approves or disapproves of every action whatsoever, according to the tendency which it appears to have to augment or diminish the happiness of the party whose interest is in question; or, what is the same thing...to promote or to oppose that happiness." In other words, Bentham believed that individuals could weigh, at least intuitively, the consequences of their behavior before acting, thus maximizing pleasure and minimizing pain. The value of any pleasure, or the tendency to avoid pain, according to Bentham, could be calculated by its intensity, duration, certainty, and immediacy (or remoteness in time).

Bentham claimed that the principles surrounding his pleasure–pain perspective were not new. "Nor is this a novel and unwarranted, any more than it is a useless theory," he wrote. "In all this there is nothing but what the practice of mankind, wheresoever they have a clear view of their own interest, is perfectly comfortable to. An article of property, an estate in land, for instance, is valuable, on what account? On account of the pleasures of all kinds which it enables a man to produce, and what comes to the same thing the pains of all kinds which it enables him to avert." Although Bentham's ideas were not new, their application to criminology was innovative at the time. In 1739, David Hume distilled the notion of utilitarianism into a philosophical perspective in his book, *A Treatise of Human Nature.* Although Hume's central concern was not to explain crime, scholars who followed Hume observed that human behavior is typically motivated by self-interest more than by anything else.

Utilitarianism is a practical philosophy, and Bentham was quite practical in his suggestions about crime prevention. All citizens, he said, should have their first and last names tattooed on their wrists for the purpose of facilitating police identification. He also recommended the creation of a centralized police force focused on crime prevention and control—a recommendation that found life in the English Metropolitan Police Act of 1829, which established London's New Police under the direction of Sir Robert Peel.

Bentham's other major contribution to criminology was his suggestion that prisons be designed along the lines of what he called a "Panopticon House." The **Panopticon**, as Bentham envisioned it, was to be a circular building with cells along the circumference, each clearly visible from a central location staffed by guards. Bentham recommended that Panopticons be constructed near or within cities, serving as examples to others of what would happen to them should they commit crimes. He also wrote that prisons should be managed by contractors, who could profit from the labor of prisoners. He further suggested that each contractor should "be bound to insure the lives and safe custody of those entrusted to him." Although a Panopticon was never built in Bentham's England, French officials funded a modified version of such a prison, eventually built at Lyons. Subsequently, three prisons modeled after the Panopticon concept were later constructed in the United States.

> Bentham advocated neither extreme nor cruel punishment—only punishment sufficiently distasteful to the offender, so that the discomfort experienced would outweigh the benefits gained from committing crimes.

Bentham's critics have been quick to point out that punishments often don't work as planned. Even death sentences appear to not affect the incidence of murder and homicidal crimes. Such critics forget Bentham's second tenet, that for punishment to be effective "it must be swift and certain." For any punishment to have teeth, Bentham said, it not only must mandate a certain degree of displeasure, but must follow immediately after judgement, and must have no avenue available for avoidance.

A Critique of Classical Criminology

Critics charge that classical thought doesn't fully explain criminal motivation. Other than claiming that crime is the result of free will, the personal attractions of crime, and individual choice, the perspective has little to say about crime causation. Why, for example, do some people choose to commit crime, while others in similar situations decide against crime commission? Critics point out that classical theory is largely missing meaningful explanations as to how a choice for or against criminal activity is made. Similarly, classical theory lacks any appreciation for the deeper sources of personal motivation. This includes those motivating factors represented by aspects of human biology, psychology, and the social environment. Moreover, the Classical School, seen first in the writings of Beccaria and Bentham, made claims without any scientific basis behind them. While such musings may make for interesting philosophical debates, their lack of grounding in practical, everyday social research means that any social policies based on them will be fraught with uncertainty.

Critics charged that the Classical School made many claims without any scientific basis.

The Panopticon design in practice—Stateville Correctional Center in Illinois. What did Classical criminology see as the motivating factors in criminal behavior?

Neoclassical Criminology

By the end of the 1800s, classical criminology, with its emphasis on free will and individual choice as the root causes of crime, was replaced by another theory of the Enlightenment era known as as "positivism." Positivism, which made use of the scientific method in studying criminality, is discussed in much greater detail in Chapter 3. For the purposes of this chapter, however, it is important to realize that positivism, in its original formulation, was based upon an acceptance of hard determinism, or the belief that much of human behavior—and therefore crime—results from forces that are beyond the control of the individual. For this reason, the original positivists completely rejected the notion of free will. They turned their attention instead to the impact of socialization, genetics, economic conditions, peer group influences, and other factors that might determine criminality. Hard determinism implied that offenders were not responsible for their crimes, and suggested that crime could be prevented by changing the conditions that produced criminality (see Figure 2–1).

Free Will	Soft Determinism	Hard Determinism
Classical Criminology		Nineteenth-Century Positivist Criminology

FIGURE 2–1 Classical Criminology versus Positivism—The Role of Free Will

Although positivism remains an important component of contemporary criminology, many of its assumptions were undermined in the 1970s. At that time, several studies showed that offenders could not be rehabilitated, no matter what method was tried to provide change in their attitudes. This precipitated a growing and widespread public fear of crime that led to "get tough on crime" policies and a cultural reaffirmation of belief in the rational nature of human beings. The result was a resurgence of classical ideals that came to be referred to as **neoclassical criminology**. Neoclassical criminology focused on the importance of character (a kind of middle ground between total free will and hard determinism), the dynamics of character development, and the rational choices that people make as they are faced with opportunities for crime.

The neoclassical movement appears to have had its start with a number of publications produced in the 1970s. One of these was **Robert Martinson's** national survey of rehabilitation programs.[5] Martinson found that when it came to the rehabilitation of offenders, nothing seemed to work, since most resume their criminal careers after release from prison. The phrase "Nothing works!" became a rallying cry of conservative policy makers everywhere, and the **nothing-works doctrine** received much public attention. Many conservative politicians, and some criminologists, began calling existing notions of crime prevention and rehabilitation into question. This was amidst claims that enhanced job skills, increased opportunities for employment, and lessened punishment did nothing to stem what was then a rising tide of crime.

In 1975, Harvard political scientist James Q. Wilson wrote *Thinking about Crime*, in which he suggested that crime is not a result of poverty or social conditions and cannot be affected by social programs.[6] Wilson argued instead for the lengthy incarceration of offenders and for the elimination of criminal opportunity. Writings by Wilson and others led to the development of the **justice model**, which was predicated on the growing belief that prisons do not rehabilitate or cure offenders, and that criminals *deserve* punishment because of the choices they make.[7]

For the next 20 to 30 years many states initiated "get tough on crime" campaigns, adapting the justice model to crime control legislation. In the spring of 1994, for example, California legislators passed the state's now-famous "three strikes and you're out" law. Amid much fanfare, then-Governor Pete Wilson signed the three-strikes measure into law, calling it "the toughest and most sweeping crime bill in California history." California's law, which is retroactive (counting offenses committed before the date the legislation was signed), requires a mandatory sentence of 25 years to life for three-time felons, with convictions for two or more serious or violent prior offenses. Criminal offenders facing a "second strike," can receive up to double the normal sentence for their most recent offense. Under the law, parole is eligible only after 80% of the sentence has been served.

A looter showing off pilfered goods. What role does free will play in crime commission?

In 2003, in two separate cases the U.S. Supreme Court upheld the three-strikes California convictions of Gary Ewing and Leandro Andrade.[8] Ewing, who had four prior felony convictions, had received a sentence of 25 years to life in a California courtroom following his conviction for felony grand theft of three golf clubs. Andrade, who also had a long record, had been sentenced to 50 years in prison for two petty-theft convictions.[9] In her opinion, noting the *Ewing* case, Justice Sandra Day O'Connor admitted that states should be able to decide when repeat offenders "must be isolated from society…to protect the public safety," even when nonserious crimes trigger the lengthy sentence. In deciding these two Eighth Amendment–based cases, the Court determined that imposing a possible life term for nonviolent felonies with a defendant who had a history of serious or violent criminal convictions was *not* cruel and unusual punishment.

In 2004, Californians voted down Proposition 66, a ballot initiative to change the state's three-strikes law. Passing the proposition would have meant that only previous convictions for violent or serious felonies brought and tried separately would have qualified for second- and third-strike sentence increases.

California's three-strikes law remains firmly in place today. It punishes anyone who commits a third felony with a mandatory sentence of 25 years to life if the first two felonies were violent or serious.

Rational Choice Theory

Rational choice theory, a product of the late 1970s and early 1980s, mirrors many principles found in classical criminology. **Rational choice theory holds that criminals make a conscious, rational, and at least partially informed choice to commit crime.** It employs cost-benefit analysis, resembling similar theories found in economics that view human behavior as resulting from personal choices made after weighing the costs and benefits of available alternatives. Rational choice theory is noteworthy for its emphasis on the rational and adaptive aspects of criminal offending. **It "predicts that individuals choose to commit crime when the benefits outweigh the costs of disobeying the law. Crime will decrease," according to such theories, "when opportunities are limited, benefits are reduced, and costs are increased."[10]**

WARNING

GUADALUPE IS A CRIME WATCH COMMUNITY

We immediately report all suspicious persons and activities to our POLICE DEPARTMENT

© 1982 THE SIGN CENTER, INC.   P.O. BOX 4097 SAN DIEGO, CA 92164

Two varieties of rational choice theory can be identified here. One, which builds on an emerging emphasis on victimization, is called **routine activities theory (RAT)**. A second, which is largely an extension of the rational choice perspective, is called **situational choice theory**.

Routine activities theory (also termed **lifestyle theory**) was proposed by **Lawrence Cohen** and **Marcus Felson** in 1979.[11] Cohen and Felson suggested that lifestyles contribute significantly to both the volume and the type of crime found in any society. The two believed that increased personal affluence and the development of social activities outside the home changed the nature of American society during the 1960s and 1970s. They felt this brought about increased rates of household theft and personal victimization by strangers. Central to the routine activities approach is the claim that crime is likely to occur when a motivated offender and a suitable target come together in the absence of a capable guardian. A **capable guardian**, simply put, is one who effectively discourages crime. So, a person who has taken steps towards crime prevention is less likely to be victimized. As Cohen and Felson observe, **"The risk of criminal victimization varies dramatically among the circumstances and locations in which people place themselves and their property."[12]** For example, a person routinely using an automated teller machine in isolated locations late at night is more likely to be preyed upon by robbers than a person who stays home after dark. Lifestyles that contribute to criminal opportunities are likely to result in crime because they increase the risk of potential victimization.[13] Although noncriminal lifestyles are partly the result of unavoidable social roles assigned to those participating in a given lifestyle, people generally make rational decisions about specific behaviors (such as going to an ATM at midnight in high crime areas). The same is true of criminal lifestyles. Here, the meshing of choices, made by both victims and criminals, contributes significantly to both the frequency and the type of criminal activity observed in society.

In a later work, Felson suggested that several "situational insights" might combine to elicit a criminal response from individual actors in a varied social world. Felson pointed out that "individuals vary greatly in their behavior from one situation to another," and said that criminality might flow from temptation, bad

company, idleness, or provocation.[14] Convenience stores, for example, create temptations toward theft by displaying merchandise within easy reach of customers. Other authors have defined the term *situation* to mean "the perceptive field of the individual at a given point in time" and have suggested that it can be described "in terms of who is there, what is going on, and where it is taking place."[15]

Situational choice theory is a kind of soft determinism. It views criminal behavior "as a function of choices and decisions made within a context of situational constraints and opportunities."[16] The theory holds that **crime is not simply a matter of motivation; it is also a matter of opportunity."[17]** Situational choice theory suggests that the probability of criminal activity can be reduced by changing the features of the environment. **Ronald V. Clarke** and **Derek B. Cornish**, developers of the situational choice perspective, review the choices available in criminal situations. They define *choice-structuring properties* as "the constellation of opportunities, costs, and benefits attaching to particular kinds of crime."[18] **Clarke and Cornish suggest using situational strategies like "cheque guarantee cards, the control of alcohol sales at football matches, supervision of children's play on public housing estates, vandal resistant materials and designs, 'defensible space' architecture, improved lighting, closed-circuit television surveillance"[19] as effective crime prevention additions to specific situations—all designed to lower criminal victimization in given instances.**

In brief, rational choice theorists concentrate on "the decision-making process of offenders confronted with specific contexts" and have shifted "the focus of the effort to prevent crime...from broad social programs to target hardening, environmental design or any impediment that would [dissuade] a motivated offender from offending."[20] Twenty-five techniques of situational crime control can be identified, and each can be classified according to the five objectives of situational prevention. Table 2–1 outlines the 25 techniques and provides examples of each.[21] As shown in the table, the five objectives are to

1. increase the effort involved in committing a crime,

2. increase the risks associated with crime commission,

3. reduce the rewards of crime,

4. reduce the provocatons that lead to criminal activity, and

5. remove the excuses that facilitate crime commission.

Although rational choice theory is similar to classical deterrence theory, earlier approaches focused largely on the balance between pleasure and pain to prevent criminal behavior. **Rational choice theory places less emphasis on pleasure and emotionality, and more on rationality and cognition.** Some rational choice theorists distinguish among the types of choices offenders make when moving toward criminal involvement. One type of choice, known as "involvement decisions," is considered "multistaged" and "includes the initial decision to engage in criminal activity as well as subsequent decisions to continue one's involvement or to desist."[22] Another type of choice, called "event decisions," relates to particular instances of criminal opportunity, such as robbing a particular person or letting him or her pass. Event decisions are usually made quickly, in contrast to involvement decisions that decided after months or years of thought.

The Seductions of Crime

One criminologist focusing on the relationship between decisions to commit crime and the rewards of those decisions is **Jack Katz**. In his book *Seductions of Crime*, Katz explains that crime is the result of "often wonderful attractions within the lived experience of criminality."[23] **Crime, Katz says, is often pleasurable for those committing it, and this pleasure of one sort or another is the major motivation behind crime.** Sometimes, however, the pleasures derived from crime are not immediately obvious. Moreover, as Katz points out, criminologists have often depicted crime as something to be avoided, and have failed to understand just how good some crimes feel to those who commit them.[24]

For many criminal offenders, crime is indeed rewarding, Katz says. It is exciting; it feels good, he tells his readers. "The particular seductions and compulsions [which criminals]

Shoplifters at work. How might situational crime control techniques be applied to reduce crimes like shoplifting?

TABLE 2–1

Twenty-Five Techniques of Situational Crime Control, with Examples

Increase the Effort	Increase the Risks	Reduce the Rewards	Reduce Provocations	Remove the Excuses

1. Harden targets
• steering column locks and immoblizers
• anti-robbery screens
• tamper-proof packaging
	6. Extend guardianship
	• take routine precautions:
	  • go out in group at night.
	  • leave signs of occupancy, carry phone
	  • "cocoon" neighborhood watch
		11. Conceal targets
		• off-street parking
		• gender-neutral phone directories
		• unmarked bullion trucks
			16. Reduce frustration and stress
			• efficient queues and polite service
			• expanded seating
			• soothing music/muted lights
				21. Set rules
				• rental agreements
				• harassment codes
				• hotel registration

2. Control access to facilities • entry phones • electronic card access • baggage screening	7. Assist natural surveillance • improved street lighting • defensible space design • support whistleblowers 12. Remove targets	• removable car radios • women's refuges • pre-paid public phone cards 17. Avoid disputes	• separate enclosures for rival fans • reduce crowding in pubs • fixed cab fares 22. Post instructions	• "No parking" • "Private property" • "Extinguish camp fires"
3. Screen exits • tickets needed for exit • export documents • electronic merchandise tags	8. Reduce anonymity • taxi driver ID's • "how's my driving?" decals • school uniforms	13. Identify property • property marking • vehicle licensing and parts marking • cattle branding	18. Reduce emotional arousal • controls on violent pornography • enforce good behavior on sports field • prohibit racial slurs	23. Alert conscience • roadside speed display signs • signatures for customs declarations • "shoplifting is stealing"
4. Deflect offenders • street closures • separate bathrooms for women • disperse pubs	9. Utilize place managers • CCTV for double-deck buses • two clerks for convenience stores • reward vigilance	14. Disrupt markets • monitor pawn shops • controls on classified ads • license street vendors	19. Neutralize peer pressure • "idiots drink and drive" • "it's OK to say NO" • disperse troublemakers at school	24. Assist compliance • easy library checkout • public lavatories • litter bins
5. Control tools/weapons • "smart" guns • disabling stolen cell phones • restrict spray paint sales to juveniles	10. Strengthen formal surveillance • red light cameras • burglar alarms • security guards	15. Deny benefits • ink merchandise tags • graffiti cleaning • speed humps	20. Discourage imitation • rapid repair of vandalism • v-chips in TVs • censor details of modus operandi	25. Control drugs/alcohol • breathalysers in pubs • server intervention • alcohol-free events

Source: Adapted from the Center for Problem Oriented Policing. Web available at http://www.popcenter.org/25techniques.htm.

experience may be unique to crime," he says, "but the sense of being seduced and compelled is not. To grasp the magic in the criminal's sensuality, we must acknowledge our own."[25] Katz describes the almost sexual attraction shoplifting held for one young offender. As one thief said, "The experience was almost orgasmic for me. There was a buildup of tension as I contemplated the danger of a forbidden act, then a rush of excitement at the moment of committing the crime, and finally a delicious sense of release."[26]

Katz's approach, which stresses the sensual dynamics of criminality, says that **for many people crime is sensually compelling.** As one writer notes, "Jack Katz argues for a redirection of the criminological gaze—from the traditional focus on background factors such as age, gender, and material conditions to foreground or situational factors that directly precipitate criminal acts and reflect crimes' sensuality."[27]

Situational Crime Control Policy

Building on the work of rational and situational choice theorists, Israeli-American criminologist David Weisburd describes the advantages of a situational approach to crime prevention. Weisburd points out that crime prevention efforts have traditionally been concerned with offenders or potential offenders. "Researchers have looked to define strategies that would deter individuals from involvement in crime or rehabilitate them," Weisburd says, "so they would no longer want to commit criminal acts. In recent years, crime prevention efforts have often focused on the incapacitation of high-rate or dangerous offenders so [that] they are not free to victimize law-abiding citizens. In the public debate over crime prevention policies, these strategies are usually defined as competing approaches."[28] However, Weisburd says, "they [agree] about crime prevention

Empty homes and their surrounding neighborhoods often become targets of crime. How can target hardening be used to protect such neighborhoods?

crime possible.[29] The situational approach does not ignore offenders; it merely places them as one part of a broader crime prevention equation centered on the context of crime. It demands shifting the approach to crime prevention from one concerned primarily with why people commit crime to one that asks why crime occurs in specific settings. It moves the context of crime into central focus and sees the offender as one of several factors that affect it. Situational crime prevention is closely associated with the idea of a "criminology of place," which is discussed in more detail in Chapter 5.

Weisburd suggests that a "reorientation of crime prevention research and policy, from the causes of criminality to the context of crime, provides much promise." Says Weisburd, "At the core of situational prevention is the concept of opportunity." In contrast to offender-based approaches to crime prevention that usually focus on the dispositions of criminals, situational crime prevention begins with the opportunity structure of the crime situation. By "opportunity structure," advocates of this perspective refer to the immediate situational and environmental components of the context of crime, not the sociological concepts of anomie (normlessness) or differential opportunity. Their approach to preventing crime is to reduce the opportunities for crime in specificically identified situations. This may involve efforts as simple and straightforward as **target hardening** or access control.[30]

The value of a situational approach lies in the fact that criminologists have found it difficult to identify who is likely to become a serious offender and to predict the timing and types of future offenses that repeat offenders are likely to commit. And, as Weisburd says, "legal and ethical dilemmas make it difficult to base criminal justice policies on models that still include a substantial degree of statistical error." Moreover, Weisburd adds, "if traditional approaches worked well, of course, there would be little pressure to find new forms of crime prevention. If traditional approaches worked well, few people would possess criminal motivation and fewer still would actually commit crimes."

Situational prevention advocates argue that the context of crime provides a promising alternative to traditional offender-based crime prevention policies.[31] They assume that situations provide a more stable and predictable focus for crime prevention efforts than do people. In part, this assumption develops from commonsense notions of the relationship between opportunities and crime. Shoplifting, for example, is by definition clustered in stores and not residences, and family disputes are unlikely to be a problem outside of the home. High-crime places, in contrast to high-crime people, cannot flee to avoid criminal justice intervention, and crime that develops from the specific characteristics of certain places cannot be easily transferred to other contexts.

Another example can be found in street robberies, which are most likely to be found in places where many pedestrians stroll (such as bus stops and business districts), where there are few police or informal guardians (for example, doormen), and where a supply of motivated offenders can be found nearby or at least within easy public transportation access.[32] Similarly, such places are not

research and policy: that efforts to understand and control crime must begin with [understanding] the offender. In all of these approaches, the focus of crime prevention is on people and their involvement in criminality."

"Although this assumption continues to dominate crime prevention research and policy," says Weisburd, "it has begun to be challenged by a very different approach that seeks to shift the focus of crime prevention efforts." The new approach developed in large part as a response to the failures of traditional theories and programs. The 1970s, in particular, saw a shattering of traditional assumptions about the effectiveness of crime prevention efforts. It led to a reevaluation of research and policy about crime prevention. For many scholars and policy makers, this meant having to rethink their assumptions about criminality and how offenders might be prevented from participating in crime. Others suggested that a more radical reorientation of crime prevention efforts was needed. They argued to shift the unit of analysis forming the basis of crime prevention efforts, instead of changing specific strategies or theories already in use at the time. This new crime prevention effort focuses not on people who commit crime, but on the context in which crime occurs.

This approach, which is called **situational crime prevention**, looks to develop greater understanding of crime and more effective crime prevention strategies through concern with the physical, organizational, and social environments that make likely to be centers for prostitution, which would favor easy access of cars (and little interference by shopkeepers who are likely to object to the obvious nature of street solicitations), or flashing, which is more likely to be found in the more anonymous environments of public parks.

Critique of Rational Choice Theory

Rational and situational choice and routine activities theories are criticized for overemphasizing the importance of individual choice with relative disregard for the role of social factors. Social factors in crime causation are poverty, poor home environment, and inadequate socialization of the would-be offender. One study, for example, found that the routine activities approach explained 28% of property crimes committed in socially disorganized (high-crime) areas of a small Virginia city and explained only 11% of offenses committed in low-crime areas.[33] In the words of the authors, "This research demonstrates more support for routine activities theory in socially disorganized areas than in socially organized areas."[34] So, although one could argue that the kinds of routine activities supportive of criminal activity are more likely to occur in socially disorganized areas, it is also true that the presence (or absence) of certain ecological characteristics (that is, the level of social disorganization) may enhance (or reduce) the likelihood of criminal victimization. As the authors state, "Those areas characterized by low socioeconomic status will have higher unemployment rates, thus creating a larger pool of motivated offenders. Family disruption characterized by more divorced or separated families will result in more unguarded living structures, thus making suitable targets more available. Increased residential mobility will result in more non-occupied housing, which creates a lack of guardianship over the property and increases the number of suitable targets."[35]

Similarly, according to another study, rational choice theory does not adequately consider the impact of emotional states on cognitive ability and the role of psychopharmacological agents (drugs or alcohol) in decision making.[36] The study examined the effects of alcohol and anger on aggression and found that "alcohol diminishes individuals' perceptions of the costs associated with aggression and, in some instances, actually increases the perceived benefits." Similarly, high arousal levels, such as those associated with anger and other emotions, appear to impair judgment. So, when acting under the influence of alcohol or when experiencing strong emotions, "the individual's capacity to anticipate gratification and aversion, success and failure, and cost is diminished."[37] The authors note that other studies show approximately 40% of offenders are under the influence of alcohol when arrested for committing their crimes. This suggests that future research on the rational choice perspective should include the role of emotions and the potential impact of psychopharmacological agents on the decisions made by people who commit crimes. Rational choice theory assumes that everyone is equally capable of making rational decisions when, in fact, such is probably not the case. Some individuals are more logical than others by virtue of temperament, personality, or socialization, whereas others are emotional, hotheaded, and unthinking. Empirical studies of rational choice theory have added scant support for the perspective's underlying assumptions, tending to show instead that criminal offenders are often unrealistic in their appraisals of the relative risks and rewards facing them.[38] Similarly, rational and situational choice theories seem to disregard individual psychology and morality, instead emphasizing external situations. Moral individuals, say critics, when faced with easy criminal opportunities, may rein in their desires and turn their backs on temptation.

Finally, the emphasis of rational and situational choice theories upon changing aspects of the immediate situation to reduce crime has been criticized for resulting in the displacement of crime from one area to another.[39] Target hardening,[40] a key crime prevention strategy among such theorists, has sometimes caused criminals to find new targets of opportunity in other areas.[41]

Punishment and Neoclassical Thought

Punishment is a central feature of both classical and neoclassical thought. Whereas punishment served as a deterrent to crime in classical thought, in neoclassical thinking it is expanded to support the ancient concept of retribution. Advocates of retribution see punishment as revenge.

If a person is attracted to crime, and chooses to violate the law, then he or she *deserves* to be punished, according to modern neoclassical thinkers. Because the consequences of crime were known to the offender before the crime was committed, the criminal *must* be punished in order to curtail future criminal behavior.

Notions of revenge and retribution are morally based. They build on a sense of community indignation at criminal behavior, and on the sense of righteousness inherent in Judeo-Christian notions of morality and propriety. Both philosophies of punishment turn a blind eye to the mundane and practical consequences of any particular form of punishment. Advocates of retributive punishment easily dismiss critics of the death penalty. Those critics are known to frequently challenge the effectiveness of court-ordered capital punishment on the basis that such sentences do little to deter others from committing the same crimes. Wider issues, including general deterrence, are irrelevant when a person focuses narrowly on the emotions that crime and victimization produce in any given instance. Simply put, from the neoclassical perspective some crimes cry out for vengeance, while others demand little more than a slap on the wrist or an apology from the offender.

Just Deserts

The old adages "He got what was coming to him" and "She got her due" summarize the thinking behind the **just deserts model** of criminal sentencing. Just deserts, a concept inherent in the justice model, means that criminal offenders deserve the punishment they receive at the hands of the law, and that any punishment imposed should be appropriate to the type and severity of crime committed. The idea of just deserts has long been a part of Western thought. The Old Testament dictum of "an eye for an eye, and a tooth for a tooth" has been cited by many as divine justification for strict punishments. Some scholars believe, however, that in reality the notion of "an eye for an eye" was intended to reduce the barbarism of existing penalties, where a victim might exact the severest of punishments for only minor offenses. In those times, even petty offenses were often punished by whipping, torture, and sometimes death.

According to the neoclassical perspective, doing justice ultimately comes down to an official doling out of what is deserved. Justice is nothing more or less than what that individual deserves after careful consideration of the circumstances.

Deterrence

True to its historical roots, **deterrence** is a hallmark of modern neoclassical thought. In contrast to early thinkers, however, today's neoclassical writers distinguish between **specific deterrence** and **general deterrence**. Specific deterrence is a goal of criminal sentencing that seeks to prevent a particular offender from repeating criminality. General deterrence, in contrast, works by way of example and seeks to prevent others from committing crimes similar to the one for which a particular offender is being sentenced.

Following their classical counterparts, modern-day advocates of general deterrence stress that for punishment to effectively impede crime, it must be swift, certain, and severe enough to outweigh rewards flowing from criminal activity. Unfortunately, those advocating punishment as a deterrent are frustrated by today's complex criminal justice system and the slow handling of cases and punishments. Court-imposed punishments are rarely swift in imposition, due to inherent delays in judicial proceedings and stalling tactics used by defense counsel. Similarly, certainty of punishment is practically nonexistent because of ongoing appeals and stumbling blocks built into the system. Often, punishments are ordered and not fully carried out. In contemporary America,

A stoning in ancient times. Why do we say that "notions of revenge and retribution" are morally based?

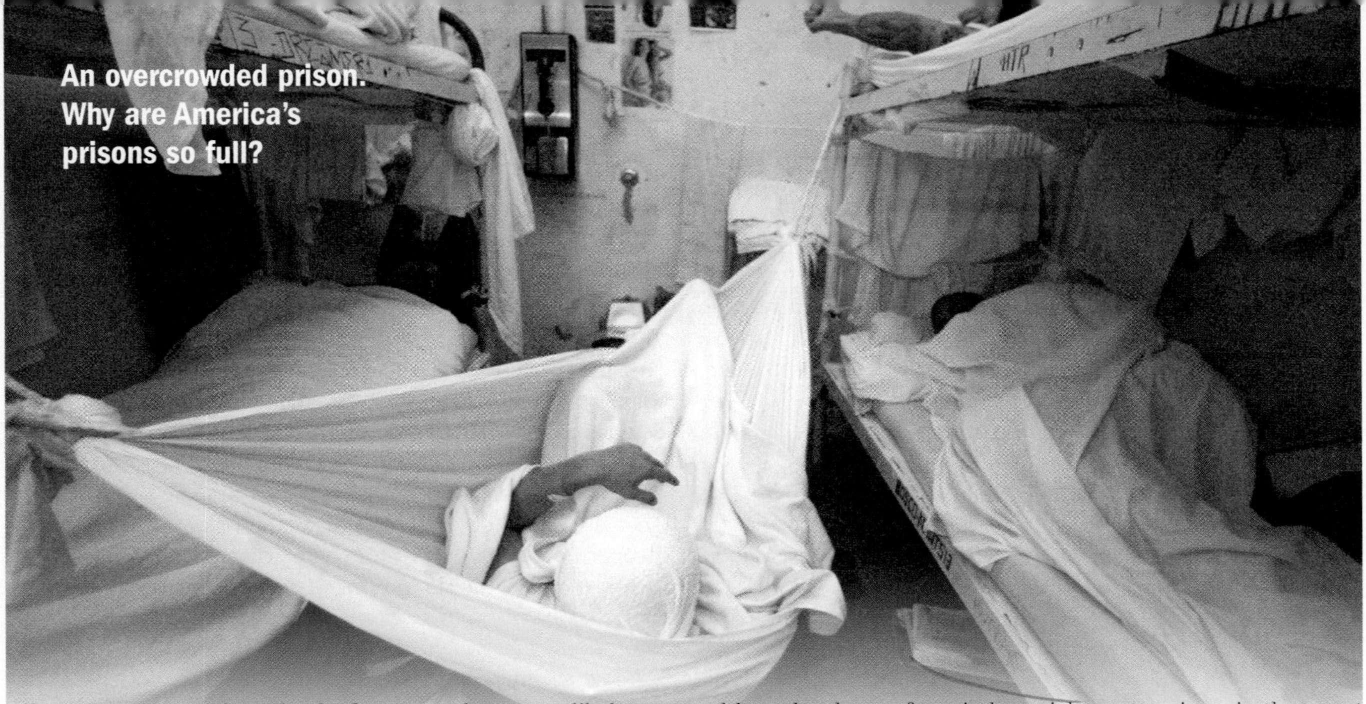

An overcrowded prison. Why are America's prisons so full?

offenders sentenced to death, for example, are unlikely to ever have their sentences finalized. For those who do, an average of nearly 12 years passes between the time a sentence of death is imposed and the time it is carried out.[42] Death row inmates and their lawyers typically solicit appeals at various courts to delay or derail the process of justice. Some win new trials while others receive overturned sentences by blanket U.S. Supreme Court rulings finding fault or trial error. Many others die of natural causes before the notion of fair process is actually served.

If the neoclassicists are correct, criminal punishments should ideally prevent a repetition of crime. Unfortunately, as high rates of contemporary recidivism indicate, punishments in America rarely accomplish that goal. **Recidivism** means repeating criminal behavior by those already involved in crime. Recidivism can also be used to measure the success of a given approach to the problem of crime. When so employed, it is referred to as a recidivism rate, expressed as the percentage of convicted offenders released from prison who are later rearrested for a new crime, generally within five years following release. Some studies show high recidivism rates, reaching 80% to 90%, meaning that eight or nine of every ten criminal offenders released from confinement are rearrested, for new crimes within five years of release. Such studies, however, do not measure how many released offenders return to crime but are not caught; nor do they identify those who return to crime more than five years after release from prison. Were such numbers available, recidivism rates would likely be even higher.

One reason American criminal justice seems so ineffectual at preventing crime and reducing recidivism may be that the punishments that contemporary criminal law provides are rarely applied to most offenders. Statistics show that few lawbreakers are ever arrested, and that of those who are, fewer still are convicted of the crimes with which they have been charged. After lengthy court proceedings, most offenders processed by the justice system are released, fined, or placed on probation. Relatively few are sent to prison,

although, short of capital punishment, prison is the most severe form of punishment available to authorities today. To represent this situation, criminal justice experts often use a diagram known as a "crime funnel." Figure 2–2 shows the crime funnel for 2008. As the figure shows, fewer than 1% of criminal law violators in America can be expected to spend time in prison as punishment for their crimes.

Complicating the situation is the fact that few inmates ever serve their full sentences. Many serve only a small fraction of their sentences, with early release for good behavior, mandated reentry training, and the practical considerations necessitated by prison overcrowding.

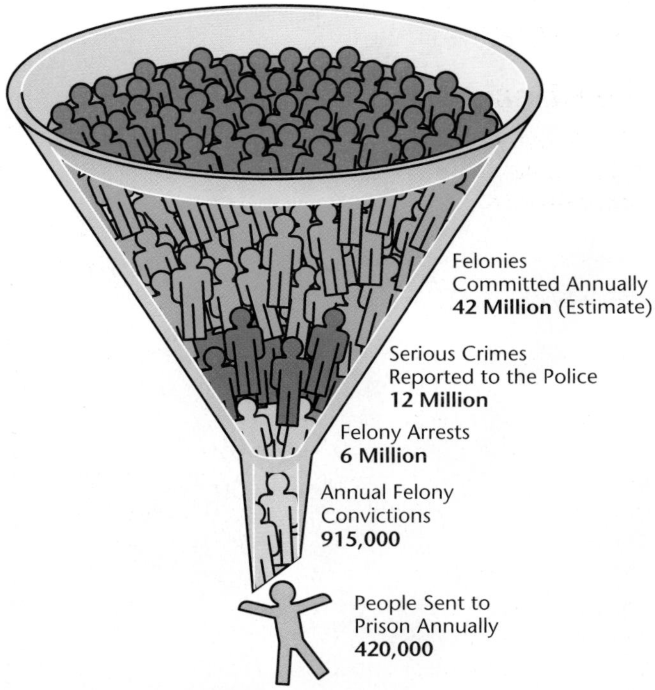

Felonies Committed Annually **42 Million** (Estimate)

Serious Crimes Reported to the Police **12 Million**

Felony Arrests **6 Million**

Annual Felony Convictions **915,000**

People Sent to Prison Annually **420,000**

FIGURE 2–2 **The Crime Funnel**

Source: Statistics derived from the Bureau of Justice Statistics, Sourcebook of Criminal Justice Statistics, 2008 (Washington, DC: National Institute of Justice, 2007).

The Death Penalty

Notions of deterrence, retribution, and just deserts all come together in **capital punishment**. The many different understandings of crime and crime control, along with arguments over free will and social determinism, combine with varying philosophies of punishment to produce considerable disagreement over death as an appropriate form of criminal sanction.

Opponents of capital punishment make ten kinds of claims:

1. Capital punishment does not deter crime.
2. The death penalty has, at times, been imposed on innocent people, with no workable system currently in place to prevent the accidental execution of innocents.
3. Human life is sacred, even the life of a murderer.
4. State-imposed death lowers society to the same moral (or amoral) level as the murderer.
5. The death penalty has been haphazardly imposed in seemingly random fashion.
6. The death penalty is imposed disproportionately on minority offenders.
7. Capital punishment goes against most fundamental precepts of organized religion.
8. The death penalty is more expensive than imprisonment.
9. Internationally, capital punishment is widely viewed as inhumane and barbaric.
10. A viable alernative exists in life imprisonment without the possibility of parole.

Advocates of capital punishment discount each of these claims by countering abolitionist arguments of injustice with the proposition that death is *deserved* by those who commit especially heinous acts. Some argue that people deserve to die as retribution for their crime. These arguments have evolved from a natural law perspective, are sometimes supported on religious grounds, and are often based on the notion of just deserts, as discussed earlier.

Strong feelings on both sides of the issue have generated studies of the effectiveness and fairness of capital punishment as a criminal sanction. Although one might expect study results to have produced some agreement, just the opposite seems to have occurred. A relative impasse exists as to the proper interpretation of most death penalty studies. How the death penalty acts as a general deterrent, for example, has been widely examined. Some researchers[43] have compared murder rates between states eliminating the death penalty and those that retain it, finding little variation in recorded murder rates. Others looked at variations in murder rates over time in jurisdictions eliminating capital punishment, with similar results.[44] A now classic 1988 Texas study provided a comprehensive review of capital punishment by correlating homicide rates with the rate of executions within the state between 1930 and 1986.[45] The study, which was especially important because Texas actively employs capital punishment, failed to find any support for the use of death as a deterrent.

Regardless of studies to the contrary, **many capital punishment advocates remain unconvinced that the threat of death cannot be an effective deterrent.** As with other punishments, a swift and certain death penalty, they point out, is likely to deter others. As noted earlier, however, modern-day capital punishment rarely meets these requirements because offenders sentenced to death are unlikely to ever have their sentences finalized.[46] Even if the threat of death does not effectively deter others, advocates of capital punishment say it will ensure that the people put to death will never commit another crime.

An anti-capital punishment protest. How do you feel about the death penalty?

Capital Punishment and Ethnicity

According to the Washington-based Death Penalty Information Center,[47] the death penalty has been imposed disproportionately on racial minorities throughout most of American history. Statistics maintained by the center show that "since 1930 nearly 90% of those executed for the crime of rape in this country were African Americans. Currently, about 50% of those on the nation's death rows are from minority populations representing 20% of the country's population." The center, a fervent anti–capital punishment organization, claims that "evidence of racial discrimination in the application of capital punishment continues. Nearly 40% of those executed since 1976 have been black [Figure 2–3], even though blacks constitute only 12% of the [nation's total] population. And in almost every death penalty case, the race of the victim is white." In 1996 alone, according to the center, "89% of the death sentences carried out involved white victims, even though 50% of the homicides in this country have black victims. Of the 229 executions that have occurred since the death penalty was reinstated [in 1972]," says the center, "only one has involved a white defendant for the murder of a black person." Figure 2–4 provides this information visually.

A 1994 congressional report by the Subcommittee on Civil and Constitutional Rights[48] reached much the same conclusion. The report, entitled *Racial Disparities in Federal Death Penalty Prosecutions 1988–1994*, had this to say about ethnicity and capital punishment under federal law:

> Racial minorities are being prosecuted under federal death penalty law far beyond their proportion in the general population or the population of criminal offenders. Analysis of prosecutions under the federal death penalty provisions of the Anti-Drug Abuse Act of 1988 reveals that 89% of the defendants selected for capital prosecution have been either African-American or Mexican-American. Moreover, the number of prosecutions under this Act has been increasing over the past two years with no decline in racial disparities. All ten of the recently approved federal capital prosecutions have been against black defendants. This pattern of inequality adds to the mounting evidence that race continues to play an unacceptable part of the application of capital punishment in American today.

The report was prepared with the assistance of the Death Penalty Information Center.

On the other hand, capital punishment advocates say that the real question is not whether differences exist in the rate of imposition among ethnic populations of the death penalty, but whether the penalty is *fairly* imposed. They argue, for example, that if 50% of all capital punishment–eligible crimes were committed by members of a particular, but relatively small, ethnic group, then anyone anticipating fairness in imposition of the death penalty would expect to see 50% of death row populations composed of members of that group—no matter how small the group. In like manner, one would also expect to see the same relative ethnicity among those executed. In short, they say, if fairness is to be any guide, those committing capital crimes should be the ones sentenced to death—regardless of ethnicity, gender, or other similar social characteristics.

Although evidence may suggest that African-Americans and other minorities in the United States have in the past been unfairly sentenced to die,[49] the present evidence is not so clear. For an accurate appraisal to be made, any claims of disproportionality must go beyond simple comparisons with racial representation in the larger population and must somehow measure both the frequency and the seriousness of capital crimes between and within racial groups. Following that line of reasoning, the Supreme Court in the 1987 case of *McCleskey* v. *Kemp*,[50] held that a simple showing of racial discrepancies in the application of the death penalty does not amount to a constitutional violation.

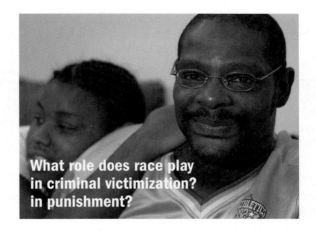

What role does race play in criminal victimization? in punishment?

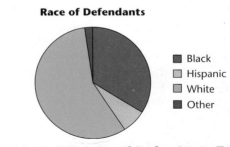

Race of Defendants

- ■ Black
- ■ Hispanic
- ■ White
- ■ Other

FIGURE 2–3 Ethnicity of Defendants Executed in the United States, 1976–2009

Source: Death Penalty Information Center. Website available at http://www.deathpenaltyinfo.org/race-death-row-inmates-executed-1976 (data current as of March 25, 2009).

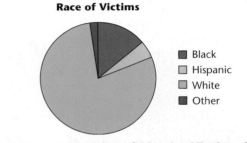

Race of Victims

- ■ Black
- ■ Hispanic
- ■ White
- ■ Other

FIGURE 2–4 Ethnicity of Murder Victims in the United States, 1976–2009

Source: Death Penalty Information Center. Website available at http://www.deathpenaltyinfo.org/race-death-row-inmates-executed-1976 (data current as of March 25, 2009).

In order to reduce the likelihood that capital punishment decisions will be influenced by a defendant's race, the Washington-based Constitution Project[51] recently recommended that "all jurisdictions that impose the death penalty should create mechanisms to help ensure that the death penalty is not imposed in a racially discriminatory manner."[52] The project said that two approaches are especially appropriate in building such mechanisms: (1) the gathering of statistical data on the role of ethnicity in the operation of a jurisdiction's capital punishment system and (2) the active involvement of members of all ethnic groups in every level of the capital punishment decision-making process.

A Flawed System?

In 1996, researchers at the Institute for Law and Justice in Alexandria, Virginia, published *Convicted by Juries, Exonerated by Science*, a report funded by the National Institute of Justice.[53] The study reviewed 28 cases where postconviction DNA evidence conclusively exonerated defendants sentenced to lengthy prison terms. The 28 cases were selected on the basis of a detailed examination of records indicating the convicted defendants actually might have been innocent. The men in the study had served an average of seven years in prison, and most were tried and sentenced prior to the widespread availability of reliable DNA testing—although eyewitness testimony and other forensic evidence sealed their convictions. In each case, the DNA results unequivocally demonstrated that the defendants were wrongfully convicted, and each defendant was ultimately set free. Although the study did not specifically involve the death penalty, *Convicted by Juries* showed just how fallible the judicial process can be for those convicted.

More recent studies focus on claimed injustices inherent in the sentencing process, leading to imposition of the death penalty and the seemingly unfair application of capital punishment sentences. In 2000, for example, a nonprofit group, the Texas Defender Service, examined hundreds of capital trials and appeals, including every published death penalty decision handed down by the Texas Court of Criminal Appeals (the state's highest criminal court) since 1976.[54] The study found, among other things, that (1) poor clients routinely received bad representation by court-appointed attorneys, (2) ethnicity influenced the administration of capital punishment because prosecutors are far more likely to ask for the death sentence in cases where the victim is white as opposed to African-American, and (3) African-Americans and Hispanics are often excluded from being chosen to serve on capital juries. The report also identified instances in which prosecutors intentionally distorted the truth in order to win convictions, cases involving the use of courtroom testimony from disbarred psychiatrists, and examples of the use of unreliable "jailhouse informers" in capital cases.

A 2000 U.S. Department of Justice (DOJ) study found significant racial and geographic disparities in the imposition of federal death sentences.[55] The study revealed that 80% of the 682 defendants who have faced capital charges in federal courts since 1995 have been African-American. Perhaps even more significant, U.S. attorneys in only 49 of the nation's 94 judicial districts have prosecuted defendants for capital crimes. Critics of the study noted that such numbers are meaningless, unless compared with actual proportions of minority defendants qualifying for capital prosecution. The fact that few crimes qualify for prosecution as capital offenses might explain the lack of death penalty prosecution. This is opposed to the belief that there might have been discretion or less-than-eager efforts exhibited by the prosecuting attorneys in seeking those death penalty convictions.

A potentially more significant study was conducted by Columbia University Law School professors James Liebman and Jeffrey Fagan. Liebman and Fagan examined 4,578 death penalty appeals during the years 1973–1995[56] and found that most cases were seriously flawed, necessitating retrials. Death sentence convictions were thrown out in 68% of the state or federal court cases analyzed. This means that appellate courts found serious, reversible errors in almost seven out of every ten cases involving capital sentences. Eighty-two percent of defendants with overturned death sentences by state appellate courts due to serious error were found to deserve a sentence less than death. Of these, 7% were found to be innocent of the capital crime charged. According to the study's authors, "Our 23 years worth of findings reveal a capital punishment system collapsing under the weight of its own mistakes."

According to the Death Penalty Information Center, 114 people in 25 states were released from death rows across the United States between 1973 and mid-2004 after proof of their innocence became available.[57] Figure 2–5 shows such releases on a state-by-state basis.

Studies like these have led to an official rethinking of the death penalty in some parts of the country, contributing to what some have called a moratorium movement focused on reform of capital punishment laws.[58] In January 2000, for example, Illinois governor George Ryan suspended executions after DNA results showed conclusively that 13 death row prisoners were innocent. Ryan appointed a commission to study capital punishment in Illinois and to determine what reforms could ensure a fair and impartial capital punishment system. In 2002, after 24 months of discussions, the governor's commission concluded that "if capital punishment is to continue to be imposed in Illinois, achieving a higher degree of confidence in the outcomes will require a significant increase in public funding at virtually every level, ranging from investigation through trial and its aftermath." The commission's report contained 85 recommendations reforming what the members of the commission saw as a broken system.[59] Recommendations included videotaping all police questioning of capital suspects and revising procedures for police lineups intended to lead to eyewitness identification. The commission also recommended limiting applicability of the death penalty to "cases where the defendant has murdered two or more persons, a police officer, firefighter; correctional institution officer or inmate; murdered to obstruct the justice system; or tortured the victim in the course of the murder." Finally, the commission recommended "the death penalty be barred in certain instances because of the character of the evidence or the defendant." Capital punishment, said the commission, should not be available when a conviction is based solely on

FIGURE 2–5 Death Row Prisoners Exonerated and Freed since 1973

Source: Death Penalty Information Center.

the testimony of a single eyewitness or evidence provided by an in-custody informant.

On May 9, 2002, Maryland became the second state to declare a moratorium on executions on order of Governor Parris N. Glendening. The governor decided that "reasonable questions have been raised in Maryland and across the country about the application of the death penalty."[60] Glendening wanted to have an opportunity to consider the results of a two-year University of Maryland study (pending release) examining the effects of racial and jurisdictional factors on imposing capital punishment.

In May 2000, the New Hampshire legislature voted to abolish the death penalty. In doing so, it became the first state legislature to cast such a vote since the U.S. Supreme Court's 1976 decision in *Gregg* v. *Georgia*,[61] which invalidated how capital punishment was imposed in a number of jurisdictions. New Hampshire's governor subsequently vetoed the legislation.

On March 18, 2009, New Mexico became the fifteenth state to abolish capital punishment when Governor Bill Richardson signed House Bill 285. The governor told reporters gathered for the signing that "This has been the most difficult decision of my political career."[62] He went on to say that "I do not have confidence in the criminal justice system as it currently operates to be the final arbiter when it comes to who lives and who dies for their crime.... If the State is going to undertake this awesome responsibility, the system to impose this ultimate penalty must be perfect and can never be wrong." The new law also created a sentence of life without the possibility of parole for those commiting the most heinous crimes.

Not all state governors are convinced that the death penalty should be abolished. Instead, some, like former Massachusetts governor Mitt Romney, believe that capital punishment should be revived. Massachusetts abolished the death penalty in 1984, and has not carried out an execution since 1947.[63] In 2003, however, Governor Romney, having campaigned in favor of the death penalty, established the Governor's Council on Capital Punishment to restore the

death penalty in his state. Romney told constituents he sought to avoid the problems that have cast the death sentencing systems of other states into doubt. The council's report, issued in 2004, included a recommended requirement that physical or scientific evidence like DNA be used to corroborate guilt during the sentencing phase of trial. Jurors would also be informed of the demonstrated fallibility of human evidence and eyewitness testimony. Were the state to follow the council's recommendations, jurors would be told that, in order to impose a sentence of death, they must find that there is "no doubt" about the defendant's guilt—a much higher standard of proof than the reasonable doubt standard used elsewhere. Finally, in 2006, the New Jersey legislature voted to suspend use of the death penalty until a state task force reported on whether capital punishment is fairly imposed.[64]

In 2004, recognizing that DNA testing exonerates the innocent, President George W. Bush signed the Innocence Protection Act[65] into law. The Innocence Protection Act provides federal funds to eliminate the backlog of unanalyzed DNA samples in the nation's crime laboratories.[66] It sets aside money to improve the capacity of federal, state, and local crime laboratories to conduct DNA analyses.[67] The act also eases access to postconviction DNA testing for those serving time in state[68] or federal prisons or on death row, and sets forth conditions under which a federal prisoner asserting innocence may obtain postconviction DNA testing of specific evidence. Similarly, the legislation requires the preservation of biological evidence by federal law enforcement agencies for any defendant under a sentence of imprisonment or death.

Not all claims of innocence are supported by DNA tests, however. In 2006, for example, DNA test results confirmed the guilt of Roger Keith Coleman, a Virginia coal miner who had steadfastly maintained his innocence until he was executed in 1992. Coleman, executed for the rape and murder of his sister-in-law, Wanda McCoy, in 1981, died declaring his innocence and proclaiming that he would one day be exonerated. His case became a rallying point for death penalty opponents, who convinced Virginia governor Mark Warner to order DNA tests on surviving evidence. Coleman's supporters claimed that the tests would provide the first scientific proof that an innocent man had been executed in the United States. Results from the tests, however, conclusively showed that blood and semen found at the crime scene had come from Coleman.[69]

Policy Implications of the Classical School

A few years ago, Lawrence Sherman of the University of Pennsylvania described four paradigms of justice, shown in Figure 2–6.[70] As shown, each form of justice is described in terms of whether it presumes either a rational or an emotional basis for crime, along with a societal response to criminality. According to Sherman, two types of justice, one rational (deterrence-focused) and the other emotional (retribution-focused), "have competed for primacy" since the dawn of the modern era. Combining those two perspectives on justice with notions of either a rational or an emotional offender yields the four paradigms in the figure.

The first paradigm, *expressive economics*, assumes that crime is a rational act. The justice philosophy that undergirds it uses "punishment as a symbolic *expression* of the emotions of anger and outrage by the state and society at the act of a criminal." Expressive economics uses the criminal law and the justice system in an emotional society as a combined means of expressing feelings and inflicting retribution on offenders who decide to violate the law. This, says Sherman, is the "paradigm that dominates current practice." It is also why so many people are unfulfilled by the justice process. "Few of us," says Sherman, "expect much justice from an expressive state that dramatizes its outrage at a rational offender who coolly calculates costs and benefits."[71]

Another important justice paradigm is a kind of *rational economics*, where an assumed-to-be-purposeful offender encounters a justice system based on rational—rather than emotional—principles. Such a system employs punishment to make the economics of crime more favorable to law-abiding rather than to lawbreaking behavior. This kind of rational economics favors deterrence and most closely mirrors the principles of classical and neoclassical thought discussed earlier.

During the past 30 years or so, a mixed American justice philosophy of expressive and rational economics has led to the rational punishment practices of determinate sentencing and truth in sentencing. The emotional consequences of long prison terms and a renewed interest in capital punishment has naturally followed as well. Since the central feature of classical and neoclassical thought is rationality, we review determinate sentencing and truth in sentencing as natural consequences of a classical view of crime and justice.

Determinate sentencing is a strategy that mandates a specified and fixed amount of time to be served for every offense category. Under determinate sentencing schemes judges may be required to impose seven-year sentences on armed robbers, but only one-year sentences on strong-armed robbers (who use no weapon). Determinate sentencing schemes build upon the twin notions of classical thought that (1) the pleasure of a given crime can be somewhat accurately

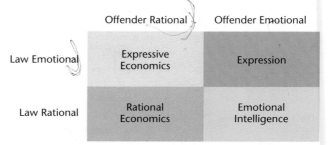

FIGURE 2–6 Lawrence W. Sherman's Paradigms of Justice

Source: Lawrence W. Sherman, "Reason for Emotion: Reinventing Justice with Theories, Innovations, and Research: The American Society of Criminology 2002 Presidential Address," *Criminology*, Vol. 41, No. 1 (2003), pp. 1-37.

assessed, and (2) a fixed amount of punishment necessary for deterrence can be calculated and specified. **Truth in sentencing** requires judges to assess and publish the actual time an offender will serve once sentenced to prison. Many recently enacted truth-in-sentencing laws require that offenders serve a large portion of their sentence (often 80%) before their release.

Because of the widespread implementation of determinate sentencing strategies and the passage of truth-in-sentencing laws during the last quarter century, prison populations today are larger than ever before. By mid-2003, the nation's state and federal prison population (excluding jails) stood at 1,380,776 inmates, a figure that represented an increase of more than 700% since 1970. Figure 2–7 shows the total U.S. prison population from 1960 to 2006.

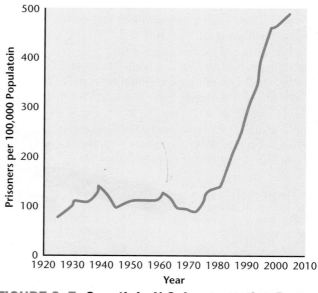

FIGURE 2–7 Growth in U.S. Incarceration Rate, 1924–2008

Source: Pennsylvania Prison Society.

Imprisonment is one component of an incapacitation strategy. **Incapacitation**, simply put, is the use of imprisonment or other means to reduce the likelihood that an offender will be capable of committing future offenses.

Proponents of modern-day incapacitation often distinguish between selective incapacitation, where crime is controlled via the imprisonment of specific individuals, and collective incapacitation, whereby changes in legislation and/or sentencing patterns lead to removing dangerous individuals from society. Advocates of selective incapacitation as a crime control strategy point to studies that show the majority of crimes are perpetrated by a small number of hard-core repeat offenders. The most famous of those studies, conducted by University of Pennsylvania Professor Marvin Wolfgang, focused on 9,000 men born in Philadelphia in 1945.[72] By the time this cohort of men had reached age 18, Wolfgang was able to determine that 627 "chronic recidivists" were responsible for the large majority of all serious violent crimes committed by the group. Other, more recent, studies show that a small core of criminal perpetrators is probably responsible for most criminal activity in the United States.

Such thinking has led to the development of incapacitation as a modern-day treatment philosophy, and to the creation of innovative forms of incapacitation without imprisonment—such as home confinement, halfway houses or career training centers for convicted felons, and psychological and/or chemical treatments designed to reduce the likelihood of future crime commission. Similarly, such thinkers argue, the decriminalization of many offenses and the enhancement of social programs designed to combat the root causes of crime—including poverty, low educational levels, a general lack of skills, and inherent or active discrimination—will result in reduced incidence of crime in the future, making high rates of imprisonment unnecessary.

Before leaving our discussion of Sherman, however, note that the figure implies the existence of two other justice paradigms. The one termed *expression* results from the combination of an emotional offender and an emotional society. In this particular interface—of emotion upon emotion—says Sherman, "the state is morally obliged to take an explicitly *emotional* stance towards a presumably emotional offender, without regard for harm to the state's self-interest in the effects of its action on the offender's future behavior."[73]

It is the fourth paradigm, however—that of *emotional intelligence*—where Sherman places the most hope for the future. Under the paradigm of emotionally intelligent justice, actors within the criminal justice system would control their emotions and would work with offenders and victims, bringing a reasonable resolution of the situation that would

repair the harm caused by crime. Emotionally intelligent justice means that governments should try to make their officials control their emotions and adopt a more rational stance while realizing that the actions of offenders and victims will often be highly emotional.[74] Sherman cites the 32% drop in executions that occurred nationwide following the growing availability of DNA evidence that helped exonerate those wrongfully convicted of capital crimes to show how intelligence and reason can begin the process of healing from even the most egregious crimes.

A Critique of Neoclassical Thought

Any perspective gains credence if actions taken on the basis of its claims bear fruit. Not surprisingly, advocates of today's neoclassical approaches to crime control take much of the credit for the recent reduction in crime rates. After all, following the implementation of "get tough on crime" policies like the determinate sentencing schemes in the just deserts model, offically reported rates of crime declined substantially. The decrease led mayors, police chiefs, and politicians throughout the country to declare victory in the battle against crime, and many took personal credit for crime's decline. Notable among them were then-New York City mayor Rudy Giuliani, Los Angeles mayor Antonio Villariagosa, and L.A. police chief William J. Bratton.

The situation, however, is not so simple. As one journalist recently expalined it, taking "responsibility for crime trends depends entirely on whether those trends are good or bad. When...crime stats decline, everyone rushes to take credit. The mayor boasts his new initiative is working exactly as he said it would. The police chief proudly declares that the strategy he implemented is a great success. Social service agencies insist their new programs are responsible. And so it goes in city after city. The only thing that varies is the identity of the initiatives, strategies, and programs said to be the cause of the crime drop....Which suggests pretty strongly that all these claims are empty."[75]

An elderly prison inmate. How does selective incapacitation work?

A prison skills training program in action. Can such programs reduce recidivism?

The fact that crime has declined significantly in almost every U.S. jurisdiction over the past 10 to 15 years means that it has gone down in areas that instituted get-tough policies, as well as in those that saw little change in their approach to crime prevention. Realistically, **those who take credit for actively reducing crime in their cities and towns must also somehow account for crime's decline in other locations over which they had no control.** In 2007, for example, after the mayor and police chief in Los Angeles claimed that their crime-fighting policies had been responsible for an 8% drop in homicides throughout the city, one Los Angeles politician looked at murder rates throughout the region and found that while murder *inside* the city was down 8%, a decline of 15% had taken place in surrounding cities. "If [Mayor] Villariagosa were doing things better than surrounding cities," he asked, "wouldn't the percentage reduction *inside* the city be greater than the reduction *outside* the city?"[76]

Contrary to neoclassical claims that enhanced criminal punishments led to decreases in crime during the get-tough on crime era of the 1990s, the most significant contributors to crime's decline may have been economic and demographic factors that were largely beyond the control of policy makers. The latter would include the aging of the population (old folks commit fewer crimes than young ones), and the relative reduction of the number of young men in their "crime-prone years." In a cogent analysis of the factors contributing to the crime drop of the mid-1990s, for example, one Canadian criminologist noted that both the United States and Canada experienced similar downward trends in the rates of major crimes during the 1990s. From 1991 to 1999, for example, homicide rates declined by 42% in the United States and 43% in Canada; cases of reported sexual assault decreased by 23% and 31%, respectively; robbery decreased by 22% and 23%; and burglary rates dropped by 38% in the United States and 35% in Canada. However, the criminal justice policies and practices of the two countries during the period could hardly have been more different. In striking contrast to the United States, which dramatically increased spending on policing and correctional services, Canada was budgeting about the same number of dollars for justice system activities at the end of the 1990s as it had at the start of that decade. As a consequence of such differences in spending, the number of police officers in the United

> ...those who take credit for actively reducing crimes in their cities and towns must also somehow account for crime's decline in other locations....

States increased by 20% between 1991 and 1999, while it fell by 3% in Canada. Similarly, because Americans passed ever-tougher criminal legislation while Canadians did not, the incarceration rate climbed by 42% in the United States during the period, while it went down by 3% in Canada.

Two things that the United States and Canada *did* have in common during the 1990s were economic expansion

> the most significant contributors to crime's decline in recent years may have been economic and demographic factors that were largely beyond the control of policy makers.

and a significant shift in demographics caused by an aging of the population. During the period, unemployment decreased by 36% in the United States and 27% in Canada, while the number of people aged 20 to 34 declined by 18% in both countries. The Canadian writer concluded that the ready availability of jobs combined with demographic shifts in the population—and not the official efforts of policy makers—to produce a noteworthy decrease in crime during the 1990s.

Finally, one last criticism of neoclassical perspectives on crime can be offered: Although neoclassical writers are sometimes credited for advancing the scientific approach to crime prevention through studies that appear to have identified effective forms of deterrence, many such thinkers defend their perspective by referring to purely philosophical ideals, such as just deserts. In this respect, they have made little progress beyond the armchair theorizing and philosophical banter of Classical perspectives.

Los Angeles Mayor Antonio Villaraigosa shakes hands with a Los Angeles firefighter in 2008. Like many big city mayors, Villaraigosa credits LAPD strategies with producing a sharp reduction in crime throughout the city over the past decade. Might there also have been other reasons for the decline?

Gary Steven Krist committed a series of juvenile offenses before being arrested as an adult and serving a series of short jail terms in California for crimes such as auto theft. In 1965, after completing a term, he married and was arrested a year later—again for auto theft. Eight months into a five-year sentence he engineered an escape during which guards shot his accomplice to death. Since California law permitted capital punishment when a prison escape led to someone's death, Krist worried that he'd get the gas chamber if he were found. So he moved his young family to Boston and created a new identity as George Deacon, an aspiring scientist.

The undeniably intelligent Krist obtained a job as a lab technician at MIT. This led, in September 1968, to his participation in a marine science expedition where the still-married Krist began an affair with a student named Ruth Eisemann Schier. Before the expedition was over a month later, Krist confessed his true identity and criminal past to her, and they formed a plan to run off to Australia.

To finance their planned new life together, Krist and Eisemann Schier plotted to kidnap Emory University student Barbara Jane Mackle, the daughter of a prominent Miami family, and bury her in a homemade box, where she would remain until they received a $500,000 ransom.

Krist and Eisemann Schier did abduct and bury Mackle, who ultimately survived 83 hours underground before police, informed by Krist of the burial site, were able to find and release her. The kidnappers were subsequently caught and tried in Decatur, Georgia, in May of 1969.

Before his trial, Krist's intellect was evaluated by a psychiatrist as "if not at the genius level, then certainly in the near genius category." But the doctor also declared him fit to stand trial, and classified Krist as "having a sociopathic character disorder with no evidence of psychosis." Found guilty, the 23-year-old Krist received a life sentence.

Paroled after ten years, Krist set about lobbying for a complete pardon, which he eventually obtained in 1989. He then enrolled in a medical school in the West Indies, and completed his M.D. degree. Several states denied him a medical license before the state of Indiana finally granted him a probationary license in 2001.[i] That license was revoked two years later when Krist's past criminal record and allegations of sexual assaults on patients surfaced.[ii]

In January 2007, 61-year-old Gary Krist, who once described himself as the "Einstein of crime," was on his way back to prison to serve a five-year, five-month sentence. A federal sting operation busted Krist and his 41-year-old stepson in early 2006 for conspiracy to bring cocaine and illegal aliens into the United States.[iii]

The Causes Behind the Crime
Gary Stephen Krist

Can Classical or Neoclassical Criminology Explain this Crime?

- Born in Aberdeen, Washington, in 1945, Gary Steven Krist was raised in a small fishing village called Pelican in Alaska's Alexander Archipelago off the western coast of Canada. Krist's father was a salmon fisherman, and Krist himself described his mother as "a well-intentioned scatterbrain."[iv] The Krist's fishing business kept his parents at sea, and the financial return was not impressive. *Seen from a classical perspective, what might Krist have learned in his early years that would have caused him to later choose a life of crime?*

- During his parents' absence, Gary and his brother, Gordon, were left in the care of others. As a preteen, Gary showed a propensity for violence when, on one occasion, he fired a shotgun over his babysitter's and brother's heads because the babysitter made him angry by being too bossy. In an article for *Life* magazine, Krist later wrote that this incident illustrated his "absolute hatred for authority." *Can classical criminology explain emotions such as hatred? If so, how would it explain them?*

Krist had been found guilty for his part in the kidnapping of Barbara Jane Mackle, and was sentenced to life in prison. Paroled after ten years, he entered a new life of crime. Why didn't he reform?

Krist being interviewed while under arrest. How might Classical or Neoclassical criminology explain Krist's criminal behavior? What of rational choice theory?

- Examination of Krist's youth by prison officials in Georgia revealed that he was known throughout the tiny Pelican community as a troublemaker. A striking discovery, however, was his parents' attitude toward the reports of theft, vandalism—including blowing up an empty oil drum—and repeated reports of frequent intercourse with an 11-year-old town girl. Krist's parents seemed to view this behavior as simply displays of typical youthful exuberance. *Classical criminology says that punishment can be effective in steering people away from crime if it is more "painful" than the rewards to be obtained from law violation. Might punishments appropriately applied in Krist's early life have prevented his future criminality?*

- As he entered his teens, Krist's delinquency bloomed into full-fledged criminality. At the age of 14, Krist was arrested with a friend for a series of burglaries, various sexual conquests, and much drinking. He later wrote in a memoir that their "crimes arose, I believe, more from an overpowering hungry curiosity coupled with excess physical energy than from any defined hostility or malice toward others." *How might Katz's "seductions of crime" perspective explain the feelings that Krist reports?*

- While on probation for these offenses, Krist stole a car. This offense got him sent to a reform school in Ogden, Utah, where he earned straight-A grades as a student in the local public school. He also unsuccessfully tried to escape on two different occasions, yet later recalled that he was "happy" in this reform school because he was "accepted." *Classical criminology says that crime can be rewarding. Might camaraderie with other offenders be one of its rewards?*

NOTES:

[i]*Cincinnati Enquirer*, The Enquirer Online Edition, "Doctor Found to Have Been Imprisoned for Kidnapping," November 16, 2002, http://www.enquirer.com/editions/2002/11/16/loc_in-felondoc16.html (accessed July 10, 2007).
[ii]Wishtv.com, "Doctor's License Revoked," August 29, 2003, *http://www.wishtv.com/Global/story.asp?S=1423007* (accessed May 21, 2007).
[iii]Steve Fennessy, "The Talented Dr. Krist." Atlanta Magazine Online, http://www.atlantamagazine.com/article.php?id=299, (accessed May 21, 2007).
[iv]MSNBC, "Georgia Man in 1960s Buried Alive Case Gets 5 Years in Drug Case," *http://www.msnbc.msn.com/id/16710294/* (accessed May 21, 2007).

Summary and Key Concepts

CLASSICAL AND NEOCLASSICAL CRIMINOLOGY

Classical and neoclassical criminology see human activity as the product of the exercise of free will, and explain crime as moral wrongdoing based on personal choice.

The Roots of Classical Criminology

The **Classical School** is a criminological perspective developed in the late 1700s and early 1800s. It had its roots in the Enlightenment and held that men and women are rational beings and that crime is the result of the exercise of free will and personal choices based on calculations of perceived costs and benefits. Therefore, punishment can be effective in reducing the incidence of crime when it negates the rewards to be derived from crime commission.

hedonistic calculus The belief, first proposed by Jeremy Bentham, that behavior holds value to any individual undertaking it according to the amount of pleasure or pain that it can be expected to produce for that person.

Panopticon A prison designed by Jeremy Bentham that was to be a circular building with cells along the circumference, each clearly visible from a central location staffed by guards.

Cesare Beccaria The purpose of punishment should be deterrence rather than retribution, and punishment should be imposed to prevent offenders from committing additional crimes. Punishment should be only severe enough to outweigh the personal benefits to be derived from crime commission.

Jeremy Bentham Individuals will weigh the consequences of their behavior before acting so as to maximize their own pleasure and minimize pain.

Q: *What is the fundamental defining feature of the Classical School?*

Neoclassical Criminology

The modern-day application of classical principles to problems of crime and crime control in contemporary society, often in the guise of get-tough social policies. **Neoclassical criminology** focuses on the importance of character, the dynamics of character development, and the rational choices that people make as they are faced with opportunities for crime.

Robert Martinson Nothing works in the area of offender rehabilitation, and most convicted offenders resume their criminal careers after release from prison.

Q: *What are the differences between the Classical School of thought and neoclassical criminology?*

How does a person's lifestyle contribute to both the volume and type of crime found in a society? Explain the routine activities theory (lifestyle theory) in your own words.

nothing-works doctrine The belief popularized by Robert Martinson in the 1970s that correctional treatment programs have little success in rehabilitating offenders.

rational choice theory A perspective that holds that criminality is the result of conscious choice and that predicts that individuals choose to commit crime when the benefits outweigh the costs of disobeying the law.

routine activities theory (RAT) A brand of rational choice theory that suggests that lifestyles contribute significantly to both the volume and the type of crime found in any society.

situational choice theory A brand of rational choice theory that views criminal behavior "as a function of choices and decisions made within a context of situational constraints and opportunities."

lifestyle theory Another term for the routine activities approach of Lawrence Cohen and Marcus Felson.

target hardening The reduction in criminal opportunity for a particular location, generally through the use of physical barriers, architectural design, and enhanced security measures.

justice model A contemporary model of imprisonment in which the principle of just deserts forms the underlying social philosophy.

Rational Choice Theory

The theory that criminals make a conscious, rational, and at least partially informed choice to commit crime. Individuals choose to commit crime when the benefits outweigh the costs of disobeying the law. Crime will decrease when opportunities are limited, benefits are reduced, and the costs of crime commission are increased.

 Q: *If criminals weigh their behavior before committing a crime, why do so many crimes seem to happen spontaneously without much thought beforehand?*

How does the idea of "rational thought" play into the widely recognized saying, "crime doesn't pay"? Do criminals think rationally before committing crimes?

lifestyle theory The theory that lifestyles contribute significantly to both the volume and the type of crime found in any society.

capable guardian One who effectively discourages crime.

situational crime prevention An approach that looks to develop greater understanding of crime and more effective crime prevention strategies through concern with the physical, organizational, and social environments that make crime possible.

The Seductions of Crime Crime is often pleasurable for those committing it, and pleasure of one sort or another is the major motivation behind crime.

Lawrence Cohen and Marcus Felson The risk of criminal victimization varies dramatically among the circumstances and locations in which people place themselves and their property.

Ronald V. Clarke and Derek B. Cornish Suggest the use of situational strategies like "cheque guarantee cards, the control of alcohol sales at football matches, supervision of children's play on public housing estates, vandal resistant materials and designs, 'defensible space' architecture, improved lighting, closed-circuit television surveillance," and the like as effective crime prevention additions to specific situations—all of which might lower the likelihood of criminal victimization in given instances.

Jack Katz A criminologist who believes that crime is sensually compelling.

Punishment and Neoclassical Thought

just deserts model The notion that criminal offenders deserve the punishment that receive at the hands of the law and that punishments should be appropriate to the type and severity of crime committed.

specific deterrence A goal of criminal sentencing that seeks to prevent a particular offender from engaging in repeat criminality.

general deterrence A goal of criminal sentencing that seeks to prevent others from committing crimes similar to the one for which a particular offender is being sentenced.

recidivism The repetition of criminal behavior.

The Death Penalty

capital punishment The legal imposition of a sentence of death upon a convicted offender.

James Liebman, Jeffrey Fagan Found that of the death penalty cases during the years 1973–1995 were seriously flawed.

Policy Implications of the Classical School

truth in sentencing A close correspondence between the sentence imposed upon those sent to prison and the time actually served prior to prison release.

incapacitation The use of imprisonment or other means to reduce the likelihood that an offender with be capable of committing future offenses.

Lawrence Sherman Describes four paradigms of justice, each described as to whether there is a rational or emotional basis for crime along with a societal response to criminality.

Biological Roots
of Criminal Behavior

It's What We Are

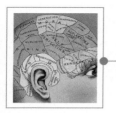

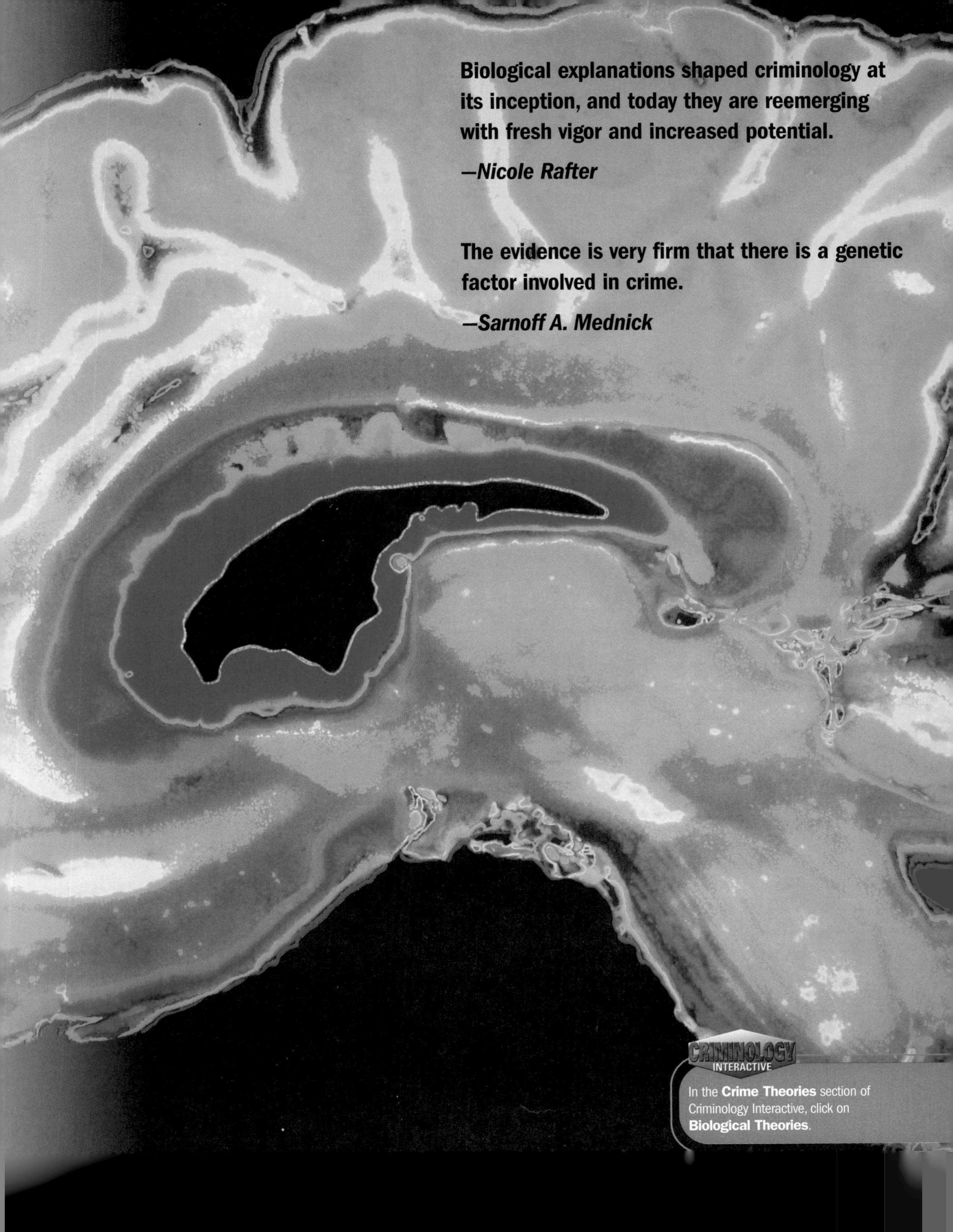

Biological explanations shaped criminology at its inception, and today they are reemerging with fresh vigor and increased potential.

—*Nicole Rafter*

The evidence is very firm that there is a genetic factor involved in crime.

—*Sarnoff A. Mednick*

CRIMINOLOGY INTERACTIVE

In the **Crime Theories** section of Criminology Interactive, click on **Biological Theories**.

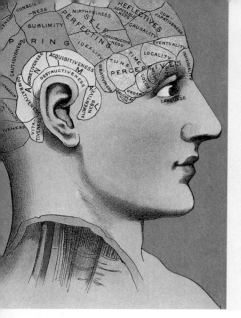

PRINCIPLES OF BIOLOGICAL THEORIES

Biological theories focus on the mind as the center of the personality and the major determinant in controlling human behavior. Unlike the classical and neoclassical tradition, which consider free will and external forces as the cause of behavior, biological theories look to internal sources, including genetic and physical makeup. According to biological theories, the source of all behavior is, for the most part, predetermined.

Early biological theorists focused on physical features and heredity as the source of criminal behavior. They considered such physical traits as facial features, body type, and the shape of the skull as causes of criminality. Several theorists proposed that criminality ran in families and could be inherited, being passed down from one generation to another. Contemporary theorists have looked at other internal sources of behavior, including diet, hormonal issues, environmental contaminants, and neurophysical conditions.

Biological theories of crime causation make certain fundamental assumptions:

- The brain is the organ of the mind and the locus of personality.

A History of Biological Theories

Numerous early perspectives on criminal biology fall into the category of criminal anthropology. **Criminal anthropology** is the scientific study of the relationship between human physical characteristics and criminality. Criminal anthropology probably derives from earlier subjective feelings, prominent for millennia, that unattractiveness, deformity, and physical disfigurement are somehow associated with evil, spiritual malaise, and general uncleanliness.

Phrenology

One of the earliest criminological anthropologists was **Franz Joseph Gall** (1758–1828). Gall hypothesized, in his theory of **phrenology** (also called "craniology"), that the shape of the human skull was indicative of the personality and could be used to predict criminality. Gall's approach contained four themes:

- The brain is the organ of the mind.

- Particular aspects of personality are associated with specific locations in the brain.

- Portions of the brain that are well developed will cause personality characteristics associated with them to be more prominent, whereas poorly developed brain areas lead to a lack of associated personality characteristics.

- The shape of a person's skull corresponds to the shape of the underlying brain and is therefore indicative of the personality.

Gall was one of the first Western writers to firmly locate the roots of personality in the brain. Prior to his time, it was thought that aspects of personality resided in various organs throughout the body—a fact reflected in expressions that survive into the present day (as, for example, when someone is described as "hard-hearted" or as having "a lot of gall" or as thinking with some organ other than the brain).

Although Gall never tested his theory, it was widely accepted by many of his contemporaries because it represented a shift away from the theological perspectives prevalent at the time and a move toward scientific understanding—a trend that was well under way by the time of his writings. Phrenology also provided for systematic evaluation of suspected offenders and was intriguing for its ease of use.

One of Gall's students, **Johann Gaspar Spurzheim** (1776–1853), brought phrenological theory to the United States and, through a series of lectures and publications on

in meiner Nachbarschaft gibt es niederträchtige L
Geschwülste!"
den lassen!" . . .

60. Die Phrenologie. 1839

The brain is the organ of the mind. Can the shape of the skull tell us anything about the personality?

- The basic determinants of human behavior, including criminal tendencies, are, to a considerable degree, constitutionally or genetically based.
- Observed gender and racial differences in rates and types of criminality may be at least partially the result of biological differences between the sexes and between racially distinct groups.
- The basic determinants of human behavior, including criminality, may be passed on from generation to generation. In other words, a tendency toward crime may be inherited.
- Much of human conduct is fundamentally rooted in instinctive behavioral responses characteristic of biological organisms everywhere. Territoriality, condemnation of adultery, and acquisitiveness are but three examples of behavior that may be instinctual to human beings.
- The biological roots of human conduct have become increasingly disguised as modern forms of indirect expressive behavior have replaced more primitive and direct ones.
- At least some human behavior is the result of biological tendencies inherited from more primitive developmental stages in the evolutionary process. In other words, some human beings may be further along the evolutionary ladder than others, and their behavior may reflect that fact.
- The interplay among heredity, biology, and the social environment provides the nexus for any realistic consideration of crime causation.

the subject, helped to spread its influence. Phrenology's prestige in the United States extended into the twentieth century, finding a place in classification schemes used to evaluate newly admitted prisoners.

The Positivist School

The Positivist school of the late-nineteenth century was built upon two principles: (1) the acceptance of social determinism, or the belief that human behavior is determined not by the exercise of free choice but by causative factors beyond the control of the individual, and (2) the application of scientific techniques to the study of crime and criminology. The term *positivism* had its roots in the writings of Auguste Comte (1798–1857), who proposed the use of the scientific method in the study of society in his 1851 work *A System of Positive Polity.*[1] Comte believed that a new "positive age" was dawning during which both society and human nature would be perfected, and his writings were an attempt to bring that age to fruition.

Positivism holds that social phenomena are observable, explainable, and measurable in quantitative terms. For a strict positivist, reality consists of a world of objectively defined facts, which can be scientifically measured and—ultimately—controlled.[2]

One of the best-known, early scientific biological theorists of the positivist school—nineteenth-century Italian army prison physician **Cesare Lombroso** (1836–1909)—coined the term **atavism** to suggest that criminality was the result of primitive urges that had survived the evolutionary process. At about this time, Charles Darwin was making a substantial impact on the scientific world with his theory of biological evolution. Darwin proposed that human beings and other contemporary living organisms were the end products of a long evolutionary process governed by such rules as natural selection and survival of the fittest. Lombroso adapted elements of Darwin's theory to suggest that primitive traits survived in present-day human populations and led to heightened criminal tendencies among individuals who harbored them.

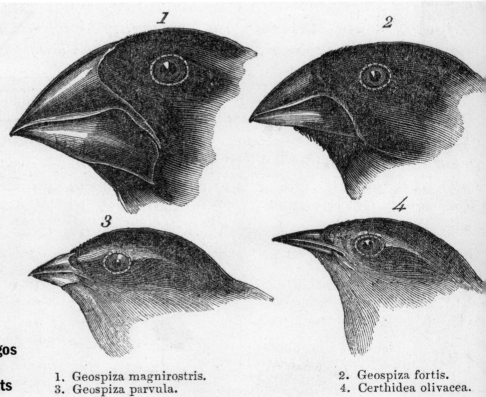

Charles Darwin's drawings of Galapagos Finches, showing the evolution of the bird's beak. Might some primitive traits survive in modern-day humans?

1. Geospiza magnirostris.
2. Geospiza fortis.
3. Geospiza parvula.
4. Certhidea olivacea.

The atavistic individual, said Lombroso in his now-classic work *L'Uomo delinquente* (1876), **was essentially a throwback to a more primitive biological state.** According to Lombroso, such an individual, by virtue of possessing a relatively undeveloped brain, is incapable of conforming his or her behavior to the rules and expectations of modern complex society. Lombroso has been called the father of modern criminology because he was the first criminologist of note to employ the scientific method—particularly measurement, observation, and attempts at generalization—in his work. Other writers have referred to him as the "father of the Italian School" of criminology in recognition of the fact that nineteenth-century positivism began in Italy.

Lombroso's scientific work consisted of postmortem studies of the bodies of executed offenders and deceased criminals in which he measured the bodies in many different ways. The body of one such well-known criminal, named Vilella, provided Lombroso with many of his findings and reinforced his belief that most offenders were biologically predisposed toward criminality. When he examined Vilella's brain, Lombroso found an unusual depression, which he named "the median occipital fossa." Lombroso identified features of Vilella's brain as being similar to those found in lower primates. Study of another offender, an Italian soldier whom Lombroso calls "Misdea" in his writings[3] and who "attacked and killed eight of his superior officers and comrades," supported his conclusions.

In addition to his examination of Vilella, Lombroso conducted autopsies on another 65 executed offenders and examined 832 living prison inmates, comparing physical measurements of their body parts with measurements taken from 390 soldiers. As a result of his work, Lombroso claimed to have found a wide variety of bodily features that could predict criminal behavior. Among them were exceptionally long arms, an index finger as long as the middle finger, fleshy pouches in the cheeks "like those in rodents," eyes that were either abnormally close together or too far apart, large teeth, ears that lacked lobes, prominent cheekbones, a crooked nose, a large amount of body hair, a protruding chin, large lips, a nonstandard number of ribs, and eyes of differing colors or hues. Lombroso went so far as to enumerate characteristics of particular types of offenders. Murderers, whom he called "habitual homicides," have, in Lombroso's words, "cold, glassy eyes, immobile and sometimes sanguine and inflamed; the nose, always large, is frequently aquiline or, rather, hooked; the jaws are strong, the cheekbones large, the hair curly, dark, and abundant; the beard is frequently thin, the canine teeth well developed and the lips delicate."[4]

Atavism implies the notion that criminals are born as criminals. Lombroso was continuously reassessing his estimates of the proportion, from among all offenders, of the born criminal population. At one point, he asserted that fully 90% of offenders committed crimes because of atavistic influences. He later revised the figure downward to 70%, admitting that normal individuals might be pulled into lives of crime.

Lombroso thought that fleshy cheek pouches, "like those of a rodent," and different colored eyes might represent atavistic traits. What is atavism?

Biological Roots of Criminal Behavior • Crime Causation

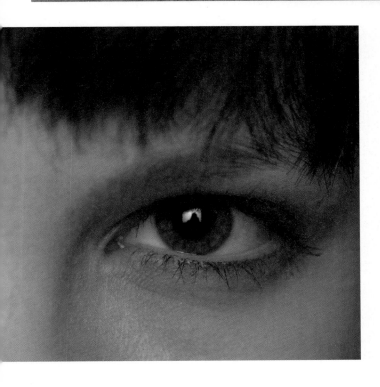

According to early biological theorists, criminals had "a love of orgies." How might such a behavioral characteristic relate to the idea of atavism?

In addition to the category of the **born criminal**, Lombroso described other categories of offenders, including the insane, "criminaloids," and criminals incited by passion. The insane were said to include mental and moral degenerates, alcoholics, drug addicts, and so forth. **Criminaloids**, also called "occasional criminals," were described as people who were pulled into breaking the law by virtue of environmental influences. Nevertheless, most criminaloids were seen by Lombroso as exhibiting some degree of atavism and hence were said to "differ from born criminals in degree, not in kind." Those who became criminals by virtue of passion were said to have surrendered to intense emotions, including love, jealousy, hatred, or an injured sense of honor.

Although he focused on physical features, Lombroso was not insensitive to behavioral indicators of criminality. In his later writings, he claimed that criminals exhibited acute sight, hearing abilities that were below the norm, insensitivity to pain, a lack of moral sensibility, cruelty, vindictiveness, impulsiveness, a love of gambling, and a tendency to be tattooed.

In 1893, Lombroso published *The Female Offender*.[5] In that book, he expressed his belief that women exhibited far

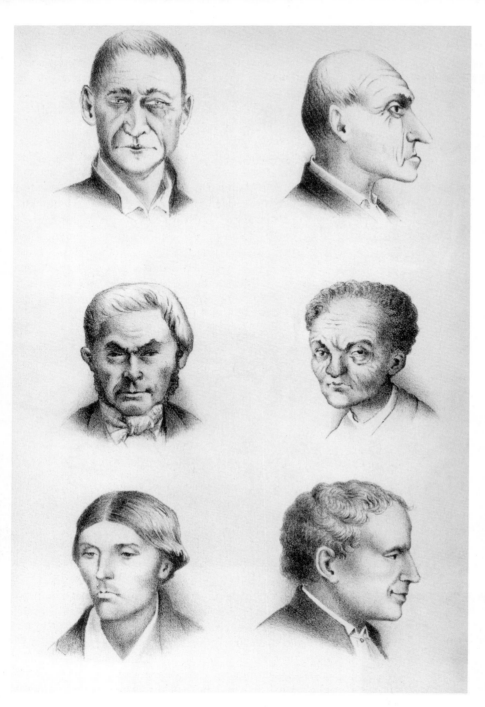

newly developed but advanced mathematical techniques to measure the degree of correlation between physiological features and criminal history, Goring examined nearly 3,000 inmates at Turin prison beginning in 1901. He concluded that "the whole fabric of Lombrosian doctrine, judged by the standards of science, is fundamentally unsound."[6] Goring compared the prisoners with students at Oxford and Cambridge universities, British soldiers, and noncriminal hospital patients and published his findings in 1913 in his lengthy treatise *The English Convict: A Statistical Study.*[7]

Constitutional Theories

Constitutional theories are those that explain criminality by reference to offenders' body types, genetics, or external observable physical characteristics. A constitutional, or physiological, orientation that found its way into the criminological mainstream during the early and mid-twentieth century was that of body types. Also called *somatotyping*, this perspective was primarily associated with the work of **Ernst Kretschmer** and **William H. Sheldon**. Kretschmer, a professor of psychiatry at the German Tübingen University, proposed a relationship between body build and personality type and created a rather detailed "biopsychological constitutional typology."[8] Kretschmer's somatotypology revolved around three basic mental categories: cycloids (also called "cyclothymes"), schizoids (or "schizothymes"), and displastics. The **cycloid** personality, which was associated with a heavyset, soft type of body, according to Kretschmer, vacillated between normality and abnormality. Cycloids were said to lack spontaneity and sophistication and were thought to commit mostly nonviolent property types of offenses. **Schizoids**, who tended to possess athletic, muscular bodies but, according to Kretschmer, could also be thin and lean, were seen as more likely to be schizophrenic and to commit violent offenses. **Displastics** were said to be a mixed group described as highly emotional and often unable to control themselves. Hence, they were thought to commit mostly sexual offenses and other crimes of passion.

less anatomical variation than do men, but that criminal behavior among women, as among men, derived from atavistic foundations. Violence among women, although a rarity in the official statistics of the late 1800s, was explained by the **masculinity hypothesis**, or the belief that criminal women exhibited masculine features and mannerisms. Lombroso saw the quintessential female offender, however, as a prostitute. Prostitutes, he claimed, act out atavistic yearnings and, in doing so, return to a form of behavior characteristic of humankind's primitive past.

Following in Lombroso's positivistic footsteps around the turn of the twentieth century, English physician **Charles Buckman Goring** (1870–1919) conducted a well-controlled statistical study of Lombroso's thesis of atavism. Using

Influenced by Kretschmer, William H. Sheldon utilized measurement techniques to connect body type with personality.[9] Sheldon felt that Kretschmer had erred in including too large an age range in his work. Therefore, he chose to limit his study to 200 boys between the ages of 15 and 21 at the Hayden Goodwill Institute in Boston. Sheldon concluded that four basic body types characterized the entire group. These types, described partly in Sheldon's words, are as follows.

- The **endomorph**, who is soft and round and whose "digestive viscera are massive and highly developed" (that is, the person is overweight and has a large stomach)

- The **mesomorph**, who is athletic and muscular and whose "somatic structures. . . are in the ascendancy" (that is, the person has larger bones and considerable muscle mass)

- The **ectomorph**, who is thin and fragile and who has "long, slender, poorly muscled extremities, with delicate, pipestem bones"

- The balanced type, a person of average build, without being overweight, thin, or exceedingly muscular

Sheldon claimed that varying types of temperament and personalities were closely associated with each of the body types he identified. Ectomorphs were said to be "cerebrotonic," or restrained, shy, and inhibited. Endomorphs were "viscerotonic," or relaxed and sociable. **The mesomorphic, or muscular, body type**, however, he said **was most likely to be associated with delinquency** or "somatotonia," which he described as "a predominance of muscular activity and. . . vigorous bodily assertiveness." Sheldon's work was supported by constitutional studies of juvenile delinquents conducted by Sheldon Glueck and Eleanor Glueck and reported in 1950.[10] The Gluecks compared 500 known delinquents with 500 nondelinquents and matched both groups on age, general intelligence, ethnic-racial background, and place of residence. Like Sheldon, the Gluecks concluded that mesomorphy was associated with delinquency. Early biological theorists like Sheldon, Lombroso, and Gall provide an interesting footnote in the history of criminological thought. **Today, however, biological theories of crime are far more sophisticated than their early predecessors**, and it is to these that we now turn.

> The mesomorphic, or muscular body type, was said to be the one most likely to be associated with crime and delinquency.

Some biological theorists claimed to have identified a relationship between body type and criminal behavior. Might there be any truth to such claims?

Modern Biological Theories: Chemical and Environmental Precursors of Crime

Today's biological theorists have made significant studies in linking violent or disruptive behavior to eating habits, vitamin deficiencies, genetic inheritance, and other conditions that affect the body. Studies of nutrition, endocrinology, and environmental contaminants have all contributed to advances in understanding such behavior.

Hypoglycemia and Diet

One of the first studies to focus on chemical imbalances in the body as a cause of crime was reported in the British medical journal *Lancet* in 1943.[11] The authors of the study linked murder to **hypoglycemia**, or low blood sugar. Low blood sugar, produced by too much insulin in the blood or by near-starvation diets, was said to reduce the mind's capacity to reason effectively or to judge the long-term consequences of behavior. More recent studies have linked excess consumption of refined white sugar to hyperactivity and aggressiveness. Popular books like *Sugar Blues* provide guides for individuals seeking to free themselves from the negative effects of excess sugar consumption.[12]

Even the courts have considered the notion that excess sugar consumption may be linked to crime. In the early 1980s, for example, Dan White, a former San Francisco police officer, was given a reduced sentence after his lawyers used what came to be known as the "Twinkie Defense."[13] They argued that White's night-long binge on large numbers of Coca-Colas and Twinkies before he murdered San Francisco mayor George Moscone and city councilman Harvey Milk, was evidence of White's unbalanced mental state. The consumption of junk food was presented as evidence of depression since White was normally very health conscious.

While studies are not conclusive about whether and how refined sugars affect behavior, studies done using positron-emission tomography (PET), in which scans of the prefrontal cortex of subjects' brains were analyzed, show interesting results. PET scans can be used to measure the "uptake" of glucose by the brain. A 1994 study of PET scans of the brains of 22 murderers (including some who had only attempted murder) revealed that the murderers showed much lower levels of glucose uptake in the prefrontal cortex than did the controls. The study concluded that deficits in the prefrontal cortex, including an inability of that portion of the brain to utilize glucose in a normal fashion, may be related to violent behavior.

Environmental Pollution

Various substances found in our environment have been shown to be linked to criminal behavior. A 1997 study showed a significant correlation between juvenile crime and high environmental levels of both lead and manganese. The toxic metals may affect individuals in complex ways. Because lead diminishes a person's normal ability to detoxify poisons, it may heighten the effects of alcohol and drugs. When brain chemistry is altered by exposure to heavy metals and other toxins, the study suggests, people lose the natural restraint that holds their violent tendencies in check.

Critique of Chemical and Environmental Precursors of Crime

Biological theories of crime based on chemical and environmental factors have been criticized because they seem to deny the role of free will. Not everyone who is exposed to the

An environmental resource specialist checks a toy for the presence of lead. What environmental contaminants might influence childhood behavior?

same chemicals behaves the same way. While some chemicals, such as strong poisons, have undeniable and powerful effects on human tissue, psychological or behavioral effects of chemicals that are said to influence behavior, especially those involving exposure over long periods of time, are less obvious, and apparently less direct. Because behavioral effects are less direct, they are also more dubious.

Critics of chemical and environmental biological theories ask that if exposure to, or ingestion of, certain chemical substances, including vitamins, can have a powerful effect on behavior, then why doesn't it happen to everyone? And to extend that argument, they ask why we don't have a diet or an injectable combination of chemicals that would cure criminality.

Studies of chemical precursors and crime, along with studies of hormones in criminality, are fundamentally flawed, critics claim, if they rely on prison inmates or arrestees as subjects in their studies. This is because not everyone who breaks the law ends up in prison. This type of theorizing neglects the notion that there is a "gray area" of criminality—people who commit crimes but who are not caught and therefore not imprisoned.

Most critics also claim theories involving chemical precursors cannot account for changes in crime rates over time. Crime rates have trended substantially downward over the past two or three decades, during the same time period that exposure to chemical substances of all types throughout the general population has expanded.

Similarly, biological theories that focus on environmental and chemical precursors of crime cannot explain why certain kinds of crime are more likely to occur in certain parts of the country, in certain types of communities, and among members of particular subcultures than in others. Such differences imply that much more is at work than chemicals themselves and suggest that cultural differences play a significant role in criminality.

Why don't we have a diet to cure criminality?

Some researchers have pointed to the role of excess sugar consumption in crime causation. What is the evidence for such a link?

Hormones and Criminality

Hormones have also been studied as potential behavioral determinants. The male sex hormone **testosterone**, for example, has been linked to aggression. Most studies on the subject have consistently shown a relationship between high blood testosterone levels and increased aggressiveness in men. More focused studies have revealed a direct relationship between the amount of the chemical present and the degree of violence used by sex offenders, while other researchers have linked steroid abuse among bodybuilders to destructive urges and psychosis. **Contemporary investigations also demonstrate a link between testosterone levels and aggression in teenagers,[17] while others show that adolescent problem behavior and teenage violence rise in proportion to the amount of testosterone in the blood of young men.[18]**

A few limited studies have attempted to measure the effects of testosterone on women. Women's bodies manufacture roughly one-tenth the amount of the hormone secreted by men. Even so, subtle changes in testosterone levels in women have been linked to changes in personality and sexual behavior.[19] One such study showed that relatively high blood levels of testosterone in female inmates were associated with "aggressively dominant behavior" in prison.[20]

Fluctuations in the level of female hormones may also bear some relationship to law violation. In 1980, a British court exonerated Christine English of charges that she murdered her live-in lover after English admittedly ran him over with her car after an argument. English's defense rested on the fact that she was suffering from premenstrual syndrome (PMS) at the time of the homicide. An expert witness, Dr. Katharina Dalton, testified at the trial that PMS had caused English to be "irritable, aggressive, . . . and confused, with loss of self-control."[21]

Although evidence linking PMS to violent or criminal behavior is far from clear, some researchers believe that a drop in serotonin levels in the female

brain just before menstruation might explain the agitation and irritability sometimes associated with PMS. Serotonin has been called a "behavior-regulating chemical," and animal studies have demonstrated a link between low levels of the neurotransmitter present in the brain and aggressive behavior. For example, monkeys with low serotonin levels in their brains have been found to be more likely to bite, slap, and chase others of their kind. Studies at the National Institute on Alcohol Abuse and Alcoholism have linked low serotonin levels in humans to impulsive crimes. Men convicted of premeditated murder, for example, have been found to have normal serotonin levels, whereas those convicted of crimes of passion had lower levels.[22]

Critique of Theories about the Role of Hormones in Criminality

Many of the same critiques identified in regard to chemical precursors can be applied to perspectives involving hormones and criminal behavior. Hormones, after all, are chemicals that are made by the body (or that are sometimes injected into the bloodstream). Just as is the case with chemical precursors, hormones apparently don't affect everyone the same way. Not all men with high testosterone levels, for example, are violent or aggressive.

Like critics of chemical precursors, those who criticize hormonal theory claim that the theories ignore the role of free choice. Critics also point to differences in socialization; upbringing; personality; and spatial, geographical, and cultural location as explanations for criminal behavior.

Female boxers in action. What role might hormones play in crime and deviant behavior?

Genetics and Crime

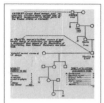

Some scholars have suggested that the tendency for crime may be inherited and that criminal tendencies are genetically based. Beginning in the late 1800s, researchers in the field of criminal anthropology focused on criminal families, or families that appeared to exhibit criminal tendencies through several generations (Figure 3–1).

One of the earliest studies focused on the **Juke family**, which was traced back to a notorious character named Max, who lived in New York in the early 1700s. Two of Max's sons married into the notorious "Juke family of girls," six sisters, all of whom were said to be illegitimate. Max's male descendants were reputed to be vicious, and one woman named Ada had an especially bad reputation. By the time of the study, almost 1,200 of Ada's descendants had been identified. Among their numbers, 7 murderers, 60 habitual thieves, 90 or so other criminals, 50 prostitutes, and 280 paupers were found. Then the crime-prone Jukes were compared to another family, the pure-blooded progeny of Jonathan Edwards, a Puritan preacher and one-time president of Princeton University. Descendants of Edwards included American presidents and vice presidents and many successful bankers and businesspeople. No one was identified among the Edwards lineage who had had a run-in with

GREAT-GRANDSON OF "DADDY" KALLIKAK.
This boy is an imbecile of the Mongolian type.

OLD AMERICAN CRIMINALS

Mosaic of Cranial, Facial, Metric and Morphological Features

MASSACHUSETTS

Narrowest face
Narrowest jaw
Thick beards
Broad, high nasal roots and bridges
Thick nasal tips
Right deflections of nasal septum
Concave profiles ①
External and median eyefolds ②
Small, attached ear lobes ③
Thin integumental lips ④
Membranous lips--upper thin, lower thick
Lip seams absent
Undershot jaw
Facial prognathism ⑤
Right facial asymmetry ⑥
Median chins

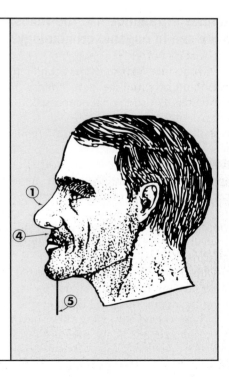

FIGURE 3–1 Hooton's "Massachusetts Criminal"

Source: Reprinted by permission of the publisher from CRIME AND THE MAN by Earnest Albert Hooton, p. 57, Cambridge, Mass.: Harvard University Press, Copyright © 1939 by the President and Fellows of Harvard College. Copyright renewed 1967 by Mary C. Hooton.

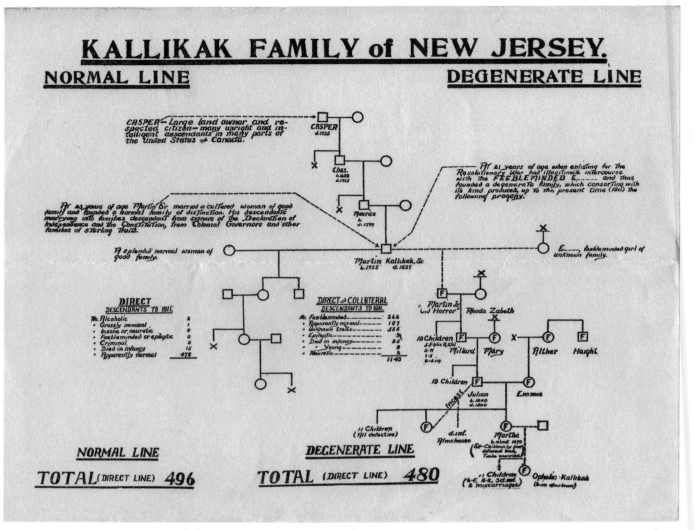

Studies of families like the Jukes and the Kallikaks supported the idea of eugenics. What dangers did some see in eugenic criminology?

the law. A follow-up study was conducted in 1916, in which an additional 715 Juke descendants, including 378 more prostitutes, 170 additional paupers, and 118 other criminals, were identified.[23]

Following in the tradition of family tree researchers, **Henry Herbert Goddard** (1866–1957) published a study of the **Kallikak family** in 1912.[24] Goddard attempted to place the study of deviant families within an acceptable scientific framework through the use of a kind of control group. For comparison purposes, he used two branches of the same family. One branch began as the result of a sexual liaison between Martin Kallikak, a Revolutionary War soldier, and a barmaid. As a result of this union, an illegitimate son (Martin, Jr.) was born. After the war, Kallikak returned home and married a righteous Quaker girl, and a second line of descent began. Although the second, legitimate branch produced only a few minor deviants, the illegitimate line resulted in 262 "feebleminded" births and various other epileptic, alcoholic, and criminal descendants. (The term *feebleminded*, which was much in vogue at the time of Goddard's study, was later recast as "mentally retarded,"

and today people exhibiting similar characteristics might be referred to as "mentally handicapped" or "mentally challenged.") Because feeblemindedness appeared to occur with some predictability in Goddard's study, whereas criminal activity seemed to be only randomly represented among the descendants of both Kallikak lines, Goddard concluded that a tendency toward feeblemindedness was inherited but that criminality was not.

Studies like these, which focused on inherited mental degeneration, led to the **eugenics** movement of the 1920s and early 1930s and to the development of **eugenic criminology**,[25] which held that the root causes of criminality were largely passed from generation to generation in the form of "bad genes." Eugenic criminology replaced the idea of the "feebleminded criminal" with the "defective delinquent," and social policies developed during the eugenics movement called for the sterilization of mentally handicapped women to prevent their bearing additional offspring.[26] Those policies were supported by the federal Eugenics Record Office, which funded studies of "cacogenic" or "bad-gened" families, and were endorsed by the 1927 U.S. Supreme Court case of ***Buck v. Bell***.[27] In

Buck, Justice Oliver Wendell Holmes, Jr., writing in support of a Virginia statute permitting sterilization, said, "It is better for all the world, if instead of waiting to execute degenerate offspring for crime, or to let them starve for their imbecility, society can prevent those persons who are manifestly unfit from continuing their kind."

The eugenics movement continued in the United Kingdom into the 1960s, but was largely discredited in this country by intense condemnation of Nazi genetic research, mass sterilization, and eugenics programs, including those that led to the Holocaust. In 1962, interest in eugenics was rekindled and an argument was made that mankind could be improved "simply by encouraging the differential reproduction of human beings exhibiting generally desirable characteristics."[28]

U.S. Supreme Court Justice Oliver Wendell Holmes. Why did his support for sterilization of the "unfit" meet with criticism?

The XYY "Supermale"

Recent developments in the field of human genetics have led to the study of the role of chromosomes, and sex-linked chromosomes in particular, in crime causation. The first well-known study of this type was undertaken by Patricia A. Jacobs,[29] a British researcher, who in 1965, examined 197 Scottish prisoners for chromosomal abnormalities through a relatively simple blood test known as "karyotyping."[30] Twelve members of the group displayed chromosomes that were unusual, and seven were found to have an XYY chromosome. "Normal" male individuals possess an XY chromosome structure, and "normal" female individuals are XX. Some other unusual combinations might be XXX, wherein a woman's genetic makeup contains an extra

A normal male karyotype. Is the concept of the "supermale" relevant today?

X chromosome, and XXY, also called Klinefelter's syndrome, in which a man might carry an extra X, or female, chromosome. Klinefelter's men often have male genitalia but are frequently sterile and evidence breast enlargement and intellectual retardation. The XYY man, however, whose incidence in the prison population was placed at around 3.5% by Jacobs, was quickly identified as potentially violent and was termed a **supermale**.

Following the introduction of the supermale notion into popular consciousness, a number of offenders attempted to offer a chromosome-based defense. In 1969, for example, Lawrence E. Hannell, who was considered a supermale, was acquitted of murder in Australia on the grounds of insanity.[31] Such a defense, however, did not work for Richard Speck, who also claimed to be an XYY man and was convicted of killing eight Chicago nursing students in 1966. It was later learned that Speck did not carry the extra Y chromosome.

To date, there have been nearly 200 studies of XYY males. Although not all researchers agree, taken as a group these studies[32] tend to show that supermales

- are taller than the average male, often standing 6'1" or more.

- suffer from acne or skin disorders.

- have less-than-average intelligence.

- are overrepresented in prisons and mental hospitals.

- come from families with a lower-than-average history of crime or mental illness.

The supermale phenomenon, also called "XYY syndrome," may have been more sensationalism than fact. Little evidence suggests that XYY men actually commit crimes of greater violence than do other men, although they may commit somewhat more crimes overall.

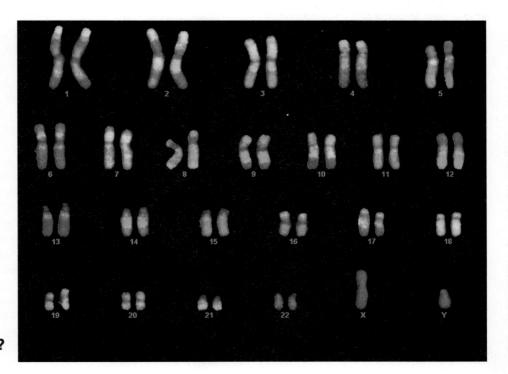

Behavioral Genetics

The field of **behavioral genetics** is the study of genetic and environmental contributions to individual variations in human behavior. Studies of the criminal tendencies of fraternal and identical twins have demonstrated the role of heredity in crime causation. Fraternal twins, also called "dizygotic (DZ) twins," develop from different fertilized eggs and share only the genetic material common among siblings. Identical twins, also called **monozygotic (MZ) twins**, develop from the same egg and carry virtually the same genetic material. Hence, if human behavior has a substantial heritable component, twins should tend to display similar behavioral characteristics despite variations in their social environment. Similarly, any observed relationship might be expected to be stronger among monozygotic twins than among dizygotic twins.

A study of twins begun in 1968 found significant statistical support for the notion that criminal tendencies are inherited. The study concluded that 52% of identical twins and 22% of fraternal siblings displayed the same degree of criminality within the twin pair. Such similarities remained apparent even among twins who had been separated at birth and who were raised in substantially different environments.

The Minnesota Twin Family Study began in 1983.[33] The study's original goal was to establish a registry of all twins born in Minnesota from 1936 to 1955 for psychological research purposes. The Minnesota database has since expanded to include twins born between 1961 and 1964. The Minnesota registry conducts personality and interests tests with more than 8,000 twin pairs and family members. One of the study's most interesting findings seems to show that monozygotic twins reared apart are about as similar as are monozygotic twins reared together. The findings apply to multiple measures of personality and temperament, occupational and leisure-time interests, and social attitudes. Study authors warn, however, that "this evidence for the strong heritability of most psychological traits, sensibly construed, does not detract from the value or importance of parenting, education, and other . . . interventions."[34]

Twin studies appear to point to criminal genes that, once inherited, inevitably produce antisocial behavior. Such a conclusion, however, is not necessarily warranted. As we shall see later in this chapter, genes may simply influence the way in which people respond to their surroundings. Hence, so-called criminal genes may be nothing more than genetic predispositions to respond in certain ways to a criminogenic environment.

The Kray twins—Ronald and Reginald—dominated organized crime in London's East End for 20 years. Could criminality have a genetic basis?

Gender Differences in Criminality

A number of contemporary writers propose that criminologists must recognize that "the male is much more criminalistic than the female."[35] With the exception of crimes like prostitution and shoplifting, the number of crimes committed by men routinely far exceeds the number of crimes committed by women in almost all categories, and when women commit crimes, they are far more likely to assume the role of followers than leaders.[36] The data on the extent of male–female criminality show surprising regularity over time. The proportion of homicides committed by men versus women, for example, has remained more or less constant for decades (see Table 3–1). Similarly, the proportion of men murdered by men versus the proportion of women murdered by women has been consistent, showing a much greater propensity for men to murder one another.

If culture exercises the major role in determining criminality, as many social scientists today suggest, then we would expect to see recognizable increases in the degree and nature of female criminality over time, especially as changes in socialization practices, cultural roles, and other ethnographic patterns increase the opportunity for women to commit what had previously been regarded as traditionally male offenses. With the exception of a few crimes, such as embezzlement, drug abuse, and liquor law violations, however, such has not been the case. Although women comprise 51% of the population of the

TABLE 3–1

Male and Female Murder Perpetrators as a Percentage of All Arrests for Homicide, 1960–2007

1960		1975		1980		1990		2000		2007	
Male	Female	Male	Female	Male	Female	Male	Female	Male	Female	Male	Female
82.5%	17.5%	84.7%	15.3%	87.2%	12.8%	89.6%	10.4%	87.5%	12.5%	89.2%	10.8%

Source: Adapted from Federal Bureau of Investigation, *Crime in the United States*, various years.

United States, they are arrested for only 18% of all violent crimes and 32% of property crimes[37]—a proportion that has remained surprisingly constant over the years since the FBI began gathering crime data more than half a century ago. Simply put, even with all the cultural changes that have created new possibilities for women in crime, few women have taken advantage of these newfound freedoms. Such apparent differences not only have existed over time but also can be seen in cross-cultural studies.

In evaluating the criminality of women based on statistics alone, however, it is dangerous to misidentify the causes in the behavior itself. Although men consistently commit more murders than women, for example, we should not jump to the conclusion that this bit of evidence shows a genetic predisposition toward interpersonal violence in men, which is absent in women. To do so would fail to recognize the role of other causal factors.

The criminality of women (or relative lack thereof) may be culturally determined to a considerable degree. Nonetheless, the consistency of data that show that women are far less likely than men to be involved in most property crimes, and less likely still to commit violent crimes, requires attention. A few authors suggest that the relative lack of testosterone in women leads them to commit fewer crimes. Some evidence supports just such a hypothesis. Studies have shown, for example, that female fetuses exposed to elevated testosterone levels during gestation develop masculine characteristics, including a muscular build and a greater tendency toward aggression later in life.[38] Even so, genetically based behavioral differences between men and women are so moderated by aspects of the social environment, including socialization, the learning of culturally prescribed roles, and the expectations of others, that definitive conclusions are difficult to reach.

Critique of Genetics Theories of Crime

Methodological problems abound in many studies that attempt to evaluate the role of genetics in crime. Glenn D. Walters and Thomas W. White mention, among other things, the lack of control or comparison groups, small sample sizes, the dropping out of subjects from study groups, biased sampling techniques, and the use of inappropriate forms of statistical analysis.

Walters and White also claim that results obtained outside the United States may not be applicable within this country. Twin studies conducted in Sweden and Denmark provide an example of this potential lack of generalizability.

Twin studies, in particular, have sometimes failed to properly establish whether a pair of twins is monozygotic or dizygotic. This is because some MZ twins are not identical in appearance, and only a few twin studies have depended on biological testing rather than on a simple evaluation of appearances.

Walters and White nonetheless conclude that "genetic factors are undoubtedly correlated with various measures of criminality," but they add that "the large number of methodological flaws and limitations in the research should make one cautious in drawing any causal inferences at this point in time."[39]

Imprisoned women share a lighter moment. How does the criminality of women differ from that of men?

Sociobiology

Sociobiology—a theoretical synthesis of biology, behavior, and evolutionary ecology—was first brought to the scientific community by **Edward O. Wilson** in his seminal 1975 work *Sociobiology: The New Synthesis*.[40] In his book, Wilson defined *sociobiology* as "the systematic study of the biological basis of all social behavior" and as "a branch of evolutionary biology and particularly of modern population biology." Wilson's major focus was to show that the primary determinant of animal *and* human behavior was the need to ensure the survival and continuity of genetic material from one generation to the next. Sociobiology considers all behaviors, including those such as mating patterns and territorial fighting, as embedded in the natural selection process.

Territoriality, a primary tenet of Wilson's writings, was said to explain much of the conflict seen among human beings, including homicide, warfare,

Mountain gorillas engaged in play fighting. How might such play contribute to natural selection?

and other forms of aggression. In Wilson's words, "Part of man's problem is that his intergroup responses are still crude and primitive, and inadequate for the extended extraterritorial relationships that civilization has thrust upon him." The "unhappy result," as Wilson terms it, may be "tribalism," expressed through the contemporary proliferation of street gangs, racial tension, and the hardened encampments of survivalist and separatist groups.

Wilson's writing propelled researchers into a flurry of studies intended to test the validity of his assertions. Some writers concluded that "murderous behavior, warfare, and even genocide were unavoidable correlates of genetic evolution, controlled by the same genes for territorial behavior that had been selected in primate evolution."[41] Others suggested that biological predispositions developed during earlier stages of human evolution color contemporary criminal activity. Male criminals, for example, tend toward robbery and burglary—crimes in which they can continue to enact their "hunter instincts" developed long ago. The criminality of women, on the other hand, is more typical of "gatherers" when it involves shoplifting, simple theft, and so on.

Critiques of Sociobiology

As sociobiology began to receive expanded recognition from American investigators, some social scientists, believing the basic tenets of their profession to be challenged by the movement, began to treat it as "criminology's anti-discipline."[42] Contemporary criminologist John Madison Memory writes, "By

Children play aggressively. Does such play support the idea that crime and aggression are "unavoidable correlates of genetic evolution"?

the early 1980s sociobiology presented such a significant threat to American criminology that it could no longer be ignored."[43] Criticisms were quick to come. Memory identifies many such critiques, including these charges:

- Sociobiology fails to convey the overwhelming significance of culture, social learning, and individual experiences in shaping the behavior of individuals and groups.

- Sociobiology is fundamentally wrong in its depiction of the basic nature of humans; there is no credible evidence of genetically based or determined tendencies to act in certain ways.

- Sociobiology is just another empirically unsupported rationale for the authoritative labeling and stigmatization of despised, threatening, powerless minorities.

- Humans are so thoroughly different from other animal species, even other primates, that there is no rational basis for the application to humans of findings from animal studies.

Sociobiology says that the primary determinant of behavior is to ensure the continuity of genetic material from one generation to the next.

Gang members show off their hand signs. Are humans territorial?

Policy Implications of Biological Theories

In his recent book, *The Blank Slate: The Modern Denial of Human Nature*,[44] MIT cognitive scientist **Steven Pinker** tells readers that **today's social scientists unjustly ignore the biological basis of human behavior, replacing it instead with three myths: (1) the myth of the blank slate, (2) the myth of the Noble Savage, and (3) the Ghost in the Machine myth.** The blank slate myth holds that the human mind has no innate traits and that the human personality is fully malleable by society. The Noble Savage myth says that human nature is essentially good. The Ghost in the Machine myth holds that each person has an individual soul-like quality that can make choices that can be completely independent of any biological predispositions. These three myths, says Pinker, comprise the standard social science model of the modern era and have led to misguided social and political policies. It is only when the impact of biology on human behavior is fully recognized, says the author, that effective social policies—including those aimed at controlling crime—can be developed.

According to **C. Ray Jeffery**, a comprehensive biologically based program of crime prevention and crime control would include the following:[45]

- "Pre- and postnatal care for pregnant women and their infants" to monitor and address potentially detrimental developmental conditions, which could lead to heightened aggression and crime later in life.

- Monitoring of children throughout the early stages of their development to identify "early symptoms of behavioral disorder."

- Monitoring of children in their early years to reduce the risk of exposure to violence-inducing experiences like child abuse and violence committed by other children.

- Neurological examinations, including CAT, PET, and MRI scans, "given when the need is evident."

- Biological research, conducted in our nation's prisons and treatment facilities, which might better identify the root causes of aggression and violence. Laws that prevent the experimental use of prison subjects, the analysis of the bodies of executed prisoners, and other similar types of biological investigations must change, says Jeffery.

Jeffery adds that the fundamental orientation of our legal system must also change to acknowledge contributions of biological criminologists. Such a change would replace or supplement our current "right to punishment" doctrine with a "right to treatment" philosophy. Jeffery concludes his analysis by saying, "If legal and political barriers prevent us from regarding antisocial behavior as a medical problem, and if we do not permit medical research on criminal behavior, how can we ever solve the crime problem?"[46]

Depending too heavily on biological approaches to crime has ethical implications for every aspect of human social life and may ultimately suggest the possible abortion of defective fetuses, capital punishment in lieu of rehabilitation, and enforced sterilization. Precedent for such fears can be found in cases like *Buck* v. *Bell*,[47] discussed earlier in this chapter, in which the U.S. Supreme Court, influenced by the genetically based perspectives of the times, sanctioned state-enforced sterilization statutes.

Potential links between race and crime, suggested by some researchers, are especially repugnant to many who criticize biological criminology, seeing it as a reemergence of the eugenics movement of the early twentieth century. Ronald Walters, a political scientist at Howard University,

A young child at play. What is the myth of the blank slate? Of the Noble Savage? The Ghost in the Machine?

for example, observes that "seeking the biological and genetic aspects of violence is dangerous to African-American youth. . . . When you consider the perception that black people have always been the violent people in this society, it is a short step from this stereotype to using this kind of research for social control."[48] According to University of Maryland criminologists Gary LaFree and Katheryn K. Russell, "[A] major reason for moving away from studies of differential crime rates by race, beginning in the 1960s, was to avoid negative associations between race and crime: blacks already were disadvantaged by the economy and the society. Thus, to imply that crime problems were more serious for blacks than for others seemed to be double victimization." However, the same authors add, "no group has suffered more than African-Americans by our failure to understand and control street crime."[49]

Although biological theories of crime may have problems, some criminologists believe that to ignore the potential contributions of biological theorists because of hypothetical policy consequences or because of the supposed danger of racial prejudice does a disservice to the science of criminology and

denies the opportunity for compassionate and objective researchers to realistically assist in the process of crime reduction. In 1993, for example, the Youth Violence Initiative, begun under President George Bush to study problem behavior among American youth, was canceled by the Clinton administration because indications were that it might identify a disproportionate number of racial and ethnic minorities as delinquent.

In 1997, in an attempt to bring biological theorizing into the criminological mainstream, Lee Ellis and Anthony Walsh expanded on the theme of genetic predispositions, noting that "in the case of behavior, nearly all of the effects of genes are quite indirect because they are mediated through complex chains of events occurring in the brain. This means that there are almost certainly no genes for something as complex as criminal behavior. Nevertheless, many genes may affect brain functioning in ways that either increase or reduce the chances of individuals learning various complex behavior patterns, including behavior patterns that happen to be so offensive to others that criminal sanctions have been instituted to minimize their recurrence."[50]

Some say that biological theories of crime hold racial implications. Is that true? If so, is that a reason to ignore their potential contributions to the field?

THE CRIME

Around midnight of July 13, 1966, a drunken Richard Speck invaded a townhouse where nursing students from nearby South Chicago Community Hospital resided.[i] Within the first hour, he was able to capture and tie up nine women. One of the most baffling elements of this crime is the mystery of how Speck was able to control all nine women without any of them attempting to escape or making enough noise to attract the attention of someone from an adjacent building.

After securing all the victims, Speck spent the next three hours systematically taking each student to another room within the townhouse and killing her. Each was violently murdered by strangulation, multiple stab wounds, and/or a cut throat; one was also raped.

Evidently distracted by these activities, Speck lost count of the number of women he had captured. As a result, one of the women survived by rolling under a bed. Speck departed the townhouse at approximately 3:30 A.M. The survivor, Corazon Amurao, huddled in terror under the bed until almost 6:00 A.M. before she finally crawled out a window and began calling for help.

During the ensuing manhunt, Speck drank his way from bar to bar, ultimately retiring to a flophouse hotel with a prostitute. Afterward, he returned to his drinking binge, ending up in a rundown hotel where he took a room. In the room, he consumed an entire bottle of wine, then went to the communal bathroom at the end of the hall, broke the bottle, and used it to cut open his wrist and inner elbow.

When Speck was found, he was placed under arrest, taken to Cook County Hospital to be treated for his injuries, and then transferred to Cook County Jail. On a change of venue motion by the defense, the case was tried in Peoria. The jury returned a guilty verdict in just 49 minutes, and Speck was sentenced to death.[ii]

Speck achieved notoriety in the national press when his lawyers offered the claim that he was an XYY supermale, apparently in the hopes that the claim could provide a defense to the charges against him. At the time the claim was made, the XYY theory was being debated in academic circles and had become popular with the public. Later tests showed, however, that Speck did not carry the extra Y chromosome.[iii]

Speck's death sentence was commuted to 50 to 100 years in prison when the U.S. Supreme Court voided the death penalty in 1972. He died of a heart attack in prison on December 5, 1991.

The Causes Behind the Crime
Richard Benjamin Speck

Can Biological Theories Explain This Crime?

- Born the seventh of eight children, on December 6, 1941, Speck's early upbringing in Kirkwood, Illinois, included strict adherence to Baptist religious teachings. When Richard was just six years old, his father died, and his mother subsequently married a hard-fisted drinker with an arrest record. *Might these events indicate that something other than biology was at work in shaping Speck's personality and behavior?*

- After the family moved to Dallas, Texas, Speck performed poorly in school and began sinking into increasingly serious delinquent behavior. His drunken stepfather's response was typically the administration of severe beatings for each of Speck's continuing transgressions. Speck himself became a heavy drinker, an affliction that would haunt him for the remainder of his life. *Could the propensity toward heavy drinking, shown by Speck, be the result of genetic predispositions? Is it more likely to be the result of learned behavior? Might it be both?*

- Interspersed with a series of incarcerations for various burglaries, thefts, check forgeries, and other low-level crimes, 18-year-old Speck married 15-year-old Shirley Malone in November 1962. Their brief marriage was marked by his repeated absence while imprisoned, punctuated by his physical abuse of both his wife and his mother-in-law whenever he was not in jail. The abuse of his wife included frequent instances of rape at knifepoint. *Might any of the biological theories discussed in this chapter provide an explanation for Speck's violent behavior? If so, which ones?*

- An examination of Speck's brain after his death by a neuropathologist at the Chicago Institute of Neurosurgery is reported to have found gross abnormalities. The boundary between two normally distinct areas of his brain—the hippocampus, which involves memory, and the amygdala, which deals with rage and other strong emotions—were found to

Lena Wilkening, the mother of Pamela, one of the eight nurses murdered by Richard Speck, wipes away tears at his parole hearing in 1976. Should Speck have been paroled?

be blurred, with cells from the areas encroaching unnaturally upon each other. *Does this sound like a plausible explanation for Speck's criminal behavior? Might social factors have also played a role?*

NOTES:

[i]David Lohr, "Richard Speck," *Crime Magazine: An Encyclopedia of Crime,* August 2003, http://crimemagazine.com/03/richardspeck,0820.htm (accessed May 22, 2007).

[ii]Troy Taylor, "Born to Raise Hell: The Life and Crimes of Richard Speck," *Weird & Haunted Chicago,* 2003, http://www.prairieghosts.com/speck.html (accessed March 14, 2009).

[iii]Scott Fornek, "Was He Evil, Crazy—or Brain-damaged?" *Chicago Sun-Times,* July 11, 2006, http://findarticles.com/p/articles/mi_qn4155/is_20060711/ai_n16528144 (accessed May 20, 2009).

Richard Speck in a jail hospital in 1966 – after his arrest. Was Speck a supermale?

Summary and Key Concepts

BIOLOGICAL ROOTS OF CRIMINAL BEHAVIOR

Biological theories adhere to the principle that the basic determinants of human behavior, including criminality, are constitutionally or physiologically based and are largely inherited.

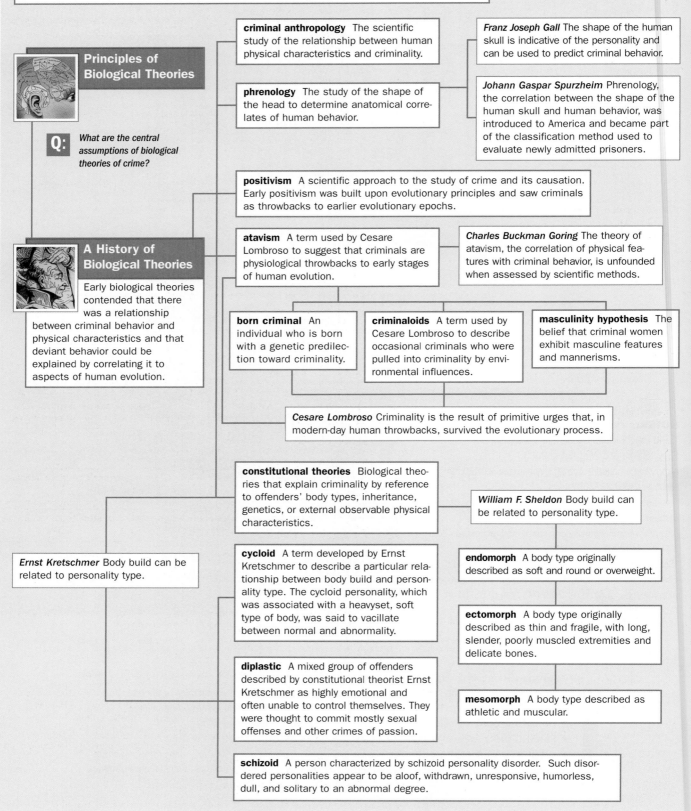

Principles of Biological Theories

Q: *What are the central assumptions of biological theories of crime?*

criminal anthropology The scientific study of the relationship between human physical characteristics and criminality.

phrenology The study of the shape of the head to determine anatomical correlates of human behavior.

Franz Joseph Gall The shape of the human skull is indicative of the personality and can be used to predict criminal behavior.

Johann Gaspar Spurzheim Phrenology, the correlation between the shape of the human skull and human behavior, was introduced to America and became part of the classification method used to evaluate newly admitted prisoners.

A History of Biological Theories

Early biological theories contended that there was a relationship between criminal behavior and physical characteristics and that deviant behavior could be explained by correlating it to aspects of human evolution.

positivism A scientific approach to the study of crime and its causation. Early positivism was built upon evolutionary principles and saw criminals as throwbacks to earlier evolutionary epochs.

atavism A term used by Cesare Lombroso to suggest that criminals are physiological throwbacks to early stages of human evolution.

Charles Buckman Goring The theory of atavism, the correlation of physical features with criminal behavior, is unfounded when assessed by scientific methods.

born criminal An individual who is born with a genetic predilection toward criminality.

criminaloids A term used by Cesare Lombroso to describe occasional criminals who were pulled into criminality by environmental influences.

masculinity hypothesis The belief that criminal women exhibit masculine features and mannerisms.

Cesare Lombroso Criminality is the result of primitive urges that, in modern-day human throwbacks, survived the evolutionary process.

constitutional theories Biological theories that explain criminality by reference to offenders' body types, inheritance, genetics, or external observable physical characteristics.

William F. Sheldon Body build can be related to personality type.

Ernst Kretschmer Body build can be related to personality type.

cycloid A term developed by Ernst Kretschmer to describe a particular relationship between body build and personality type. The cycloid personality, which was associated with a heavyset, soft type of body, was said to vacillate between normal and abnormality.

endomorph A body type originally described as soft and round or overweight.

ectomorph A body type originally described as thin and fragile, with long, slender, poorly muscled extremities and delicate bones.

diplastic A mixed group of offenders described by constitutional theorist Ernst Kretschmer as highly emotional and often unable to control themselves. They were thought to commit mostly sexual offenses and other crimes of passion.

mesomorph A body type described as athletic and muscular.

schizoid A person characterized by schizoid personality disorder. Such disordered personalities appear to be aloof, withdrawn, unresponsive, humorless, dull, and solitary to an abnormal degree.

Modern Biological Theories: Chemical and Environmental Precursors of Crime

Biological theories utilize chemical influences, including hormones, food additives, allergies, vitamins, and other chemical substances, to explain criminal behavior.

hypoglycemia A medical condition characterized by low blood sugar.

 Q: *What have research studies in the field of genetics had to say about possible causes of crime?*

Hormones and Criminality

Some studies demonstrate a link between testosterone levels and aggression; fluctuations in levels of female hormones may also influence behavior and lead to law violation.

testosterone The primary male hormone. Produced in the testes, its function is to control secondary sex characteristics and sexual drive.

Q: *Are high blood levels of testosterone linked to criminality?*

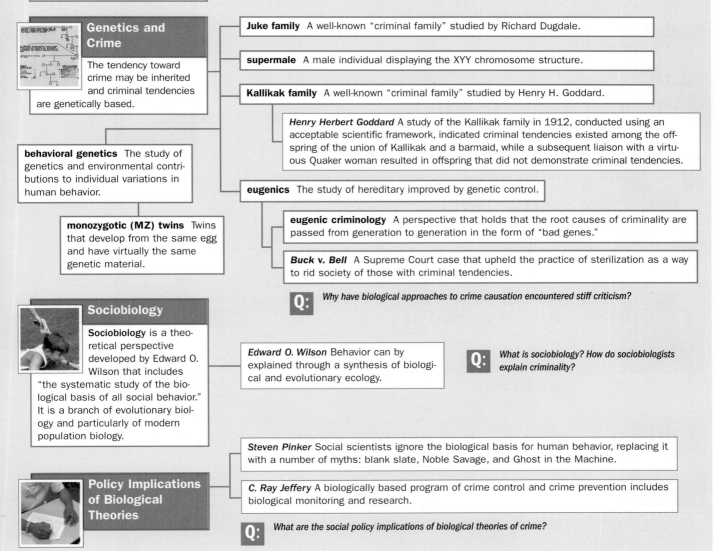

Genetics and Crime

The tendency toward crime may be inherited and criminal tendencies are genetically based.

Juke family A well-known "criminal family" studied by Richard Dugdale.

supermale A male individual displaying the XYY chromosome structure.

Kallikak family A well-known "criminal family" studied by Henry H. Goddard.

Henry Herbert Goddard A study of the Kallikak family in 1912, conducted using an acceptable scientific framework, indicated criminal tendencies existed among the offspring of the union of Kallikak and a barmaid, while a subsequent liaison with a virtuous Quaker woman resulted in offspring that did not demonstrate criminal tendencies.

behavioral genetics The study of genetics and environmental contributions to individual variations in human behavior.

eugenics The study of hereditary improved by genetic control.

eugenic criminology A perspective that holds that the root causes of criminality are passed from generation to generation in the form of "bad genes."

monozygotic (MZ) twins Twins that develop from the same egg and have virtually the same genetic material.

Buck v. Bell A Supreme Court case that upheld the practice of sterilization as a way to rid society of those with criminal tendencies.

Q: *Why have biological approaches to crime causation encountered stiff criticism?*

Sociobiology

Sociobiology is a theoretical perspective developed by Edward O. Wilson that includes "the systematic study of the biological basis of all social behavior." It is a branch of evolutionary biology and particularly of modern population biology.

Edward O. Wilson Behavior can by explained through a synthesis of biological and evolutionary ecology.

 Q: *What is sociobiology? How do sociobiologists explain criminality?*

Steven Pinker Social scientists ignore the biological basis for human behavior, replacing it with a number of myths: blank slate, Noble Savage, and Ghost in the Machine.

C. Ray Jeffery A biologically based program of crime control and crime prevention includes biological monitoring and research.

Policy Implications of Biological Theories

Q: *What are the social policy implications of biological theories of crime?*

CHAPTER 4

Psychological and Psychiatric Foundations of Criminal Behavior
It's How We Think

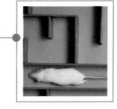

The antisocial child tends to become the antisocial teenager and then the antisocial adult, just as the antisocial adult then tends to produce another antisocial child.

—David Farrington

[The psychopath] lacks those normal human sentiments without which life in common is impossible.

—Gordon Allport

CRIMINOLOGY INTERACTIVE

In the **Crime Theories** section of Criminology Interactive, click on **Psychological Theories**.

PRINCIPLES OF PSYCHOLOGICAL AND PYSCHIATRIC THEORIES

Psychological determinants of deviant or criminal behavior may be couched in terms of exploitative personality characteristics, poor impulse control, emotional arousal, an immature personality, and so on. Before beginning a discussion of psychological theories, however, it is necessary to provide a brief overview of the terminology used to describe the psychological study of crime and criminality. **Forensic psychology**, one of the fastest-growing subfields of psychology, is the application of the science and profession of psychology to questions and issues relating to law and the legal system.[1] Forensic psychology is sometimes referred to as **criminal psychology**, and forensic psychologists are also called "criminal psychologists," "correctional psychologists," and "police psychologists." Unlike forensic psychologists (who

History of Psychological Theories

Two major ideas characterized early psychological theories. One view emphasized behavioral **conditioning**; the other focused mostly on personality disturbances and diseases of the mind. Together, these two theories formed the early foundation of psychological criminology.

Behavioral Conditioning

The concept of conditioned behavior was popularized through the work of Russian physiologist Ivan Pavlov (1849–1936), whose work with dogs won the Nobel Prize in physiology and medicine in 1904. The dogs, which salivated when food was presented to them, were always fed in the presence of a ringing bell. Soon, Pavlov found, the dogs would salivate as if in preparation for eating when the bell alone was rung, even when no food was present. Hence, salivation, an automatic response to the presence of food, could be conditioned to occur in response to some other stimulus, demonstrating that animal behavior could be predictably altered via association with external changes arising from the environment surrounding the organism.

The Psychopath

The other idea that informed early psychological theories was that of mental disease, or psychopathy. Psychologists and psychiatrists distinguish between the terms *psychopathy* and *psychopathology*. In the psychological literature, *psychopathology* "refers to any sort of psychological disorder that causes distress either for the individual or for those in the individual's life."[3] Hence, depression, **schizophrenia**, attention deficit hyperactivity disorder, alcoholism, bulimia, etc., can all be considered forms of psychopathology. *Psychopathy*, on the other hand, "refers to a very specific and distinctive type of psychopathology"[4]—a personality disorder characterized by antisocial behavior and a lack of feelings, especially empathy or sensitivity toward others.

The term *psychopathy* comes from the Greek words *psyche* (meaning "soul" or "mind") and *pathos* ("suffering" or "illness"). The **psychopath**, also called a **sociopath**, has been historically viewed as perversely cruel, often without thought or feeling for his or her victims.[5] By the Second World War, the role of the psychopathic personality in crime causation had become central to psychological theorizing. The concept of a psychopathic personality, which by its very definition is asocial, was fully developed by neuropsychiatrist **Hervey M. Cleckley** in his 1941 book *The Mask of Sanity*[6]—a work that had considerable impact on the field of psychology. Cleckley described the psychopath as a "moral idiot," or as one who does not feel empathy with others, even though that person may be fully aware of what is happening around him or her. The central defining

Ivan Pavlov (with beard), demonstrating a conditioned reflex in a dog. Might some human behavior also be explained through the concept of a conditioned response?

generally hold Ph.D.'s), forensic psychiatrists are medical doctors, and **forensic psychiatry** is a medical sub-specialty that applies psychiatry to the needs of crime prevention and solution, criminal rehabilitation, and issues of criminal law.[2]

Psychological and psychiatric theories of crime causation make the following fundamental assumptions:

- The individual is the primary unit of analysis.
- Personality is the major motivational element within individuals because it is the seat of drives and the source of motives.
- Crimes result from abnormal, dysfunctional, or inappropriate mental processes within the personality.

- Criminal behavior, although condemned by the social group, may be purposeful for the individual insofar as it addresses certain felt needs. Behavior can be judged "inappropriate" only when measured against external criteria purporting to establish normality.
- *Normality* is generally defined by social consensus—that is, what the majority of people in any social group agree is "real," appropriate, or typical.
- Defective, or abnormal, mental processes may have a variety of causes, including a diseased mind, inappropriate learning or improper conditioning, the emulation of inappropriate role models, and adjustment to inner conflicts.

characteristic of a psychopath is described as a "poverty of affect," or the inability to accurately imagine how others think and feel. Therefore, it becomes possible for a psychopath to inflict pain and engage in cruelty without appreciation for the victim's suffering. Charles Manson, for example, whom some regard as a psychopath, once told a television reporter, "I could take this book and beat you to death with it, and I wouldn't feel a thing. It'd be just like walking to the drugstore."[7]

In *The Mask of Sanity*, Cleckley describes numerous characteristics of the psychopathic personality, some of which are listed here:

- Superficial charm and "good intelligence"
- Absence of delusions, hallucinations, or other signs of psychosis
- Absence of nervousness or psychoneurotic manifestations
- Inability to feel guilt or shame
- Unreliability
- Chronic lying
- Ongoing antisocial behavior
- Poor judgment and inability to learn from experience
- Self-centeredness and incapacity to love
- Unresponsiveness in general interpersonal relations
- An impersonal, trivial, and poorly integrated sex life
- Failure to follow any life plan

For Cleckley, "psychopathy was defined by a constellation of dysfunctional psychological processes as opposed to specific behavioral manifestations."[8] Cleckley noted that in cases he had observed the behavioral manifestations of psychopathy varied with the person's age, gender, and socioeconomic status.

Even though psychopaths have a seriously flawed personality, they can easily fool others into trusting them—hence the title of Cleckley's book. According to Cleckley, indicators of psychopathy appear early in life, often in the teenage years. They include lying, fighting, stealing, and vandalism. Even earlier signs may be found, according to some authors, in bed-wetting, cruelty to animals, sleepwalking, and fire setting.[9] Others have described psychopaths as "individuals who display impulsiveness, callousness, insincerity, pathological lying and deception, egocentricity, poor judgment, an impersonal sex life, and an unstable life plan."[10]

Antisocial Personality Disorder

In recent years, the terms *sociopath* and *psychopath* have fallen into disfavor. In the attempt to identify sociopathic individuals, some psychologists have come to place greater emphasis on the type of *behavior* exhibited, rather than on identifiable personality traits. By 1968, the American Psychiatric Association's (APA's) *Diagnostic and Statistical Manual of Mental Disorders* had completely discontinued using the words *sociopath* and *psychopath*, replacing them with the terms *antisocial* and *asocial personality*.[11] In that year, the APA manual changed to a description of **antisocial (asocial) personality** types as "individuals who are basically unsocialized and whose behavior pattern brings them repeatedly into conflicts with society. They are incapable of significant loyalty to individuals, groups, or social values. They are grossly selfish, callous, irresponsible, impulsive, and unable to feel guilt or to learn from experience and punishment. Frustration tolerance is low. They tend to blame others or offer plausible rationalization for their behavior."[12] In most cases, individuals exhibiting, through their behavioral patterns, an antisocial personality are said to be suffering from *antisocial personality disorder* (sometimes referred to in clinical circles as "APD," "ASPD," or "ANPD").

Charles Manson. What characteristics of a psychopath does Manson demonstrate?

The Psychoanalytic Perspective

Perhaps the best-known psychiatrist of all time is **Sigmund Freud** (1856–1939). Freud coined the term **psychoanalysis** in 1896 and based an entire theory of human behavior on it. From the point of view of psychoanalysis, criminal behavior is maladaptive, or the product of inadequacies in the offender's personality. Significant inadequacies may result in full-blown mental illness, which can be a direct cause of crime. The psychoanalytic perspective encompasses diverse notions like personality, **neurosis**, and **psychosis** and more specific concepts like transference, **sublimation**, and repression. **Psychotherapy**, referred to in its early days as the "talking cure" because it relied on patient–therapist communication, is the attempt to relieve patients of their mental disorders through the application of psychoanalytic principles and techniques.

According to Freud, the personality is made up of three components—the id, the ego, and the superego—as shown in Figure 4–1. The **id** is the fundamental aspect of the personality from which drives, wishes, urges, and desires emanate. Freud focused primarily on love, aggression, and sex as fundamental drives in any personality. The id operates according to the pleasure principle, seeking full and immediate gratification of its needs. Individuals, however, according to Freud, are rarely fully aware of the urges that manifest (occasionally into awareness) from the id because it is a largely unconscious region of the mind. Nonetheless, from the Freudian perspective, each of us carries within our id the prerequisite motivation for criminal behavior. We are, each one of us, potential murderers, sexual aggressors, and thieves—our drives and urges kept in check only by other, controlling aspects of our personalities.

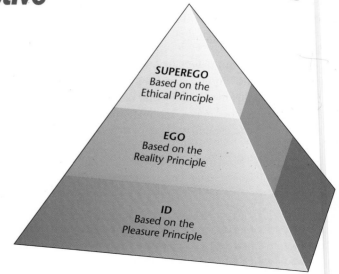

FIGURE 4–1 The Psychoanalytic Structure of Personality

The **ego** is primarily charged with reality testing. Freud's use of the word *ego* should not be confused with popular usage, whereby a person might talk about an "inflated ego" or an "egotistical person." For Freud, the ego was primarily concerned with how objectives might be best accomplished. The ego tends to effect strategies for the individual that maximize pleasure and minimize pain. It lays out the various paths of action that can lead to wish fulfillment. The ego inherently recognizes that it may be necessary to delay gratification to achieve a more fulfilling long-term goal.

The **superego** is much like a moral guide to right and wrong. If properly developed, it evaluates the ego's plans, dismissing some as morally inappropriate while accepting others as ethically viable. The id of a potential rapist, for example, might be filled with lustful drives, and his ego may develop a variety of alternative plans whereby those drives might be fulfilled, some legal and some illegal. His superego will, if the individual's personality is relatively well integrated and the

Sigmund Freud at work in his study in the 1930s. Which of the three aspects of the personality posited by psychoanalysis can be expected to contribute the most to criminal behavior?

superego is properly developed, turn the individual away from law-violating behavior based on his sensual desires and guide the ego to select a path of action that is in keeping with social convention. When the dictates of the superego are not followed, feelings of guilt may result. The superego is one of the most misunderstood of Freudian concepts. In addition to elements of conscience, the superego also contains what Freud called the "ego-ideal," which is a symbolic representation of what society values. The ego-ideal differs from the conscience in that it is less forceful in controlling behavior in the absence of the likelihood of discovery.

Although Freud did not directly address crime, he did spend much of his time examining abnormal behaviors, many of which might lead to violations of the criminal law. One way in which a person might be led into crime, according to the perspective of psychoanalysis, is as the result of a poorly developed superego. In the individual without a fully functional superego, the mind is left to fall back on the ego's reality-testing ability. To put it simply, the ego, operating without a moral guide, may select a path of action that, although expedient at the time, violates the law. Individuals suffering from poor superego development are likely to seek immediate gratification without giving thought to the long-term consequences of the choices they make.

Critique of the Psychoanalytic Perspective

Freudian theory has been criticized on several levels. The first and most fundamental criticism of this perspective is its lack of scientific support. Critics point out that Freud's theories are not research-based and that there is not substantial support for his concepts. As such, Freudian theory has been seen as less of a scientific explanation for human behavior based on sound methodology, and more of a belief system, valuable as a tool for literary and philosophical interpretation.[13]

Freud has also been criticized for failing to put the particular elements of his theory into a wider context for society as a whole. According to Freud critic Reinhold Niebuhr, Freud's theories "seemed to reconstruct pessimism about human nature upon the basis of modern science and thus gave modern man a secular view of the inevitability of egoist corruptions of creativity."[14]

Freudian theory was very popular during the middle part of the twentieth century. By the 1980s, however, the notions of ego and id were considered antiquated by most psychiatrists. Attention shifted to the study of chemical imbalances in the brain, and psychopharmacology, or the use of drugs to treat psychiatric symptoms and disorders, has supplemented—if not replaced—the earlier ideas of Freud and his followers. Recently, however, the field of psychiatry has seen a rekindling of interest in Freudian psychology. The reason, according to some contemporary thinkers, is that psychopharmacology has been unable to provide an alternative grand theory of personality, emotion, and motivation.[15] Moreover, today's neuroscientists are busily creating a chemical map of the mind that seems to validate the general sketch that Freud provided decades ago. Soon a new and unified perspective that reconciles the work of neurologists and psychiatrists may emerge.

This is the famous couch used by Freud during psychoanalysis sessions with his patients. What are some criticisms of the Freudian perspective?

Crime as Adaptive Behavior

One pressing need of many criminals, according to some psychologists, is the need to be punished, which arises, according to psychiatric theory, from a sense of guilt. Psychiatrists who suggest that the need to be punished is a motivating factor in criminal behavior are quick to point out that this need may be a closely guarded secret, unknown even to the offender. Hence, from the psychiatric point of view, many drives, motives, and wishes are unconscious or even repressed by people who harbor them. **The concept of repression holds that the human mind may choose to keep certain aspects of itself out of consciousness, possibly because of shame, self-loathing, or a simple lack of adequate introspection.** The desire for punishment, however, sometimes comes to the fore. In 1993, for example, Westley Alan Dodd was hanged to death by authorities in Washington State for the kidnapping, rape, and murder of three little boys four years earlier. Dodd, who said he had molested dozens of children over the course of a decade, sought the death penalty after he was convicted, saying he deserved to die and vowing to sue the American Civil Liberties Union or anyone else who sought to save him.[16]

Crime can be adaptive in other ways as well. Some psychiatrists see it as an adaptation to life's stresses. According to **Seymour L. Halleck**, a psychiatrist and adjunct professor of law at the University of North Carolina at Chapel Hill, turning to crime can provide otherwise disenfranchised individuals with a sense of power and purpose.[17] Halleck says that crime can also provide "excellent rationalizations" for perceived inadequacies—especially for those whose lives have been failures when judged against the benchmarks of the wider society. "The criminal is able to say. . ., 'I could have been successful if I had not turned to crime. All my troubles have come to me because I have been bad.'" Thus, crime, according to Halleck, provides "a convenient resource for denying, forgetting or ignoring. . . other inadequacies."[18]

Insofar as the choice of crime reduces stresses that the individual faces by producing changes in the environment (empowerment), it is referred

Young boys playing a video game. How might such play be a form of adaptation?

to as **alloplastic adaptation**. When crime leads to stress reduction as a result of internal changes in beliefs, value systems, and so forth, it is called **autoplastic adaptation**. The offender who is able to deny responsibility for other failures by turning to crime is said to be seeking autoplastic adaptation. Because other forms of behavior may also meet many of the same needs as crime, Halleck points out, an individual may select crime over various other behavioral alternatives only when no reasonable alternatives are available or when criminal behavior has inherent advantages—as might be the case under instances of economic or social oppression. (That is, individuals who are actively discriminated against may find personal and political significance in violating the laws of the oppressing society.)

Finally, we should recognize that perceptions vary and that although criminal behavior may appear to be a valid choice for some individuals who are seeking viable responses to perceived stresses and oppression, their perceptions may not be wholly accurate.

A group of playground bullies. How might the concept of alloplastic adaptation explain future delinquency on the part of the victim?

Modeling Theory

On December 1, 1997, 14-year-old Michael Carneal walked up to a student prayer group in his Kentucky high school and opened fire with a .22-caliber pistol. Like a trained marksman, he squeezed off eight shots, killing three students and wounding five others. Lieutenant Colonel Dave Grossman, a retired army ranger and former West Point assistant professor of psychology, was amazed at the accuracy of Carneal's shooting. "He . . . got eight hits on eight different targets, five of them head shots," says Grossman. It was, Grossman says, a "truly, truly stunning" feat of marksmanship.[19]

Where did Carneal learn to shoot like that? And what made him *want* to shoot? The local sheriff couldn't understand Carneal's motivation and fielded questions about a possible conspiracy or an anti-Christian terror campaign.[20] But no conspiracy ever came to light, and Carneal and his family were churchgoers themselves. Although not a criminologist, Grossman thinks he knows what caused the shootings. The colonel reviewed Carneal's psychiatric records and found that the teenager had spent hundreds of hours playing violent computer games—including *Quake*, *Redneck Rampage*, and *Resident Evil*—for months before the shooting. Grossman calls the games "hypnotic murder simulators" and says that they are surprisingly similar to military combat-training programs. "This boy was doing exactly what he was drilled to do," says Grossman. Some young men, like Carneal, says Grossman, "play these video games not twice a year, but hours every night, and they shoot every living creature in sight until they run out of bullets or run out of targets."[21]

Do violent computer games lead to violent crime? While the jury is still out on that question, the importance of imitation and **modeling** in shaping behavior has long been studied. One of the earliest attempts to explain crime and deviance as learned behavior can be found in the work of **Gabriel Tarde** (1843–1904), a French social theorist of the late 1800s. Tarde discounted the biological theories of Lombroso and others. **The basis of any society, Tarde believed, was imitation, the tendency of people to pattern their behavior after the behavior of others.** Tarde developed a theory of human behavior that built upon three laws of imitation and suggestion.[22] **Tarde's first law held that individuals in close intimate contact with one another tend to imitate each other's behavior. His second law stated that imitation moves from the top down.** This means that poor people tend to imitate wealthy people, youngsters tend to emulate those older than themselves, lower-class people tend to imitate members of the upper class, and so on. **The third law of imitation is the law of insertion, which says that new acts and behaviors tend to either reinforce or replace old ones.** Hence, the music of each generation replaces the music of the one that preceded it, the politics of young people eventually become the politics of the nation, faddish drugs are substituted for traditional ones, and new forms of crime tend to take the place of older ones (as when, for example, computer criminals become a more serious threat to financial institutions than bank robbers).

More recently, **Albert Bandura** developed a comprehensive **modeling theory** of aggression. Although everyone is capable of aggression, Bandura says, "people are not born with . . . repertories of aggressive behavior. They must learn them."[23] **Modeling theory, a form of social learning theory, asserts that people learn how to act by observing others.** In some of his early work, Bandura experimented with children who observed adult role models striking inflatable cartoon characters. When the children were observed following their

A father and son go hunting together. What can modeling theory tell us about this young boy's future behavior?

encounter with adult behavior, they, too, exhibited similarly aggressive behavior. Bandura also studied violence on television and concluded that "television is an effective tutor. Both laboratory and controlled field studies in which young children and adolescents are repeatedly shown either violent or nonviolent fare, disclose that exposure to film violence shapes the form of aggression and typically increases interpersonal aggressiveness in everyday life."[24] A later study by other researchers showed that even after ten years, the level of violence engaged in by young adults was directly related to the degree of violent television they had been exposed to as children.[25]

Aggression can be provoked, Bandura suggests, through physical assaults and verbal threats and insults, as well as by thwarting a person's hopes or obstructing his or her goal-seeking behavior. Deprivation and "adverse reductions in the conditions of life" (a lowered standard of living, the onset of disease, a spouse leaving or caught cheating, for example) are other potential triggers of aggression. Bandura adds, however, that a human being's ability to foresee the future consequences of present behavior adds another dimension to the activation of learned patterns of aggression. That is, aggressive behavior can be perceived as holding future benefits for individuals exhibiting it. In short, it can be seen as a means to a desired end.

Bandura also says that individuals sometimes become aggressive because they are rewarded for doing so. The early twentieth-century American concept of a "macho"—virile and masculine—male figure, for example, was often associated with the expectation of substantial reward. Whether this perception was accurate, it was nonetheless subscribed to by a significant proportion of American men and, for many decades, served as a guide to daily behavior.

Another form of reward can flow from aggression. Bandura called it the "reduction of aversive treatment." By this he meant that simply standing up for oneself can improve the way one is treated by others. For example, standing up to a bully may be the most effective way of dealing with the harassment one might otherwise face. Bandura recognized that everyone has self-regulatory mechanisms that can inhibit the tendency toward aggression. People reward or punish themselves, Bandura said, according to internal standards they have for judging their own behavior. Thus, aggression may be inhibited in people who, for example, value religious, ethical, or moral standards of conduct like compassion, thoughtfulness, and courtesy. Bandura concluded that people who devalue aggression may still engage in it via a process he called "disengagement." **Disengagement** may result from (1) "attributing blame to one's victims"; (2) dehumanization through bureaucratization, automation, urbanization, and high social mobility; (3) vindication of aggressive practices by legitimate authorities; and (4) desensitization resulting from repeated exposure to aggression in any of a variety of forms.

Critique of Modeling Theory

Modeling theory has been criticized for lacking comprehensive explanatory power. How, for example, can striking differences in sibling behavior, when early childhood experiences were likely much the same, be explained? Similarly, why do apparent differences exist between the sexes with regard to degree and type of criminality, irrespective of social background and early learning experiences? More recent versions of modeling theory, sometimes called "cognitive social learning theory,"[26] attempt to account for such differences by hypothesizing that reflection and cognition play a significant role in interpreting what one observes and in determining responses. Hence, few people are likely to behave precisely as others, because they will have their own ideas about what observed behavior means and about the consequences of imitation.

A child imitates her parent's behavior. Which of the three laws of imitation is most applicable here?

Behavior Theory

Behavior theory has sometimes been called the **stimulus-response** approach to human behavior. When an individual's behavior results in rewards or feedback that the individual regards as pleasurable and desirable, then it is likely that the behavior will become more frequent. Under such circumstances, the behavior in question is reinforced. Conversely, when punishment follows behavior, chances are that the frequency of that type of behavior will decrease. The individual's responses are termed **operant behavior** because a person's behavioral choices effectively operate on the surrounding environment to produce consequences for the individual. Similarly, stimuli provided by the environment become behavioral cues that elicit conditioned responses from the individual. Responses are said to be conditioned according to the individual's past experiences, wherein behavioral consequences effectively defined some forms of behavior as desirable and others as undesirable. Behavior theory is often used by parents seeking to control children through a series of **rewards** and **punishments**. Young children may be punished, for example, with spanking, the loss of a favored toy, a turned-off television, and so forth. Older children are often told what rules they are expected to obey and what rewards they can anticipate receiving if they

B. F. Skinner demonstrates the "Skinner box," used for operant conditioning. What criticisms of this perspective can you offer?

A time out corner. What can operant conditioning tell us about raising children?

adhere to those rules. They also know that punishments will follow if they do not obey the rules.

Rewards and punishments have been further divided into four conceptual categories: (1) positive rewards, which increase the frequency of approved behavior by adding something desirable to the situation—as when a "good" child is given a toy; (2) negative rewards, which increase the frequency of approved behavior by removing something distressful from the situation—as when a "good" child is permitted to skip the morning's chores; (3) positive punishments, which decrease the frequency of unwanted behavior by adding something undesirable to the situation—as when a "bad" child is spanked; and (4) negative punishments, which decrease the frequency of unwanted behavior by removing something desirable from the situation—as when a "bad" child's candy is taken away. **According to behavior theory, it is through the application of rewards and punishments that behavior is shaped.**

Behavior theory differs from other psychological theories in that the major determinants of behavior are envisioned as existing in the environment surrounding the individual rather than actually in the individual. **Perhaps the best-known proponent of behavior theory is B. F. Skinner (1904–1990). Skinner, a former Harvard professor, rejected unobservable psychological constructs, focusing instead on patterns of responses to external rewards and stimuli.** Skinner did extensive animal research involving behavioral concepts and created the notion of programmed instruction, which allows students to work at their own pace and provides immediate rewards for learning accomplishments.

Critique of Behavior Theory

Behavior theory has been criticized for ignoring the role that cognition plays in human behavior. Martyrs, for example, persist in what may be defined by the wider society as undesirable behavior, even in the face of severe punishment—including the loss of their own lives. No degree of punishment is likely to deter a martyr who answers to some higher call. Similarly, criminals who are punished for official law violations may find that their immediate social group interprets criminal punishment as status-enhancing.

Self-Control Theory

Self-control refers to a person's ability to alter his or her own states and responses.[27] Many people, regardless of what they have learned or of any flaws in their personality, are able to exercise enough self-control to keep from getting into trouble with the law, even under the most challenging of circumstances. Many psychologists suggest that "the capacity to override and alter the self's responses is a vital characteristic that sets human beings apart from other species."[28] Self-control is most obvious in the face of adversity, as when people override their own natural tendencies to act or when they act contrary to their preferences and impulses.

In the field of psychology, four types of self-control have been identified (Figure 4–2). The first type is impulse control, in which people resist temptations and refrain from acting on impulses that they consider to be socially or personally undesirable. Impulses subject to control include those to eat or drink, to take drugs, to act violently or aggressively, to engage in sexual activity, and so forth. A second type of self-control is exercised over the contents of the mind and includes suppression of unwanted thoughts, the focusing of thoughts or concentration, reasoning and analysis, and inference and guided intuition. A third type of self-control can be exercised over one's emotional and mood states, and a fourth type involves controlling performance—as when a person persists in the face of adversity or physical challenges.

Self-control enables people who are able to exercise it to adjust themselves to a much wider range of circumstances than they otherwise could. Psychologists sometimes argue that the majority of today's personal and social problems (which include things like drug abuse, violence, school failure, alcoholism, unwanted pregnancy, venereal disease, irresponsible money management, underachievement, poor eating habits and obesity, lack of exercise, cigarette smoking, and delinquency and criminality) stem from deficiencies or failures in self-control.[29]

A somewhat different perspective on self-control is offered by criminologists **Michael R. Gottfredson** and **Travis Hirschi** as part of their **general theory of crime**. Gottfredson and

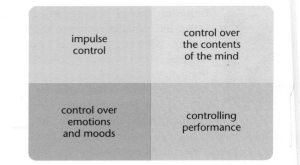

impulse control	control over the contents of the mind
control over emotions and moods	controlling performance

FIGURE 4–2 The Four Types of Self-Control

Hirschi define *self-control* as the degree to which a person is vulnerable to temptations of the moment.[30] They propose that self-control is acquired early in life and that low self-control is the premier individual-level cause of crime. Self-control, say Gottfredson and Hirschi, develops by the end of childhood and is fostered through parental emotional investment in the child, which includes monitoring the child's behavior, recognizing deviance when it occurs, and punishing the child.

Gottfredson and Hirschi recognize the sociological dimensions of criminality by noting that the link between self-control and crime depends substantially upon criminal opportunity, which in itself is a function of the structural or situational circumstances that an individual encounters. Thus, these theorists suggest that "the link between self-control and crime is not deterministic, but probabilistic, affected by opportunities and other constraints."[31]

Recent research appears to show that low self-control tends to lead to peer rejection and isolation—especially

A mother mentors her daughter in the kitchen. What can we learn about self-control from those around us?

A beer bong in action. People learn self-control at an early age, and higher levels of self-control are associated with fewer problems in living. Might members of this group lose control?

> People with little self-control are drawn to activities that are adventurous and exciting.

among juveniles.[32] Consequently, young people with low self-control tend to associate with their deviant peers, meaning that those with low levels of self-control are essentially self-selected into groups of people who share their characteristics. Building on the work of Gottfredson and Hirschi, **Harold G. Grasmick** identifies some of the characteristics of individuals with low levels of self-control.[33] According to Grasmick, such people are impulsive and seek immediate gratification. Those with higher levels of self-control are more inclined to defer gratification in favor of long-term gains. People with less self-control lack diligence, tenacity, and persistence, says Grasmick, and prefer simple tasks and want "money without work, sex without courtship, [and] revenge without court delays."[34] Grasmick also believes that risk seeking is an important determinant of self-control, and he says that people with little self-control are drawn to activities that are adventurous and exciting. Similarly, says Grasmick, these people prefer physical activity over contemplation or conversation and tend to be indifferent or insensitive to the needs of others. While those who lack self-control are not necessarily antisocial or malicious, they are predisposed to being self-centered. Finally, according to Grasmick, self-control is inversely associated with a low frustration tolerance and with an inclination to handle conflict through confrontation.

Critique of Self-Control Theory

One of the major criticisms of self-control theory concerns the definition of self-control itself. Because the theory, in essence, ties self-control directly to crime, their definitions are fundamentally the same. In other words, where there is low self-control, crime naturally exists. Self-control theory, then, cannot stand up to rigorous evaluation and will always appear to be proven correct. Issues also remain about how to measure self-control. For instance, smoking is an indicator of low self-control, but is not necessarily related to crime.

Another debate regarding self-control concerns the generalization that individual differences in criminal behavior remain consistent over the course of one's life. External factors, critics of self-control theory argue, affect an individual's tendency to commit crime at various times in the individual's life.

Finally, the general theory of crime has been criticized because it is considered to oversimplify the causes for crime. Human behavior is more complex, especially in terms of criminal behavior, than Gottfredson and Hirschi take into account, critics contend. Some well-adjusted teenagers, for example, participate in crime during their teen years and then become law-abiding once they reach adulthood.[35]

Insanity and the Law

Unfortunately for criminologists, psychological conceptions of mental illness, antisocial personality, and even psychopathy are not readily applicable to the criminal justice system, which relies instead on the legal concept of **insanity**.[36] Insanity, for purposes of the criminal law, is strictly a legal, not a clinical, determination. Seen this way, *insanity* is a term that refers to a type of defense allowable in criminal courts. While the legal concept of insanity is based upon claims of mental illness, it has no precise counterpart in the jargon of contemporary psychologists or psychiatrists, who speak instead in terms of mental status or, at most, psychosis and personality disorder. As a consequence, legal and psychiatric understandings of mental impairment rarely coincide.

One of the first instances within the Western legal tradition where insanity was accepted as a defense to criminal liability can be found in the case of Daniel M'Naughten (also spelled "McNaughton" and "M'Naghton"). M'Naughten was accused of the 1843 killing of Edward Drummond, the secretary of British prime minister Sir Robert Peel. By all accounts, M'Naughten had intended to kill Peel, but because he was suffering from mental disorganization, he shot Drummond instead, mistaking him for Peel. At his trial, the defense presented information to show that M'Naughten was suffering from delusions, including the belief that Peel's political party waspersecuting him. The court accepted his lawyer's claims, and the defense of insanity was established in Western law. Other jurisdictions were quick to adopt the *M'Naughten* rule, as the judge's decision in the case came to be called. The **M'Naughten rule** holds that individuals cannot be held criminally responsible for their actions if at the time of the offense either (1) they did not know what they were doing or (2) they did not know that what they were doing was wrong. Today the *M'Naughten* rule is still followed by many states when insanity is at issue in criminal cases. Critics of the *M'Naughten* rule say that although the notion of intent inherent within it appeals greatly to lawyers, "it is . . . so alien to current concepts of human behavior that it has been vigorously attacked by psychiatrists. An obvious difficulty with the *M'Naughten* rule is that practically everyone, regardless of the degree of his [mental] disturbance, knows the nature and quality and rightness or wrongness of what he is doing."[37]

Daniel M'Naughten's trial in 1843. How do legal conceptions of insanity differ from psychological and psychiatric understandings?

CENTRAL CRIMINAL COURT, OLD BAILEY—M'NAUGHTEN'S TRIAL.

John W. Hinckley Jr., who attempted to assassinate President Ronald Reagan in 1981, arrives at the Marine Corps base at Quantico, Virginia, following a battery of psychiatric tests. Eventually, Hinckley was found not guilty by reason of insanity—leading to enactment of GBMI laws nationally. What are the likely consequences of a GBMI finding?

The *M'Naughten* ruling opened the floodgates for other types of insanity claims offered as defenses to charges of criminal activity. One interesting claim is that of irresistible impulse. The **irresistible-impulse test**—employed by 18 states, some of which also follow the dictates of the M'Naughten rule—holds that a defendant is not guilty of a criminal offense if the person, by virtue of his or her mental state or psychological condition, was not able to resist committing the action in question.

Guilty but Mentally Ill (GBMI)

A **GBMI** verdict means that a person can be held responsible for a specific criminal act, even though a degree of mental incompetence may be present. In most GBMI jurisdictions, a jury must return a finding of "guilty but mentally ill" if (1) every statutory element necessary for a conviction has been proved beyond a reasonable doubt, (2) the defendant is found to have been *mentally ill* at the time the crime was committed, and (3) the defendant was not found to have been *legally insane* at the time the crime was committed. The difference between mental illness and legal insanity is crucial because a defendant can be mentally ill by standards of the medical profession but sane for purposes of the law.

Upon return of a GBMI verdict, a judge may impose any sentence possible under the law for the crime in question. Offenders declared GBMI are, in effect, found guilty of the criminal offense with which they are charged but, because of their mental condition, are generally sent to psychiatric hospitals for treatment rather than to prison. Once they have been declared "cured," however, such offenders can be transferred to correctional facilities to serve out their sentences.

Social Policy and Psychiatric and Psychological Foundations of Criminal Behavior

Can past behavior predict future behavior? Do former instances of criminality presage additional ones? Are there other identifiable characteristics that violent offenders might manifest that could serve as warning signs to criminal justice decision makers faced with the dilemma of whether to release convicted felons? This, like many other areas, is one in which criminologists are still learning. One recent study found a strong relationship between childhood behavioral difficulties and later problem behavior.[38] According to the authors of the study, "Early antisocial behavior is the best predictor of later antisocial behavior. It appears that this rule holds even when the antisocial behavior is measured as early as the preschool period." Prediction, however, requires more than generalities. It is one thing to say, for example, that generally speaking 70% of children who evidence aggressive behavior will show violent tendencies later in life and quite another to be able to predict which specific individuals will engage in future violations of the criminal law.

Selective incapacitation is a policy based on the notion of career criminality.[39] Career criminals, also called "habitual offenders," are people who repeatedly violate the criminal law. Research has shown that only a small percentage of all offenders account for most of the crimes reported to the police. Some studies have found that as few as 8% of all offenders commit as many as 60 serious crimes each per year.[40] A recent Wisconsin study found that imprisonment of individuals determined to be career offenders saved the state approximately $14,000 per year per offender when the cost of imprisonment was compared with the estimated

Our nation's most secure federal prison, the Administrative Maximum facility in Florence, Colorado. What kinds of policies might work best with career criminals?

Women inmates participate in a substance-abuse meeting at the Julia Tutwiler prison in Alabama. Why do some researchers say that prison pays? Do you agree?

cost of new crimes.[41] Researchers in the Wisconsin study concluded that "prison pays" and suggested that the state continue pursuing a policy of aggressive imprisonment of career offenders, even in the face of escalating costs and vastly overcrowded prisons. The strategy of selective incapacitation, however, which depends on accurately identifying potentially dangerous offenders in existing criminal populations, has been criticized by some authors for yielding a rate of "false positives" of over 60%.[42] Potentially violent offenders are not easy to identify, even on the basis of past criminal records, and sentencing individuals to long prison terms simply because they are thought likely to commit crimes in the future would no doubt be unconstitutional.

The federal 1984 Comprehensive Crime Control Act,[43] which established the U.S. Sentencing Commission, targeted career offenders. Guidelines created by the commission contain, as a central feature, a "criminal history" dimension, which substantially increases the amount of punishment an offender faces based on his or her history of law violations. The sentencing guidelines originally classified a defendant as a career offender if "(1) the defendant was at least 18 years old at the time of the . . . offense, (2) the . . . offense is a crime of violence or trafficking in a controlled substance, and (3) the defendant has at least two prior felony convictions of either a crime of violence or a controlled substance offense."[44] The definition, however, later came under fire for casting individuals with a history of minor drug trafficking into the same category as serial killers and the like. ﹨

Definitions of **dangerousness** are fraught with difficulty because, as some authors have pointed out, "dangerousness is not an objective quality like obesity or brown eyes, rather it is an ascribed quality like trustworthiness."[45] Dangerousness is not necessarily a personality trait that is stable or easily identifiable. Even if it were, some studies of criminal careers seem to show that involvement in crime decreases with age.[46] Hence, as one author states, if "criminality declines more or less uniformly with age, then many offenders will be 'over the hill' by the time they are old enough to be plausible candidates for preventive incarceration."[47]

No discussion of social policy as it relates to the insights of criminal psychology would be complete without mention of correctional psychology. **Correctional psychology** is concerned with the diagnosis and classification of offenders, the treatment of correctional populations, and the rehabilitation of inmates and other law violators. Perhaps the most commonly used classification instrument in correctional facilities today is the Minnesota Multiphasic Personality Inventory, better known as the MMPI. Based on the results of an MMPI, an offender may be assigned to a security level, a correctional program, or a treatment program. Psychological treatment, when employed, typically takes the form of individual or group counseling. Psychotherapy, guided group interaction, cognitive therapy, behavioral modification, and various forms of interpersonal therapy are representative of the range of techniques used.

Few crimes have shocked American society as deeply as the drowning of five young children by their mother, Andrea Pia (Kennedy) Yates, in a bathtub in their suburban Houston, Texas, home on January 20, 2001. Her subsequent trial, conviction, life sentence, successful appeal, and second trial brought the insanity defense based on a claim of postpartum psychosis under intense scrutiny.

Yates's early life showed promise for future success. High school valedictorian and swim team captain, she went on to earn an undergraduate degree in nursing from the University of Texas. After obtaining a job as a registered nurse, she met Rusty Yates. Their shared deep Christian faith was a significant factor in their attraction to one another.

When Andrea and Rusty finally married, they planned on having as many children as God intended them to have. The birth of their first child, Noah, a year after their marriage, however, brought unexpected difficulties.

Unaware of the extent of mental illness that had plagued her own family, the new mother was tormented when she began to have violent visions of stabbings and came to believe that Satan was speaking directly to her. Yates hid these frightening experiences from everyone, including her husband. The Yateses had two more children, after which Andrea miscarried. She then had their fourth child, but the birth was followed by pronounced depressive manifestations—including chewed fingers, uncontrollable shaking, hallucinations, voices in her head, suicidal and homicidal thoughts, and two suicide attempts. Soon, she entered into a series of psychiatric counseling sessions with various doctors. A wide variety of drug therapies were tried, many of which Andrea rejected by flushing the prescriptions down the toilet.

Despite extensive hospitalizations and medication for her ongoing depression and emerging psychosis, and against the advice of her psychiatrist, Yates became pregnant again, delivering her fifth child, Mary, in November 2000. The pregnancy had resulted from the urging of her husband, who also ignored the strong medical opposition to the birth of another child.[i]

When Yates's father died just 4 1/2 months after her fifth child was born, her mental health declined dramatically.[ii] Both a hospitalization at the end of March and her medication, however, were terminated by her psychiatrist, Dr. Mahommed Saeed, because, he claimed, she did not seem psychotic. Yates returned to the hospital again for 10 days in May. Upon her release, she was advised to think positive thoughts and to see a psychologist.

Two days later, she systematically drowned each of her five children.

Following a sensational trial, Yates was convicted and sentenced to life in prison. That conviction was subsequently overturned. In July 2006, Yates was retried, but this time she was acquitted of capital murder charges and found not guilty by reason of insanity. She was immediately ordered to commitment in a mental hospital, where she will remain until she is no longer considered to be a threat to herself or others.[iii]

The Causes Behind the Crime
Andrea Yates

Can Psychiatric Theories Explain This Crime?

- Andrea Yates exhibited signs of mental illness and depression. *Could she have been considered a psychopath? Why or why not?*

- Andrea Yates had a family history of mental illness. Depression, for Yates, seemed to follow the birth of a child or other traumatic life event. *How could Yates's mental issues be seen in light of Freudian theory?*

- Yates considered herself a traditional Christian woman. *How might modeling theory have explained her behavior?*

Andrea Yates on her way to trial. What can the Yates case teach us about the psychology of criminal offending?

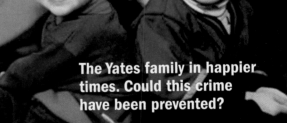

The prosecutor in the Yates case showing photos of the child victims to the jury. What reason did Yates gave for killing her children?

The Yates family in happier times. Could this crime have been prevented?

- Presumably, Andrea Yates eventually succumbed to the Satanic voice and visions she was experiencing. *Might self-control theory be applicable to Yates? Why or why not?*

- Two days after Yates's psychiatrist terminated her medication and hospitalization, she drowned her five children. *Could the irresistible-impulse test be applicable to Yates's case? The M'Naughten rule? Which seems to fit best?*

NOTES:

[i]Charles Montaldo, "Profile of Andrea Yates," About: Crime/Punishment, 2007, http://crime.about.com/od/current/p/andreayates.htm (accessed June 16, 2007).

[ii]Ibid.

[iii]"Jury: Yates Not Guilty by Reason of Insanity," July 26, 2006, MSNBC/ Associated Press, http://www.msnbc.msn.com/id/14024728 (accessed June 16, 2007).

Go to mycrimekit.com to explore the following resources for Chapter 4:

- **MULTIMEDIA:** Interactive review about psychological theories and videos about Sigmund Freud, Behavior Theory, and Gabriel Tarde
- **PRACTICE QUIZ:** Multiple-choice, true/false, short-answer, and essay questions
- **FLASHCARDS:** Twenty-six flashcards to test your knowledge of the chapter's key terms
- **WEB EXTRAS & LIBRARY EXTRAS:** Links to websites, online articles, and resources relating to antisocial personality disorder, behavioral development, and correctional and forensic psychology

Summary and Key Concepts

PSYCHOLOGICAL AND PSYCHIATRIC FOUNDATIONS OF CRIMINAL BEHAVIOR

Psychological and psychiatric perspectives explain crime by examining the mental processes of individual offenders.

Principles of Psychological and Psychiatric Theories

Psychological and psychiatric theories of criminology are derived from the behavioral sciences and focus on the individual as the unit of analysis.

forensic psychology (also called **criminal psychology**) The application of the science and profession of psychology to questions and issues relating to law and the legal system.

forensic psychiatry A branch of psychiatry having to do with the study of crime and criminality.

Q: *What are the major principles of psychological perspectives as they relate to criminal behavior?*

History of Psychological Theories

The psychiatric approach envisions a complex set of drives and motives operating from recesses deep within the personality to determine behavior.

conditioning A psychological principle that holds that the frequency of any behavior can be increased or decreased through reward, punishment, or association with other stimuli.

schizophrenia A form of mental illness in which the sufferer is out of touch with reality and suffers from disjointed thinking.

psychopath An individual who has a personality disorder, especially one manifested in aggressively antisocial behavior, and who is lacking in empathy.

antisocial (asocial) personality A term used to describe individuals who are basically unsocialized and whose behavior patterns bring them repeatedly into conflict with society.

sociopath A term used interchangeably with psychopath.

Hervey M. Cleckley A psychopath is a "moral idiot," or one who does not feel empathy with others, even though that person may be fully aware of what is happening around him or her.

● Psychological and Psychiatric Foundations of Criminal Behavior ● Crime Causation

88

The Psychoanalytic Perspective

This psychiatric approach developed by Austrian psychiatrist Sigmund Freud emphasizes the role of personality in human behavior and sees deviant behavior as the result of dysfunctional personalities.

Sigmund Freud According to Freud, the personality is made up of three components—the id, the ego, and the superego.

psychoanalysis A technique for examining the contents of human consciousness developed by Freud. From the point of view of psychoanalysis, criminal behavior is the product of inadequacies in the offender's personality.

neurosis A functional disorder of the mind or of the emotions involving anxiety, phobia, or other abnormal behavior.

psychosis A form of mental illness in which sufferers are said to be out of touch with reality.

sublimation The psychological process whereby one aspect of consciousness comes to be symbolically substituted for another.

psychotherapy A form of psychiatric treatment based on psychoanalytical principles and techniques.

id The aspect of the personality from which drives, wishes, urges, and desires emanate. More formally, the division of the psyche associated with instinctual impulses and demands for immediate satisfaction of primitive needs.

ego The reality-testing part of the personality. Also called the reality principle. More formally, the personality component that is conscious, most immediately controls behavior, and is most in touch with external reality.

superego The moral aspect of personality, much like the conscience. More formally, the division of the psyche that develops by the incorporation of the perceived moral standards of the community, is mainly unconscious, and includes the conscience.

 Q: *Describe the role of the id, ego, and superego in Freudian psychoanalysis.*

Crime as Adaptive Behavior

alloplastic adaptation A form of adjustment that results from change in the environment surrounding an individual.

autoplastic adaptation A form of adjustment that results from changes with an individual.

Seymour Halleck Crime provides otherwise disenfranchised individuals with a sense of power and purpose.

 Q: *From a psychological perspective, how can criminal behavior be seen as a type of maladaptive behavior?*

Modeling Theory

Modeling theory is a psychological perspective that contends that people learn how to behave by modeling themselves after others whom they have the opportunity to observe.

modeling The process of learning how to behave by observing others.

disengagement The process of devaluing aggression by those who may still engage in it.

Gabriel Tarde The basis for a society is imitation, the tendency of people to pattern their behavior after the behavior of others.

Albert Bandura According to the comprehensive modeling theory of aggression, everyone is capable of aggression, but people must learn aggressive behaviors.

Q: *How does modeling theory explain criminal behavior?*

Behavior Theory

Behavior theory posits that individual behavior that is rewarded will increase in frequency, while that which is punished will decrease.

stimulus-response Alternate name of behavior theory.

operant behavior Behavior that affects the environment in such a way as to produce responses or further behavioral clues.

reward A desirable behavioral consequence likely to increase the frequency of occurrence of that behavior.

punishment An undesirable behavioral consequence likely to decrease the frequency of occurrence of that behavior.

B.F. Skinner A proponent of behavior theory who rejected unobservable psychological constructs, focusing instead on patterns of responses to external rewards and stimuli.

Q: *How can rewards and punishments shape behavior?*

Self-Control Theory

Self-control theory says the root cause of crime can be found in a person's inability to exercise socially appropriate controls over the self.

self-control A person's ability to alter his or her own states and responses.

general theory of crime A theory that attempts to explain all (or at least most) forms of criminal conduct through a single, overarching approach.

Harold Grasmick Those who have high social control tend to defer gratification in favor of long-term gains.

Michael R. Gottfredson and *Travis Hirschi* Low self-control accounts for all crime, from vandalism to homicide, from rape to white-collar crime.

Q: *How can a lack of self-control lead to crime? What can be done to enhance self-control?*

Insanity and the Law

insanity A type of defense allowed in criminal courts.

***M'Naughten* rule** A standard for judging legal insanity that requires that offenders did not know what they were doing, or if they did, that they did not know it was wrong.

irresistible-impulse test A standard for judging legal insanity that holds that a defendant is not guilty of a criminal offense if the person, by virtue of his or her mental state or psychological condition, was not able to resist committing the crime.

GBMI Guilty But Mentally Ill. A GBMI verdict means that a person can be held responsible for a specific criminal act, even though a degree of mental incompetence may be present.

Q: *What's the difference between legal understandings of insanity and psychiatric notions of mental illness?*

Social Policy and Psychiatric and Psychological Foundations of Criminal Behavior

correctional psychology The branch of forensic psychology concerned with the diagnosis and classification of offenders, the treatment of correctional populations, and the rehabilitation of inmates and other law violators.

dangerousness The degree of criminal threat that an offender represents.

selective incapacitation An imprisonment policy based on the notion of career criminality; that is, on the long-term confinement of career criminals.

Q: *What types of crime-control policies might be based on psychological understandings of criminality?*

Social Structure

It's How We Live

Society prepares the crime; the criminal commits it.
—*Chinese proverb*

CRIMINOLOGY
INTERACTIVE

In the **Crime Theories** section of Criminology Interactive, click on **Social Structure Theories**.

MAJOR PRINCIPLES OF SOCIOLOGICAL THEORIES

Theories that explain crime by examining the structure of society are only one of three major sociological approaches to crime causation. Although sociological perspectives on crime causation are diverse, most build upon the following assumptions:

- Social groups, social institutions, the arrangements of society, and social roles all provide the proper focus for criminological study.
- Group dynamics, group organization, and subgroup relationships form the causal nexus out of which crime develops.

- The structure of society and its relative degree of organization or disorganization are important factors contributing to criminal behavior.
- Although it may be impossible to predict the specific behavior of a given individual, statistical estimates of group characteristics are possible. Hence, the probability that a member of a given group will engage in a specific type of crime can be estimated.

Sociological theories analyze institutional arrangements within society (that is, **social structure**) and the interaction among social institutions, individuals, and groups (that is, **social processes**) as they affect socialization and have an impact on social behavior (that is, **social life**). Sociological theories examine the nature of existing power relationships between social groups and focus on the influ-

Principles of Social Structure Theories

Social structure theories explain crime by reference to the economic and social arrangements of society. They see the various formal and informal arrangements between social groups (that is, the structures of society) as the root causes of crime and deviance. Structural theories predict that negative aspects of societal structures, such as disorganization within the family, poverty or income inequality within the economic arrangements of society, disadvantages brought about by a lack of success for some in the educational process, and so on, produce criminal behavior.

Although different kinds of social structure theories have been advanced to explain crime, they all have one thing in common: They highlight those arrangements within society that contribute to the low socioeconomic status of identifiable groups as significant causes of crime. Social structure theorists view members of socially and economically disadvantaged groups as being more likely to commit crime, and they see economic and social disenfranchisement as fundamental causes of crime. Poverty, lack of education, an absence of salable skills, and subcultural

values conducive to crime are all thought to be predicated on the social conditions surrounding early life experiences, and they provide the foundations of social structure theories. Environmental influences, socialization, and traditional and accepted patterns of behavior are all used by social structuralists to portray the criminal as a product of his or her social environment—and the immediate social environment is itself viewed as a consequence of the structure of the society to which the offender belongs. Although criminality is recognized as a form of acquired behavior, it is depicted as the end result of social injustice, racism, and feelings of disenfranchisement to which existing societal arrangements give rise. Similarly, social structure, insofar as it is unfair and relatively unchangeable, is believed to perpetuate the fundamental conditions that cause crime. Consequently, viewed from a social structure perspective, crime is seen largely as a lower-class phenomenon, while the criminality of the middle and upper classes is generally discounted as less serious, less frequent, and less dangerous.

This chapter describes three major types of social structure theories: (1) social disorganization theory (also called the "ecological approach"), (2) strain theory, and (3) culture

> Social structure theories explain crime by reference to the economic and social arrangements of society.

ences that various social phenomena bring to bear on the types of behaviors that tend to characterize *groups* of people. In contrast to more individualized psychological theories, which have what is called a "micro" focus, sociological approaches utilize a "macro" perspective, stressing the type of behavior likely to be exhibited by group members rather than attempting to predict the behavior of specific individuals.

Although all sociological perspectives on crime share the characteristics identified in this section, particular theories give greater or lesser weight to the various components of social life. Hence, we can identify three key sociological explanations for crime:

- Crime is the result of an individual's location within the structure of society. This approach focuses on the social and economic conditions of life, including poverty, alienation, social disorganization, weak social control, personal frustration, relative deprivation, differential opportunity, alternative means to success, and deviant subcultures and subcultural values, that conflict with conventional values. (These are the primary features of *social structure theories*, which are discussed in this chapter.)

- Crime is the end product of various social processes, especially inappropriate socialization and social learning. This approach stresses the role of interpersonal relationships, the strength of the social bond, a lack of self-control, and the personal and group consequences of societal reactions to deviance as they contribute to crime. (These are the primary characteristics of social *process theories* and *social development theories*, which are discussed in Chapter 6.)

- Crime is the product of class struggle. This perspective emphasizes the nature of existing power relationships between social groups, the distribution of wealth within society, the ownership of the means of production, and the economic and social structure of society as it relates to social class and social control. (These are the primary features of *conflict theories*, which are discussed in Chapter 7.)

conflict theory (also called "cultural deviance" theory). All have a number of elements in common, and the classification of a theory into one subcategory or another is often a matter of which aspects a writer chooses to emphasize rather than the result of any clear-cut definitional elements inherent in the perspectives themselves.

Volunteer workers feed the economically unfortunate. How can economic conditions contribute to crime?

Social Structure Theories—From Past to Present

Social disorganization theory is closely associated with the ecological school of criminology. Much early criminology in the United States is rooted in the human ecology movement of the early twentieth century. The idea of the community as a functional whole that directly determines the quality of life for its members was developed and explored around the beginning of the twentieth century by sociologists like **Emile Durkheim** (1858–1917),[1] Ferdinand Toennies (1855–1936),[2] and Georg Simmel (1858–1918).[3] **Durkheim believed that crime was a normal part of all societies and that law was a symbol of social solidarity. Hence, for Durkheim, an act was "criminal when it offends strong and defined states of the collective conscience."[4]**

Because ecological models build upon an organic analogy, it is easy to portray social disorganization as a disease or pathology.[7] Hence, **social ecologists who studied crime developed a disease model built around the concept of social pathology.** In its initial statement, social pathology was defined as "those human actions which run contrary to the ideals of residential stability, property ownership, sobriety, thrift, habituation to work, small business enterprise, sexual discretion, family solidarity, neighborliness, and discipline of will."[8] The term referred simply to behavior not in keeping with the prevalent norms and values of the social group. Over time, however, the concept of social pathology changed, and it came to represent the idea that aspects of society may be somehow pathological, or "sick," and may produce deviant behavior among individuals and groups who live under or are exposed to such social conditions.

Social disorganization and, therefore, social pathology may arise when a group is faced with "social change, uneven development of culture, maladaptation, disharmony, conflict, and lack of consensus."[9] Due to the rapid influx of immigrant populations at the beginning of the twentieth century, American cities were caught up in swift social change, and Park and Burgess saw in them an ideal focus for the study of social disorganization. Park and Burgess viewed cities in terms of concentric zones, which were envisioned much like the circles on a target (see Figure 5-1). Each zone had its unique characteristics wherein

City and suburban environments are contrasted in these two photos. How are lifestyles likely to vary between the two locales? How about crime?

The Chicago School

Some of the earliest sociological theories to receive widespread recognition can be found in the writings of **Robert Park** and **Ernest Burgess**.[5] In the 1920s and 1930s, Park and Burgess, through their work at the University of Chicago, developed what became known as **social ecology**, or the ecological school of criminology. **The social ecology movement, which was influenced by the work of biologists on the interaction of organisms with their environments, concerned itself with how the structure of society adapts to the quality of natural resources and to the existence of other human groups.[6]**

Students enjoying their time at school. What was the greatest contribution made by the ecological school to criminological literature?

unique populations and typical forms of behavior could be found. Park and Burgess referred to the central business zone as Zone I, or the "Loop," in which retail businesses and light manufacturing were typically located. Zone II, surrounding the city center, was home to recent immigrant groups and was characterized by deteriorated housing, factories, and abandoned buildings. Zone II was an area that was in transition from residential to business uses. Zone III contained mostly working-class tenements, while Zone IV was occupied by middle-class citizens with single-family homes, each with its own yard and garage. Zone V, consisting largely of suburbs, was called the "commuter zone." Significantly, Park and Burgess noticed that residents of inner-city zones tended to migrate to outer zones as their economic positions improved.

Clifford Shaw and **Henry McKay**, other early advocates of the ecological approach, applied the concentric zone model to the study of juvenile delinquency. They conducted empirical studies of arrest rates for juveniles in Chicago during the years 1900–1906, 1917–1923, and 1927–1933. These years were associated with high rates of neighborhood transition, during which one immigrant group after another moved in rapid succession from the inner city toward the suburbs—a process that was repeated with the arrival of each new wave of immigrants. Shaw and McKay found that rates of offending remained relatively constant over time within zones of transition, and they concluded that delinquency was caused by the nature of the environment in which immigrants lived rather than by some characteristic of the immigrant groups themselves.[10] Shaw and McKay saw social disorganization as the inability of local communities to solve common problems, and they believed that the degree of disorganization in a community was largely caused by the extent of residential mobility and racial heterogeneity present in that community. In effect, as a new immigrant group, like the Polish, replaced an old immigrant group, like the Irish, and became dominant in a particular location, the process of succession was complete. As a result of their studies, they developed the idea of **cultural transmission**, which held that traditions of delinquency were transmitted through successive generations of the same zone in the same way that language, roles, and attitudes were communicated.

Because early **ecological theories**, including those of Park and Burgess, were developed through a close focus on selected geographic locals, the methodology upon which they were predicated came to be known as "area studies," and because 1920s Chicago served as the model for most such studies, they were soon collectively referred to as the **Chicago School of criminology**.

Although the applicability of these early studies to other cities or to other time periods was questionable, it was generally accepted that the Chicago School had demonstrated the tendency for criminal activity to be associated with urban transition zones, which, because of the turmoil or social disorganization that characterized them, were typified by lower property values, impoverished lifestyles, and a general lack of privacy.

The greatest contribution the ecological school made to criminological literature can be found in its claim that society, in the form of the community, wields a major influence on human behavior.[11] Similarly, ecological theorists of the Chicago School formalized the use of two sources of information: (1) official crime and population statistics and (2) ethnographic data. Population statistics, or demographic data, when combined with crime information, provided empirical material that gave scientific weight to ecological investigations. Ethnographic information, gathered in the form of life stories, or ethnographies, described the lives of city inhabitants. By comparing demographic data with ethnographic data, ecological investigators were able to show that life experience varied from one location to another and that personal involvement in crime had a strong tendency to be associated with place of residence.

The Criminology of Place

Ecological approaches to crime causation have found a modern rebirth in the **criminology of place**. The criminology of place, also called **environmental criminology**, is an emerging perspective that emphasizes the importance of geographic location and architectural features as they are associated with the prevalence of victimization. Such "hot spots" of crime, including neighborhoods, specific streets, and even individual houses and businesses, have been identified by recent writers. Lawrence W. Sherman, for example, tells of a study that revealed that 3% of places (addresses and intersections) in Minneapolis produce 50% of all calls to the police.[12] Crime, noted Sherman, although relatively rare in Minneapolis and similar urban areas, is geographically concentrated.

Reflecting the questions first addressed by Shaw and McKay, another contemporary researcher, Rodney Stark, asks, "How is it that neighborhoods can remain the site of high crime and deviance rates despite a complete turnover in their populations?. . . There must be something about places as such that sustains crime."[13] Stark has developed a theory of deviant neighborhoods. It consists of 30 propositions, including the following:[14]

- To the extent that neighborhoods are dense and poor, homes will be crowded.

- Where homes are more crowded, there will be a greater tendency to congregate outside the home in places and

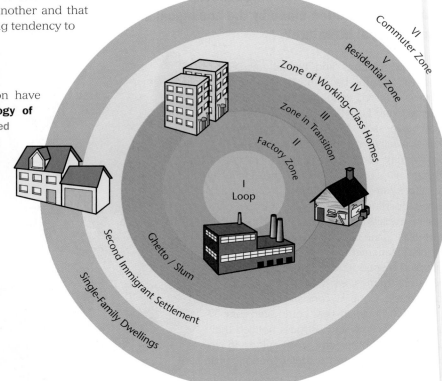

FIGURE 5–1 Concentric Zones

circumstances that raise levels of temptation and offer opportunity to deviate.

- Where homes are more crowded, there will be lower levels of supervision of children.

- Reduced levels of child supervision will result in poor school achievement, with a consequent reduction in stakes in conformity and an increase in deviant behavior.

- Poor, dense neighborhoods tend to be mixed-use neighborhoods.

- Mixed use increases familiarity with and easy access to places offering the opportunity for deviance.

Central to the criminology of place is the **broken windows thesis**, which holds that physical deterioration and an increase in unrepaired buildings lead to increased concerns for personal safety among area residents.[15] Heightened concerns, in turn, lead to further decreases in maintenance and repair and to increased delinquency, vandalism, and crime among local residents, which cause even further deterioration

A rundown building in a deteriorating neighborhood. What is the broken windows thesis?

Rates of crime in a community are influenced by the area's perceived vulnerability. What does this well-tended garden say about the watchfulness of its keepers?

Environmental criminology says that physical disorder in a community leads to crime.

in both a sense of safety and the physical environment. Offenders from other neighborhoods are then increasingly attracted by the area's perceived vulnerability. In short, physical evidence of disorder, left unchecked, leads to crime by driving residents indoors and sending a message to would-be offenders that a neighborhood is out of control.[16]

Critique of Ecological Theory

Some authors have suggested that ecological theories give too much credence to the notion that spatial location determines crime and delinquency. The nature of any given location changes over time, they say, and evolutions in land-use patterns, such as a movement away from homeownership and toward rental or low-income housing, may seriously affect the nature of a neighborhood and the character of the social organization found there. Similarly, rates of neighborhood crime and delinquency may be "an artifact of police decision-making practices"[17] and may bear little objective relationship to the actual degree of law violation in an area. Such police bias (that is, enforcement efforts focused on low-income inner-city areas) may seriously mislead researchers into categorizing certain areas as high in crime

when enforcement decisions made by police administrators merely make them appear that way.

Another critique of the ecological school can be found in its seeming inability to differentiate between the condition of social disorganization and the things such a condition is said to cause. What, for example, is the difference between social disorganization and high rates of delinquency? Isn't delinquency a form of the very thing said to cause it? As Stephen J. Pfohl has observed, early ecological writers sometimes used the incidence of delinquency as "both an example of disorganization and something caused by disorganization,"[18] making it difficult to gauge how accurate their explanatory approach is.

Similarly, those who criticize the ecological approach note that many crimes occur outside of geographic areas said to be characterized by social disorganization. Murder, rape, burglary, incidents of drug use, assault, and so on all occur in affluent, "well-established" neighborhoods as well as in other parts of a community. Likewise, white-collar, computer, environmental, and other types of crime may actually occur with a greater frequency in socially well-established neighborhoods than elsewhere. Hence, the ecological approach is clearly not an adequate explanation for all crime, nor for all types of crime.

Strain Theory

Strain theory depicts delinquency as a form of adaptive, problem-solving behavior, usually committed in response to problems involving frustrating and undesirable social environments. Strain can be thought of as the pressure that individuals feel to reach socially determined goals (Figure 5–2).[19]

The classic statement of **strain theory** was offered in 1938 by **Robert K. Merton**, who developed the concept of anomie. *Anomie*, a French word meaning "normlessness," was popularized by Emile Durkheim in his 1897 book *Suicide*.[20] Durkheim used the term to explain how a breakdown of predictable social conditions can lead to feelings of personal loss and dissolution. In Durkheim's writings, *anomie* was a feeling of strain that resulted from not being embedded personally in society. It marked the loss of a sense of belonging.

Merton's use of the term *anomie* was somewhat different. In Merton's writings, **anomie** came to mean a disjunction between socially approved means to success and legitimate goals.[21] Merton maintained that legitimate goals, involving such things as wealth, status, and personal happiness, are generally portrayed as desirable for everyone. The widely acceptable means to these goals, however, including education, hard work, financial savings, and so on, are not equally available to all members of society. As a consequence, crime and deviance tend to arise as alternative means to success when individuals feel the strain of being pressed to succeed in socially approved ways but find that the tools necessary for such success are not available to them. Strain increases as the gulf between goals and the availability of the means necessary to achieve them widens. Complicating the picture further, Merton maintained, is the fact that not everyone accepts the legitimacy of socially approved goals. Merton diagrammed possible combinations of goals and

TABLE 5–1

Goals and Means Disjuncture

		GOALS		
		accepts	rejects	replaces
MEANS	accepts	conformist	ritualist	
	rejects	innovator	retreatist	
	replaces			rebel

Source: Author adaptation from Robert K. Merton, SOCIAL THEORY AND SOCIAL STRUCTURE, (The Free Press, 1967).

means as shown in Table 5–1, referring to each combination as a mode of adaptation.

The upper-left box in Table 5–1 signifies acceptance of the goals that society holds as legitimate for everyone, with ready availability of the means approved for achieving those goals. The mode of adaptation associated with this combination of goals and means, conformity, typifies most middle- and upper-class individuals.

Innovation, the second form of adaptation, arises when an emphasis on approved goal achievement combines with a lack of opportunity to participate fully in socially acceptable means to success. This form of adaptation is experienced by many lower-class individuals who have been socialized to desire traditional success symbols, such as expensive cars, large homes, and big bank accounts, but who do not have ready access to approved means of acquiring them, such as educational opportunity. Innovative behavioral responses, including crime, can be expected to develop when individuals find themselves so deprived.

The third form of adaptation, *ritualism*, describes the form of behavior that arises when members

A graduation celebration. What kind of future would strain theory predict for these graduates?

Merton's last category, *rebellion*, signifies a person, or rebel, who wishes to replace socially approved goals and means with some other system. Political radicals, revolutionaries, and antiestablishment agitators may fit into this category. Merton believed that conformity was the most common mode of adaptation prevalent in society, whereas retreatism was least common.

Relative Deprivation

Relative deprivation refers to the economic and social gap that exists between rich and poor people who live in close proximity to one another. This contemporary version of Merton's anomie theory has been proposed by Steven F. Messner and Richard Rosenfeld, who suggest that inconsistencies in the ability to achieve the American Dream are to be blamed for most criminal activity.

According to sociologists **Judith Blau** and **Peter Blau**, two proponents of the relative deprivation concept, people assess their position in life by comparing themselves with things and people they already know.[22] Inner-city inhabitants, for example, develop an increasing sense of relative deprivation when they grow up in impoverished communities and witness well-to-do lifestyles in nearby neighborhoods. According to the Blaus, relative deprivation creates feelings of anger, frustration, hostility, and social injustice on the part of those who experience it. Relative deprivation is also related to the notion of **distributive justice**, which refers to an individual's perception of his or her rightful place in the reward structure of society. Thus, according to the principle of distributive justice, even wealthy and socially privileged individuals may feel slighted or shortchanged if they feel they have been inadequately rewarded for their behavior or their accomplishments.

FIGURE 5–2 Strain Theory

of society participate in socially desirable means but show little interest in goal achievement. A ritualist may get a good education, work every day in an acceptable occupation, and appear outwardly to be leading a solid middle-class lifestyle, yet that person may care little for the symbols of success, choosing to live an otherwise independent lifestyle.

Retreatism describes the behavior of those who reject both the socially approved goals and means. They may become dropouts, drug abusers, or homeless persons or participate in alternative lifestyles, like communal living. Such individuals are often socially and psychologically quite separate from the larger society around them.

General Strain Theory (GST)

In 1992, strain theory was reformulated by **Robert Agnew** and others who molded it into a comprehensive perspective called **general strain theory (GST)**.[23] GST sees lawbreaking behavior as a coping mechanism that enables those who engage in it to deal with the socioemotional problems generated by negative social relations. According to GST, strain occurs when others do the following: (1) prevent or threaten to prevent an individual from achieving positively valued goals, like autonomy or financial success; (2) remove or threaten to remove positively valued stimuli that a person possesses, such as the loss of a romantic partner or the death of a loved one; or (3) present or threaten to present someone with noxious or negatively valued stimuli, like verbal insults or physical abuse. In 2006, Agnew restated the six central propositions of general strain theory as follows:[24]

1. Strains refer to events and conditions that are disliked by individuals. There are three major types of strain: Individuals may (a) lose something they value, (b) be treated in an aversive or negative manner by others, and (c) be unable to achieve their goals.

2. Strains increase the likelihood of *particular* crimes primarily through their impact on a range of negative emotional states. Certain kinds of strains, for example, might lead to revenge seeking, while others cause those who experience them to steal things of value, and so forth.

3. Those strains most likely to cause crime (a) are perceived as high in magnitude or (b) as unjust; (c) are associated with low self-control; and (d) create some pressure or incentive to engage in criminal coping.

4. The likelihood that individuals will react to strains with criminal behavior depends on a range of factors that influence the individual's (a) ability to engage in legal coping, (b) costs of crime, and (c) disposition of crime.

5. Patterns of offending over the life course, group differences in crime, and community and societal differences in crime can be partly explained in terms of differences in the exposure to strains conducive to crime (males, for example, are more often exposed to strains conducive to crime, and are more likely than females to cope with strains through crime).

6. Crime can be reduced by reducing individuals' exposure to strains that are conducive to crime, and by reducing their likelihood of responding to strains with crime.

Factors that increase the likelihood of criminal (as opposed to conformist) coping include poor conventional coping skills and resources, the availability of criminal skills and resources, low levels of conventional social support, routine association with criminal others, personal beliefs and values that are favorable to crime, frequent exposure to situations where the costs of crime are low, low levels of social control, including weak bonds to conventional others, and a lack of investment in conventional institutions.

Strategies for reducing exposure to strains include eliminating strains conducive to crime, altering strains to make them less conducive to crime, removing individuals from exposure to strain, and equipping

Inside a modern-day commune. Explain Merton's concept of retreatism.

A homeless person in Beverly Hills. How does this photograph illustrate the concept of relative deprivation?

A graffiti artist at work. What are the six central propositions of GST?

individuals with the traits and skills needed to avoid strains that are conducive to crime.

GST expands on traditional strain theory in several ways. First, it significantly widens the focus of strain theory to include all types of negative relations between an individual and others. Second, GST maintains that strain is likely to have a cumulative effect on delinquency after reaching a certain threshold. Third, general strain theory provides a more comprehensive account of the cognitive, behavioral, and emotional adaptations to strain than traditional strain approaches. Finally, GST more fully describes the wide variety of factors affecting the choice of delinquent adaptations to strain.

Agnew sees the crime-producing effects of strain as cumulative and concludes that whatever form it takes, "strain creates a predisposition for delinquency in those cases in which it is chronic or repetitive."[25] Predispositions may be manifested in the form of **negative affective states**, or emotions such as anger, fear, depression, and disappointment.

An analysis by Agnew of other strain theories found that all such theories share at least two central explanatory features.[26] Strain theories, Agnew said, (1) focus "explicitly on negative relationships with others, relationships in which the individual is not treated as he or she wants to be treated," and (2) argue that "adolescents are pressured into delinquency by the negative affective states—most notably anger and related emotions—that often result from negative relationships."[27]

Critique of Strain Theory

From a social responsibility perspective, those who criticize strain theory note that Merton's original formulation of strain theory is probably less applicable to American society today than it was in the 1930s. That's because in recent times, considerable effort has been made toward improving opportunities for success for all Americans, regardless of ethnic heritage, race, or gender. Hence, it is less likely that individuals today will find themselves without the opportunity for choice, as was the case decades ago. Travis Hirschi criticizes contemporary strain theory for its inability "to locate people suffering from discrepancy" and notes that human beings are naturally optimistic—a fact, he says, that "overrides. . . aspiration-expectation disjunction." Hirschi concludes that "expectations appear to affect delinquency, but they do so regardless of aspirations, and strain notions are neither consistent with nor required by the data."[28] Similarly, recent studies have found that, contrary to what might be expected on the basis of strain theory, "delinquents do not report being more distressed than other youth."[29] Delinquent youths who are not afforded the opportunities for success that are available to others appear to be well shielded from sources of stress and despair through their participation in delinquency. Hence, "although strain theorists often have portrayed the lives of delinquents in grim terms. . . this depiction does not square well with the lived world of delinquency."[30]

Young athletes preparing for competition. Why does GST say that positive relationships reduce the likelihood of delinquency?

Culture Conflict Theory

Culture conflict theory (also called "cultural deviance theory") suggests that the root cause of criminality can be found in a clash of values between differently socialized groups over what is acceptable or proper behavior. The culture conflict concept is inherent in ecological criminology and its belief that zones of transition, because they tend to be in flux, harbor groups of people whose values are often at odds with those of the larger, surrounding society.

In his 1938 book *Culture Conflict and Crime*,[31] **Thorsten Sellin** maintained that the root cause of crime could be found in different values about what is acceptable or proper behavior. According to Sellin, **conduct norms**, or expectations for human behavior within a social group, are acquired early in life through childhood socialization. The clash of norms between variously socialized groups results in crime. Because crime is a violation of laws established by legislative decree, the criminal event itself, from this point of view, is nothing other than a disagreement over what should be acceptable behavior. For some social groups, what we tend to call "crime" is simply part of the landscape—something that can be expected to happen to you unless you take steps to protect yourself. From this point of view, those to whom crime happens are not so much victimized as they are simply ill-prepared.

Sellin described two types of culture conflict. The first type, *primary conflict*, arises when a fundamental clash of cultures occurs. Sellin's classic example was that of an immigrant father who kills his daughter's lover following an old-world tradition that demands that a family's honor be kept intact. The other type of conflict, *secondary conflict*, arose, according to Sellin, when smaller cultures within the primary one clashed. Because criminal laws are based on middle-class values, the social phenomenon called crime occurs when middle-class values are at odds with inner-city or lower-class norms.

In Sellin's day, prostitution and gambling provided plentiful examples of secondary conflict. Many lower-class inner-city groups accepted gambling and prostitution as a way of life. Today, drug use and abuse provide more readily understandable examples. In some parts of America, drug dealing is an acceptable form of business. To those who make the laws, however, it is not. It is from the clash of these two opposing viewpoints that conflict and crime emerge.

Subcultural Theory

Subcultural theory is a sociological perspective that emphasizes the contribution made by variously socialized cultural groups to the phenomenon of crime. Like the larger culture of which it is a part, a **subculture** is a collection of values and preferences that is communicated to subcultural participants through a process of socialization. Subcultures differ from the larger culture in that they claim the allegiance of smaller groups of people. Whereas the wider American culture, for example, may proclaim that hard work and individuality are valuable, a particular subculture may espouse the virtues of deer hunting, male bonding, and recreational alcohol consumption. Although it is fair to say that most subcultures are not at odds with the surrounding culture, some subcultures do not readily conform to the parameters of national culture. Countercultures, which tend to reject and invert the values of the surrounding culture, and criminal subcultures, which may actively espouse deviant activity, represent the other extreme.

In 1958, **Walter Miller** attempted to detail the values that drive members of lower-class subcultures into delinquent pursuits. Miller described *lower-class culture* as "a long established, distinctively patterned tradition with integrity of its own."[32]

Miller also outlined what he termed the **focal concerns**, or key values, of delinquent subcultures. Such concerns included trouble, toughness, smartness, excitement, fate, and autonomy. Miller concluded that subcultural crime and deviance are not the direct consequences of poverty and lack of opportunity but emanate from specific values characteristic of such subcultures. Just as middle-class concerns with achievement, hard work, and delayed gratification lead to socially acceptable forms of success, said Miller, so, too, do lower-class concerns provide a path to subculturally recognized success for lower-class youth.

Miller found that trouble is a dominant feature of lower-class culture. Getting into trouble, staying out of trouble, and dealing with trouble when

A group of Arizona Hell's Angels. How might the values of biker subculture conflict with the values of wider American culture?

it arises become focal points in the lives of many members of lower-class culture. Miller recognized that getting into trouble is not necessarily valued in and of itself but is seen as an oftentimes necessary means to valued ends. In Miller's words, "[For] men, 'trouble' frequently involves fighting or sexual adventures while drinking; for women, sexual involvement with disadvantageous consequences."

Like many theorists of the time, Miller was primarily concerned with the criminality of men. The lower-class masculine concern with toughness that he identified, Miller admitted, may have been a product of the fact that many men in the groups he examined were raised in female-headed families. Miller's "toughness," then, may reflect an almost obsessive concern with masculinity as a reaction to the perceived threat of over identification with female role models. Miller described "smartness" as the "capacity to outsmart, outfox, outwit, dupe, take, [or] con another or others and the concomitant capacity to avoid being outwitted, taken or duped oneself. . . . In its essence," said Miller, "smartness involves the capacity to achieve a valued entity—material goods, personal status— through a maximum use of mental agility and a minimum of physical effort."

Excitement was seen as a search for thrills—often necessary to overcome the boredom inherent in lower-class lifestyles. Miller claimed that fighting, gambling, picking up women, and making the rounds were all derived from the lower-class concern with excitement. Fate is related to the quest for excitement and to the concept of luck or of being lucky. As Miller stated, "Many lower-class persons feel that their lives are subject to a set of forces over which they have relatively little control. These . . . relate to a concept of 'destiny' or man as a pawn. . . . This often implicit world view is associated with a conception of the ultimate futility of directed effort toward a goal."

Autonomy, as a focal concern, manifests itself in statements like "I can take care of myself" and "No one's going to push me around." Autonomy produces behavioral problems from the perspective of middle-class expectations when it occurs in work environments, public schools, or other social institutions built on expectations of conformity.

Miller's work is derived almost entirely from his study of black inner-city delinquents in the Boston area in the 1950s. As such, it may have less relevance to members of lower-class subcultures in other places or at other times.

Delinquency and Drift

Members of delinquent subcultures are, to at least some degree, participants in the larger culture that surrounds them. How is it, then, that subcultural participants may choose behavioral alternatives that seemingly negate the norms and values of the larger society?

Gresham Sykes and **David Matza** suggested that offenders and delinquents are aware of conventional values, understand that their offending is wrong, but overcome feelings of responsibility through **techniques of neutralization**.[33] When involved in crime commission offenders may use one or more of these five types of justification (Figure 5–3):

- *Denying responsibility*, by pointing to one's background of poverty, abuse, lack of opportunity, and so on. Example: "The trouble I get into is not my fault."

- *Denying injury*, by explaining how insurance companies, for example, cover losses. Claims that "everyone does it" or that the specific victim could "afford it" fall into this category. Example: "They're so rich, they'll never miss it."

- *Denying the victim*, or justifying the harm done by claiming that the victim, for whatever reason, deserved the victimization. Example: "I only beat up drunks."

- *Condemning the condemners*, by asserting that authorities are corrupt or responsible for their own victimization. Offenders may also claim that society has made them into what they are and must now suffer the consequences. Example: "They're worse than we are. They're all on the take."

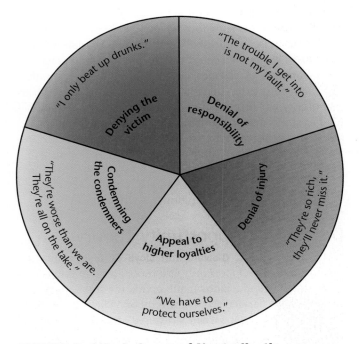

FIGURE 5–3 Techniques of Neutralization

A cock fighting ring. How might techniques of neutralization be used by the people shown here?

- *Appealing to higher loyalties,* as in defense of one's family honor, gang, significant other, or neighborhood. Example: "We have to protect ourselves."

A few years later, Matza went on to suggest that delinquents tend to drift into crime when available techniques of neutralization combine with weak or ineffective values espoused by the controlling elements in society. In effect, said Matza, the delinquent "drifts between criminal and conventional action," choosing whichever is the more expedient at the time. By employing techniques of neutralization, delinquents need not be fully alienated from the larger society. When opportunities for crime present themselves, such techniques provide an effective way of overcoming feelings of guilt and of allowing for ease of action. Matza used the phrase "soft determinism" to describe drift, saying that delinquents are neither forced to make choices because of fateful experiences early in life, nor are they entirely free to make choices unencumbered by the realities of their situation.

Some subcultures are decidedly violent and are built around violent themes and around values supporting violent activities. **Franco Ferracuti** and **Marvin Wolfgang** drew together many of the sociological perspectives previously advanced to explain delinquency and crime and claimed that violence is a learned form of adaptation to certain problematic life circumstances.[34] Learning to be violent, then, takes place within the context of a subculture that emphasizes the advantages of violence over other forms of adaptation. Such subcultures are characterized by songs and stories that glorify violence, by gun ownership, and by rituals that tend to stress macho models. They are likely to teach that a quick and decisive response to insults is necessary to preserve one's prestige within the group. Subcultural group members have a proclivity for fighting as a means of settling disputes. Subcultures of violence both expect violence from their members and legitimize it when it occurs.

Differential Opportunity Theory

In 1960, **Richard A. Cloward** and **Lloyd E. Ohlin** published *Delinquency and Opportunity,*[35] a report on the nature and activities of juvenile gangs that blended the subcultural thesis with ideas derived from strain theory. Cloward and Ohlin identified two types of socially structured opportunities for success: illegitimate and legitimate. They observed that whereas **legitimate opportunities** are generally available to individuals born into middle-class culture, participants in lower-class subcultures are often denied access to them. As a consequence, illegitimate opportunities for success are often seen as quite acceptable by participants in so-called illegitimate subcultures.

Cloward and Ohlin used the term **illegitimate opportunity structure** to describe preexisting subcultural paths to success that are not approved of by the wider culture. Where illegitimate paths to success are not already in place, alienated individuals may undertake a process of ideational evolution through which "a collective delinquent solution" or a "delinquent means of achieving success" may be decided upon by members of a gang. Because the two paths to success, legitimate and illegitimate, differ in their availability to members of society, Cloward and Ohlin's perspective has been called "differential opportunity."

According to Cloward and Ohlin, delinquent behavior may result from the ready availability of illegitimate opportunities and the effective replacement of the norms of the wider culture with subcultural rules. Hence, delinquency and criminality may be seen as legitimate in the eyes of gang members and may even form the criteria used by other subcultural participants to judge successful accomplishments.

Cloward and Ohlin noted that a delinquent act can be "defined by two essential elements: it is behavior that violates basic norms of the society, and, when officially known, it evokes a judgment by agents of criminal justice that such norms have been violated."[36] For Cloward and Ohlin, however, deviance is just as much an effort to conform, albeit to subcultural norms and expectations, as is conformity to the norms of the wider society. Cloward and Ohlin described three types of delinquent subcultures: (1) criminal subcultures, in which criminal role models are readily available for adoption by those being socialized into the subculture; (2) conflict subcultures, in which participants seek status through violence; and (3) retreatist subcultures, where drug use and withdrawal from the wider society predominate. Each subculture is thought to emerge from a larger, all-encompassing "parent" subculture of delinquent values. According to Cloward and Ohlin, delinquent subcultures have at least three identifiable features: (1) "acts of delinquency that reflect subcultural support are likely to recur with great frequency," (2) "access to a successful adult criminal career sometimes results from participation in a delinquent subculture," and (3) "the delinquent subculture imparts to the conduct of its members a high degree of stability and resistance to control or change."[37]

Reaction Formation

Another criminologist whose work is often associated with both strain theory and the subcultural perspective is **Albert Cohen**. Like Cloward and Ohlin, Cohen's work focused primarily on the gang behavior of delinquent youth. Cohen argued that young people from all backgrounds are generally held accountable to a "middle-class measuring rod" of expectations related to school performance, language proficiency, cleanliness, punctuality, neatness, nonviolent behavior, and allegiance to other similar standards. Like strain theorists, Cohen noted that unfortunately not everyone is prepared, by virtue of the circumstances surrounding his or her birth and subsequent socialization, for effectively meeting such expectations.[38]

Children, especially those from deprived backgrounds, turn to delinquency, Cohen claimed, because they experience status frustration when judged by adults and others according to middle-class standards and goals, which they are unable to achieve. Because it is nearly impossible for nonmainstream children to succeed in middle-class terms, they may overcome anxiety through the process of reaction formation, in which hostility toward middle-class values develops. Cohen adapted **reaction formation** from psychiatric perspectives and used it to mean "the process in which a person openly rejects that which he wants, or aspires to, but cannot obtain or achieve."[39]

Cohen discovered the roots of delinquent subcultures in what he termed the "collective solution to the problem of status."[40] When youths who experience the same kind of alienation from middle-class ideals band together, they achieve a collective and independent solution and create a delinquent subculture.

The Code of the Street

Elijah Anderson, a University of Pennsylvania sociology professor, studied African-American neighborhoods along Philadelphia's Germantown Avenue and published the results of his findings in a 1990 book entitled *The Code of the Street*.[41] In *Code*, Anderson details aspects of contemporary street code that stress a hyperinflated notion of manhood that rests squarely on the idea of respect. "At the heart of the code is the issue of respect," says Anderson, "loosely defined as being treated 'right' or being granted one's 'props' (or proper due) or the deference one deserves." In street culture, a man's sense of worth is determined by the respect he commands when in public. The violent nature of street subculture, however, means that a man cannot back down from threats—no matter how serious they may be. Working-class African-American families place high value on the man as head of the household, and he is expected to be a provider and strict disciplinarian. Economic and social circumstances, however, conspire to limit opportunities for legitimate success—driving many families to alternative means of making money. Men who are not able to live up to the role of provider tend to abandon their mates and their children and may then move through a series of unsuccessful relationships.

A crucial distinction between both families and individuals in inner-city neighborhoods like Germantown can be expressed as what Anderson calls the "decent family" and the "street family." "Decent" and "street" are labels that residents themselves use, says Anderson, and they mark people as either trying to uphold positive values or being oriented toward the street. Street life, he says, involves displays of physical strength and intellectual prowess meant to demonstrate that "I can take care of myself" and "I can take care of my own." Those who wholeheartedly embrace the street code are proud to live the "thug life" and identify with role models like Tupac Shakur and Snoop Dogg. A street orientation, says Anderson, means that people and situations become obstacles to be overcome or subdued. Hence, individuals who are street-wise learn to outsmart or "hustle" others while avoiding being hustled themselves.

Gangs Today

Gangs have become a major source of concern in contemporary American society. Although the writings of investigators like Cohen, Thrasher, and Cloward and Ohlin focused on the illicit activities of juvenile gangs in the nation's inner cities, most gang-related crimes of the period involved vandalism, petty theft, and battles over turf. The ethnic distinctions that gave rise to gang culture in the 1920s through the 1950s are today largely forgotten. Italian, Hungarian, Polish, and Jewish immigrants, whose children made up many of the early gangs, have been, for the most part, successfully integrated into the society that is modern America.

Tupac and Suge Knight prior to Shakur's death in 1996. His performing group was named Thug Life. How do today's street codes influence behavior?

Today's gangs are quite different from the gangs of the first half of the twentieth century. More than one-third of jurisdictions covered by the 2007 National Youth Gang Survey (NYGS) reported experiencing gang problems in 2007, the highest annual estimate since before 2000.[42] Within the areas surveyed, 86% of law enforcement agencies that serve larger cities, 50% of agencies that serve suburban counties, 35% of agencies that serve smaller cities, and 15% of agencies that serve rural counties reported experiencing youth gang problems in 2007. Overall, an estimated 3,550 jurisdictions served by city and county law enforcement agencies reported gang problems. Survey results also indicated that an estimated 788,000 gang members and 27,000 gangs were active in the United States during 2007.

The 2007 NYGC Survey confirmed previous findings that gang members are often involved in a variety of serious and violent crimes. Almost half of the law enforcement agencies reporting gang problems are involved in collaborative efforts with other law enforcement and criminal justice agencies to combat youth gangs and the serious and violent crimes they commit.

In addition to conducting the National Youth Gang surveys, the NYGC provides a compilation of gang-related legislation, maintains a repository of gang-related literature, analyzes gang-related data and statistics, and coordinates the activities of the Youth Gang Consortium.

Although its data are older than data available through the NYGC, the National Gang Crime Research Center's Project Gangfact provides a profile of gangs and gang members nationwide. The latest Gangfact report, based on data collected by 28 researchers in 17 states, found the following:[43]

- The average age for joining a gang, nationally, is 12.8 years of age.

- Over half who joined gangs have tried to quit.

- More than two-thirds of gangs have written rules for members to follow.

- Over half of all gangs hold regular weekly meetings.

- Nearly 30% of gangs require their members to pay dues.

- Approximately 55% of gang members were recruited by other gang members, while the remainder sought out gang membership.

- Most gang members (79%) said they would leave the gang if given a "second chance in life."

- Four-fifths of gang members reported that their gangs sold crack cocaine.

- Most gangs (70%) are not racially exclusive and consist of members drawn from a variety of ethnic groups.

- One-third of gang members report that they have been able to conceal their gang membership from their parents.

- Most gangs (83%) report having female members, but few allow female members to assume leadership roles.

- Many gang members (40%) report knowing male members of their gangs who had raped females.

Members of modern youth gangs generally identify with a name (such as the "Crips" and "Bloods," which are well-known Los Angeles–area gangs), a particular style of clothing, symbols, tattoos, jewelry, haircuts, and hand symbols.

Gangs can be big business. In addition to traditional criminal activities like burglary, extortion, vandalism, and protection rackets, drug dealing has become a mainstay of many inner-city gangs. Los Angeles police estimate that at least four city gangs earn over $1 million each per week through cocaine sales.[44] The potential for huge drug-based profits appears to have changed the nature of gangs themselves, making them more prone to violence and cutthroat tactics. Gang killings, including the now infamous drive-by shootings, have become commonplace in our nation's cities.

Rodney Dailey, a self-avowed former Boston-area drug dealer and gun-wielding gang member, says that in today's gang world, "shoot before you get shot is the rule." According to Dailey, "Things that normally people would have had fist-fights about can get you shot or stabbed" today.[45] Dailey is the founder of Gang Peace, an outreach group that tries to reduce gang-related violence.

Guns have become a way of life for many young gang members. As a young man named Jamaal, hanging around with friends outside Boston's Orchard Park housing project, recently put it, "We don't fight, we shoot." Police in the area describe how values among youth have changed over the past decade or two. Today they "think it's fun to pop someone," they say.[46]

Female gang members. Why do young people join gangs? Why do young *women* join gangs?

Critique of Culture Conflict Theories

Subcultural approaches, which constitute the last of the three types of social structure explanations for crime discussed in this chapter, have been questioned by some criminologists who see them as lacking in explanatory power. Canadian criminologist Gwynn Nettler, for example, criticizes the notion of violent subcultures by insisting that it is tautological, or circular. Nettler argues that saying that people fight because they are violent or that "they are murderous because they live violently" does little to explain their behavior. Attributing fighting to "other spheres of violence," he says, may be true, but it is fundamentally "uninformative."[47]

The subcultural approach has also been criticized for being racist because many so-called violent subcultures are said to be populated primarily by minorities. Margaret Anderson says that "the problem with this explanation is that it turns attention away from the relationship of black communities to the larger society and it recreates dominant stereotypes about blacks as violent, aggressive, and fearful. Although it may be true that rates of violence are higher in black communities, this observation does not explain the fact."[48] In sociological jargon, one might say that an observed correlation between race and violence does not necessarily provide a workable explanation for the relationship.

Policy Implications of Social Structure Theories

Theoretical approaches that fault social structure as the root cause of crime point in the direction of social action as a solution. In the 1930s, for example, Clifford Shaw, in an effort to put his theories into practice, established the **Chicago Area Project**. Through the Chicago Area Project, Shaw sought to reduce delinquency in transitional neighborhoods. Shaw analyzed oral histories gathered from neighborhood citizens to determine that delinquents were essentially normal youngsters who entered into illegal activities at early ages, often through street play. Hence, he worked to increase opportunities for young people to embark on successful work careers.

The Chicago Area Project attempted to reduce social disorganization in slum neighborhoods through the creation of community committees. Shaw staffed these committees with local residents rather than professional social workers. The project had three broad objectives: (1) improving the physical appearance of poor neighborhoods, (2) providing recreational opportunities for youths, and (3) involving project members directly in the lives of troubled youths through school and courtroom mediation. The program also made use of "curbside counselors," street-wise workers who could serve as positive role models for inner-city youth. Although no effective assessment programs were established to evaluate the Chicago Area Project during the program's tenure, in 1984 Rand Corporation reviewers published a 50-year review of

the program, declaring it "effective in reducing rates of juvenile delinquency."[49]

Similarly, Mobilization for Youth, which operated in New York City during the 1960s, provides a bold example of the treatment

A still scene from the movie _Gangs of New York_. What policies based on social structure theories might be used to reduce the prevalence of gangs in American society?

implications of social structure theories. Mobilization for Youth sought not only to provide new opportunities, but to change the fundamental arrangements of society and thereby address the root causes of crime and deviance through direct social action. Leaders of Mobilization for Youth decided that "what was needed to overcome. . . formidable barriers to opportunity. . . was not community organization but community action" that attacked entrenched political interests. Accordingly, the program promoted "boycotts against schools, protests against welfare policies, rent strikes against 'slum landlords,' lawsuits to ensure poor people's rights, and voter registration."[50] A truly unusual government-sponsored program for its time, Mobilization for Youth was eventually disbanded amid protests that "the mandate of the President's Committee was to reduce delinquency, not to reform urban society or to try out sociological theories on American youths."[51]

The War on Poverty declared by the Kennedy and Johnson administrations during the 1960s and subsequent federal and state-run welfare programs that provide supplemental income assistance have been cited[52] as examples of programs that at least held the potential to reduce crime rates by redistributing wealth in American society.[53] Such programs, however, have come under increasing fire recently, and the federal Welfare Reform Reconciliation Act of 1996[54] reduced or eliminated long-term benefits that had previously been available through avenues like the federal Aid to Families with Dependent Children (AFDC) program. The 1996 legislation also established stricter work requirements for welfare recipients through a new Welfare-to-Work program under the Personal Responsibility and Work Opportunity Reconciliation Act of 1996.[55]

Born in the tumultuous 1960s (1963), 11-year-old Kody Scott (he adopted the name Sanyika Shakur in prison some years later) earned initiation into the infamous Crips street gang—and into a life of persistently violent criminal conduct—with eight blasts from a shotgun at a group of the notorious Bloods, a rival gang. His teen years were an odyssey of violent crime interspersed with repeated stays in various juvenile detention centers and, ultimately, the California State Penitentiary.

His "Monster" moniker came from one such crime. After robbing and beating a man, the victim had the audacity to strike Shakur in the face. In retaliation, Shakur further "beat him, and stomped him and disfigured him," leaving the young man in a coma.[i] The severity of the damage caused one investigating police officer to observe that whoever had done the beating was a monster. Shakur decided to adopt the name later that night when he saw the looks on the faces of the people in his neighborhood. "[I]t was just power," he says proudly. "And I felt it. And I just took that name."[ii]

Feared even by his fellow Crips, Shakur rose through the gang's leadership ranks until he eventually became one of its top leaders and achieved status as an Original Gangster (O.G.), the highest "honor" a gang member can receive. Throughout his autobiography, Shakur speaks with pride of committing his crimes out of an honor-bound "duty" to stand with his fellow Crips. To his way of thinking, adherence to the code of the gang justifiably trumps social prohibitions against killing and maiming—as long as one does so for the purpose of supporting the criminal activities of one's fellow lawbreakers.

The Causes Behind the Crime
Sanyika Shakur, aka Monster Kody Scott

Can Social Structure Theories Explain This Crime?

- Shakur shrouds his behavior in a cloak of inevitability, asserting that there are no other options available to him and those like him by which they can achieve success within the legitimate American social system. He "portrays himself as the inevitable product of a hellish environment."[iii] *How is Shakur demonstrating the principles of reaction formation?*

- Shakur speaks out against what he perceives as a contrived systematic mechanism for preventing minorities from advancement, and gives one the sense that he is attempting to create a Robin Hood-esque mystique about his criminality. *Sykes and Matza suggest that offenders use five techniques of neutralization to justify their actions, even when they know offending is wrong. Which of these techniques might Shakur be expressing?*

- Shakur has been dubbed an "iconic figure" of the hip-hop culture by independent filmmaker Billy Wright, who further asserts that Shakur's "real life encapsulates what hip hop imagery is all about."[iv] Wright's current project, entitled *Can't Stop, Won't Stop,* tells the story of Shakur's life. Wright describes the film as a "tribute" to close friend Shakur. *How is Wright demonstrating Cloward and Ohlin's notion of*

Sanyika Shakur, aka "Monster Kody," inside a prison visiting area. What role did "duty" play in Shakur's crimes?

illegitimate opportunity structure to explain his admiration of Shakur?

- In December 2006, already a fugitive for numerous parole violations (he was, at the time, out on parole from yet another term in the California State Penitentiary), Shakur allegedly broke into a man's home and beat him in order to steal the victim's car. Arrested for the offense on March 7, 2007, Shakur now faces a possible life sentence. *How might strain theory be used to explain Shakur's actions in this last case?*

NOTES:

[i]Mandalit Del Barco, "Gang Member Turned Author Arrested in L.A.," *Morning Edition*. National Public Radio. March 9, 2007, http://www.npr.org/templates/story/story.php?storyId=7793148 (accessed July 14, 2007).

[ii]Ibid.

[iii]Mark Horowitz, "In Search of Monster," *The Atlantic*, December 1993, http://www.theatlantic.com/doc/199312/monster (accessed July 2, 2009).

[iv]"America's O. G. Gangster—Monster Kody (aka Sanyika Shakur)." RapIndustry.com. 2007.

Go to mycrimekit.com to explore the following resources for Chapter 5:

- **MULTIMEDIA:** Videos about social structure, social disorganization, the Chicago School, concentric zone theory, strain theory, Robert Merton, Walter Miller, Albert Cohen, Cloward and Ohlin, and Sykes and Matza
- **PRACTICE QUIZ:** Multiple-choice, true/false, short-answer, and essay questions
- **FLASHCARDS:** Twenty-four flashcards to test your knowledge of the chapter's key terms
- **WEB EXTRAS & LIBRARY EXTRAS:** Links to websites, online articles, and resources about social disorganization theories, the Chicago School, crime maps, strain theory, Park and Burgess, Shaw and McKay, the National Youth Gang Center, and other information related to social structure
- **ENDNOTES:** Chapter 5 bibliography

PEARSON **mycrimekit**

Summary and Key Concepts

SOCIAL STRUCTURE

Social structure approaches emphasize the role of poverty, lack of education, absence of marketable skills, and subcultural values as fundamental causes of crime. Social structure approaches portray crime as the result of an individual's location within the structure of society and focus on the social and economic conditions of life.

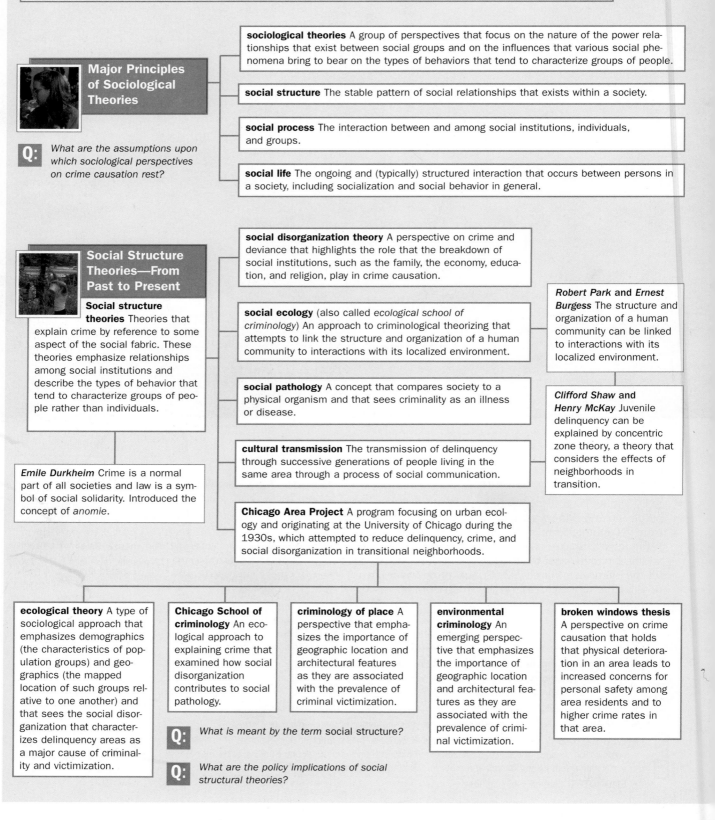

Major Principles of Sociological Theories

Q: *What are the assumptions upon which sociological perspectives on crime causation rest?*

sociological theories A group of perspectives that focus on the nature of the power relationships that exist between social groups and on the influences that various social phenomena bring to bear on the types of behaviors that tend to characterize groups of people.

social structure The stable pattern of social relationships that exists within a society.

social process The interaction between and among social institutions, individuals, and groups.

social life The ongoing and (typically) structured interaction that occurs between persons in a society, including socialization and social behavior in general.

Social Structure Theories—From Past to Present

Social structure theories Theories that explain crime by reference to some aspect of the social fabric. These theories emphasize relationships among social institutions and describe the types of behavior that tend to characterize groups of people rather than individuals.

Emile Durkheim Crime is a normal part of all societies and law is a symbol of social solidarity. Introduced the concept of *anomie*.

social disorganization theory A perspective on crime and deviance that highlights the role that the breakdown of social institutions, such as the family, the economy, education, and religion, play in crime causation.

social ecology (also called *ecological school of criminology*) An approach to criminological theorizing that attempts to link the structure and organization of a human community to interactions with its localized environment.

social pathology A concept that compares society to a physical organism and that sees criminality as an illness or disease.

cultural transmission The transmission of delinquency through successive generations of people living in the same area through a process of social communication.

Chicago Area Project A program focusing on urban ecology and originating at the University of Chicago during the 1930s, which attempted to reduce delinquency, crime, and social disorganization in transitional neighborhoods.

Robert Park and *Ernest Burgess* The structure and organization of a human community can be linked to interactions with its localized environment.

Clifford Shaw and *Henry McKay* Juvenile delinquency can be explained by concentric zone theory, a theory that considers the effects of neighborhoods in transition.

ecological theory A type of sociological approach that emphasizes demographics (the characteristics of population groups) and geographics (the mapped location of such groups relative to one another) and that sees the social disorganization that characterizes delinquency areas as a major cause of criminality and victimization.

Chicago School of criminology An ecological approach to explaining crime that examined how social disorganization contributes to social pathology.

criminology of place A perspective that emphasizes the importance of geographic location and architectural features as they are associated with the prevalence of criminal victimization.

environmental criminology An emerging perspective that emphasizes the importance of geographic location and architectural features as they are associated with the prevalence of criminal victimization.

broken windows thesis A perspective on crime causation that holds that physical deterioration in an area leads to increased concerns for personal safety among area residents and to higher crime rates in that area.

Q: *What is meant by the term* social structure?

Q: *What are the policy implications of social structural theories?*

Strain Theory

Strain theory points to a lack of fit between socially approved success goals and the availability of socially approved means to achieve those goals. As a consequence, according to the perspective of strain theory, individuals who are unable to succeed through legitimate means turn to other avenues that promise economic and social recognition.

Q: *How might the organization and structure of a society contribute to criminality?*

anomie A social condition in which norms are uncertain or lacking.

relative deprivation A sense of social or economic inequality experienced by those who are unable, for whatever reason, to achieve legitimate success within the surrounding society.

distributive justice The rightful, equitable, and just distribution of rewards within a society.

general strain theory (GST) A perspective that suggests that lawbreaking behavior is a coping mechanism that enables those who engage in it to deal with the socioemotional problems generated by negative social relations.

negative affective states Adverse emotions that derive from the experience of strain, such as anger, fear, depression, and disappointment.

Robert K. Merton The classic statement of strain theory as a disjunction between socially approved means to success and legitimate goals.

Judith and *Peter Blau* People assess their position in life by comparing themselves with things and people they already know.

Robert Agnew Lawbreaking behavior is a coping mechanism that enables those who engage in it to deal with the socioemotional problems generated by negative social relations.

Culture Conflict Theory

Culture conflict relies on the proposition that the root cause of crime is a clash of values between variously socialized groups over what is acceptable or proper behavior.

Franco Ferracuti and *Marvin Wolfgang* Violence is a learned form of adaptation to certain problematic life circumstances and that learning to be violent takes place within the context of a subculture that emphasizes the advantages of violence.

Q: *Describe some subcultures in contemporary society that might be in conflict with the wider culture.*

Richard A. Cloward and *Lloyd E. Ohlin* There are two types of socially structured opportunities for success: illegitimate and legitimate.

culture conflict theory A sociological perspective on crime that suggests that the root cause of criminality can be found in a clash of values between variously socialized groups over what is acceptable or proper behavior.

conduct norms Shared expectations of a social group relative to personal conduct.

subcultural theory A sociological perspective that emphasizes the contribution made by variously socialized cultural groups to the phenomenon of crime.

subculture A collection of values and preferences that is communicated to subcultural participants through a process called socialization.

focal concerns The key values of any culture, especially the key values of a delinquent subculture.

techniques of neutralization Culturally available justifications that can provide criminal offenders with the means to disavow responsibility for their behavior.

legitimate opportunities Opportunities generally available to individuals born into middle-class culture; participants in lower-class subcultures are often denied access to them.

illegitimate opportunity structure Subcultural pathways to success of which the wider society disapproves.

reaction formation The process by which a person openly rejects that which he or she wants or aspires to but cannot obtain or achieve.

Thorsten Sellin The root cause of crime could be found in different values about what is acceptable or proper behavior.

Walter Miller Lower-class culture is "a long established distinctively patterned tradition with integrity of its own."

Gresham Sykes and *David Matza* Offenders understand that their offending is wrong, but engage in neutralizing self-talk before offending to mitigate the anticipated shame and guilt associated with violating societal norms.

Albert Cohen Young people from all backgrounds are generally held accountable to the norms of the wider society through a "middle-class measuring rod" of expectations related to school performance, language proficiency, cleanliness, punctuality, neatness, nonviolent behavior, and allegiance to other similar standards.

Social Process and Social Development

It's What We Learn

**What is the interactionist perspective?
How did social process and social development
theories evolve?** 116

**How do social control theories explain
crime?** 118

How does labeling help create criminals? 122

**What are the policy implications of social
process theories?** 125

**How does the social development perspective
explain criminality?** 126

**What are the policy implications of social
development theories?** 137

On April 16, 2007, Virginia Tech University suffered a terrible tragedy. Today, my thoughts and prayers are with the victims and their families and the entire Virginia Tech community.

—*Virginia Gov. Timothy M. Kaine*

CRIMINOLOGY
INTERACTIVE

In the **Crime Theories** section of Criminology Interactive, click on **Social Process Theories**.

THE PERSPECTIVE OF SOCIAL INTERACTION

The theories discussed in the first part of this chapter are called **social process theories**, or *interactionist perspectives*, because they depend on the process of interaction between individuals and society for their explanatory power. The various types of social process theories include social learning theory, social control theory, and labeling theory. The second part of this chapter focuses on **social development theories**, which tend to offer an integrated perspective and which place a greater emphasis on changes in offending over time.

Principles of Social Process and Social Development Theories

- Social process theories of crime causation assume that everyone has the potential to violate the law and that criminality is not an innate human characteristic.
- Criminal behavior is learned in interaction with others, and the socialization process that occurs as the result of group membership is seen as the primary route through which learning occurs. Among the most important groups contributing to the process of socialization are family, peers, work groups, and reference groups with which one identifies.

History of Social Process and Social Development Theories

Social **learning theory** says that all behavior is learned in much the same way and that crime, like other forms of behavior, is also learned. People learn to commit crime from others by learning the norms, values, and patterns of behaviors conducive to crime. Hence, according to learning theory, criminal behavior is a product of the social environment and not an innate characteristic.

Differential Association

One of the earliest and most influential forms of learning theory was advanced by **Edwin Sutherland** in 1939. Sutherland's thesis was that criminality is learned through a process of **differential association** with others who communicate criminal values and who advocate the commission of crimes.[1] Sutherland emphasized the role of social learning as an explanation for crime because he believed that many of the concepts popular in the field of criminology at the time—including social pathology, genetic inheritance, biological characteristics, and personality flaws—could not fully explain why an otherwise normal individual turns to crime. Sutherland was the first well-

Differential association theory says that all behavior is learned through interaction with others. What will this child likely learn as it matures?

known criminologist to suggest that all significant human behavior is learned and that crime, therefore, is not substantively different from any other form of behavior.

Although Sutherland died in 1950, the tenth edition of his famous book, *Criminology,* was published in 1978 under the authorship of Donald R. Cressey, a professor at the University of California at Santa Barbara. The 1978 edition of *Criminology* contained the finalized principles of differential association (which, for all practical purposes, were complete as early as 1947). Nine in number, the principles read as follows:[2]

1. Criminal behavior is learned.

2. Criminal behavior is learned in interaction with others in a process of communication.

3. The principal part of the learning of criminal behavior occurs within intimate personal groups.

4. When criminal behavior is learned, the learning includes (a) techniques of committing the crime, which are sometimes very complicated and sometimes very simple, and (b) the specific direction of motives, drives, rationalizations, and attitudes.

5. The specific direction of motives and drives is learned from definitions of the legal codes as favorable or unfavorable.

- The process through which criminality is acquired, deviant self-concepts are established, and criminal behavior results are active, open-ended, and ongoing throughout a person's life.
- Individuals who have low stakes in conformity are more likely to be influenced by the social processes and contingent experiences that lead to crime. Criminal choices, once made, tend to persist because they are reinforced by the reaction of society to those whom it has identified as deviant.
- The social development perspective understands that development begins at birth (and perhaps even earlier), and occurs primarily within a social context.
- Human development occurs on many levels simultaneously, including psychological, biological, familial, interpersonal, cultural, societal, and ecological. Hence, social development theories tend to be integrated theories, or theories that combine various points of view on the process of development.
- Social development theories focus more on individual rates of offending and seek to understand both increases and decreases in rates of offending over the individual's lifetime. Social development theories generally use longitudinal (over time) measurements of delinquency and offending, and they pay special attention to the transitions that people face as they move through the life cycle.
- Most theories of social development recognize that a critical transitional period occurs as a person moves from childhood to adulthood.

6. A person becomes delinquent because of an excess of definitions favorable to law violation over definitions unfavorable to law violation.

7. Differential associations may vary in frequency, duration, priority, and intensity.

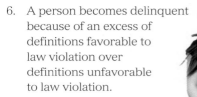

Social development perspectives say that a critical transitional period occurs as a person moves from childhood to adulthood. How would you describe that transition?

8. The process of learning criminal behavior by association with criminal and anticriminal patterns involves all of the mechanisms that are involved in any other learning.

9. While criminal behavior is an expression of general needs and values, it is not explained by those general needs and values, since noncriminal behavior is an expression of the same needs and values.

Differential association found considerable acceptance among mid-twentieth-century theorists because it combined then-prevalent psychological and sociological principles into a coherent perspective on criminality. Crime as a form of learned behavior quickly became the catchword of mid-twentieth-century criminology, and biological and other perspectives were largely abandoned.

Critique of Differential Association

Perhaps the most potent criticism of differential association is the claim that Sutherland's initial formulation of the approach is not applicable at the individual level because even people who experience an excess of definitions favorable to law violation may still not become criminal. Likewise, those who rarely associate with recognized deviants may still turn to crime. In addition, the theory is untestable because most people experience a multitude of definitions—both favorable and unfavorable to law violation—and it is up to them to interpret just what those experiences mean. Hence, classifying experiences as either favorable or unfavorable to crime commission is difficult at best.

Other critics suggest that differential association alone is not a sufficient explanation for crime. If it were, then we might expect correctional officers, for example, to become criminals by virtue of their constant and continued association with prison inmates. Similarly, wrongly imprisoned people might be expected to turn to crime upon release from confinement. Little evidence suggests that either of these scenarios actually occurs. In effect, differential association theory does not seem to provide for free choice in individual circumstances, nor does it explain why some individuals, even when surrounded by associates who are committed to lives of crime, are still able to hold onto other, noncriminal values. Finally, differential association theory fails to account for the emergence of criminal values, addressing only the communication of those values.

Social Process: Social Control Theories

According to Charles R. Tittle, a sociologist with a specialty in crime and deviance, **social control theories**, which fall under the general category of the social process perspective, emphasize "the inhibiting effect of social and psychological integration with others whose potential negative response, surveillance, and expectations regulate or constrain criminal impulses."[3] In other words, **social control theorists seek to identify those features of the personality and the environment that keep people from committing crimes.** Social control theorists, however, take a step beyond static aspects of the personality and physical features of the environment in order to focus on the *process* through which social integration develops. It is the extent of a person's integration with positive social institutions and with significant others that determines that person's resistance to criminal temptations; social control theorists focus on the process through which such integration develops. **Rather than stressing causative factors in criminal behavior,** however, **social control theories tend to ask** *why* **people actually obey rules instead of breaking them.**[4]

Containment Theory

In the 1950s, **Walter C. Reckless** tackled head-on the realization that most sociological theories lacked the ability to predict precisely which individuals, even those exposed to various causes of crime, would become criminal. Crime, Reckless wrote, was the consequence of social pressures to involve oneself in violations of the law, as well as of failure to resist such pressures. Reckless called his approach **containment theory**, and he compared it with a biological immune response, saying that only some people exposed to a disease actually come down with it. Thus sickness, like crime, results from the failure of control mechanisms—some internal to the person, and others external.

In the case of crime, Reckless wrote, *external containment* consists of **"the holding power of the group."**[5] Under most circumstances, Reckless said, "the society, the state, the tribe, the village, the family, and other nuclear groups are able to hold the individual within the bounds of the accepted norms and expectations."[6] *Inner containment*, said Reckless, **"represents the ability of the person to follow the expected norms, to direct himself."**[7] Such ability is said to be enhanced by a positive self-image, a focus on socially approved goals, personal aspirations that are in line with reality, a good tolerance for frustration, and a general adherence to the norms and values of society. A person with a positive self-image can avoid the temptations of crime simply by thinking, "I'm not that kind of person." A focus on socially approved goals helps keep people on the straight and narrow path. Reckless's containment theory is diagrammed in Figure 6–1. "Pushes toward Crime" represents those factors in an individual's background that might propel him or her into criminal behavior. They include a criminogenic background or upbringing that involves participation in a delinquent subculture, deprivation, biological propensities toward deviant behavior, and psychological maladjustment. "Pulls toward Crime" signifies all the perceived rewards crime may offer, including financial gain, sexual satisfaction, and higher status. **Containment** is a stabilizing force and, if effective, blocks such pushes and pulls from leading the individual toward crime.

Critique of Reckless's Containment Theory

Reckless's pushes and pulls against crime have been cited as purely personal interpretation. They are not part of a fixed formation of psychological impulses and drives, many critics claim, but simply the feelings of the moment that may have been conditioned through individual thought processes.

Containment theory says that crime results from a failure of control mechanisms. How might the theory apply to this situation?

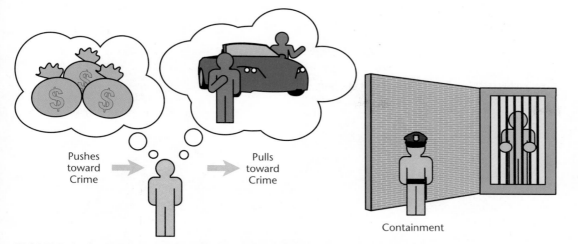

Pushes toward Crime → Pulls toward Crime

Containment

The Criminal Event

FIGURE 6–1 A Diagrammatic Representation of Containment Theory

Delinquency and Self-Esteem

An innovative perspective on social control was offered by **Howard B. Kaplan** in the mid–1970s.[8] Kaplan proposed that people who are ridiculed by their peers suffer a loss of self-esteem, assess themselves poorly, and, as a result, abandon the motivation to conform.

A number of studies appear to support the idea that **low self-esteem** fosters delinquent behavior.[9] At the same time, however, delinquency seems to also enhance self-esteem, at least for some delinquents.[10] One study has found that delinquent behavior enhances self-esteem in adolescents whose self-esteem is already very low.[11]

Social Bond Theory

An important form of control theory called *social bond theory* was popularized by **Travis Hirschi** in his 1969 book *Causes of Delinquency*.[12] Hirschi argued that through successful socialization, a bond forms between individuals and the social group. When that bond is weakened or broken, deviance and crime may result. There are four components of the **social bond**:

- Attachment: a person's shared interests with others
- Commitment: the amount of energy and effort put into activities with others
- Involvement: the amount of time spent with others in shared activities
- Belief: a shared value and moral system

In his writings, Hirschi cites the psychopath as an example of the kind of person whose attachment to society is nearly nonexistent.[13] Other relatively normal individuals may find their attachment to society loosened through "the process of becoming alienated from others [which] often involves or is based on active interpersonal conflict," says Hirschi. "Such conflict could easily supply a reservoir of socially derived hostility sufficient to account for the

A number of studies link low self-esteem and delinquent behavior. How does peer group acceptance build self-esteem?

Social bond theory highlights the importance of the bond between individuals and the group. What are the four major components of the social bond?

aggressiveness of those whose attachments to others have been weakened."[14]

The second component of the social bond—commitment—reflects a person's investment of time and energies into conforming behavior versus the potential loss of the rewards that would otherwise accrue from that behavior. In Hirschi's words, "The idea, then, is that the person invests time, energy, himself, in a certain line of activity—say, getting an education, building up a business, acquiring a reputation for virtue. Whenever he considers deviant behavior, he must consider the costs of this deviant behavior, the risk he runs of losing the investment he has made in conventional behavior."[15] For such a traditionally successful person, says Hirschi, "a ten-dollar-holdup is stupidity" because the potential for losing what has already been acquired through commitment to social norms far exceeds what stands to be gained. Recognizing that his approach applies primarily to individuals who have been successfully socialized into conventional society, Hirschi adds, "The concept of commitment assumes that the organization of society is such that the interests of most persons would be endangered if they were to engage in criminal acts."[16]

Involvement, for Hirschi, means "engrossment in conventional activities."[17] In explaining the importance of involvement in determining conformity, Hirschi cites the old saying that "idle hands are the devil's workshop." Time and energy, he says, are limited, and if a person is busy at legitimate pursuits, he or she will have little opportunity for crime and deviance.

Belief, the last of Hirschi's four aspects of the social bond, sets his control theory apart from subcultural approaches. Hirschi says that unlike subcultural theory, "control theory assumes the existence of a common value system within the society or group whose norms are being violated. We not only assume the deviant has believed the rules, we assume he believes the rules even as he violates

them."[18] How can a person simultaneously believe it is wrong to commit a crime and still commit it? Hirschi's answer is that "many persons do not have an attitude of respect toward the rules of society."[19] That is, although they know the rules exist, they basically do not care. They invest little of their sense of self in moral standards.

In 1990, Hirschi, in collaboration with **Michael Gottfredson**, proposed a **general theory of crime** based on the concepts advanced earlier in control theory.[20] Nearly all crimes, they claim, are mundane, simple, trivial, easy acts aimed at satisfying desires of the moment. Hence, their general theory is built on a classical or rational choice perspective—that is, the belief that crime is a natural consequence of unrestrained human tendencies to seek pleasure and avoid pain. Crime, say Gottfredson and Hirschi, is little more than a subset of general deviant behavior. Hence, they conclude, crime bears little resemblance to the explanations offered in the media, by law enforcement officials, or by most academic thinkers on the subject.

According to Gottfredson and Hirschi, the offender is neither the diabolical genius of fiction nor the ambitious seeker of the American Dream often portrayed by other social scientists. On the contrary, offenders appear to have little control over their own desires. When personal desires conflict with long-term interests, those who lack self-control often opt for the desires of the moment, thus contravening legal restrictions and becoming involved in crime.[21] Central to Gottfredson and Hirschi's thesis is the belief that a well-developed social bond will result in the creation of effective mechanisms of self-control.

Critique of General Theory of Crime and Social Bond Theory

Hirschi's social bond theory has been criticized for its basic premise that those who commit deviant behavior know that it is against social norms and the law, but commit it anyway. Social bonds do not seem strong enough to negate the propensity toward that behavior. In addition Hirschi's and

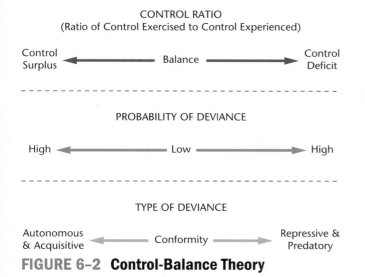

CONTROL RATIO
(Ratio of Control Exercised to Control Experienced)

Control
Surplus ←————————— Balance —————————→ Control
Deficit

- -

PROBABILITY OF DEVIANCE

High ←————————— Low —————————→ High

- -

TYPE OF DEVIANCE

Autonomous
& Acquisitive ←————— Conformity —————→ Repressive &
Predatory

FIGURE 6–2 Control-Balance Theory

Gottfriend's general theory of crime has been criticized for exactly what it is—a general view of crime that is overly simplistic and ignores the complexity of the criminal process.

Control-Balance Theory

A novel form of control theory can be found in **Charles R. Tittle**'s control-balance perspective.[22] **Tittle's control-balance approach results from a blending of the social bond and containment perspectives.** Too much control can be just as dangerous as too little. **The crucial concept in the approach is what is called the control ratio.** The control ratio is the amount of control to which a person is subject versus the amount of control that person exerts over others. The control ratio is said to predict not only the probability that one will engage in deviance but also the specific form that deviance will take (Figure 6–2).

High levels of control, or overcontrol, are termed "control surplus," while low levels are called "control deficit." Individuals with *control surpluses* are able to exercise a great deal of control over others and will work to extend their degree of control even further. Their efforts lead to deviant actions involving exploitation, plunder, and decadence—frequently seen in cases of white-collar crime and political corruption.[23] Control surpluses are built upon "the fundamental drive toward autonomy." Such a drive involves "a desire to extend control as far as possible" and results in forms of deviance that Tittle terms "autonomous."[24]

A *control deficit* exists for people unable to exercise much control over others (and who are hence overly controlled).

Control deficits result in deviance as an attempt to escape repressive controls. Deviance caused by control deficit takes the form of predation (physical violence, theft, sexual assault, robbery, and so on), defiance (challenges to conventional norms, including vandalism, curfew violations, and sullenness), or submission (which Tittle describes as "passive,

unthinking, slavish obedience to the expectations, commands, or anticipated desires of others"[25]). Thus control imbalance only sets the stage for deviance. Deviance ultimately occurs once a person realizes, at some level, that acts of deviance can reset the control ratio in a favorable way. Finally, opportunity also plays a significant role. "No matter how favorable the motivational and constraint configuration," says Tittle, "the actual likelihood of deviance occurring depends on there being an opportunity for it to happen."[26]

Critique of Social Control Theories

Social control theories have been criticized because they make the assumption that all people are automatically nonconformist unless they are socialized through control mechanisms. Human choice, then, is minimized in favor of creating the right kind and level of social self-controls to help individuals avoid deviance and achieve conformity. Consequently, the individual is seen as somehow naturally "evil" and it is society's job to institute moral order to bring about conformity.

Just as troubling to critics of social control theories is the fact that these theories do not recognize the role of human motivation or the conditions that propel people to associate and learn from others. Instead, the assumption is simply made that most of us would commit crime if we had the chance. While associations and relationships can mitigate or escalate deviant behavior, it is unclear how those relationships are formed.

Control-balance theory says that conformity results from just the right balance between control surpluses and control deficits. Explain the concept of control ratio.

Labeling Theory

Society's response to known or suspected offenders determines the individual futures of those labeled as criminals and contributes to the incidence of criminality by reducing the behavioral options available to labeled offenders.

Tagging is a term that explains what happens to offenders following arrest, conviction, and sentencing. From the community's point of view the individual who used to do bad and mischievous things becomes a bad and unredeemable human being."[27]

Once a person has been defined as bad, few legitimate opportunities remain open to him or her. As a consequence, the offender finds that only other people who have been similarly defined by society as bad are available to associate with him or her. This continued association with negatively defined others leads to continued crime.

One of the best-known views of labeling comes from **Edwin M. Lemert**. Lemert called an offender's initial acts of deviance **primary deviance** and the offender's continued acts of deviance, especially those resulting from forced association with other offenders, **secondary deviance**. Primary deviance may be undertaken to solve some immediate problem or to meet the expectations of one's subcultural group. Hence, the robbery of a convenience store by a college student temporarily desperate for tuition money, although not a wise undertaking, may be the first serious criminal offense ever committed by the student. The student may well intend for it to be the last, but if arrest ensues and the student is tagged with the status of a criminal, then secondary deviance may occur as a means of adjustment to the negative status. Secondary deviance becomes especially important because of the forceful role it plays in causing tagged individuals to internalize the negative labels that have been applied to them. Through such a process, labeled individuals assume the role of the deviant.

The name most often associated with labeling theory is that of **Howard Becker**, who described the deviant subculture of jazz musicians and the process by which an individual becomes a marijuana user, among other things. His primary focus, however, was to explain how a person becomes labeled as an *outsider*, as "a special kind of person, one who cannot be trusted to live by the rules agreed on by the group."[28] The central fact about deviance, says Becker, is that society creates both deviance and the deviant person by its response to circumscribed behaviors. The person who engages in sanctioned behavior is, as part of the process, labeled a deviant.[29] For Becker, as for other labeling theorists, no act is intrinsically deviant or criminal but is defined as such by others. Becoming deviant involves a sequence of steps that eventually lead to commitment to a deviant identity and participation in a deviant career.

In developing labeling theory, Becker attempted to explain how some rules come to carry the force of law, while others have less weight or apply only within the context of marginal subcultures. His explanation centered on the concept of **moral enterprise**, a term he used to encompass all the efforts a particular interest group makes to have its sense of propriety embodied in law.

An early example of moral enterprise can be found in the Women's Christian Temperance Union (WCTU), a group devoted to the prohibition of alcohol. From 1881 to 1919, the WCTU was highly visible in its nationwide fight against alcohol—holding marches and demonstrations, closing drinking establishments, and lobbying legislators. Press coverage of the WCTU's activities swayed many politicians into believing that the lawful prohibition of alcoholic beverages was inevitable, and an amendment to the U.S. Constitution soon followed, ushering in the age of prohibition. Moral enterprise is similarly used, Becker claimed, by other groups seeking to support their own

interests with the weight of law. Often the group that is successful at moral enterprise does not represent a popular point of view. The group is simply more effective than others at maneuvering through the formal bureaucracy that accompanies legislation.

Becker was especially interested in describing deviant careers—the processes by which individuals become members of deviant subcultures and take on the attributes associated with the deviant role. Becker argued that most deviance, when it first occurs, is unlikely to occur again. However, deviance can become part of a person's behavioral repertoire through the labeling process. **Once a person is labeled "deviant," most opportunities that remain open are deviant ones.** Hence, throughout the person's career, the budding deviant increasingly exhibits deviant behavior because his or her choices are restricted by society. Additionally, successful deviants must acquire the techniques and resources necessary to undertake the deviant act (be it drug use or bank robbery) and must develop the mind-set characteristic of others like them. Near the completion of a deviant career, the person who has been labeled a deviant internalizes society's negative label, assumes a deviant self-concept, and is likely to become a member of a deviant subgroup. In this way, says Becker, deviance finally becomes a "self-fulfilling prophecy." **Labeling, then, is a cause of crime insofar as society's calling the rule-breaker "deviant" pushes the person further in the direction of continued deviance.**

Labeling theory contributed a number of unique ideas to the criminological literature, including the following:

- Deviance is the result of social processes involving the imposition of definitions, rather than the consequence of any quality inherent in human activity itself.

- Deviant individuals achieve their status by virtue of social definition, rather than because of inborn traits.

- The reaction of society to deviant behavior and to those who engage in such behavior is the major element in determining the criminality of the person and of the behavior in question.

- Negative self-images do not precede delinquency but rather result from processing by the criminal justice system.

- Labeling by society and handling by the justice system tend to perpetuate crime and delinquency rather than reduce it.

Becker's typology of delinquents demonstrates the labeling approach (Figure 6–3). It consists of (1) the pure deviant, (2) the falsely accused deviant, and (3) the secret deviant. The pure deviant is one who commits norm-breaking behavior and whose behavior is accurately appraised as such by society. An example might be the burglar who is caught in the act of burglary and then tried and convicted. Such a person, we might say, has gotten what he or she deserves. The falsely accused individual is one who, in fact, is not guilty but is labeled "deviant" nonetheless. The falsely accused category in Becker's typology demonstrates the power of social definition. Innocent people sometimes end up in prison, and one can imagine that the impact of conviction and of the experiences that attend prison life can leave the falsely accused with a negative self-concept and with group associations practically indistinguishable from those of the

Juvenile offenders shield their faces from the camera. Why is labeling theory especially applicable to youthful offenders?

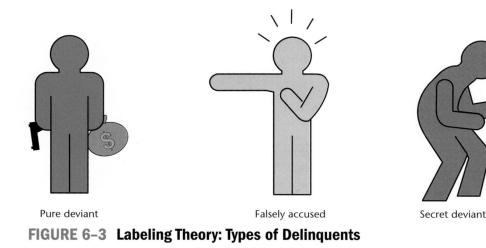

Pure deviant   Falsely accused   Secret deviant

FIGURE 6–3 Labeling Theory: Types of Delinquents

true deviant. In effect, the life of the falsely accused is changed just as thoroughly as is the life of the pure deviant by the process of labeling. Finally, the secret deviant violates social norms, but his or her behavior is not noticed, and negative societal reactions do not follow. The secret deviant again demonstrates the power of societal reaction—in this case, by the very lack of consequences.

Although labeling theory fell into disregard during the late 1970s and early 1980s due to accusations that it was vague and ambiguous, criminologists have recently recast the theory as one that points out the cumulative effects over time of official intervention on future life chances and opportunities for approved success. Contemporary proponents of the labeling perspective, however, generally see labeling as only one factor contributing to cumulative disadvantages in life chances. In 2003, Jon Gunnar Bernburg and Marvin D. Krohn studied the impact of negative official intervention on young men in Rochester, New York. Data on the men were available from the time they were (on average) 13.5 years old until they reached the age of 22. In keeping with what labeling theory would predict, Bernburg and Krohn found that official intervention during adolescence led to increased criminality in early adulthood because it reduced life chances for educational achievement and successful employment.

Critique of Labeling Theory

The labeling approach, although it successfully points to the labeling process as a reason for continued deviance and as a cause of stabilization in deviant identities, has been criticized because it does little to explain the origin of crime and deviance. In addition, few, if any, studies seem to support the basic tenets of the theory. Critics of labeling have pointed to its "lack of firm empirical support for the notion of secondary deviance," and "many studies have not found that delinquents or criminals have a delinquent or criminal self-image."[30] There is also a lack of unequivocal empirical support for the claim that contact with the justice system is fundamentally detrimental to the personal lives of criminal perpetrators. Even if that supposition were true, however, one must ask whether it would ultimately be better if offenders were not caught and forced to undergo the rigors of processing by the justice system. Although labeling theory hints that official processing makes a significant contribution to continued criminality, it seems unreasonable to expect that offenders untouched by the system would forego the rewards of future criminality. Finally, labeling theory has little to say about *secret deviants*, or people who engage in criminality but are never caught. An important question about secret deviants, for example, is whether they can be expected to continue in lives of deviance if never caught.

Labeling theory has been criticized for doing little to explain the origin of crime and deviance.

124

Policy Implications of Social Process Theories

Social process theories suggest that crime prevention programs should work to enhance self-control and to build **prosocial bonds**. One program that seeks to build strong prosocial bonds while attempting to teach positive values to young people is the **Juvenile Mentoring Program (JUMP)** of the Office of Juvenile Justice and Delinquency Prevention (OJJDP). Fundamentally a social control initiative, JUMP was funded by Congress in 1992 under an amendment to the Juvenile Justice and Delinquency Prevention Act of 1974.[31] OJJDP-sponsored JUMP programs commenced operation in 1996. JUMP places at-risk youth in a one-on-one relationship with favorable adult role models. At-risk youths are defined as those who are at risk of delinquency, gang involvement, educational failure, or dropping out of school. General demographic information is used in conjunction with scores on a standardized risk-assessment instrument known as the Problem Oriented Screening Instrument for Teens in order to identify potential JUMP participants.

Most recent data show 9,200 youths were enrolled in more than 200 JUMP programs nationwide. The average age at the time of enrollment was just under 12 years. Although complete evaluation data are only beginning to come in on the project, both youth and mentors were very positive when rating various aspects of their mentoring experiences. Another social control–based program is **Preparing for the Drug Free Years (PDFY)**.[32] PDFY is designed to increase effective parenting and is part of the Strengthening America's Families Project. OJJDP, which runs the program, says, "The PDFY curriculum is guided theoretically by the social development model, which emphasizes the role of bonding to family, school, and peers in healthy adolescent development. The model specifies that strong bonding to positive influences reduces the probability of delinquency and other problem behaviors."[33]

PDFY works with parents of children in grades four to eight in an effort to reduce drug abuse and behavioral problems in adolescents. It seeks to teach effective parenting skills as a way to decrease the risks that juveniles face. PDFY incorporates both behavioral skills training and communication-centered approaches into parent training. Through a series of 10 one-hour sessions, parents learn to (1) increase their children's opportunities for family involvement, (2) teach needed family-participation and social skills, and (3) provide reinforcement for positive behavior and appropriate consequences for misbehavior. Early studies show that program participation (session attendance) tends to be high and that the program is effective at improving general child-management skills among parents.[34]

A program that emphasizes the development of self-control is the **Montreal Preventive Treatment Program**.[35] It addresses early childhood risk factors for gang involvement by targeting boys from poor socioeconomic backgrounds who display disruptive behavior while in kindergarten. The program offers training sessions for parents that are designed to teach family crisis management, disciplining techniques, and other parenting skills. The boys participate in training sessions that emphasize the development of prosocial skills and self-control. At least one evaluation of the program showed that it was effective at keeping boys from joining gangs.[36]

Strong social bonds and effective mechanisms of self-control are central to preventing crime under social process theories. Seen this way, why did Prohibition fail?

The Social Development Perspective

Over the past 25 years, an emerging appreciation for the process of **human development** has played an increasingly important role in understanding criminality.[37] Human development refers to the relationship between the maturing individual and his or her changing environment and to the social processes that relationship entails. The **social development perspective** acknowledges that human development begins at birth and takes place within a social context. Students of human development recognize that the process of development occurs through reciprocal and dynamic interactions that take place between individuals and various aspects of their environment.

The Life Course Perspective

Developmental theories of crime and delinquency demonstrate that criminal behavior tends to follow a distinct pattern across the life cycle. Criminality is relatively uncommon during childhood; it tends to begin as sporadic instances of delinquency during late adolescence and early adulthood and then diminishes and sometimes completely disappears by age 30 or 40. Of course, some people never commit crimes or do so only rarely, while others become career criminals and persist in lives of crime.

The life course perspective, which is quite popular among criminologists today, shifted the traditional focus away from asking why people begin offending, to questions about the dimensions of criminal offending over the entire life course.[38] Also known as **life course criminology**, the contemporary life course perspective has its roots in a 1986 National Academy of Sciences (NAS) panel report.[39] The NAS report emphasized the importance of the study of criminal careers and of crime over the life course. The NAS panel defined a **criminal career** as "the longitudinal sequence of crimes committed by an individual offender."[40] The report was especially important for its analysis of "offending development," a concept that underlies the life course perspective (Figure 6–4).

The panel noted (Figure 6–5) that criminal careers can be described in terms of four dimensions: participation, frequency, duration, and seriousness. *Participation,* which refers to the fraction of a population that is criminally active, depends on the scope of criminal acts considered and the length of the observation period.[41] *Frequency* refers to the number of crimes committed by an individual offender per unit of time. Hence, a burglar who commits one burglary a year has a much lower frequency than one who is active monthly or weekly. Frequency is generally not constant and varies over the life course—even for habitual offenders. *Duration* refers to the length of the criminal career. A criminal career

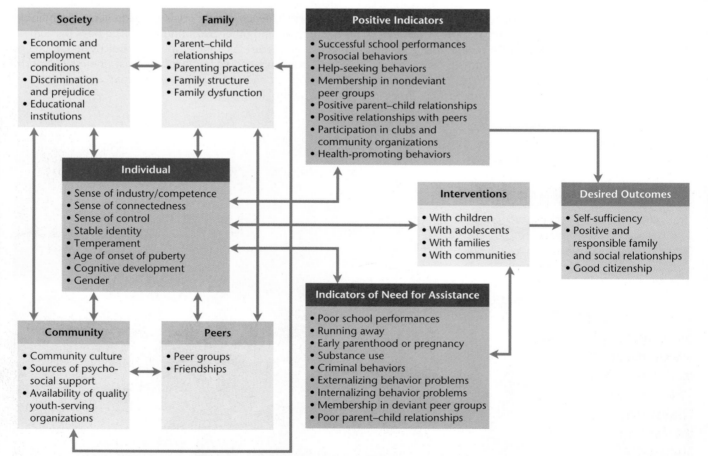

FIGURE 6–4 A Conceptual Model of Adolescent Development

| participation | frequency | duration | seriousness |

FIGURE 6–5 Aspects of Criminal Careers

can be very short, consisting of only one offense, or it can be quite long, as in the case of habitual or chronic criminals. *Seriousness* is relatively self-explanatory, although it is worthwhile to note that some offenders with long criminal careers commit only petty crimes, while others are serious habitual offenders, and still others commit offenses with a mixed degree of seriousness.

Life course criminology was given its name in a book written by **Robert J. Sampson** and **John H. Laub** in 1993.[42] Earlier, the **life course** concept had already been defined as "pathways through the life span involving a sequence of culturally defined, age-graded roles and social transitions enacted over time."[43] Life course theories, which build on social learning and social control principles, recognize that criminal careers may develop as the result of various criminogenic influences, which affect individuals over the course of their lives.

Researchers who focus on the life course as it leads to delinquency, crime, and criminal identities are interested in evaluating the prevalence, frequency, and onset of offending, as well as identifying different developmental pathways to delinquency. Life course researchers ask a variety of questions: How do early childhood characteristics (for example, antisocial behavior) lead to adult behavioral processes and outcomes? How do life transitions (for example, shifts in relationships from parents to peers, transitions from same-sex peers to opposite-sex peers, transitions from attending school to beginning work, marriage, divorce, and so on) influence behavior and behavioral choices? How do offending and victimization interact over the life cycle?[44]

Life course researchers examine "trajectories and transitions through the age-differentiated life span."[45] A trajectory is a pathway or line of development through life that is marked by a sequence of transitions in such areas as work, marriage, parenthood, and criminal behavior. "Trajectories refer to longer-term patterns and sequences of behavior, whereas transitions are marked by specific life events (for example, first job or the onset of

crime) that are embedded in trajectories and evolve over shorter time spans."[46] The concept of age differentiation (or age grading) recognizes the fact that certain forms of behavior and some experiences are more appropriate (in terms of their social consequences) in certain parts of the life cycle than in others. Having a baby, for example, is more manageable when a woman is married, has a spouse with a dependable job and income, is covered by health insurance, and so on, than during adolescence. Life course theorists search for evidence of continuity between childhood or adolescent experiences and adult outcomes or lifestyles.

Three sets of dynamic concepts are important to the life course perspective: (1) activation, (2) aggravation, and (3) desistance.[47] *Activation* refers to the factors that stimulate delinquent behaviors, once initiated, and the processes that shape the continuity, frequency, and diversity of delinquency. Three types of activation are possible: (1) acceleration, or increased frequency of offending over time; (2) stabilization, or increased continuity over time; and (3) diversification, or the tendency of individuals to become involved in more diverse delinquent activities. *Aggravation*, the second dynamic process, refers to the existence of a developmental sequence of activities that escalate or increase in seriousness over time. *Desistance*, the third process, describes a slowing down in the frequency of offending

A multi-generational family reunion. What do life course researchers mean when they talk about "trajectories" and "transitions" through the "age-differentiated life span"?

(deceleration), a reduction in its variety (specialization), or a reduction in its seriousness (deescalation).[48] Desistance is discussed in greater detail later in this chapter.

Another central organizing principle of life course theories is linked lives. The concept of linked lives refers to the fact that human lives "are typically embedded in social relationships with kin and friends across the life span."[49] Family, friends, and coworkers exercise considerable influence on the life course of most people.

Glen H. Elder, Jr., has identified four important life course principles, which, taken together, provide a concise summary of life course theory.[50]

1. **The principle of historical time and place.** The life course of individuals is embedded in and shaped by the historical times and places they experience over their lifetime. Hence, children born in the United States during the Great Depression or in Nazi Germany during World War II were no doubt strongly influenced by the conditions around them. Similarly, surviving children whose parents were lost in the Holocaust experienced trajectories in their life course that would probably have been far different had they been born elsewhere or at a different time.

2. **The principle of timing in lives.** The developmental impact of a succession of life transitions or events is contingent on when they occur in a person's life. Early marriage, for example, or childbearing at an early age can significantly influence the course of people's lives through the long-term consequences of such events. People who start families early may find themselves excluded from further schooling by the demands of parenthood, and those who leave home and marry early may find that parental financial support is not as readily available to them as it might have been if they were still living at home.

3. **The principle of linked lives.** Lives are lived interdependently and social and historical influences are expressed through this network of shared relationships. If a child or a spouse develops a serious illness, for example, the lives of other family members are likely to be affected. Caring for an ill family member is emotionally and financially costly, and it takes time. Because of such costs, opportunities that might have been otherwise available are likely to be lost.

4. **The principle of human agency. Human agency,** which is closely related to the concept of free will, refers to the fact that individuals construct their own life course through the choices they make and the actions they take within the opportunities and constraints of history and social circumstances. The example that Elder gives is of hard-pressed Depression-era parents who "moved their residence to cheaper quarters and sought alternative forms of income." In making such choices, they were involved in the process of building a new life course.

Life course theories are supported by research dating back well over half a century. During the 1930s, for example, **Sheldon Glueck** and **Eleanor Glueck** studied the life cycles

of delinquent boys.[51] The Gluecks followed the careers of 500 nondelinquents and 500 known delinquents in an effort to identify the causes of delinquency. Study group participants were matched on age, intelligence, ethnicity, and neighborhood residence. Data were originally collected through psychiatric interviews with subjects, parent and teacher reports, and official records obtained from police, court, and correctional files. Surviving subjects were interviewed again between 1949 and 1965.

Significantly, the Gluecks investigated possible contributions to crime causation on four levels: sociocultural (socioeconomic), somatic (physical), intellectual, and emotional-temperamental. They concluded that family dynamics played an especially significant role in the development of criminality, and they observed that "the deeper the roots of childhood maladjustment, the smaller the chance of adult adjustment."[52] Delinquent careers, then, tend to carry over into adulthood and frequently lead to criminal careers.

Critique of Life Course Theory

Like the social structure approaches discussed in Chapter 5, life course theories are intimately associated with the social problems approach. For policy makers, an important question is what role individual choice plays, if any, in human development. Do people actively select components of the life course? Do they influence their own trajectories? Since so many important life course determinants are set in motion in early childhood and during adolescence, should those who make wrong choices be held accountable?

Laub and Sampson's Age-Graded Theory

A few years ago, John H. Laub and Robert J. Sampson analyzed 60 cartons of nearly forgotten data that had been collected by the Gluecks and were stored in the basement of the Harvard Law School.[53] Laub and Sampson found that children who turned to delinquency were frequently those who had trouble at school and at home and who had friends who were already involved in delinquency. They also found that two events in the life course—marriage and job stability—seemed to be especially important in reducing the frequency of offending in later life.

Using a sophisticated computerized analysis of the Gluecks' original data, Laub and Sampson developed an "age-graded theory of informal social control."[54] Laub and Sampson suggest that delinquency is more likely to occur when an individual's bond to society is weak or broken. Their theory, however, also recognizes "that social ties embedded in adult transitions (for example, marital attachment, job stability) explain variations in crime unaccounted for by childhood deviance."[55] Hence, although it incorporates elements of social bond theory, Laub and Sampson's perspective also emphasizes the significance of continuity and change over the life course.

Central to Laub and Sampson's approach is the idea of turning points in a criminal career. According to the age-graded

Life course theory stresses the importance of turning points. How might the child shown here represent a significant turning point in this young man's life?

theory, "the interlocking nature of trajectories and transitions may generate turning points or a change in the life course."[56] **One highly significant turning point, for example, may occur when a person becomes a first-time parent and decides to settle down and abandon a carefree or even "fringe" lifestyle.** Given the importance of turning points—which may turn a person either toward or away from criminality and delinquency—a clear-cut relationship between early delinquency and criminality later in life cannot be assumed.

Although turning points can occur at any time in the life course, Sampson and Laub identified two especially significant turning points: employment and marriage. Employers who are willing to give "troublemakers" a chance and marriage partners who insist on conventional lifestyles seem to be able to successfully redirect the course of a budding offender's life. Other important turning points can occur in association with leaving home, having children, getting divorced, graduating from school, receiving a financial windfall, and so on. Even chronic offenders can be reformed when they experience the requisite turning points, while individuals with histories of conventionality can begin offending in response to events and circumstances that undermine previously restraining social bonds.[57]

Because transitions in the life course are typically associated with age and because events (like marriage) either enhance or weaken the social bond, Sampson and Laub contend that "age-graded changes in social bonds explain changes in crime." Since these events are not the result of

"purposeful efforts to control," they are dubbed "informal social controls."[58]

Another important concept in Laub and Sampson's theory is **social capital**. **Laub and Sampson use the concept of social capital to refer to the degree of positive relationships with other people and with social institutions that individuals build up over the course of their lives.**[59] Social capital can be enhanced by education, a consistent employment background, enriching personal connections, a "clean" record, a good marriage and family life, and so on. Social capital impacts directly on life course trajectories: **The greater a person's social capital, the less the chance of criminal activity.**[60]

Critique of Age-Graded Theory

Age-graded theory, while supported by research, still leaves a number of research questions unanswered. For instance, why does social capital prevent some individuals from participating in criminal activity and not others? A second key question is this: Does social capital actually change a criminal's behavior or simply limit his or her access to crime? Of course, just what constitutes a "positive" relationship is open to interpretation. And some otherwise positive relationships might actually increase the opportunity for crime, as when an individual who has been successful in the world of business finds him- or herself introduced to corrupt politicians or is offered bribes to bend the rules and regulations that should be followed in the normal course of business activities.

Moffitt's Dual Taxonomic Theory

Criminologists have long noted that although adult criminality is almost always preceded by antisocial behavior during adolescence, most antisocial children do not become adult criminals. Psychologist **Terrie E. Moffitt** developed a two-path (dual taxonomic) theory of criminality that helps to explain this observation.[61] **Moffitt's theory contends that as a result of neuropsychological deficits (specifically, early brain damage or chemical imbalances) combined with poverty and family dysfunction, some people come to display more or less constant patterns of misbehavior throughout life.**[62] These people are called "life course–persistent offenders" or "life course persisters." Life course persisters tend to fail in school and become involved in delinquency at an early age. As a consequence, their opportunities for legitimate success are increasingly limited with the passage of time.

Other teenagers, says Moffitt, go through limited periods where they exhibit high probabilities of offending. Probabilities of offending are generally highest for these people, says Moffitt, during the mid-teen years. This second group, called "adolescence-limited offenders," is led to offending primarily by structural disadvantages, according to two-path theory. The most significant of these disadvantages is the status anxiety of teenagers that stems from modern society's inadequacy at easing the transition from adolescence to adulthood for significant numbers of young people. Moffitt hypothesizes that a significant source of adolescent strain arises from the fact that biological maturity occurs at a relatively early age (perhaps as early as age 12) and brings with it the desire for sexual and emotional relationships, as well as personal autonomy.[63] Society, however, does not permit the assumption of autonomous adult roles until far later (around age 18). **As adolescents begin to desire autonomy, they are prevented from achieving it because of preexisting societal expectations and societally limited opportunities, resulting in what Moffitt calls a "maturity gap."** They might be told, "You're too young for that," or "Wait until you grow up." Lacking the resources to achieve autonomy on their own, they are drawn into delinquent roles by lifelong deviants who have already achieved autonomy and who serve as role models for others seeking early independence. At least an appearance of autonomy is achievable for adolescence-limited offenders by engaging in actions that mimic those routinely undertaken by life course–persistent offenders. Once adolescence-limited offenders realize the substantial costs of continuing misbehavior, however, they abandon such social mimicry and the participation in delinquent acts that characterizes it. As they mature, they begin to aspire toward achieving legitimate autonomy. Those who fail to successfully make the transition add to the ranks of the life course–persistent population.

Moffitt notes that adolescence-limited offenders display inconsistencies in antisocial behavior from one place to another. They might, for example, participate in illicit drug use with friends or shoplift in stores. They might also experiment sexually. Still, their school behavior is likely to remain within socially acceptable bounds, and they will probably act with respect toward teachers, employers, and adults.

Life course–persistent offenders, on the other hand, consistently engage in antisocial behavior across a wide spectrum of social situations.

Research findings indicate that positive developmental pathways are fostered when adolescents are able to develop (1) a sense of industry and competency, (2) a feeling of connectedness to others and to society, (3) a belief in their ability to control their future, and (4) a stable identity.[64] Adolescents who develop these characteristics appear more likely than others to engage in prosocial behaviors, exhibit positive school performances, and be members of nondeviant peer groups. Competency, connectedness, control, and identity are outcomes of the developmental process. They develop through a person's interactions with his or her community, family, school, and peers. The following kinds of interactions appear to promote development of these characteristics:

- Interactions in which children engage in productive activities and win recognition for their productivity

- Interactions in which parents and other adults control and monitor adolescents' behaviors in a consistent and caring manner while allowing them a substantial degree of psychological and emotional independence

- Interactions in which parents and other adults provide emotional support, encouragement, and practical advice to adolescents

- Interactions in which adolescents are accepted as individuals with unique experiences based on their temperament, gender, biosocial development, and family, cultural, and societal factors.

Social capital refers to the degree of positive relationships with other people and with social institutions that individuals build up over the course of their lives. How does education enhance social capital?

intense periods of criminal involvement during the teenage years, with continued involvement into their twenties and even thirties. By age 35 or so, however, spontaneous desistance seems to occur. Marvin Wolfgang described the process as one of "spontaneous remission." The Gluecks later developed the concept of maturational reform to explain the phenomenon and suggested that the "sheer passage of time" caused delinquents to "grow out" of this transitory phase and to "burn out" physiologically. "Ageing is the only factor," they concluded, "which emerges as significant in the reformative process."[65]

In 1985, Walter R. Grove proposed a maturational theory of biopsychosocial desistance that sees the desistance phenomenon as a natural or normal consequence of the aging process.[66] Grove wrote, "As persons move through the life cycle, (1) they will shift from self-absorption to concern for others; (2) they will increasingly accept societal values and behave in socially appropriate ways; (3) they will become more comfortable with social relations; (4) their activities will increasingly reflect a concern for others in their community; and (5) they will become increasingly concerned with the issue of the meaning of life."[67]

Longitudinal studies of crime in the life course conducted by **David P. Farrington** and **Donald J. West** have shown far greater diversity in the ages of desistance than in the ages of onset of criminal behavior.[68] In 1982, in an effort to explain the considerable heterogeneity of developmental pathways, Farrington and West began tracking a cohort of 411 boys born in London in 1953. The study, known as the **Cambridge Study in Delinquent Development**, is ongoing. It uses self-reports of delinquency as well as psychological tests and in-depth interviews. To date, participants have been interviewed nine times. Although respondents are now 48-years-old, the earliest interviews were conducted at age eight.

The Cambridge study reveals that life course patterns found in the United States are also characteristic of English delinquents. Farrington found that the study's persistent offenders suffered from "hyperactivity, poor concentration, low achievement, an antisocial father, large family size, low family income, a broken family, poor parental supervision, and parental disharmony."[69] Other

Critique of Moffitt's Dual Taxonomic Theory

Moffit has been criticized because her research could not definitely show that family and psychological dysfunction was directly related to parent control or individual trajectories. Generally, however, her ideas are well supported and have achieved broad acceptance within the field of criminology.

Farrington's Delinquent Development Theory

Life course theorists use the term **persistence** to describe continuity in crime, or continual involvement in offending. **Desistance**, on the other hand, refers to the cessation of criminal activity or to the termination of a period of involvement in offending behavior (that is, abandoning a criminal career). In **Farrington's delinquent development theory**, desistance (which was mentioned briefly earlier in this chapter) can be unaided or aided. *Unaided desistance* refers to desistance that occurs without the formal intervention or assistance of criminal justice agencies like probation or parole agencies, the courts, or prison or jail. *Aided desistance*, which does involve agencies of the justice system, is generally referred to as "rehabilitation." As noted earlier in our discussion of adolescence-limited offenders, delinquents often mature successfully and grow out of offending. Even older persistent offenders, however, may tire of justice system interventions or lose the personal energy required for continued offending. Such offenders are said to have "burned out."

A number of early criminologists noted the desistance phenomenon where offenders appear to undergo relatively

131

risk factors for delinquency included harsh discipline, negative peer influences, and parents with offense histories of their own. Chronic offenders were found to have friends and peers who were also offenders, and offending was found to begin with early antisocial behavior, including aggressiveness, dishonesty, problems in school, truancy, hyperactivity, impulsiveness, and restlessness. Consistent with other desistance studies, Farrington found that offending tends to peak around the age of 17 or 18 and then declines. By age 35, many subjects were found to have assumed conforming lifestyles, although they were often separated or divorced with poor employment records and patterns of residential instability. Many former offenders were also substance abusers and consequently served as very poor role models for their children.

In 1990, Rolf Loeber and Marc LeBlanc identified four components of desistance.[70] Desistance, they said, can be conceptualized in terms of (1) *deceleration*, or a slowing down in the frequency of offending; (2) *specialization*, or a reduction in the variety of offenses; (3) *deescalation*, or a reduction in the seriousness of offending; and (4) *reaching a ceiling*, or remaining at a certain level of offending and not committing more serious offenses. Until desistance is better defined and conceptualized, it will remain difficult for researchers to investigate the topic.

Critique of Farrington's Delinquent Development Theory

Delinquent development theory has been criticized for its methodology. While studies of desistance are becoming increasingly common, one of the main methodological problems for researchers is determining when desistance has occurred. Some theorists conceptualize desistance as the complete or absolute stopping of criminal behavior of any kind, while others see it as the gradual cessation of criminal involvement.[71]

Some criminologists argue, however, that the claim that aging causes desistance is meaningless because it doesn't explain the actual mechanisms involved in the desistance phenomenon. In other words, the claim that an offender "ages out" of crime offers no more explanatory power than the claim that turning 16 causes delinquency.

Evolutionary Ecology

Because life course theory uses a developmental perspective in the study of criminal careers, life course researchers typically use longitudinal research designs involving cohort analysis. **Cohort analysis** usually begins at birth and traces the development of a population whose members share common characteristics, until they reach a certain age. One well-known analysis of a birth cohort, undertaken by **Marvin Wolfgang** during the 1960s, found that a small nucleus of chronic juvenile offenders accounted for a disproportionately large share of all juvenile arrests.[72] Wolfgang studied male individuals born in Philadelphia in 1945 until they reached age 18. He concluded that a small number of violent offenders were responsible for most of the crimes committed by the cohort. Six percent of cohort members accounted for 52% of all arrests. A follow-up study found that the seriousness of the offenses among the cohort increased in adulthood but that the actual number of offenses decreased as the cohort aged.[73] More recently, Wolfgang published a cohort analysis of 5,000 individuals born in the Wuchang district of the city of Wuhan in China. The study, from which preliminary results were published in 1996, used Chinese-supplied data to compare delinquents with nondelinquents. It found "striking differences in school deportment, achieved level of education, school dropout rate, type of employment, and unemployment rate" between the two groups.[74]

The ecological perspective on crime control, pioneered by **Lawrence E. Cohen** and **Richard Machalek**, provides a contemporary example of a life course approach.[75] Like other life course theories, **evolutionary ecology** blends elements of previous perspectives—in this case, building upon the

Desistance refers to the termination of involvement in offending behavior. Why is only one person in this photo not smoking?

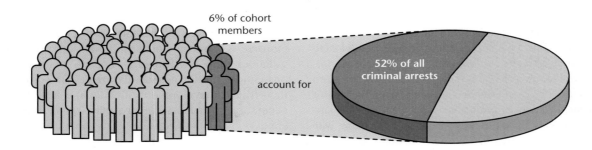

6% of cohort members account for 52% of all criminal arrests

approach of social ecology—while emphasizing developmental pathways encountered early in life. According to University of Wyoming criminologist Bryan Vila, "the evolutionary ecological approach draws attention to the ways people develop over the course of their lives. Experiences and environment early in life, especially those that affect child development and the transmission of biological traits and family management practices across generations, seem particularly important."[76] According to Vila, evolutionary ecology "attempts to explain how people acquire criminality—a predisposition that disproportionately favors criminal behavior—when and why they express it as crime, how individuals and groups respond to those crimes, and how all these phenomena interact as a dynamic self-reinforcing system that evolves over time."[77]

Critique of Evolutionary Ecology

Wolfgang's analysis has since been criticized for its lack of a second cohort, or control group, against which the experiences of the cohort under study could be compared.[78] Similarly, the dropping out of cohort members can bias the results of any cohort analysis. Such dropping out can occur when contact is lost with members, when cohort members move away, or when they die. It can be expected, for example, that the most crime-prone individuals in any cohort are the most likely to be difficult to keep in touch with, and may themselves suffer death or incapacitation—making it impossible to determine what their future behavior might have entailed.

Thornberry's Interactional Theory

Terence Thornberry has proposed what he calls an **interactional theory** of crime, which integrates social control and social learning explanations of delinquency.[79] In constructing his approach, Thornberry was attentive to the impact of social structure on behavior and noted how delinquency and crime seem to develop within the context of reciprocal social arrangements. Reciprocity was especially important to Thornberry because he believed that too many other theories were simplistic in their dependence on simple unidirectional causal relationships.

The fundamental cause of delinquency according to interactional theory is a weakening of a person's bond to conventional society.[80] Thornberry points out that adolescents who are strongly attached to their parents and family and who strive to achieve within the context of approved social arrangements, such as education, rarely turn to serious delinquency. It takes more than weak conventional bonds, however, for delinquency to develop. A further requirement is the presence of an environment in which delinquency can be learned and in which rule-violating behavior can be positively rewarded. Delinquent peers are especially important in providing the kind of environment necessary for criminal behavior to develop, and gang membership can play a highly significant role in the development and continuation of such behavior. **Associating with delinquent peers, says Thornberry, leads to delinquent acts, but also creates a causal loop because those who commit delinquent acts continue associating with others like themselves, reinforcing the behavior and creating escalating levels of criminal activity.** Thornberry also predicts that delinquents will seek out association with ever-more delinquent groups if their delinquency continues to be rewarded. Hence, delinquency, from the perspective of interactional theory, is seen as a process that unfolds over the life course.

In a test of interactional theory,[81] Thornberry used data drawn from the Rochester Youth Development Study, a multiwave panel study designed to examine drug use and delinquent behavior among adolescents in the Rochester, New York, area. Study findings, discussed in more detail in the next section, supported the loop-back aspects of interactional theory and showed that delinquency is part of a dynamic social process, and not merely the end result of static conditions. The study also found that the development of beliefs supportive of delinquent behavior tends to follow that behavior in time. In other words, **commitment to delinquent values may be more a product of delinquent behavior that is rewarded than an initial cause of such behavior.**

Critique of Thornberry's Interactional Theory

Those who criticize Thornberry say that his theory does not fully appreciate the notion of childhood maltreatment (as measured by official records) as an important element of the developmental process leading to delinquency.[82] Researchers have also found that the degree of maltreatment experienced in childhood bears at least some relationship to the extent of delinquent involvement later in life. While maltreatment appears to weaken the bond to conventionality, it also weakens the family bond.

Developmental Pathways

Researchers have found that manifestations of disruptive behaviors in childhood and adolescence are often age dependent, reflecting a developing capability to display different behaviors with age.[83] Budding behavioral problems can often be detected at an early age. In 1994, for example, Rolf Loeber and Dale F. Hay described the emergence of opposition to parents and aggression toward siblings and peers as a natural developmental occurrence during the first two years of life.[84] Loeber and Hay found, however, that as toddlers develop the ability to speak, they become increasingly likely to use words to resolve conflicts. As a consequence, oppositional behaviors decline between ages three and six. Children who are unable, for whatever reason, to develop adequate verbal coping skills, however, distinguish themselves from the norm by committing acts of intense

aggression, initiating hostile conflict, and being characterized by parents as having a difficult temperament.[85] Figure 6–6 shows the order in which disruptive and antisocial childhood behaviors tend to manifest between birth and late adolescence. Figure 6–7, in contrast, shows the order of development of skills and attitudes deemed necessary for successful prosocial development during childhood and adolescence.

One of the most comprehensive studies to date that has attempted to detail life pathways leading to criminality began in 1986. The study, called the Program of Research on the Causes and Correlates of Delinquency, is sponsored by the U.S. Department of Justice's Office of Juvenile Justice and Delinquency Prevention. The program, a longitudinal study that is producing ongoing results, intends to improve the understanding of serious delinquency, violence, and drug use by examining how youths develop within the context of family, school, peers, and community.[86] It has compiled data on 4,500 youths from three distinct but coordinated projects: the Denver Youth Survey, conducted by the University of Colorado; the Pittsburgh Youth Study, undertaken by University of Pittsburgh researchers; and the Rochester Youth Development Study, fielded by professors at the State University of New York at Albany.

The Causes and Correlates projects all use a similar research design. All of the projects are longitudinal investigations involving repeated contacts with youths during a substantial portion of their developmental years. In each project, researchers conduct individual, face-to-face interviews with inner-city youths considered to be at high risk for involvement in delinquency and drug abuse. Multiple perspectives on each child's development and behavior are obtained through interviews with the child's primary caretakers and in interviews with teachers. In addition to interview data, the studies collect extensive information from official agencies, including police, courts, schools, and social services.[87]

Program results show that (1) delinquency is related to individual risk factors like impulsivity; (2) the more seriously involved in drugs a youth is, the more seriously that juvenile will be involved in delinquency; (3) children who are more attached

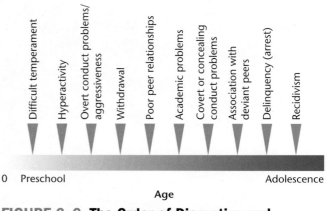

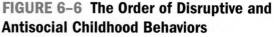

FIGURE 6–6 The Order of Disruptive and Antisocial Childhood Behaviors

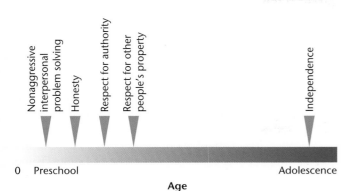

FIGURE 6–7 The Order of Development of Skills and Attitudes Necessary for Successful Prosocial Development

to and involved with their parents are less involved in delinquency; (4) greater risks exist for violent offending when a child is physically abused or neglected early in life; (5) students who are not highly committed to school have higher rates of delinquency, and delinquency involvement reduces commitment to school; (6) poor family life, and especially poor parental supervision, exacerbates delinquency and drug use; (7) affiliation with street gangs and illegal gun ownership are both predictive of delinquency; (8) living in a "bad" neighborhood doubles the risk for delinquency; and (9) family receipt of public assistance (welfare) is associated with the highest risk of delinquency (followed by low socioeconomic status).[88] Results also showed that peers who were delinquent or used drugs had a great impact on other youth. In terms of desistance, program results show that "the best predictors of success were having conventional friends, having a stable family and good parental monitoring, having positive expectations for the future, and not having delinquent peers."[89]

Perhaps the most significant result of the Causes and Correlates study is the finding that three separate developmental pathways to delinquency exist. The pathways identified by the study are shown in Figure 6–8. They are the following:[90]

- The *authority conflict pathway*, on which subjects appear to begin quite young (as early as three or four years of age). "The first step," says the study authors, "was stubborn behavior, followed by defiance around age 11, and authority avoidance—truancy, staying out late at night, or running away."

- The *covert pathway*, which begins with "minor covert acts such as frequent lying and shoplifting, usually around age 10." Delinquents following this path quickly progress "to acts of property damage, such as firestarting or vandalism, around age 11 or 12, followed by moderate and serious forms of delinquency."

- The overt *pathway*, in which the first step is marked by minor aggression such as "annoying others and bullying—around age 11 or 12." Bullying was found to escalate into "physical fighting and violence as the juvenile progressed along this pathway." The overt pathway eventually leads to violent crimes like rape, robbery, and assault.

Researchers have found that these three different pathways are not necessarily mutually exclusive and can at times converge (see Figure 6–9). Self-report data show that simultaneous progression along two or more pathways leads to higher rates of delinquency than would otherwise occur.[91]

Critique of Developmental Pathways

As with other social development theories, the idea of developmental pathways suffers from definitional issues. What, for example, do life course concepts like turning points and pathways really mean? A related fundamental question, especially for policy makers, is the role that individual choice plays, if any, in human development.

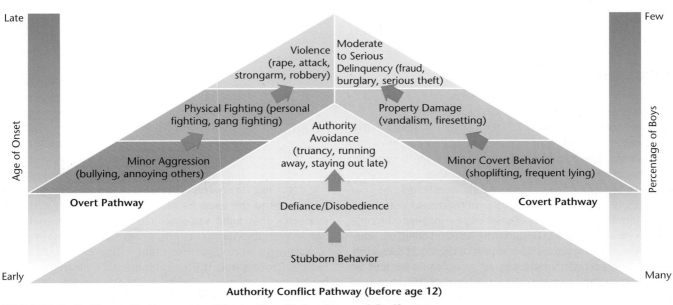

FIGURE 6–8 Three Pathways to Disruptive Behavior and Delinquency

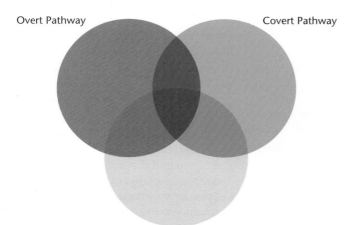

Overt Pathway   Covert Pathway

Authority Conflict Pathway

FIGURE 6–9 Single or Multiple Disruptive Pathways

The Chicago Human Development Project

Another study that could produce substantially significant results began in 1990. It is known as the **Project on Human Development in Chicago Neighborhoods (PHDCN)**,[92] and is directed by physician Felton J. Earls, professor of human behavior and development at Harvard University's School of Public Health. Also involved in the project are Robert Sampson, professor of sociology at the University of Chicago, and Stephen Raudenbush, professor of education at Michigan State University. Earls and Albert J. Reiss describe the ongoing research as "the major criminological investigation of this century."[93]

PHDCN, which consists of a longitudinal analysis of how individuals, families, institutions, and communities evolve together, is now "tracing how criminal behavior develops from birth to age 32."[94] It involves experts from a wide range of disciplines, including psychiatry, developmental and clinical psychology, sociology, criminology, public health and medicine, education, human behavior, and statistics.

The project is actually two studies combined into a single, comprehensive design. The first is an intensive study of Chicago's neighborhoods. This aspect of the project is evaluating the social, economic, organizational, political, and cultural components of each neighborhood. It seeks to identify changes that took place in the neighborhoods over the study's eight-year data-gathering period. The second project component consists of a series of coordinated longitudinal evaluations of 7,000 randomly selected children, adolescents, and young adults. This aspect of the study is looking at the changing circumstances of people's lives and is attempting to identify personal characteristics that may lead toward or away from antisocial behavior. Researchers are exploring a wide range of variables—from prenatal drug

exposure, lead poisoning, and nutrition to adolescent growth patterns, temperament, and self-image—as they try to identify which individuals might be most at risk for crime and delinquency. Additional features of the project include a study of children's exposure to violence and its consequences and an evaluation of child care and its impact on early childhood development. A variety of study methodologies is being used, including self-reports, individualized tests and examinations, direct observation, the examination of existing records, and reports by informants. The questions being explored can be described as follows:[95]

- **Communities.** Why do some communities experience high rates of antisocial behavior while other, apparently similar communities are relatively safe?

- **School.** Some children have achievement problems early in schools. Others have behavioral or truancy problems. Some exhibit both kinds of problems, and others neither. Why do these differences exist? What are the causes and effects?

- **Peers.** Delinquent youths tend to associate with delinquent peers and usually act in groups. Does the association lead to delinquency or is it simply a case of "file finding like"? Are the influences of peers equally important for girls and for boys, or are their development pathways entirely different?

- **Families.** Poor parenting practices are strongly associated with substance abuse and delinquency, but are they the cause of such behavior? If so, then social programs in parenting skills could make a difference. But what if there are underlying factors, such as a temperamental characteristics or social isolation, that cause problems in both parents and children?

- **Individual differences.** What health-related, cognitive. intellectual and emotional factors in children promote positive social development? What factors put children at risk of developing antisocial behaviors?

PHDCN is producing results and has led to targeted interventions intended to lower rates of offending. According to Sampson, "Instead of external actions (for example, a police crackdown), we stress in this study the effectiveness of 'informal' mechanisms by which residents themselves achieve public order. In particular, we believe that collective expectations for intervening on behalf of neighborhood children is a crucial dimension of the public life of neighborhoods."[96] Life course perspectives, like the perspective that informs PHDCN, often point to the need for early intervention with nurturing strategies that build self-control through positive socialization. As Bryan Vila points out, "There are two main types of nurturing strategies: those that improve early life experiences to forestall the development of strategic styles based on criminality, and those that channel child and adolescent development in an effort to improve the match between individuals and their environment."[97]

Life course perspectives point to the need for early intervention using nurturing strategies that build self-control.

Policy Implications of Social Development Theories

Social development strategies have been widely applied to juvenile justice and human services settings. **The Office of Juvenile Justice and Delinquency Prevention has adopted the social development model as the foundation for its Comprehensive Strategy for Serious, Violent, and Chronic Juvenile Offenders program**. The Comprehensive Strategy Program provides participating communities with a framework for preventing delinquency, intervening in early delinquent behavior, and responding to serious, violent, and chronic offending. It assists communities in establishing or modifying a juvenile justice "continuum of care" through risk-focused prevention, risk and needs assessment, structured decision making, and graduated sanctions training and technical assistance. OJJDP's Comprehensive Strategy Program centers around the following six components:

- Strengthening families in their role of providing guidance and discipline and instilling sound values as the first and primary teacher of children

- Supporting core social institutions, including schools, churches, and other community organizations, so that they can reduce risk factors and help children develop their full potential

- Promoting prevention strategies that enhance protective factors and reduce the impact of negative risk factors affecting the lives of young people at risk for high delinquency

- Intervening immediately and constructively when delinquent behavior first occurs

- Identifying and controlling a small segment of violent and chronic juvenile offenders

- Establishing a broad spectrum of *sanctions* that ensure accountability and a continuum of services

Another contemporary example of social intervention efforts tied to a developmental model is Targeted Outreach, a program operated by Boys and Girls Clubs of America.[98] The program has its origins in the 1972 implementation of a youth development strategy based on studies undertaken at the University of Colorado, which showed that at-risk youths could be effectively diverted from the juvenile justice system through the provision of positive alternatives. Using a wide referral network made up of local schools, police departments, and various youth service agencies, club officials work to end what they call the "inappropriate detention of juveniles."[99]

The program's primary goal is to provide a positive, productive alternative to gangs for the youths who are most vulnerable to their influences or are already entrenched in gang activity. Currently, the program recruits at-risk youngsters—many as young as seven years old—and diverts them into activities that are intended to promote a sense of belonging, competence, usefulness, and self-control. **A sense of belonging is fostered through clubs that provide familiar settings where each child is accepted. Competence and usefulness are developed through opportunities for meaningful activities, which young people in the club program can successfully undertake. Finally, Targeted Outreach provides its youthful participants with a chance to be heard and, consequently, with the opportunity to influence decisions affecting their future.** To date, Targeted Outreach has served more than 10,000 at-risk youths. Organizers hope that Targeted Outreach will eventually involve more than 1.5 million youngsters between the ages of 7 and 17. Mobilization for Youth and Targeted Outreach both stand as examples of the kinds of programs that theorists who focus on the social structure typically seek to implement.

Young members of the Challengers Boys and Girls Club of south Los Angeles work with TV station personnel. Which OJJDP strategy is reflected in the club's efforts?

The Crime

Shortly after 7:00 A.M. on April 16, 2007, Seung-Hui Cho shot and killed two people near the Virginia Polytechnic Institute and State University (Virginia Tech) campus in Blacksburg, Virginia. Cho, an English major at the university, was in his senior year, and had previously been accused of stalking two female students. When police mistakenly believed the shootings to have been the result of a lovers' quarrel between one of the victims and her off-campus boyfriend, Cho found the time he needed to make his final preparations for another attack.[i]

Entering the campus' Norris Hall around 9:30 A.M., Cho secured the interior door handles with chains, then systematically set about slaughtering everyone he encountered. During the next 15 minutes, he fired more than 175 rounds of ammunition from two weapons, leaving 30 people dead within Norris Hall. When Cho heard police blast through the entrance doors to gain access to the building, he turned the gun on himself. His rampage is the worst event of its kind in U.S. history,[ii] leaving a total of 32 victims dead. Seventeen other were wounded by gunshots, and still more when they jumped out of the building's second-story windows to escape.

The attacks on the Virginia Tech campus were planned and executed with near-military precision. Cho acquired two handguns in the weeks before the shootings, extra magazines, ammunition, and lengths of chain with which to secure the doors of classroom buildings so that potential victims would be unable to escape. Just days before the killings, he videotaped a raging manifesto-like diatribe/suicide note in which he blamed society for making him into what he'd become.[iii] In the video, Cho praised the Columbine High School shooters as martyrs, pronounced himself a Christ figure, and ranted against the hedonistic behavior, trust funds, and high-class living of the financially elite.[iv]

On April 18, 2007, a package from Cho was delivered to NBC News. The date and time post marked on the mailing showed a time between the first and second shooting episodes, showing that Cho had made a trip to the post office before continuing his shooting spree. Inside the package were an 1,800-word manifesto, photos, and 27 digitally recorded videos in which Cho likened himself to Jesus Christ and expressed his hatred of the wealthy. In the video he proclaimed, "You forced me into a corner and gave me only one option.... You just loved to crucify me. You loved inducing cancer in my head, terror in my heart and ripping my soul all this time."

The Causes Behind the Crime
Seung-Hui Cho

A still image from a home video made by Seung-Hui Cho before the attacks. Were there warning signs of what was to come?

Can the Social Process or Social Development Perspective Explain This Crime?

- Seung-Hui Cho was born on January 18, 1984. He rarely talked and possessed a disassociated manner that has been described as an "empty face," as he displayed little reaction to what was occurring around him. Some people think that he may have had symptoms of autism. Cho came to the United States from the Republic of Korea when he was just eight years old, a sullen, withdrawn, and brooding child. *Which social process or social development perspective might apply to Cho?*

- After coming to the United States and moving to the tight-knit Korean community in Centreville, Virginia, the family maintained an "uncommonly private"[v] existence. Cho's progression through elementary school was unremarkable. At nearby Chantilly, Virginia's Westfield High School, the slight, slender boy appeared to be too young to be there. The taciturn Cho was teased and bullied more than most, especially about his poor English and deep-throated voice, which didn't seem to fit his small body.[vi] *Might the life-course approach help explain Cho's later behavior? If so, how?*

- While others in the success-oriented community were heralded in the community newspaper for making the selection lists at some of the most elite Ivy League universities, Cho's good but less-than-stellar grades kept him off such lists. Instead, he attended Virginia Tech in southwest Virginia's Blue Ridge Mountains. *What turning points can you identify in Cho's life?*

- Cho's freshman, sophomore, and junior years as an English major at Virginia Tech were noteworthy for the anger in his writings. Although he never threatened killing people or mentioned guns, the disturbingly violent nature of his papers caused the

Emergency personnel assist some of Seung-Hui Cho's many victims. What motivated Cho?

chairperson of the English Department to remove him from a creative writing class. She attempted to teach him one-on-one, then sought assistance from the university's counseling department and other university officials. *Might there be value in a control-balance perspective when examining Cho's behavior? If so, how?*

- The anger that seethed within Cho was also of concern to his fellow students, who openly discussed whether he could become a school shooter. In a perceptive article after the shootings, *New York Times* columnist Benedict Carey eloquently explained that "the tragedy illustrates how human social groups, whether in classrooms, boardrooms or dormitories, are in fact exquisitely sensitive to a threat in their midst."[vii] *Which of the three pathways to delinquent behavior described in this chapter seem most applicable to Cho?*

Author's note: Not long after the events described here, the then-governor of Virginia, Timothy M. Kaine, established a panel of nationally-recognized experts from a variety of fields to perform an independent review of the shootings. The group, known as the Virginia Tech Review Panel, studied the shooting incident in detail, and released a comprehensive report that can be viewed at http://www.vtreviewpanel.org/report/index.html. A psychological profile of Cho, prepared by panel member and forensic behavioral scientist Roger L. Depue, was included in the report, and is available separately at http://www.vtreviewpanel.org/report/report/32_APPENDIX_N.pdf.

NOTES:

[i]Ned Potter, David Schoetz, Richard Esposito, Pierre Thomas, and the staff of ABC News, "Killer's Note: You Caused Me to Do This," ABC News, April 28, 2007, http://abcnews.go.com/US/Story? id=3048108&page=1 (accessed July 1, 2007).

[ii]Aamer Madhani, E. A. Torriero, and Rex W. Huppke, "Danger Signs Festered Below Aloof Surface," *Chicago Tribune*, April 17, 2007.

[iii]Ibid.

[iv]"High School Classmates Say Gunman Was Bullied," MSNBC, April 19, 2007.

[v]Benedict Carey, "When the Group Is Wise," *New York Times*, April 22, 2007, http://www.nytimes.com/2007/04/22/weekinreview/22carey.html?_r=1&ref=weekinreview&oref=slogin (accessed July 1, 2007).

[vi]Ned Potter, David Schoetz, Richard Esposito, Pierre Thomas, and the staff of ABC News, "Killer's Note: You Caused Me to Do This," ABC News, April 28, 2007, http://abcnews.go.com/US/Story? id=3048108&page=1 (accessed July 1, 2007).

[vii]N. R. Kleinfield, "Before Deadly Rage, a Life Consumed by Troubling Silence," *New York Times*, April 22, 2007, http://www.nytimes.com/2007/04/22/us/22vatech.html?_r=1&n=Top%2fReference%2fTimes%20Topics%2fPeople%2fC%2fCho%2c%20Seung%2dHui&oref=slogin (accessed July 1, 2009).

Go to mycrimekit.com to explore the following resources for Chapter 6:

- **MULTIMEDIA:** Videos about the major principles of social process, concentric zone theory, life histories, Edwin H. Sutherland, differential association, labeling, societal reaction, Edwin Lemert, Howard Becker, learning theory, punishment vs. reward, social control, Travis Hirschi, and self-control theory
- **PRACTICE QUIZ:** Multiple-choice, true/false, short-answer, and essay questions
- **FLASHCARDS:** Thirty-four flashcards to test your knowledge of the chapter's key terms
- **WEB EXTRAS & LIBRARY EXTRAS:** Links to websites, online articles, and resources for labeling theory, causes and prevention of delinquency, child development and the transition to adulthood, adolescent drug use, and social capital
- **ENDNOTES:** Chapter 6 bibliography

Summary and Key Concepts

SOCIAL PROCESS AND SOCIAL DEVELOPMENT

Both social process and social development theories see criminal behavior as a product of the social environment and not as an innate characteristic.

The Perspective of Social Interaction

social process theories suggest that criminal behavior is learned in interaction with others and that socialization and learning processes occur as the result of group membership and relationships.

social development theories An integrated view of human development that examines multiple levels of maturation simultaneously, including the psychological, biological, familial, interpersonal, cultural, societal, and ecological levels.

 Q: *How does the process of social interaction contribute to criminal behavior?*

History of Social Process and Social Development Theories

learning theory A perspective that places primary emphasis upon the role of communication and socialization in the acquisition of learned patterns of criminal behavior and the values that support that behavior.

differential association An explanation for crime and deviance that holds that people pursue criminal or deviant behavior to the extent that they identify themselves with real or imaginary people from whose perspective their criminal or deviant behavior seems acceptable.

Edwin Sutherland All significant behavior is learned and crime, therefore, is not substantively different from any other form of behavior.

Q: *What are the various social process perspectives discussed in this chapter?*

Social Process: Social Control Theories

social control theories A perspective that predicts that when social constraints on antisocial behavior are weakened or absent, delinquent behavior emerges.

containment theory A form of control theory that suggests that a series of both internal and external factors contributes to law-abiding behavior.

containment The stabilizing force that, if effective, blocks pushes and pulls from leading an individual toward crime.

low self-esteem Low self-esteem is linked to delinquency.

social bond The link created through individuals and the society of which they are a part.

general theory of crime A theory that attempts to explain all (or at least most) forms of criminal conduct through a single, overarching approach, and which holds that low self-control accounts for all crime at all times.

control ratio The amount of control to which a person is subject versus the amount of control that person exerts over others.

Walter Reckless Crime is like sickness because it results from the failure of control mechanisms, some internal to the person, and others external.

Howard B. Kaplan People who are ridiculed by their peers suffer a loss of self-esteem, assess themselves poorly, and, as a result, abandon the motivation to conform.

Travis Hirschi Through successful socialization, a bond forms between individuals and the social group. When that bond is weakened or broken, deviance and crime may result.

Michael Gottfredson and *Travis Hirschi* Nearly all crimes are mundane, simple, trivial, easy acts aimed at satisfying the desires of the moment.

Charles R. Tittle The control-balance approach results from a blending of social bond and containment perspectives.

Labeling Theory

Q: *Why do people tend to accept the labels applied to them?*

tagging A term that explains what happens to offenders following arrest, conviction, and sentencing.

primary deviance Initial deviance often undertaken to deal with transient problems in living.

secondary deviance Deviant behavior that results from official labeling and from association with others who have been so labeled.

moral enterprise The efforts made by an interest group to have its sense of moral ethical propriety enacted into law.

Edwin M. Lemert Primary deviance is undertaken to solve an immediate problem. Secondary deviance is important after an arrest has taken place and an individual is "tagged" as a deviant. The deviance then becomes more forceful and serious.

Howard Becker Society creates both deviance and the deviant person by its response to circumscribed behaviors.

Policy Implications of Social Process Theories

Social process theories suggest that crime prevention programs should work to enhance self-control and to build prosocial bonds.

Q: *What kinds of social policy initiatives might be based on social process theories of crime causation?*

prosocial bonds Bonds between the individual and the social group that strengthen the likelihood of conformity. Prosocial bonds are characterized by attachment to conventional social institutions, values, and beliefs.

Juvenile Mentoring Program (JUMP) A program that places at-risk youth in a one-on-one relationship with favorable adult role models.

Preparing for the Drug-Free Years (PDFY) A program designed to increase effective parenting for children in grades four to eight in an effort to reduce drug abuse and behavioral problems.

Montreal Prevention Treatment Program A program designed to address early childhood risk factors for gang involvement by targeting boys in kindergarten who exhibit disruptive behavior.

The Social Development Perspective

Q: *What are the central concepts of social development theories?*

human development The relationship between the maturing individual and his or her changing environment, as well as the social processes that the relationship entails.

social development perspective An integrated view of human development that examines multiple levels of maturity simultaneously, including the psychological, biological, familial, interpersonal, cultural, societal, and ecological levels.

life course criminology A developmental perspective that draws attention to the fact that criminal behavior tends to follow a distinct pattern across the life cycle.

criminal career The longitudinal sequence of events committed by an individual offender.

life course Pathways through the life span involving a sequence of culturally defined, age-graded roles and social transitions enacted over time.

social capital The degree of positive relationships with others and with social institutions that individuals build up over the course of their lives.

human agency Individuals construct their own life course through the choices they make and the actions they take within the opportunities and constraints of history and social circumstances.

Sheldon Glueck and *Eleanor Glueck* Family dynamics plays an especially significant role in the development of criminality, and the deeper the maladjustment is, the smaller the chance that these same children will adjust into nondeviant adults.

Terrie E. Moffitt Neuropsychological deficits combined with poverty and dysfunction cause patterns of misbehavior throughout life.

John H. Laub and *Robert J. Sampson* After re-examining the Gluecks' data, found that two events in the life course—marriage and job stability—were especially important in reducing the frequency of offending in later life.

Glen Elder, Jr. There are four important life course principles: historical time and place, timing in lives, linked lives, human agency.

Farrington's Delinquent Development Theory Persistence describes continuity in crime. Desistance refers to cessation of criminal activity or to a termination in a period of involvement in offending behavior.

persistence Continuity in crime, or continual involvement in offending.

desistance The cessation of criminal activity or the termination of a period of involvement in offending behavior (that is, abandoning a criminal career).

Cambridge Study in Delinquent Development A longitudinal (life-course) study of crime and delinquency tracking a cohort of 411 boys in London.

David P. Farrington and *Donald J. West* There is a far greater diversity in the ages of distance than in the ages of onset behavior.

cohort analysis A social scientific technique that studies over time a population with common characteristics. Cohort analysis usually begins at birth and traces the development of cohort members until they reach a certain age.

Marvin Wolfgang Through cohort analysis, found that a small nucleus of chronic juvenile offenders accounted for a disproportionately large share of all delinquents.

evolutionary ecology Blends elements of previous perspectives—building upon social ecology while emphasizing developmental pathways.

Lawrence E. Cohen and *Richard Machalek* Blends social ecology while emphasizing the pathways encountered early in life.

interactional theory A theoretical approach to exploring crime and delinquency that blends social control and social learning perspectives.

Terence Thornberry Interactional theory of crime integrates social control and social learning explanations of delinquency.

Project on Human Development in Chicago Neighborhoods (PHDCN) A longitudinal analysis of how individuals, families, institutions, and communities evolve together.

Policy Implications of Social Development Theories Based on the belief that at-risk youth can be effectively diverted from the juvenile justice system through the provision of positive alternatives.

Chronic Strategy for Serious, Violent, and Chronic Juvenile Offenders Program A program that works to strengthen families and core institutions in their efforts to reduce risk factors and develop their full potential.

 Q: *What kinds of social policy initiatives might be suggested by social development perspectives?*

Social Conflict

It's How We Relate

Social stratification breeds envy, and that leads to crime.
–*Natalya Lemesheva, Russian Schoolteacher*

To move beyond criminal justice is to move beyond capitalism.
–*Richard Quinney*

In the **Crime Theories** section of Criminology Interactive, click on **Social Conflict Theories**.

PRINCIPLES OF THE SOCIAL CONFLICT PERSPECTIVE

The social conflict perspective, which is shared among social sciences generally, says that conflict is a fundamental aspect of social life that can never be fully resolved. At best, the conflict perspective says, formal agencies of social control, including the police, the courts, and the correctional establishment, merely coerce the unempowered or the disenfranchised to comply with the rules established by those in power.

Social order, rather than being the result of any consensus, is seen as resting upon the *exercise of power through law*. From the conflict point of view, laws are a tool of the powerful, useful in keeping the unempowered from wresting control over important social institutions. Those in power must work ceaselessly to remain there, although the structure that they impose on society—including patterns of wealth-building that they define as acceptable and circumstances under which they authorize the exercise of legal power and military might—gives them all the advantages they are likely to need. Hence, according to the conflict perspective, the body of laws that characterize any society is a political statement, and crime is a political definition imposed largely upon those whose interests lie outside of those that the powerful, through the law, define as acceptable. In short, from a conflict perspective crime is defined in terms of the concept of oppression.[1]

A History of Social Conflict Theory in Criminology

Marx: Social Conflict as Class Struggle

The conflict perspective in the social sciences has a long history. One of the best-known early writers on social conflict is **Karl Marx**. Born in Germany in 1818, Marx became well known as a revolutionary economist and sociologist following the publication of *The Communist Manifesto* in 1848. His writings, including another famous book, *Das Kapital*, focused on conflicts inherent in capitalism and led to the formulation of communist ideals, becoming part of the intellectual foundation of twentieth-century communist societies.

According to Marx, two fundamental social classes exist within any capitalist society: the haves and the have-nots. Marx called these two groups the **bourgeoisie** and the **proletariat**. He defined the bourgeoisie, also called capitalists, as the wealthy owners of the means of production (for example, factories, businesses, land, and natural resources). Marx's proletariat encompasses the large mass of people, those who are relatively uneducated and who are without power. In short, the proletariat comprises the workers.

According to Marx, the proletariat, possessing neither capital nor the means of production, must earn their living by selling their labor. The bourgeoisie, from their very position within society, stand opposed to the proletariat in an ongoing class struggle. Marx saw the struggle between classes as inevitable in the evolution of any capitalist society, and believed that its natural outcome would be the overthrow of the capitalist social order and the birth of a truly classless, or communist, society.

Although Marx concerned himself with only two social classes, most social scientists today refer to at least three groups—the upper, middle, and lower classes—with some, such as sociologist Vance Packard, distinguishing up to five while further subdividing classes "horizontally" according to ascribed characteristics such as race and religion.[3] Societies, including our own, vary as to the relative proportion of each class, although a number of commentators have noted what they call a shrinking of the middle class in a number of today's post-industrial countries.

In 1905, Dutch sociologist Willem Bonger echoed Marx, describing the ongoing struggle between the haves and the have-nots as a natural consequence of capitalist society.[4] Bonger advanced the notion that in such societies only those who lack power are routinely subject to the criminal law. In 1908 German sociologist Georg Simmel highlighted the role of social conflict in two- and three-person groups, which Simmel called diads and triads.[5] The notion of culture conflict, proposed in 1938 by University of Pennsylvania criminologist Thorsten Sellin, incorporates the idea of social conflict.

Vold: Crime as Political Conflict

In his 1958 book *Theoretical Criminology*, **George B. Vold** describes crime as the product of political conflict between groups, a natural expression of the ongoing struggle for power, control, and material well-being.[6] According to Vold, conflict is "a universal form of interaction," and groups are naturally in conflict because their interests and purposes "overlap, encroach on one another and [tend to] be competitive."[7] Vold also addresses the issue of social cohesion, noting, "It has long been realized that conflict between groups tends to develop and intensify the loyalty of group members to their respective groups."[8] Vold, whose writings led to the development of **conflict theory** in criminology, succinctly observes conflict's contribution to crime: "The whole political process of law making, law breaking, and law enforcement becomes a direct reflection of deepseated and fundamental conflicts between interest groups. Those who produce legislative majorities win control over the power and dominate the policies that decide who is likely to be involved in violation of the law."[9]

Central to the social conflict perspective is the notion of **social class**. The concept of social class entails distinctions made among individuals on the basis of significant defining characteristics, such as race, religion, education, profession, income, wealth, family background, housing, artistic tastes, aspirations, cultural pursuits, child-rearing habits, speech, accent, and so forth. Individuals are assigned to classes by others and by themselves on the basis of characteristics that are both ascribed and achieved. *Ascribed characteristics* are those with which a person is born, such as race or gender, while *achieved characteristics* are acquired through personal effort or chance over the course of one's life and include such things as level of education, income, place of residence, and profession.

The six key elements of the social conflict perspective are as follows:[2]

1. Society is made up of diverse social groups. Diversity is based on distinctions that people believe to be significant, such as gender, sexual orientation, and social class.
2. Each group holds to differing definitions of right and wrong. Moralistic conceptions and behavioral standards vary from group to group.
3. Conflict between groups is unavoidable. Conflict is based on differences held to be socially significant (such as ethnicity, gender, and social class) and is unavoidable because groups defined on the basis of these characteristics compete for power, wealth, and other forms of recognition.
4. The fundamental nature of group conflict centers on the exercise of political power. Political power is the key to the accumulation of wealth and to other forms of power.
5. Law is a tool of power and furthers the interests of those powerful enough to make it. Laws allow those in control to gain what they define (through the law) as legitimate access to scarce resources and to deny (through the law) such access to the politically disenfranchised.
6. Those in power are inevitably interested in maintaining their power against those who would usurp it.

According to Vold, powerful groups make laws, and those laws express and protect their interests. He compares the criminal with a soldier, fighting through crime commission for the very survival of the group whose values he or she represents: "The individual criminal is then viewed as essentially a soldier under conditions of warfare: his behavior may not be 'normal' or 'happy' or 'adjusted'—it is the behavior of the soldier doing what is to be done in wartime."[10] Vold's analogy, probably influenced by World War II, expresses the idea that crime is a manifestation of denied needs and values—that is, the cultural heritage of disenfranchised groups who are powerless to enact their interests in legitimate fashion. Hence, theft becomes necessary for many poor people, especially those left unemployed or unemployable by the socially acceptable forms of wealth distribution defined by law.

According to Marx, two fundamental social classes exist within any capitalist society: the haves and the have-nots.

Crime, Social Class, Power, and Conflict

Writers on social conflict in the early and mid-1900s saw in social class the rudimentary ingredients of other important concepts such as authority, power, and conflict. German sociologist **Ralf Dahrendorf**, for example, wrote in the 1950s that "classes are social conflict groups the determinant of which can be found in the participation in or exclusion from the exercise of authority."[11] For Dahrendorf, conflict is ubiquitous, a fundamental part of and coextensive with any society. "Not the presence but the absence of conflict is surprising and abnormal," he writes, "and we have good reason to be suspicious if we find a society or social organization that displays no evidence of conflict."[12]

From Dahrendorf's perspective, it is power and authority that are most at issue between groups and over which **class conflicts** arise. Dahrendorf also recognized that situations characterized by conflict are rarely static and that conflict is a source of change, whether destructive or constructive. Destructive change brings about a lessening of social order; constructive change increases cohesiveness within society. Dahrendorf's 1959 *Class and Class Conflict in Industrial Society* set the stage for the radical writers of the 1960s and 1970s.

Another theorist, University of California sociologist **Austin Turk**, states that when searching to explain criminality, "one is led to investigate the tendency of laws to penalize persons whose behavior is more characteristic of the less powerful than of the more powerful and the extent to which some persons and groups can and do use legal processes and agencies to maintain and enhance their power position vis-à-vis other persons and groups."[13] In 1969's *Criminality and Legal Order*, Turk writes that in any attempt to explain criminality, "it is more useful to view the social order as mainly a pattern of conflict" rather than to offer explanations for crime based on behavioral or psychological approaches.[14] Like most other conflict criminologists, **Turk saw the law as a powerful tool in the service of prominent social groups seeking continued control over others. Crime is the natural consequence of such intergroup struggle because it results from the definitions imposed by the laws of the powerful upon the disapproved strivings of the unempowered.**

Modern Radical-Critical and Marxist Criminology

During the late 1960s and early 1970s, the term *Marxist criminology* came into vogue. **Marxist criminology** was the intellectual child of three important historical circumstances: (1) the ruminations of nineteenth-century social utopian thinkers, including Karl Marx, Friedrich Engels, Georg W. F. Hegel, and others; (2) the rise of the conflict perspective in the social sciences around 1900; and (3) the dramatic radicalization of American academia in the 1960s and 1970s.

Radical-critical criminology is an outgrowth of Marxist criminology, although both forms of thought coexisted and influenced each other throughout much of the 1970s. Consistent to its roots, contemporary radical-critical criminology holds that the causes of crime can be found in social conditions that empower the wealthy and the politically well organized but disenfranchise those who are less fortunate. Some writers distinguish between radical and critical criminology, saying that the latter simply critiques social relationships that lead to crime, whereas the former constitutes a proactive call for change in the underlying social conditions.

Chambliss: Crime and Economic Stratification

William J. Chambliss gained prominence during this period, giving voice to the theories of contemporary and earlier Marxist and radical-critical criminologists. He succinctly summarizes the theoretical perspective: "What makes the behavior of some criminal is the coercive power of the state to enforce the will of the ruling class."[15] In 1971, Chambliss and **Robert T. Seidman** coauthored the critically acclaimed *Law, Order, and Power*, which represented something of a bridge between earlier writers on social conflict and Marxist and radical-critical criminologists. Emphasizing social class, class interests, and class conflict, *Law, Order, and Power* presents a Marxist perspective stripped of overt references to capitalism as the root cause of crime. "The more economically stratified a society becomes," Chambliss and Seidman write, "the more it becomes necessary for the dominant groups in the society to

enforce through coercion the norms of conduct which guarantee their supremacy."[16] They outline their position in four propositions:[17]

- The conditions of one's life affect one's values and norms. Complex societies are composed of groups with widely different life conditions.

- Complex societies are therefore composed of highly disparate and conflicting sets of norms.

- The probability of a given group's having its particular normative system embodied in law is not distributed equally but is closely related to the political and economic position of that group.

- The higher a group's political or economic position, the greater the probability that its views will be reflected in laws.

Inherent in this perspective is the notion that no act is instrinsically criminal or immoral, but is made so by the successful application of negative labels to individuals and activities through the exercise of legislative power by those who are in control of government.

Chambliss also believes that middle- and upper-class criminals are more apt to escape apprehension and punishment by the criminal justice system, not because they are any smarter or more capable of hiding their crimes than are lower-class offenders but because of a "very rational choice on the part of the legal system to pursue those violators that the community will reward them for pursuing and to ignore

Marx defined the *bourgeoisie* as wealthy capitalists who owned the factories of his day. The *proletariat* were the workers. Is the study of social class still relevant to criminology today?

Some say that communism's rise and later fall in Eastern Europe means that only capitalism can provide a stable economic basis for society. Do you agree?

those violators who have the capability for causing trouble for the agencies."[18]

Through the 1970s, Chambliss's radical-critical writings assumed a more directly Marxist flavor. In 1975 he once again recognized the huge power gap separating the haves from the have-nots.[19] Crime, he said, is created by actions of the ruling class that define as criminal such undertakings and activities that contravene the interests of the rulers. At the same time, members of the ruling class will inevitably be able to continue to violate the criminal law with impunity because it is their own creation: "As capitalist societies industrialize and the gap between the bourgeoisie and the proletariat widens, penal law will expand in an effort to coerce the proletariat into submission."[20]

For Chambliss, the economic consequences of crime within a capitalist society are partially what perpetuate it: "Crime reduces surplus labor by creating employment not only for the criminals but for law enforcers, welfare workers, professors of criminology, and a horde of people who live off the fact that crime exists."[21]

Socialist societies, Chambliss claims, should reflect much lower crime rates than capitalist societies because a "less intense class struggle should reduce the forces leading to and the functions of crime."[22]

> Socialist societies, Chambliss claims, should reflect much lower crime rates than capitalist societies because a "less intense class struggle should reduce the forces leading to and the functions of crime."

Quinney: Capitalism and Crime

Although Chambliss provides much of the intellectual bedrock of contemporary radical-critical criminology, it finds its most eloquent expression in the writings of social philosopher **Richard Quinney**. In 1974, Quinney, in an attempt to challenge and change American social life for the better, set forth his six Marxist propositions for an understanding of crime:

- American society is based on an advanced capitalist economy.

- The state is organized to serve the interests of the dominant economic class—that is, the capitalist ruling class.

- Criminal law is an instrument of the state and ruling class used to maintain and perpetuate the existing social and economic order.

- Crime control in a capitalist society is accomplished through a variety of institutions and agencies established and administered by a governmental elite, representing ruling-class interests, for the purpose of establishing domestic order.

- The contradictions of advanced capitalism—the disjunction between existence and essence—require that the subordinate classes remain oppressed by whatever means necessary, especially through the coercion and violence of the legal system.

- Only with the collapse of the capitalist society and the creation of a new society, based on socialist principles, will there be a solution to the crime problem.[23]

Quinney's portrayal of criminology as closely associated with capitalist modes of production in contemporary society underlies conflict criminology to this day. "Criminological theory and practice," he writes, "are materially based. Moreover, criminology is a cultural producton under the late stages of capitalism. It is a form of production: the production of knowledge and consciousness."[24]

A few years later, Quinney further contributed to the development of radical-critical criminology with *Class, State, and Crime,* in which he argues that almost all crimes committed by members of the lower classes are necessary for the survival of individual members of those classes. Crimes, writes Quinney—reminiscent of Vold's criminal as soldier—are actually an attempt by the socially disenfranchised "to exist in a society where survival is not assured by other, collective means."[25] **Quinney concludes that "crime is inevitable under capitalist conditions" because crime is "a response to the material conditions of life. Permanent unemployment—and the acceptance of that condition—can result in a form of life where criminality is an appropriate and consistent response."[26]** His solution to the problem of crime is the development of a socialist society. "The ultimate meaning of crime in the development of capitalism," he writes, "is the need for a socialist society."[27]

Critique of Radical-Critical and Marxist Criminology

Radical-critical criminology has been criticized for its nearly exclusive emphasis on mechanisms of social change at the expense of developed, testable theory. As William V. Pelfrey explains, "It is in the Radical School of Criminology that theory is almost totally disregarded, except as something to criticize, and radical methods are seen as optimum."[28]

Radical-critical criminologists may also be criticized for failing to recognize what appears to be a fair degree of public consensus about the nature of crime—that crime is undesirable and that criminal activity is to be controlled. Were criminal activity a true expression of the sentiments of the politically and economically disenfranchised, then public opinion might be expected to offer support for at least certain forms of crime. However, even the sale of illicit drugs—a type of crime that may provide an alternative path to riches for the otherwise disenfranchised—is frequently condemned by residents of working-class communities.[29]

An effective criticism of Marxist criminology, in particular, is that by allowing personal values and political leanings to enter the criminological arena, Marxist criminologists have frequently appeared to sacrifice their objectivity. Jackson Toby, for example, claims that Marxist and radical thinkers are simply building upon an "old tradition of sentimentality toward those who break social rules," which can be easily discounted when we realize that "color television sets and automobiles are stolen more often than food and blankets."[30] In a now-classic critique of radical criminology,[31] Carl Klockars in 1979 charged that Marxists are unable to explain low crime rates in some capitalist countries, such as Japan, and seem equally unwilling to acknowledge or address the problems of communist countries, which often have terrible human rights records. Klockars claimed that Marxist criminologists behaved more like "true believers" in a "new religion" who were unwilling to objectively evaluate their beliefs.[32]

Marxist criminology has also been criticized for failing to appreciate the multiplicity of issues that contribute to the problem of crime. For example, criminologist Hermann Mannheim showed how "subsequent developments" have revealed that Marx was wrong in thinking that there could be only two classes in a capitalist society.[33] Mannheim pointed out that the development of a semiskilled workforce along with the advent of highly skilled and well-educated workers has resulted in a multiplicity of classes within contemporary capitalist societies, effectively spreading the available wealth in those societies where such workers are employed and reducing the likelihood of revolution.

The Evolution of Radical-Critical Criminology

Radical-critical criminology attributes much of the existing propensity toward criminality to differences in social class, and in particular to those arrangements within society that maintain class differences. As Quinney puts it, "Classes are an expression of the underlying forces of the capitalist mode of production."[34] "Thus," he writes, "all social life, including everything associated with crime, must be understood in terms of the objective economic conditions of production and the subjective struggle between classes that is related to those conditions."[35]

Elliott Currie amplifies Quinney, stating that "'market societies'—those in which the pursuit of private gain becomes the dominant organizing principle of social and economic life—are especially likely to breed high levels of violent crime."[36] The conditions endemic to market societies—free enterprise, free market economies, the pursuit of personal wealth—lead to high crime rates because they undercut and overwhelm more traditional principles that "have historically sustained individuals, families, and communities." The United States is the world's premier market society, says Currie, and its culture provides "a particularly fertile breeding ground for serious violent crime." Similarly, the recent and dramatic rise in crime rates in former communist countries throughout Europe can be explained by the burgeoning development of new market societies in those nations.

Marxist criminology has suffered a considerable loss of prestige among many would-be followers in the wake of the collapse of the former Soviet Union and its client states in Eastern Europe and other parts of the world. With the death of Marxist political organizations and their agendas, Marxist criminology seems to have lost much of its impetus. Consequently, today's radical-critical criminologists have largely rescinded calls for revolutionary change and no longer employ traditional Marxist rhetoric. They continue, nonetheless, to escalate their demands for the eradication of gender, racial, and other inequalities in the criminal justice system; for the elimination of prisons; for the abolition of capital punishment; and for an end to police misconduct.

The ideas associated with mid- to late-twentieth-century Marxist criminology, and the more recent radical-critical criminology, contributed to the formation of a number of new and innovative social conflict theory–based approaches to crime and criminology. Four of the most interesting emerging theories are those of peacemaking, feminist, convict, and postmodern criminology.

Four of the most interesting emerging theories are those of peacemaking, feminist, convict, and postmodern criminology.

Some say that market societies, or those based on free enterprise, are especially likely to have high levels of violent crime. Why?

Emerging Theory: Peacemaking Criminology

Throughout the development of Western culture, formal agencies of social control, especially the police, officials of the courts, and correctional personnel, have been seen as pitted against criminal perpetrators and would-be wrongdoers in a kind of epic struggle in which only one side can emerge victorious. Since the late 1980s, however, **peacemaking criminology**, a form of postmodern criminology with its roots in Christian and Eastern philosophies, has advanced the notion that social control agencies and the citizens they serve should work together to alleviate social problems and human suffering and thus reduce crime.[37] Also called "compassionate criminology," it includes the notion of service to others and suggests that "compassion, wisdom, and love are essential for understanding the suffering of which we are all a part and for practicing a criminology of nonviolence."[38]

Peacemaking criminology has been popularized by the works of **Harold E. Pepinsky**[39] and Richard Quinney,[40] who restate the problem of crime control from one of "how to stop crime" to one of "how to make peace" within society and between citizens and criminal justice agencies. Peacemaking criminology draws attention to such issues as (1) perpetuating violence through social policies based on current criminological theory, (2) the role of education in peacemaking, (3) "commonsense theories of crime," (4) crime control as human rights enforcement, and (5) conflict resolution within community settings.[41]

Quinney and John Wildeman summarize well the theoretical underpinnings: "A criminology of peacemaking—a nonviolent criminology of compassion and service—seeks to end suffering and thereby eliminate crime."[42] Elsewhere, Quinney writes, "A society of meanness, competition, greed, and injustice is created by minds that are greedy, selfish, fearful, hateful, and crave power over others. Suffering on the social level can be ended only with the ending of suffering on the personal level. . . . We must become one with all who suffer from lives of crime and from the sources that produce crime. Public policy must then flow from this wisdom."[43]

Contributors to peacemaking criminology include **Bo Lozoff**, **Michael Braswell**, and **Clemens Bartollas**. In *Inner*

Peacemaking criminology aims to end human suffering as a way of stopping crime. It's an idealistic theory, but can it work?

Corrections, Lozoff and Braswell claim that "we are fully aware by now that the criminal justice system in this country is founded on violence. It is a system which assumes that violence can be overcome by violence, evil by evil. Criminal justice at home and warfare abroad are of the same principle of violence. This principle sadly dominates much of our criminology."[44]

Bartollas and Braswell apply New Age principles to correctional treatment. "Most offenders suffered abusive and deprived childhoods," they write. "Some New Age teachings tempered by the ancient spiritual traditions may offer offenders the hope they can create a future that . . . may include growing out of the fear of victimization, becoming more positive and open to possibilities, . . . understanding the futility of violence, and attaining emotional and financial sufficiency."[45]

In a fundamental sense, **peacemaking criminologists exhort their colleagues to transcend personal dichotomies to** end the political and ideological divisiveness that separates people, asking "If we ourselves cannot know peace, how will our acts disarm hatred and violence?"[46] As Lozoff and Braswell write, "Human transformation takes place as we change our social, economic and political structure. And the message is clear: without peace within us and in our actions, there can be no peace in our results. Peace is the way."[47]

Critique of Peacemaking Criminology

Peacemaking criminology has been criticized as being naïve and utopian, as well as for failing to recognize the realities of crime control and law enforcement. Few victims, for example, would expect to gain much from attempting to make peace with their victimizers (although such strategies do occasionally work). Such criticisms, however, may be improperly directed at a level of analysis that peacemaking criminologists have not assumed. In other words, peacemaking criminology, while it involves work with individual offenders, envisions positive change on the societal and institutional levels and does not suggest that victims attempt to effect personal changes in offenders.

TRADITIONAL PUNISHMENT
Once an ex-con always an ex-con

I drew a circle that shut him out.

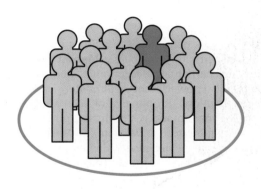

THE PEACEMAKING PROCESS
Reintegration into society

We drew a circle that drew him in.

153

Emerging Theory: Feminist Criminology

Feminist criminology applies various forms of feminist thought to infuse gender awareness into mainstream criminology. **Feminism, generally speaking, is a way of seeing the world.** Feminist thought views gender in terms of power relationships, revealing the inequities inherent in patriarchal structures. **Patriarchy** refers to "social relations of power in which the male gender appropriates the labor power of women and controls their sexuality."[48] The patriarchal structure of Western society has long excluded women from much socially significant decision making, affecting both fundamental social roles and personal expectation at all levels.

According to feminist criminologists, evidence of patriarchy can be found throughout criminology. Crime is often seen as an act of aggression, for example, which helps perpetuate the idea that men have a biologically aggressive nature that must be channeled and controlled. This belief has led to the socialization of women as passive actors, excluding them from criminological study and making them more susceptible to continued victimization by men. In other words, **traditional criminology, like the larger society, has been male centered, and women have been largely ignored by criminologists, heightening their sense of powerlessness and dependence upon men.**

As one author observes, "Women have been virtually invisible in criminological analysis until recently and much theorizing has proceeded as though criminality is restricted to men."[49] Another puts it this way: "Criminological theory assumes a woman is like a man."[50]

Feminist Thought and Criminological Theory

The forms of feminist thought that have most influenced criminology are radical, liberal, socialist, and Marxist feminism, each of which argues that conflict in society derives from gender-based inequalities, although they differ in their focus. **Radical feminism** asserts that because in patriarchical society men control the law, women are defined as subjects. Women who act reasonably to avoid men's exploitation may thus become criminalized. **Liberal feminism** asserts that gender inequalities arise from "separate and distinct spheres of influence and traditional attitudes about the appropriate role of men and women."[51] **Socialist feminism** sees gender oppression as a consequence of the economic structure of society. **Marxist feminism** sees capitalism as perpetuating economic inequality, dependence, and political powerlessness, ultimately leading to unhealthy gender relations. Proponents of each advocate eliminating male domination and restructuring power relationships to reduce crime rates for women and "even [to] precipitate a decrease in male violence against women."[52]

Early feminist criminological works include **Freda Adler's** *Sisters in Crime*[53] and **Rita J. Simon's** *Women and Crime,*[54] both published in 1975. These authors attribute gender divergences in crime rates primarily to socialization rather than to biology. Carol Smart, in *Women, Crime and Criminology* (1977),[55] asserts that men and women experience and perceive the world in different ways, and thus women must have a voice in interpreting the behavior of other women.

Feminist theorizing has heightened awareness of the need to apply feminist thinking to criminological analysis. Two contemporary proponents, **Kathleen Daly** and **Meda Chesney-Lind**, suggest that feminist thought is more important for the way it informs and challenges existing criminology than for the new theories it offers, and state that more research on gender-related issues is badly needed. **Traditional understandings of what is "typical" about crime are derived from a study of men only** or, more precisely, from that relatively small group of men who commit most crimes. They write, "criminologists should begin to appreciate that their discipline and its questions are a product of white, economically privileged men's experiences"[56] and note that rates of female criminality, lower than those of males (Table 7–1)—a fact

TABLE 7–1		
Male and Female Involvement in Crime: Offense Patterns, 2008		
Percentage of All Arrests		
UCR Crime	**Males**	**Females**
Murder and nonnegligent manslaughter	89.2	10.8
Rape	98.8	1.2
Robbery	88.4	11.6
Aggravated assault	78.5	21.5
Burglary	85.4	14.6
Larceny-theft	58.7	41.3
Motor vehicle theft	82.8	17.2
Arson	84.1	15.9
Forgery and counterfeiting	62.1	37.9
Fraud	56.5	43.5
Embezzlement	48.3	51.7

Gender Differences

- *Men are more likely than women to be arrested for "serious" crimes, such as murder, rape, robbery, and burglary.*
- *Arrest, jail, and prison data all suggest that more women than men who commit crimes are involved in property crimes, such as larceny, forgery, fraud, and embezzlement, and in drug offenses.*

Source: Federal Bureau of Investigation, *Crime in the United States, 2008* Washington, DC: U.S. Dept. of Justice, 2009).

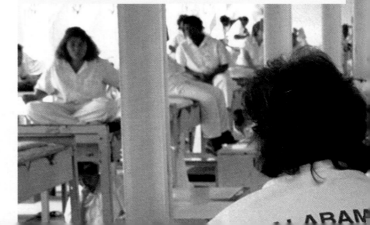

rarely accorded criminological significance—"suggest that crime may not be so normal after all."[57] Hence, feminism's fundamental challenge to criminology: Do existing theories of crime causation apply as well to women as they do to men? Or, as Daly and Chesney-Lind ask, "Do theories of men's crime apply to women?"[58]

Other feminists have analyzed the legislative process itself and have concluded that criminal statutes reflect traditionally male ways of organizing the social world.[59] For example, *assault* (or, more precisely, battery) is defined as an attack by one person upon another. Until the close of the twentieth century, however, in many jurisdictions domestic violence statutes tended to downplay the seriousness of such attacks, implying that occurrences within the home—whose victims were typically women—weren't as important to the justice system as other forms of assault.[60] Similarly, some argue, legal definitions of prostitution, pornography, and rape derive primarily from men's understanding of the behavior in question and not from women's experiences. Hence, women receive special protection because they are considered vulnerable to crime, but women's experiences do not define the nature of the law or of the justice system's response.

John Hagan, in a perspective known as **power-control theory**, suggests that "family class structure shapes the social reproduction of gender relations, and in turn the social distribution of delinquency."[61] Hagan believes that power relationships existing in the wider society are "brought home" to domestic settings and are reflected in everyday relationships among men, women, and children within the context of family life. Hagan writes, "Work relations structure family relations, particularly relations between fathers and mothers and, in turn, relations between parents and their children, especially mothers and their daughters."[62] In most middle- and upper-middle-class families, says Hagan, a paternalistic model, in which the father works and the mother supervises the children, is the norm. Under the paternalistic model, girls are controlled by both parents—through male domination and by female role modeling. Boys, however, are less closely controlled and are relatively free to deviate from social norms, resulting in higher levels of delinquency among males. In lower- and lower-middle-class families, however, the paternalistic model is frequently absent. Hence, in such families there is less "gender socialization and less maternal supervision of girls," resulting in higher levels of female delinquency.[63]

In the area of social policy, feminist thinkers have pointed to the need for increased controls over men's violence toward women, for the creation of alternatives (to supplement the home and traditional family structures) for women facing abuse, and for the protection of children. Most agree that the structure of the justice system itself—gender biased from years of male domination—must change. Many advocate a balanced approach, believing that individuals of both genders have much to contribute to a workable justice system.[64]

Critique of Feminist Criminology

Critics argue that in the area of theoretical development, feminist criminology has yet to live up to its promise. As one writer puts it, **"Feminist theory is a theory in formation."**[65] From the late-1970s through the early 1990s, few comprehensive feminist theories of crime were proposed; feminist criminology instead focused on descriptive studies of female involvement in crime,[66] and on women's victimization. To date, feminist analysis has hardly advanced beyond a framework for the "deconstruction" and reevaluation of existing theories in light of feminist insights.[67] A fair assessment would probably conclude that the greatest contributions of thought to criminological theory building are yet to come.

Feminist criminology has also faced other criticism. Predicted increases in female crime rates have failed to materialize as social opportunities available to both genders have become more balanced. The **gender gap** in crime—males accounting for much more law violation than females—continues to exist. As criminologist Karen Heimer notes, "The relationship holds, regardless of whether the data analyzed are arrest rates, victimization incidence reports on characteristics of offenders, or self-reports of criminal behavior [and] as far as we can tell, males have always been more criminal than females, and gender differences emerge in every society that has been studied systematically."[68]

Some critics argue that a feminist criminology is impossible. Daly and Chesney-Lind, for example, agree that although feminist thought may inform criminology, "a feminist criminology cannot exist because neither feminism nor criminology is a unified set of principles and practices."[69] Even with such a caveat, however, it should still be possible to construct a gender-aware criminology that incorporates feminist concerns.

Women in prison. Why is there a gender gap in crime?

Emerging Theory: Convict Criminology

The newest radical paradigm to emerge within the field of criminolgy is convict criminology. Formalized in 2001 with the publication of "Introducing the New School of Convict Criminology" by **Stephen C. Richards** in the journal *Social Justice*,[70] convict criminology (also called "alternative criminology") is not so much a school of thought as it is a body of writings and musings on criminology by convicted felons and ex-inmates who have acquired academic credentials, or who are associated with credentialled others. In 2002, with the publication of *Convict Criminology* by Ian Ross and Stephen Richards, the writings of convict crimiologists went mainstream and began receiving attention from within the discipline and from the media.

Convict criminology offers a blend of writings by credentialled ex-inmates and critical criminologists who have joined forces in distrust of mainstream criminology.[71] Convict criminology is largely issues-based and personal. As its adherents admit, convict criminology is not without an agenda, and tends to assume a critical perspective with regard to the justice system—especially corrections. Similarly, the language of convict criminologists is different from that of academic criminologists who do not share their convict background. Convict criminologists tend to write about "convicts" instead of "offenders," and "inmates" instead of "prisoners." The distinction is an important one, because the terminology used by academic criminologists

is "managerial" in the sense that it is consistent with the language of controlling agents in the justice system—police officers, correctional officers, probation and parole officers, court officials, and so on. **By using the language of convict insiders, convict criminologists signify their allegiance to an insider's perspective, and refer to traditional criminology as managerial criminology.**[72]

The primary method used by convict criminologists is ethnographic. *Ethnography* is a branch of anthropology that involves studying other cultures, in this case, inmate society. Ethnographers depend upon lived experiences and oral communicatons about them (for example, interviews, stories, and long hours spent listening to those whom they are studying). The advantage of convict criminologists is that they are their own subjects, and the long hours needed to gather experiences have already been spent—usually in prison or in personal interaction with the justice system.

The prototype convict criminologist is **John Irwin**, who spent five years in California's Soledad Prison in the 1950s for armed robbery. While imprisoned, Irwin earned college credits and after release went on to attend San Francisco State College and UCLA. Irwin says, "The point is, I made my transition from the life of a thief, drug addict, and convict to one of a 'respectable' professional . . . ." Irwin went on to write *The Felon*,[73] an academic work that shared the career criminal's point of view with interested readers.

Some of the most recent works in the area of convict criminology are the result of collaboration between traditional criminologists and ex-convicts. Among them are *Behind a Convict's Eyes*[74] and *Prison, Inc.*[75] —both by the author team of **K. C. Carceral** (a convict serving life in prison who holds an associate's degree in paralegal studies), **Thomas J. Bernard** (a criminologist at Penn State University), and others.

The prisons shown in these pictures are often thought of as places of violence and despair. What can we learn from convict criminology?

Convict criminology is the source of a number of recommendations for improving the justice system, stemming primarily from the lived experiences of the convict criminologists themselves and not from traditional forms of social scientific research. Nonetheless, the claim is sometimes made that experience is itself a kind of research, albeit a very personal one. Convict criminologists say the following:[76]

1. Prisons hold far too many people, do not effectively reduce crime, and hold too many people who have committed minor crimes.

2. Prison expansion has disproportionately and unfairly impacted the nation's poor—especially young men of color—who have made bad decisions in their lives and committed relatively harmless and bothersome crimes.

3. A substantial reduction in the number of federal and state prisoners is needed. Convict criminologists point out that many of today's prisoners are nonviolent drug offenders who committed property crimes in support of drug habits, or those who were caught with drugs in their possession either for personal use or resale. Diversion and treatment are recommended as viable alternatives to incarceration. Similarly, the nation's war on drugs—which they see as having a negative impact on all of society— should be terminated.

4. Corrections today can benefit significantly from the use of smaller prisons in place of the large institutions that now characterize many state facilities. Smaller prisons should become a model for U.S. corrections because they are less dangerous than large ones, and tend to result in heightend rates of rehabilitation.

5. Treatment should be given precedence over security because most inmates will eventually return to society, and it is treatment that offers the best hope for desistance from crime. Not only should institutional priorities be reversed, but treatment programs need to receive top-level funding.

Critique of Convict Criminology

Convict criminology has been critiqued by those who say that most of the authors working in the field are white males, and not all are ex-convicts.[77] Feminist nonconvict criminologists have also begun contributing to the literature through their prison research, moving the field even further from its roots.

Convict criminologists have been faulted for their activism and partisan approach, and their research has been questioned in light of their thinly veiled agendas. Finally, not everyone agrees that convict criminology offers an edge over traditional criminology. Critics say that having been in prison might actually distort a criminologist's view of his or her field rather than enhance it. Moreover, personal experience rarely gives anyone the entire picture needed to understand a phenomenon. Focusing on the injustices of prison life, for example, might keep one from appreciating the reformative effects of punishment.

Convict criminologists tend to write about "convicts" instead of "offenders," and "inmates" instead of "prisoners." The distinction is an important one, because the terminology used by academic criminologists is "managerial" in the sense that it is consistent with the language of controlling agents in the justice system

There are a variety of prisons: Although the style of housing prisoners may vary from prison to prison the overall outcome does not change significantly; convicts emerge from the system poorly equipped to succeed in the "real world."

157

Emerging Theory: Postmodern Criminology

Postmodern criminology applies understandings of social change inherent in postmodern philosophy to criminological theorizing and to issues of crime control. **Postmodern philosophy, which developed primarily in Europe after World War II, represents "a rejection of the enlightenment belief in scientific rationality as the main vehicle to knowledge and progress."[78]** As a philosophical movement, postmodernism is skeptical of scence and the scientific method.[79] One important aspect of postmodern social thought can be found in its efforts to demonstrate the systematic intrusion of sexist, racist, capitalist, colonialist, and professional interests into the very content of science. Feminist scholar Joycelyn M. Pollock puts it this way: "Post-modernism questions whether we can ever 'know' something objectively; so-called neutral science is considered a sham and criminology's search for causes is bankrupt because even the question is framed by **androcentric**, sexist, classist, and racist definitions of crime, criminals, and cause."[80]

Postmodernist thought began to influence criminology in the late-1980s. Today's postmodernist criminology is not so much a theory as it is a group of new criminological perspectives that have emerged since 1990 and that are all informed by the tone of postmodernism. At the leading edge of post-modern criminology can be found novel paradigms with such intriguing names as "chaos theory," "discourse analysis," "topology theory," "catastrophe theory," "Lacanian thought," "Godel's theorem," "constitutive theory," and "anarchic criminology."[81]

All postmodern criminologies build on the feeling that past criminological approaches have failed to realistically assess the true causes of crime and have therefore failed to offer workable solutions for crime control—or if they have, that such theories and solutions may once have been appropriate but do not apply to the postmodern era. Hence, much postmodern criminological theory is deconstructionist. **Deconstructionist theories** are approaches that challenge existing perspectives to debunk them and that attempt to replace them with approaches more relevant to the postmodern era. They intend to offer freedom from perceived oppressive forms of thought by deconstructing—pulling apart the foundations of—existing thought, knowledge, and belief in modern Western culture.

Henry and Milovanovic: Constituitive Criminology

Two especially notable authors in the field of postmodern criminology are **Stuart Henry** and **Dragan Milovanovic**,[82] whose **constitutive criminology** claims that crime and crime control are not "object-like entities," but, rather, constructions produced through a social process in which offender, victim, and society are all involved.[83]

A central feature of constitutive criminology is its assertion that individuals shape their world, while also being shaped by it. Hence, the behaviors of those who offend and victimize others cannot be understood in isolation from the society of which they are a part. Individuals, however, tend to remain unaware of the role they play in the social construction of their subjective worlds, and generally fail to realize that, at least to some degree, they are able to create new meanings while freeing themselves from old biases.

One area that demonstrates such constructionist notions is the sociology of law, which highlights the inherent interrelatedness between law and social structure. Milovanovic, for example, suggests the application of semiotics to the study of law.[84] *Semiotics* is a term akin to semantics; both derive from the Greek *sêma*, meaning "sign." Milovanovic sees semiotics as being especially useful in the study of law and criminology because everything we know, say, do, think, and feel is mediated through signs—a sign being anything that stands for something else. Hence, language, gestures, sensations, objects, and events are all interpreted by the human mind through the use of signs. A semiotic criminology is concerned, therefore, with identifying how language systems (for example, those of medicine, law, education, gangs, sports, prison communities, criminal justice practitioners, and criminologists)

Members of a polygamist family. What does constitutive criminology mean by saying individuals shape their world, while also being shaped by it?

communicate uniquely encoded values. Such values are said to "oppress those who do not communicate meaning from within the particular language system in use" because they may prevent effective discourse with those in power.[85]

The application of **semiotics** to the study of law can be illustrated by the term mental illness. As a sign, this term is imbued with multiple—perhaps even contradictory—meanings, including a disease in need of treatment and a person needing psychiatric services. Moreover, mental illness means something different in the law (wherein the proper phrase is legal insanity) than it does in medicine or in the lay community. Different interpretations reflect different values, and these values can be traced to divergent interest groups. Moreover, as Milovanovic notes, the meaning of mental illness has changed over time—and continues to change.

Semiotics can also be applied directly to the notion of crime, as crime itself is a "socially constructed category," or sign. In the words of Henry and Milovanovic, crime "is a categorization of the diversity of human conflicts and transgressions into a single category 'crime,' as though these were somehow all the same. It is a melting of differences reflecting the multitude of variously motivated acts of personal injury into a single entity."[86] Such a statement, to the minds of constitutive criminologists, lays bare the true meaning of the word crime, effectively "deconstructing" it.

Crime should be understood, say Henry and Milovanovic, as an integral part of society—not as something separate and apart from it. From this perspective, a kind of false consciousness, or lack of awareness, gives rise to criminal activity. **According to Werner Einstadter and Stuart Henry, crime is seen to be the culmination of certain processes that allow persons to believe that they are somehow not connected to other humans and society.** These processes place others into categories or stereotypes and make them different or alien, denying them their humanity. These processes result in the denial of responsibility for other people and to other people. Hence, from a constitutive point of view, crime is simply "the power to deny others," and crime is caused by "the structure, ideology and invocation of discursive practices that divide human relations into categories, that divide responsibility from others and to others into hierarchy and authority relations."[87]

Modern society exhibits a broad range of values, as the wall graffiti shown above demonstrates. How can semiotics, as the analysis of systems of communication, be applied to the study of crime?

What are the major criticisms of postmodern perspectives?

Critique of Postmodern Criminology

Ian Taylor, a British sociologist who lent focus to radical-critical criminology in the 1970s with the publication of two well-received books,[88] **criticizes postmodern approaches to crime and deviance for their "increasing incoherence."**[89] Not only do postmodern criminologists employ vaguely defined terminology, but, Taylor seems to say, the "battle with orthodox criminology" has led postmodern approaches to increasingly obscure their most basic claims. A second result, says Taylor, "has been the development of a social account of crime that entirely lacks a value or ethical foundation."[90] Deconstructionism, for example, may challenge traditional theories, but unless it offers viable alternatives for crime control and prevention, it does little good. Taylor criticizes what he calls "privileged academic commentators working within the postmodern tradition" for being "nihilistic."[91]

Policy Implications of Conflict Criminology

Three different levels of policy implications emanate from conflict theory in criminology. The first relates to the macro, or wider societal, level, advocating widespread social change intended to redistribute wealth on the premise that crime rates will fall as poverty and social inequalities are eliminated. Raymond J. Michalowski summarizes well the idealistic policy directions envisioned by some radical-critical criminologists when he says, **"We cannot be free from the crimes of the poor until there are no more poor; we cannot be free from domination of the powerful until we reduce the inequalities that make domination possible; and we cannot live in harmony with others until we begin to limit the competition for material advantage over others that alienates us from one another."**[92]

As noted previously, radical-critical criminologists have had to come to terms with the collapse of the Soviet Union, a society that represented utopian Marxism in practice. They have also had to recognize that a sudden and total political reversal within the United States is highly unlikely. As a consequence, many have begun to focus on the second policy level, promoting a gradual transition to socialism and to socialized forms of government activity as a means for crime reduction. These mid-level approaches involve "equal justice in the bail system, the abolition of mandatory sentences, prosecution of corporate crimes, increased employment opportunities, and promoting community alternatives to imprisonment,"[93] and include programs to reduce prison overcrowding, efforts to highlight current injustices, the elimination of racism and other forms of inequality in the handling of both victims and offenders, and increased equality in criminal justice system employment.

Participatory and Restorative Justice

It is safe to say that few radical-critical criminologists expect to see dramatic social or cultural changes in the near future. Consequently, a third, and some would say more pragmatic, approach to reducing crime lies in applying conflict resolution principles at the micro level—that of the individual and the community. Peacemaking criminology suggests that effective crime control at these levels can best be achieved by adopting a model based on cooperation rather than retribution. **This peace model of crime control focuses on effectively developing a shared consensus on critical issues that may seriously affect the quality of life.** These issues may include major crimes such as murder and rape but also extend to gambling, drug use, sexual preference, nonviolent sexual deviance, noise complaints, simple child custody claims, and minor public offenses—all of which require few resources beyond those immediately available in the community.

> Many have begun to focus on the second policy level, promoting a gradual transition to socialism and to socialized forms of government activity as a means for crime reduction.

Alternative dispute resolution mechanisms play an important role in peacemaking perspectives.[94] Mediation programs, such as neighborhood justice centers, are characterized by cooperative efforts to resolve disputes rather than by the adversarial-like proceedings characteristic of most U.S. courts. **Dispute resolution programs are based on the principle of participatory justice, in which all parties to a dispute accept a kind of binding arbitration by neutral parties.** Currently operating in over 200 areas throughout the country, dispute resolution centers often utilize administrative hearings and ombudsmen and are staffed by volunteers who work to resolve disputes without assigning blame.

Many alternative dispute resolution strategies are forms of restorative justice. Postmodern writers describe restorative justice as "a new system based on remedies and restoration rather than on prison, punishment and victim neglect,"[95] and see it as **"a system rooted in the concept of a caring community."[96]** It is in fact a modern social movement meant to reform the criminal justice system. Restorative justice stresses healing rather than retribution and is based on three principles. The first is a view of crime "as more than simply law-breaking, an offense against governmental authority; [instead] crime is understood to cause multiple injuries to victims, the community and even the offender. Second, proponents argue that the criminal justice process should help repair those injuries. Third, they protest the government's apparent monopoly over society's response to crime,"[97] insisting that victims, offenders, and their communities must also be involved in a concerted effort to heal the harm caused by crime. Restorative justice programs differ from traditional approaches in that their central features prescribe clear outcomes directed at the three primary stakeholders in the justice system—offenders, victims, and the community. These outcomes, in turn, provide the basis for developing concrete performance measures to gauge the success of justice system programs, agencies, and interventions.

TABLE 7–2

Differences between Retributive and Restorative Justice

Retributive Justice	Restorative Justice
Crime is an act against the state, a violation of a law, an abstract idea.	Crime is an act against another person or the community.
The criminal justice system controls crime.	Crime control lies primarily with the community.
Offender accountability is defined as taking punishment.	Offender accountability is defined as assuming responsibility and taking action to repair harm.
Crime is an individual act with individual responsibility.	Crime has both individual and social dimensions of responsibility.
Victims are peripheral to the process of resolving a crime.	Victims are central to the process of resolving a crime.
The emphasis is on adversarial relationships.	The emphasis is on dialogue and negotiation.
Pain is imposed to punish, deter, and prevent.	Restitution is a means of restoring both parties; the goal is reconciliation.
The response is focused on the offender's past behavior.	The response is focused on harmful consequences of the offender's behavior; the emphasis is on the future and on reparation.
There is dependence on proxy professionals.	There is direct involvement by both the offender and the victim.

Source: Adapted from Gordon Bazemore and Mark S. Umbreit, Balanced and Restorative Justice: Program Summary (Washington, DC: Office of Juvenile Justice and Delinquency Prevention, 1994), p. 7.

Restoration, or repairing the harm done by crime and rebuilding relationships in the community, is the primary goal of restorative justice. The effectiveness of restorative justice programs is measured by how much relationships are healed rather than by how much punishment is inflicted on the offender. Table 7–2 highlights significant differences between traditional (retributive) justice and **restorative justice**.

The Balanced and Restorative Justice (BARJ) Model

One form of restorative justice is the **Balanced and Restorative Justice Model** (Figure 7–1). Under this model, the community, victim, and offender should all receive balanced attention, and all three should gain tangible benefits from their interactions with the justice system. Its three components may be described as follows:[98]

- **Accountability**. When an offense occurs, an obligation to the victim results. Victims and communities should have their losses restored by the actions of offenders making reparation, and victims should be empowered as active participants in the justice process.

- **Community protection**. The public has a right to a safe and secure community and must be protected during the time the offender is under supervision. The justice system must provide a range of intervention alternatives geared to the varying risks presented by the offenders.

- **Competency development**. Offenders who come within the jurisdiction of the court should leave the system capable of being productive and responsible in the community. Rather than simply receiving treatment and services aimed at suppressing problem behavior, offenders should make measurable improvements in their ability to function as productive, responsible citizens.

Restorative justice programs make use of a number of techniques, but central to all of them is restorative conferencing, also called community conferencing, in which victim, offender, and affected community members meet face-to-face in a safe setting with an impartial facilitator to discuss the facts and the impact of a particular offense.[99] The victim can ask questions and express directly to the offender how the crime has affected his or her life. Conferencing provides the victim with greater access to the criminal justice process and a strong voice in the process.[100] Conferencing also humanizes the incident for the offender so that he or she may better understand the real human consequences of his or her wrongdoing. The offender can propose steps that he or she can take to help restore the harm caused to the victim and the community. Participation in conferences is voluntary for victims and offenders. In some cases, a victim unwilling to participate in a face-to-face meeting may make a written statement to be used in the conference, or a surrogate victim may take his or her place.

RESTORATIVE JUSTICE

Competency Development · Community Protection · Accountability

FIGURE 7–1 The Balanced and Restorative Justice (BARJ) Model
Source: Office of Juvenile Justice and Delinquency Prevention, Balanced and Restorative Justice: Program Summary (Washington, D.C.: OJJDP, no date)., p. 1. NCJ 149727.

Between 1978 and 1995, Theodore John ("Ted") Kaczynski left or sent a total of 16 homemade pipe bombs, primarily targeting universities and airlines-related activities. (The FBI designated the investigation the "Unabomb"—or Unabomber—case from these early university targets.) The bombing campaign caused three deaths and numerous serious injuries.

Kaczynski's intermittent attacks were shrouded in anonymity, a trait he inexplicably broke when he sent letters to a newspaper threatening to bomb an airplane. He also stated that he would stop the bombings if his 35,000-word manifesto was published in the *Washington Post*. In this manifesto, Kaczynski railed against contemporary life, claiming that "The Industrial Revolution and its consequences have been a disaster for the human race."[i]

Upon reading the manifesto, David Kaczynski, Ted's younger brother, immediately recognized that its tone and approach "almost had the feeling for me of one of Ted's angry letters over the years. . . . Some of those letters were addressed to the theme of technology just as the manifesto was."[ii] Although not convinced that his brother was the long-sought Unabomber, David Kaczynski contacted the FBI.

That slim investigative thread led the FBI to Kaczynski's cabin in the Montana wilderness, where they found overwhelming evidence that he was, in fact, the Unabomber. A live bomb, meticulous notes of past bombings, bomb-making materials, and the original copy of his infamous manifesto made the ensuing trial almost anticlimactic, and its results an almost foregone conclusion.

On January 22, 1998, Kaczynski pled guilty in the U.S. District Court in Sacramento to four bombings that occurred in 1985, 1993, and 1995. In accordance with his plea agreement, Kaczynski admitted to the three deaths his bombings had caused, all other pending charges were resolved, and he was sentenced to a life term without parole. Kaczynski remains imprisoned at the maximum-security federal prison in Florence, Colorado.

The Causes Behind the Crime
Theodore John "Ted" Kaczynski (The Unabomber)

Can the Social Conflict Perspective Explain This Crime?

- Kaczynski was a shy, intelligent youth who did not socialize easily or well, and who periodically underwent episodes of intense and brooding withdrawal. As he grew older, the episodes were increasingly accompanied by a seething rage. *Although Kaczynski is not a criminologist, it is likely that he would agree with some of the principles of the social conflict perspective. With which of those principles do you think he would be most comfortable? Why?*

- Upon completing his Ph.D., Kaczynski accepted an assistant professorship in mathematics at the University of California at Berkeley in 1967. However, in June 1969, declaring that there was "no relevance" to what he was doing, he quit his teaching post. *Why might he have seen "no relevance" in what he was doing?*

- From 1969 through his arrest in 1996, he worked sporadically, including a brief time at the University of Michigan, and he usually worked only out of financial necessity. He ended up living off the land, assuming a hermit's existence of self-exile in a ramshackle cabin in the remote Montana wilderness that was to last almost 25 years. *How does Kaczynski's being a loner fit with the crimes he committed? Might it indicate that he was in conflict with the wider society?*

Kaczynski's Montana cabin. Why did he seek solitude?

Inside Theodore Kaczynski's cabin

Kaczynski lived in a one-room, wooden cabin, approximately 10 feet by 12 feet. Inside there was a wood stove, platform bed, table and chair, and storage loft, all handmade. There was no electricity, running water or sanitary facilities. What investigators found:

Bomb-making equipment: Electrical wire, electrical and watch parts, pipes, chemicals, batteries, and metal parts in empty oatmeal, corn meal, baking powder and cocoa cannisters and flour bags; a pipe bomb.

Manifesto: Handwritten draft of the Unabomber's manifesto; a carbon copy of the typed manifesto sent to the New York Times; Kaczynski's autobiography, nine binders of bombing experiments. One journal entry reads: "EXPERIMENT 97. DEC. 11, 1985 I PLANTED BOMB DISGUISED TO LOOK LIKE SCRAP OF LUMBER BEHIND RENTECH COMPUTE STORE IN SACRAMENTO... THE 'OPERATOR'...OF THE STORE WAS KILLED, BLOWN TO BITS, ON DEC. 12."

Typewriters: Three manual typewriters, one of which investigators say was used to type all identifiable Unabomber correspondence since 1982 - including correspondence sent with seven bombs and a letter to the New York Times in which the Unabomber claimed responsibility for 17 years of bombing.

Clothing: Blue zippered sweatshirt, green hooded jacket and sunglasses. A Unabomber bombing witness said a man at the scene as wearing a hooded sweat shirt and aviator glasses, resulting in the sketch distributed nationwide.

SOURCES: Court documents, KRT Photos

- Kaczynski also experienced lifelong difficulties with sexual relationships. While at the University of Michigan, he came to believe that he should undergo a sex change operation because fantasies of being a woman intensely excited him. He initiated the process at the school's health care facility but, when finally seen by a doctor, he claimed to be there for a different reason entirely, then left in a rage. He described the experience as shameful and humiliating. Later, he infrequently sought health system support as he attempted to establish meaningful relationships with women, but was never able to do so. *How might Kaczynski's difficulties with gender relationships provide further evidence of his difficulties with social life in general?*

- As he retreated deeper into his isolationist lifestyle, Kaczynski wrote his angry manifesto criticizing modern technology's impact on humanity. Read this document at http://www.washingtonpost.com/wp-srv/national/longterm/unabomber/manifesto.text.htm. *What similarities do you see between his writings and those of Karl Marx (learn more about Marx at http://www.philosophypages.com/ph/marx.htm)?*

Kaczynski under arrest. Why did he spend so much time writing his "manifesto"?

AUTHOR'S NOTE:

Kaczynski's entire manifesto remains available in the *Washington Post* achieves at http://www.washingtonpost.com/wp-srv/national/longterm/unabomber/manifesto.text.htm

An FBI video showing the inside of the Kaczynski cabin can be viewed at http://www.newseum.org/exhibits_th/fbi_feat/fbi_feat_vid/video.aspx?item=unabombercabin_vid.

NOTES:

[i] Theodore Kaczynski, *Industrial Society and Its Future* (no date).

[ii] "When Your Brother Is the Unabomber," Interview with David Kaczynski, MSNBC News, December 29, 2006. Web available at http://www.msnbc.msn.com/id/16304477 (accessed July 4, 2009).

Go to mycrimekit.com to explore the following resources for Chapter 7:

- **MULTIMEDIA:** Videos about an introduction to the conflict perspective, definition of conflict theory, basic principles of conflict theory, Karl Marx, and Richard Quinney
- **PRACTICE QUIZ:** Multiple-choice, true/false, short-answer, and essay questions
- **FLASHCARDS:** Twenty-five flashcards to test your knowledge of the chapter's key terms
- **WEB EXTRAS & LIBRARY EXTRAS:** Links to websites, online articles, and resources relating to the conflict perspective

Summary and Key Concepts

SOCIAL CONFLICT PERSPECTIVE

Social conflict theories in criminology emphasize the central significance of conflict within society, which is seen as a natural consequence of inequities that exist between social classes.

A History of Social Conflict Theory in Criminology

Conflict theory applies the principles and concepts developed by Karl Marx to the study of crime, and holds that the causes of crime are rooted in social conditions that empower the wealthy and the politically well-organized but disenfranchise those who are less fortunate. Also sometimes referred to as **Marxist criminology**.

For the most part Marxist criminology has been replaced by radical-critical criminology.

social class Distinctions made between individuals on the basis of important defining social characteristics.

class conflict Crime is a result of conflict, often between those with power and those without.

bourgeoisie The class of people who own the means of production.

proletariat The working class.

Karl Marx There are two fundamental social classes within any capitalist society—the haves and the have-nots—which creates conflict.

George B. Vold Conflict is a natural result of the struggle for power in society.

Ralf Dahrendorf Conflict is a a fundamental part of any society.

Austin Turk The actions of the less powerful are penalized by those who are more powerful.

Q: *Does the Marxist perspective hold any significance for contemporary American society? Why?*

Modern Radical-Critical and Marxist Criminology

True to its Marxist roots, **radical-critical criminology** is a conflict perspective that sees crime as engendered by the unequal distribution of wealth, power, and other resources that its adherents believe is especially characteristic of capitalist societies.

William J. Chambliss and **Robert T. Seidman** The more stratified a society becomes, the more the dominant members will use coercion to enforce their will. No act is intrinsically criminal, but is determined to be so by those in power.

Richard Quinney Advanced capitalistic society requires that the subordinate classes remain oppressed, especially through the coercion and violence of the legal system.

Elliot Currie Market societies are especially likely to breed high levels of violent crime.

These ideas contribute to the formation of a number of new theories, the most interesting of which are peacemaking, feminist, convict, and postmodern criminology.

Q: *Does the radical-critical perspective hold any significance for contemporary American society? Why?*

Emerging Theory: Peacemaking Criminology

Peacemaking criminology holds that crime control agencies and the citizens they serve should work together to alleviate social problems and human suffering and thus reduce crime.

Harold E. Pepinsky Peacemaking promotes a nonviolent criminology of compassion and service, seeking to end suffering and thereby eliminate crime.

Bo Lozoff The criminal justice system is founded on violence.

Michael Braswell and **Clemens Bartollas** Human transformation takes place when we change our social, economic, and political structure.

Q: *Does the peacemaking perspective hold any significance for contemporary American society? Why?*

Emerging Theory: Feminist Criminology

A self-conscious corrective model intended to redirect the thinking of mainstream criminologists to include gender awareness.

Freda Adler and **Rita J. Simon** Differences in crime rates by gender is attributable to socialization rather than biology.

Kathleen Daly and **Meda Chesney-Lind** Traditional understanding of what is "typical" about crime is derived from the study of men.

John Hagan Family structure and social structure are intertwined.

Q: *How would feminists change the study of crime?*

● Social Conflict ● Crime Causation

164

radical feminism A perspective that holds that any significant change in the social status of women can be accomplished only through substantial changes in social institutions such as the family, law, and medicine.

liberal feminism A perspective that holds that the concerns of women can be incorporated within existing social institutions through conventional means and without the need to drastically restructure society.

Marxist feminism A perspective that sees capitalism as the root cause of women's oppression because it perpetuates economic inequality, dependence, and political powerlessness, ultimately leading to unhealthy social relations between men and women.

socialist feminism A perspective that examines social roles and the gender-based division of labor within the family, seeing both as a significant source of women's subordination within society.

patriarchy The tradition of male dominance.

androcentric A single-sex perspective, as in the case of criminologists who study only the criminality of males.

gender gap The observed differences between male and female rates of criminal offending in a given society, such as the United States.

power-control theory A perspective that holds that the distribution of crime and delinquency within society is to some degree founded upon the consequences that power relationships within the wider society hold for domestic settings and for the everyday relationships among men, women, and children within the context of family life.

Emerging Theory: Convict Criminology

A new radical paradigm consisting of writings on the subject matter of criminology by convicted felons and ex-inmates who have acquired academic credentials, or who are associated with credentialled others.

Convict criminologists say the following:

Prisons are too crowded.

Poor people are more likely to be incarcerated.

Too many nonviolent offenders are imprisoned.

Prisons should be smaller.

Rehabilitation should be the priority of prisons.

Stephen C. Richards, *John Irwin*, *K.C. Carceral*, and *Thomas J. Bernard*. Much can be learned from the lived experiences of convicts themselves.

 How would convict criminology change the study of crime?

Emerging Theory: Postmodern Criminology

A brand of criminology that developed following World War II and that builds on the tenets inherent in postmodern social thought.

deconstructionist theories A postmodern perspective that challenges existing criminological theories in order to debunk them and that works toward replacing traditional ideas with concepts seen as more appropriate to the postmodern era.

constitutive criminology The assertion that individuals shape their world, while also being shaped by it.

semiotics Everything we know, say, do, think, and feel is mediated through signs. Semiotic criminology identifies how language systems communicate uniquely encoded values.

Stuart Henry and *Dragan Milovanovic* Crime and crime control are constructions produced through a social process in which offender, victim, and society are involved.

Ian Taylor Deconstructionism does not offer viable alternatives for crime control and prevention.

 What does it mean to say that traditional theories of crime need to be "deconstructed"? What role does deconstructionist thinking play in postmodern criminology?

Policy Implications of Conflict Criminology

Widespread social change is needed to redistribute wealth in the belief that crime rates will fall as poverty and social inequalities are eliminated.

Balanced and Restorative Justice Model (BARJ) A model of restorative justice in which the community, victim, and offender should all receive balanced attention.

participatory justice A relatively informal type of criminal justice case processing that makes use of local community resources rather than requiring traditional forms of official intervention.

restorative justice A postmodern perspective that stresses "remedies and restoration rather than prison, punishment and victim neglect."

peace model An approach to crime control that focuses on effective ways for developing a shared consensus on critical issues that could seriously affect the quality of life.

The Crime
Picture—
It's Not Pretty

Crimes against Persons
What We Fear

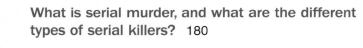

I'm a student of violence because I'm a student of the human heart.

–Sam Peckinpah

It's not the bullet with my name on it that worries me. It's the one that says "To whom it may concern."

–Anonymous

CRIMINOLOGY INTERACTIVE

In the **Types of Crime** section of Criminology Interactive, click on **Violent Crimes**.

Crime Facts

In order to fully understand the nature of crime, it is necessary to gain an appreciation for crime statistics—including how they are gathered, how they affect our understanding of crime, and how they are accessed. Such an appreciation helps criminologists keep types of crime in perspective and also allow us to track increases and decreases in kinds of criminal activity.

The government-sponsored gathering of crime data for the nation as a whole began in the United States around 1930. Before then, the gathering of statistics was random at best and most accounts were anecdotal and spread either by word of mouth or printed in local newspapers (or both).

Today's official U.S. crime statistics come from the Bureau of Justice Statistics (BJS), which conducts the annual **National Crime Victimization Survey (NCVS)**, and from the Federal Bureau of Investigation (FBI), which publishes yearly data under its summary-based **Uniform Crime Reporting (UCR) Program** and its more detailed incident-driven **National Incident-Based Reporting System (NIBRS)**. NIBRS data provide a more complete picture of crimes reported and committed.

NCVS data appear in a number of annual reports, the most important of which is *Criminal Victimization in the United States.* FBI data take the form of the annual publication *Crime in the United States.* Numerous other surveys and reports are made available through the Bureau of Justice Statistics (BJS). Such surveys not only cover the incidence of crime and criminal activity in the United States but also extend to many other aspects of the criminal justice profession, including justice system expenditures, prisons and correctional data, probation and parole populations, jail inmate information, data on law enforcement agencies and personnel, and information on the activities of state and federal courts. These and other reports

Government-sponsored national crime reporting began in the 1930s. What are the two major official sources of national crime statistics today?

are generally made available free of charge to interested parties through the National Criminal Justice Reference Service (NCJRS).[1] The largest collection of facts about all aspects of U.S. crime and criminal justice is the *Sourcebook of Criminal Justice Statistics*, which is compiled yearly by the BJS and made available in various formats.

The UCR/NIBRS and the NCVS each use their own specialized definitions in deciding which events should be scored as crimes. Sometimes the definitions vary considerably between programs, and none of the definitions used by the reporting agencies are strictly based on federal or state statutory crime classifications.

The National Crime Victimization Survey (NCVS)

The NCVS began collecting data in 1972. It differs from FBI-sponsored programs in one significant way: Rather than depending on reports of crimes to the police, the data contained in the NCVS consist of information from interviews with members of randomly selected households throughout the nation. Hence, the NCVS uncovers a large number of crimes that may not have been reported, and it is therefore regarded by many researchers

The National Crime Victimization Survey uses civilian interviewers to collect data about crime. How does it differ from the FBI's Uniform Crime Reporting Program?

as a more accurate measure of the actual incidence of crime in the United States than the UCR/NIBRS.

NCVS interviewers ask questions about the incidence of rape, personal robbery, aggravated and simple assault, household burglary, personal and household theft, and motor vehicle theft as they have affected household members during the past six months. Information is gathered on victims (including sex, age, race, ethnicity, marital status, income, and educational level), offenders (sex, age, race, and relationship to the victim), and crimes (time and place of occurrence, use of weapons, nature of injury, and economic consequences of the criminal activity for the victim). Questions also cover protective measures used by victims, the possibility of substance abuse by offenders, and the level of previous experience victims may have had with the criminal justice system.

The number of victimizations counted by the NCVS for any single reported criminal occurrence is based on the number of people victimized by the event. Hence, a robbery may have more than one victim and will be so reported in NCVS data. Although this distinction is applied to personal crimes, households are treated as individual units, and all household crimes are counted only once, no matter how many members the household contains.

According to the NCVS,[2] on average only 49% of violent victimizations and 38% of property crimes are reported to the police. While violent crimes are most likely to be reported to the police, personal thefts are the least likely crimes to be reported. NCVS data show that around 80% of motor vehicle thefts are reported to the police, making this the most highly reported of crimes. Larcenies, at 32%, are least likely to be reported. An interest in recovering property or in receiving insurance payments motivates many victims of property crimes to report their victimization to the police. The two most common reasons for not reporting violent victimizations are that the crime is a personal or private matter and that the offender was unsuccessful and the crime was only attempted.

Critique of the NCVS

Just as the UCR/NIBRS has been criticized for underestimating the actual incidence of criminal activity within the United States, the NCVS can be criticized for possible overreporting. No comprehensive attempt is made to verify the actual occurrence of any of the crimes reported to NCVS interviewers. Hence, no reliable measure exists of the number of crimes that might be falsely reported or of the number of crimes that might be underreported in NCVS data.

Although the proportion is not known, it is likely that some individuals, when approached by NCVS interviewers, may be unable to resist embellishing crime reports pertaining to their households and may even concoct criminal incidence data for purposes of self-aggrandizement or in an attempt to please the interviewer by providing copious amounts of data.

The NCVS program is much newer than the FBI's UCR Program, and comparisons between the programs are not available for the years before 1973. As with the UCR/NIBRS, definitions of crimes measured by the NCVS do not necessarily correspond to any federal or state statutes or to definitions used for other purposes, making comparisons with other state and federal crime records difficult. Complicating matters still further, changes in NCVS categories have resulted in the inability to easily compare NCVS findings of even a decade ago with current NCVS data.[3]

Not all crimes are reported to the police. What are some reasons victims may have for not reporting?

The Uniform Crime Reporting Program

The UCR Program was created by the FBI in 1929 as an official crime data-gathering program covering the entire United States. The UCR Program developed out of a national initiative by the International Association of Chiefs of Police (IACP), whose goal was to develop a set of uniform crime statistics for use by police agencies and policy makers. **The FBI was designated to serve as a national clearinghouse on crime facts, and police agencies around the country began submitting data under the UCR Program.** In its initial year of operation, 400 police departments representing cities and towns in 43 states participated in the program.

Early UCR data were structured in terms of seven major offense categories: murder, rape, robbery, aggravated assault, burglary, larceny, and motor vehicle theft. These crimes, called **Part I offenses**, formed the FBI's Crime Index. The Crime Index provided a crime rate that could be compared over time and from one geographic location to another. Rates of crime under the UCR/NIBRS Program are generally expressed as "*x* number of offenses per 100,000 people." The 2008 rate of criminal homicide, for example, was 5.4 murders for every 100,000 people in the U.S. population.

In 1979, Congress mandated that arson be added to the list of major crimes offenses. Unfortunately, the inclusion of arson as an eighth index offense made it difficult to compare pre- and post-1979 Crime Indexes. For this and other reasons, the FBI officially discontinued use of the term *crime index* beginning with its report of crime data for 2005.[4]

In today's UCR/NIBRS reports, Part I offenses are subdivided into two categories: violent personal crimes consisting of murder, rape, robbery, and aggravated assault (which will be specifically discussed in this chapter) **and property crimes consisting of burglary, larceny, motor vehicle theft, and arson** (which will be discussed in subsequent chapters). Table 8–1 lists violent personal crimes, showing the number of offenses reported to the police in 2008. UCR/NIBRS trend data for personal crimes over the past 50 years are shown graphically in Figure 8–1.

Each year, when the FBI issues its annual report, *Crime in the United States*, it includes information within each Part I offense category on the percentage of crimes that have

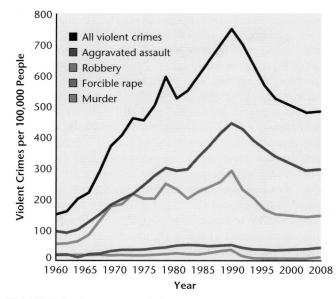

FIGURE 8–1 Violent Crime Trend Data, 1960–2008

Source: Federal Bureau of Investigation, *Crime in the United States* (Washington, DC: FBI, various years).

been "cleared." *Cleared crimes* are those for which an arrest has been made or for which the perpetrator is known but an arrest is not possible (as when the offender is deceased or is out of the country). Cleared crimes are also referred to as "solved." Those charged with a crime that is scored as cleared by the FBI may not yet have been adjudicated. In official UCR/NIBRS terminology, a Part I offense is regarded as cleared or solved when (1) "a law enforcement agency has charged at least one person with the offense" or (2) "a suspect has been identified and located and an arrest is justified, but action is prevented by circumstances outside law enforcement control."[5] Clearance rates are reported for each Part I crime category. A **clearance rate** is the proportion of reported or discovered crimes within a given offense category that are solved. Figure 8–2 shows clearance rates for 2008 for violent crimes.

The most significant feature of the UCR Program is indicated by its name. It is a *reporting* program. In other words, only crimes that are reported to the police (or that are discovered by the police or by others who then report them to the police) are

TABLE 8–1			
Violent Crimes Known to the Police, 2008			
Offense	Number	Rate Per 100,000	Clearance Rate (%)
Personal/Violent Crimes			
Murder	16,272	5.4	63.6
Forcible rape	89,000	58.6	40.4
Robbery	441,855	145.3	26.8
Aggravated assault	834,885	274.6	54.9

a. Rate shown is per 100,000 females.
Source: Federal Bureau of Investigation, *Crime in the United States, 2008.*

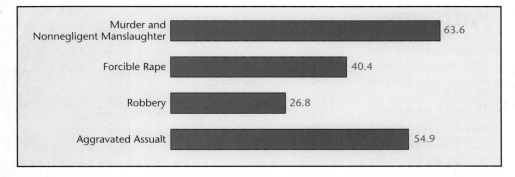

FIGURE 8–2 Percent of Violent Crimes Cleared, 2008

Source: Federal Bureau of Investigation, *Crime in the United States*, *2008* (Washington, DC: FBI, 2009).

included in the statistics compiled by the program. Most complaints are made by victims.

Because UCR/NIBRS data are based on *reported* crime, the program has been criticized for seriously underestimating the true incidence of criminal activity within the United States—a measurement that would also include unreported crimes. Some experts say, for example, that rape is the most underreported crime in the FBI data, with four to five times as many rapes occurring each year as are reported. Reasons for not reporting a crime like rape are numerous and include fear of the perpetrator, shame, fears the victim may have of not being believed, and fear of participation in the justice system.

Although rape is indeed seriously underreported (a conclusion drawn from comparison of NCVS and UCR/NIBRS rape statistics), many other crimes are underreported as well. The most seriously underreported crime may be larceny because the theft of small items may never make it into official police reports.

NIBRS: The New UCR Data Format

Recently, the UCR Program has undergone a number of significant changes, and more are scheduled to be implemented shortly as a new, enhanced, incident-driven crime-reporting system is phased in. The new system, the National Incident-Based Reporting System (NIBRS), revises the definitions of a number of offenses for reporting purposes, but its "incident-driven" nature is its most important feature. Incident-driven means that the FBI will use the NIBRS system to collect detailed data on the circumstances surrounding each serious criminal incident. NIBRS reports are much more detailed than those previously provided under the UCR Program. The NIBRS data-collection format focuses on each single incident and arrest within 22 crime categories, with incident, victim, property, offender, and arrestee information being gathered when available. The 22 NIBRS crime categories are, in turn, made up of 46 specific crimes called "Group A offenses" (as compared with only 8 major offenses on which the old UCR Program gathered data). In addition to Group A offenses, there are 11 Group B offense categories for which only arrest data are reported. The goal of NIBRS is to make data on reported crime more useful by relating them more completely than the old system did to other available information, such as victim and offender characteristics.[6] Because the UCR Program is currently undergoing a transition in format that involves more complete use of NIBRS data, we refer to UCR information that is cited in this chapter as UCR/NIBRS data.

The National Incident-Based Reporting System (NIBRS), an enhancement to the original Uniform Crime Reporting (UCR) Program, provides a more complete picture of crimes committed. What additional details does it report?

Changing Crime Patterns

Since official crime statistics were first gathered around 1930, there have been three major shifts in crime rates. The first occurred during the early 1940s at the outbreak of the Second World War when crime decreased sharply due to the large number of young men who entered military service. Young males make up the most "crime-prone" segment of the population, and their participation in the war efforts abroad did much to lower crime rates at home. From 1933 to 1941, the Crime Index declined from 770 to 508 offenses per every 100,000 members of the U.S. population.[7]

The second significant shift in offense statistics was a dramatic increase in most forms of crime that began in the 1960s and ended in the 1990s. Many criminologists believe that this shift also had a link to World War II. With the end of the war and the return of millions of young men to civilian life, birth rates skyrocketed between 1945 and 1955, creating a postwar baby boom. By 1960, baby boomers were entering their teenage years. A disproportionate number of young people in the U.S. population produced a dramatic increase in most major crimes.

Other factors contributed to the increase in reported crime during the same period. Crimes that may have gone undetected in the past began to figure more prominently in official statistics. Similarly, the growing professionalization of some police departments resulted in more

accurate and increased data collection, making some of the most progressive departments appear to be associated with the largest crime increases.[8] Finally, the 1960s were tumultuous years, punctuated as they were by the Vietnam War, a vibrant civil rights struggle, the heady growth of secularism, dramatic increases in the divorce rate, diverse forms of "liberation," and the influx of psychedelic and other drugs. As a consequence, social norms were blurred, and group control over individual behavior declined substantially. According to the FBI, from 1960 to 1980 crime rates rose from 1,887 to 5,950 offenses per every 100,000 members of the U.S. population.

Crime rates recorded by the FBI continued their upward swing, with the exception of a brief decline in the early 1980s, when postwar boomers began to "age out" of the crime-prone years and U.S. society emerged from the cultural drift that had characterized the previous 20 years. About the same time, however, an increase in drug-related criminal activity led crime rates to soar once again, especially in the area of violent crime. Crime rates peaked about 1991 and have since shown a third major shift, with decreases in the rates of most major crimes being reported since that time. Between 1991 and 2008, the crime rate decreased from 5,897 to 3,667 offenses per every 100,000 citizens, sending it down to levels not seen since 1975.

Decreases in crime since the mid-1990s may have been largely due to an "aging out" of the

BRIG. GEN. Wᵐ E. H

A significant decline in crime rates in this country took place during the early 1940s, as many young men went off to war. What other significant shifts in the crime rate have been noted?

post–World War II baby-boomer generation (members of which are now mostly too old to continue active criminal lifestyles), new strict laws, expanded justice system and police funding, changes in crime-fighting technologies, and economic factors.

While the two-decade long decline in crime that took place beginning in 1991 is noteworthy, it did not even begin to bring the overall rate of crime in this country anywhere close to the low crime rates characteristic of the early 1940s and the 1950s. From a long-term perspective, even with recent declines, crime rates in this country remain more than seven times what they were in 1940.

Recent evidence seems to indicate that the decline in crime is ending, and that we may be on the cusp of a new cycle of increased crime. Some criminologists think that recent economic uncertainty, an increased jobless rate among unskilled workers, the growing number of ex-convicts who are back on the streets, the recent growth in the teenage population in this country, the increasing influence of gangs, copycat crimes, and the lingering social disorganization brought on by natural disasters like Hurricane Katrina in 2005 may lead to sustained increases in crime.[9]

Unreported Crime

As the NCVS shows, many crimes are not reported, leading criminologists to talk about the "dark figure of crime."[10] The **dark figure of crime** refers to the large number of unreported crimes that never make it into official crime statistics. Crime's dark figure is sometimes glimpsed through offender self-reports, also known as offender **self-report surveys**, in which anonymous respondents without fear of disclosure or arrest are asked to report confidentially any violations of the criminal law that they have committed. Unfortunately for researchers, self-reports of crime are too often limited to asking questions only about petty offenses (such as shoplifting or simple theft), are usually conducted among young people like high school or college students (and hence may not provide results that

are representative of the wider population), typically focus on juvenile delinquency rather than adult criminality, and cannot guarantee that respondents have told the truth. Limitations aside, some criminologists believe that "the development and widespread use of the self-report method of collecting data on delinquent and criminal behavior was one of the most important innovations in criminological research in the twentieth century."[11]

Some of the more recent and best-known self-report surveys include the **National Youth Survey (NYS)** and the **Monitoring the Future** study. Begun in 1976, the NYS surveyed a national sample of 1,725 youths between the ages of 11 and 17.[12] Members of the group (or "panel") were interviewed each year for five years between 1977 and 1981 and later at three-year intervals. The survey, which was last conducted in 1993, followed the original respondents into their thirties. Self-report data were compared with official data over time, and data were gathered on a wide variety of variables. Among other things, researchers found that (1) females were involved in a much higher proportion of crime than previously thought, (2) race differentials in crime were smaller than traditional data sources (that is, the UCR/NIBRS) indicated, and (3) violent offenders begin lives of crime much earlier than previous estimates provided by official statistics indicated. The NYS also found a consistent progression from less serious to more serious acts of delinquency over time.

Monitoring the Future[13] is an ongoing national self-report study of the behaviors, attitudes, and values of U.S. secondary school students, college students, and young adults. The study began in 1975, and each year, a total of almost 50,000 eighth-, tenth-, and twelfth-grade students are surveyed. (Twelfth graders have been surveyed since 1975, eighth and tenth graders since 1991.) In addition, annual follow-up questionnaires are mailed to a sample of each graduating class for a number of years after their initial participation.

Self-report surveys can tell us much about the dark figure of crime. Why are some victimizations not reported to the police?

Murder

The terms *homicide* and **murder** are often used interchangeably, although they are not the same. Homicide is the willful killing of one human being by another, whereas murder is an unlawful homicide. Some homicides, such as those committed in defense of oneself or one's family, may be justifiable and therefore legal. The term used by most courts and law enforcement agencies to describe murder is **criminal homicide**. In legal parlance, *criminal homicide* means the causing of the death of another person without legal justification or excuse. According to the UCR/NIBRS, 16,272 murders were committed throughout the United States in 2008.[14] The 2008 rate of criminal homicide was 5.4 people murdered for every 100,000 individuals in the U.S. population.

Jurisdictions generally distinguish among various types of murder. Among the distinctions made are **first-degree murder**, also called "premeditated murder"; **second-degree murder**; and third-degree murder, or **negligent homicide**. First-degree murder differs from the other two types of murder in that it is planned. It involves what some statutes call "malice aforethought," which may become evident by someone "lying in wait" for the victim but can also be proved by a murderer's simple action of going into an adjacent room to find a weapon and returning with it to kill. In effect, any activity in preparation to kill that demonstrates the passage of time, however brief, between formation of the intent to kill and the act of killing itself is technically sufficient to establish the legal requirements needed for a first-degree murder prosecution.

Second-degree murder, on the other hand, is a true crime of passion. It is an unlawful killing in which the intent to kill and the killing itself happen almost simultaneously. Hence, a person who kills in a fit of anger is likely to be charged with second-degree murder, as is one who is provoked into killing by insults, physical abuse, and the like. For a murder to be second-degree, however, the killing must follow immediately upon the abuse. Time that elapses between abuse or insults and the murder itself allows the opportunity for thought to occur and hence for premeditation.

Both first- and second-degree murderers intend to kill. Third-degree murder, although it varies in meaning between jurisdictions, most often refers to homicides that are the result of some other action that is unlawful or negligent. Hence, it is frequently called "negligent homicide," "negligent manslaughter," "manslaughter," or "involuntary manslaughter." Under negligent homicide statutes, for example, a drunk driver who causes a fatal accident may be charged with third-degree murder, even though that person had not the slightest intent to kill.

Some jurisdictions have created a special category of **felony murder**, whereby an offender who commits a crime during which someone dies can be found guilty of first-degree murder, even though the person committing the crime had no intention of killing anyone. Bank robberies in which one of the robbers is shot to death by police, for example, or in which a bank patron succumbs to a fear-induced heart attack may leave a surviving robber subject to the death penalty under the felony murder rule. Hence, felony murder is a special class of criminal homicide whereby an offender may be charged with first-degree murder when that person's criminal activity results in another person's death.

Significant contributions to the understanding of the crime of homicide are being made today by the Homicide Research Working Group (HRWG). Prior to the creation of the HRWG, work in lethal violence had been scattered among numerous disciplines and was largely uncoordinated. To address this lack of coordination, homicide experts from various disciplines, including criminology, public health, demography, medicine, sociology, criminal

Criminal homicide refers to the causing of the death of another person without legal justification or excuse. It is the same thing as murder. What different kinds of murder can you identify?

Under negligent homicide statutes, a drunk driver who causes a fatal accident may be charged with third-degree murder, even though that person had not the slightest intent to kill. Does that seem fair?

justice, and other fields, joined together to create the HRWG.

While homicide offenders include men and women, young and old, rich and poor, homicide offending is very much patterned in terms of certain sociodemographics, with members of some groups being disproportionately represented as offenders. **Distinctive patterns of homicide can be identified by such factors as individual characteristics, cultural norms, community characteristics, geographic region, availability of weapons and weapons used, gang activity and affiliation, and the victim–offender relationship.** All of these sociodemographic features have been used to further our understanding of homicide patterns and to create typologies surrounding homicide.

> The subculture of violence thesis holds that certain groups share norms and values that contribute to lifestyles involving violence.

The Subculture of Violence Thesis

Within the United States there has been strong research interest in the subculture of violence thesis originally formulated by Marvin Wolfgang and Franco Ferracuti,[15] which was discussed in Chapter 6. These authors stressed that certain groups share norms and values in lifestyles of violence. Ethnic and racial differences in criminal activity rely on interaction with others, including a shared sense of history, language, values, and beliefs. A subculture requires a sufficient number of people who share not only values and beliefs, but also a share a social forum that expresses membership. Such a forum may be something as elusive as a street corner. It is primarily the nature of this situation that makes it difficult to test empirically. **The subculture of violence thesis has been the primary theoretical perspective used to explain the similarity between homicide victims and offenders.** First, homicide statistics reveal that victims and offenders share similar sociodemographic characteristics, such as age, gender, and race. African-Americans are disproportionately represented in the homicide statistics as both victims and offenders.[16] Second, victims and offenders who know each other well are disproportionately represented in homicide statistics. An analysis of supplemental homicide reports shows that approximately 60% of victims and offenders have some prior relationship.[17]

The subculture of violence thesis has also been explored at the community level, where the emphasis is on the importance of "critical masses" as support for the existence of subcultures.[18] Early research argued that the disproportionate rate at which African-Americans commit homicide is associated with the presence of a large African-American population, the "critical mass" necessary for the "transmission of violence-related models" and subcultural behavior patterns.[19] However, most of the research that found higher homicide rates to be associated with higher percentages of African-Americans in the population did not take into consideration things like socioeconomic status, level of education, and so on.[20] Research by Robert Sampson using more sophisticated measures and stronger research designs revealed that the racial composition of an area alone did not have a significant effect on the homicide rates for either whites or blacks.[21]

Homicide: A Closer Look

Marvin Wolfgang's now-famous 1958 study of homicides in Philadelphia revealed that approximately 25% of all homicides were between family members and that women were far more likely than men to be both offenders and victims within this category than within any other.[22] Males were more likely to be killed by friends and strangers than by their family members. However, when a male was killed by a female, the offender was most likely to be his spouse.[23] Other researchers have emphasized qualitative differences in the pattern of homicide within the victim–offender relationship. Figure 8–3 shows the relationship between killers and their victims.

Instrumental and Expressive Homicide

Not all homicide offenders intend to kill their victims. This may be the case when the incident begins as a robbery motivated by instrumental ends, such as getting money. An argument may also precede a homicide, but this circumstance is expressive rather than instrumental because "the dominant motivation is the violence itself," even if lethal violence is not planned in advance.[24] The importance of instigating incidents is explored in research by Carolyn Rebecca Block and Richard Block.[25] The Blocks use the term **sibling offense** to refer to the incident that begins the homicide. A sibling offense may be a crime, such as robbery, or another incident, such as a lovers' quarrel. It is crucial to take these sibling offenses into

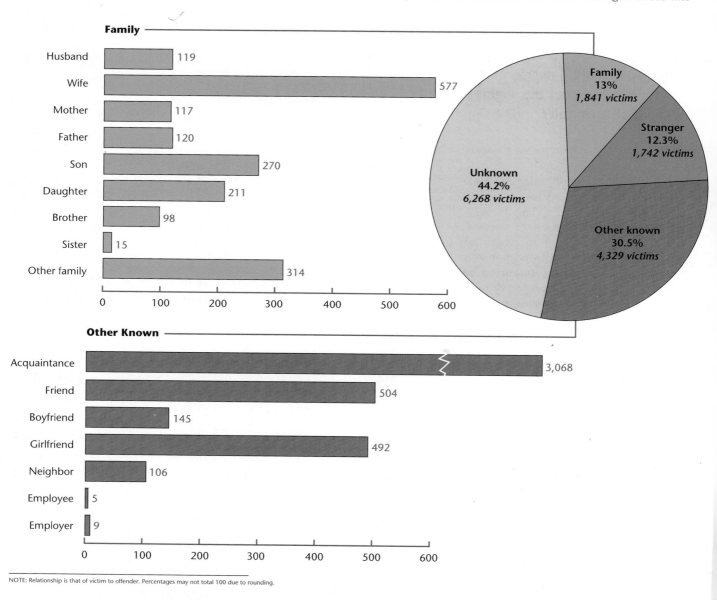

NOTE: Relationship is that of victim to offender. Percentages may not total 100 due to rounding.

FIGURE 8–3 Murder by Relationship, 2008

Source: Federal Bureau of Investigation, *Crime in the United States, 2008* (Washington, DC: FBI, 2009).

account, because they help explain why some robberies end in murder, while others do not. The Blocks developed an elaborate typology of homicide to illustrate how an understanding of the patterns of nonlethal violence can assist in the prevention of lethal violence. For example, there are a great many incidents of street gang violence, most of which do not end in death, and understanding those nonlethal incidents can assist in preventing homicides.[26]

Victim Precipitation

The concept of **victim precipitation** focuses on the characteristics of victims that may have precipitated their victimization. Victim precipitation seems to blame the victim, which makes it quite controversial. From a scholarly point of view, however, the thrust of the concept of victim precipitation is not to blame the victim for the event but to examine both individual and situational factors that may have contributed to and initiated the crime. This is especially important in studying patterns of homicide because quite often a homicide begins as a fight or an argument between people who know each other. The circumstances of the particular encounter determine whether the event will end as some type of assault or as a homicide.

Wolfgang also identified alcohol use as a factor in homicide cases where the "victim is a direct, positive precipitator in the crime."[27] He concluded that the positive and significant association between alcohol and victim-precipitated homicides may be explained by the fact that the victim was the "first to slap, punch, stab, or in some other manner commit an assault" and that if the victim had not been drinking, he or she would have been less violent.[28] Wolfgang's research on homicide revealed that most victims of spousal homicide had been drinking at the time of the incident, a situation that did not apply to homicide offenders.[29]

Weapon Use

There are different perspectives on the role that weapons play in crime, with most of the discussion centering on the role of firearms in

homicide. In examining the relationship between guns and homicide, it is important to differentiate between instrumentality and availability. *Instrumentality* refers to the fact that the type of weapon used in a particular encounter has an effect on whether the encounter ends in death. For example, the involvement of a gun may mean the difference between a criminal event ending as an assault or as a homicide. When guns are used in robberies, the fatality rate is "three times as high as for robberies with knives and 10 times as high as for robberies with other weapons."[30]

Availability refers to issues surrounding how access to guns may increase their presence in all types of interactions, including criminal ones.[31] The ease of availability is important, given the relative spontaneity of some violent encounters. The availability of guns is important at the individual level as well as the community level because the greater the presence of guns in a particular neighborhood, the easier the access for individuals beyond their immediate households. Gun availability, then, may be a much stronger factor in explaining lethal violence than gun instrumentality.[32]

Studies of victim precipitation examine both individual and situational factors that contribute to and initiate crime. How might victim precipitation be relevant to the scene shown here?

Serial Murder

Serial murder is a criminal homicide that "involves the killing of several victims in three or more separate events."[33] Criminologists **James Alan Fox** and **Jack Levin** have written extensively on both serial killing and mass murder.

Contrary to some commonly held beliefs, the vast majority of serial killers are not legally insane or medically psychotic. "They are more cruel than crazy," according to Fox and Levin. "Their crimes may be sickening but their minds are not necessarily sick."[34] Many serial killers are diagnosed as sociopaths, a term for those with antisocial personalities. Since they lack a conscience, sociopaths do not consider the needs or basic humanity of others in their decision making or their view of the world. They do not see themselves as being bound by conventional rules or by the expectations of others. Sociopaths view other people as "tools to be manipulated for the purpose of maximizing their personal pleasure."[35] However, many sociopaths are neither serial killers nor involved in violent crime, even though "they may lie, cheat, or steal."[36]

Although not an exclusive characteristic of serial killers, sexual sadism is a strong pattern. In many of the typologies developed by researchers, this characteristic forms the basis for a type of serial killer. Typologies of serial killers are organized around different, but generally related, themes. Some criminologists identify four different types of serial killers: **Visionary serial killers** hear voices and have visions that are the basis for a compulsion to murder, **comfort serial killers** are motivated by financial or material gain, **hedonistic serial killers** murder because they find it enjoyable and derive psychological pleasure from killing, and **power seekers** operate from some position of authority over others, and their killings usually involve a period where the killer plays a kind of cat-and-mouse game with the victim.[37] Fox and Levin offer a three-part typology. They classify serial murderers as thrill motivated, mission oriented, or expedience directed. *Thrill-motivated killers*, the most common type of serial killer, may be of two types: the sexual sadist and the dominance killer. *Mission-oriented killers* are not as common and generally have either a reformist or a visionary orientation. Reformists want to rid the world of evil, and visionaries hear voices commanding them to do certain activities. Visionary killers are quite rare and tend to be genuinely psychotic. *Expedience-directed serial killers* are driven by either profit or protection. Profit-driven killers may kill for financial or material gain, and protection-oriented killers commit murder to mask other crimes, such as robbery.[38]

Female Serial Killers

Although the vast majority of serial killers are male, there have been female serial killers, and the patterns of their activities are sometimes distinct from those of male serialists.[39] Female serial killers typically select their victims from among people who are known to them, unlike male serial killers, who tend to target strangers.[40] A type of serial killer found primarily among women is the *disciple killer*, who murders as the result of the influence of a charismatic personality. The women who killed at the behest of Charles Manson were of this type. The geographic area in which serial killers operate may be either stable or transient, with no clear preference among male serial killers. However, geographic stability characterizes almost all of the known female serial killers.[41]

Michael D. Kelleher and C. L. Kelleher researched female serial killers from a historical perspective and developed a typology based on motivation. Arguing that there are two broad categories of female serial killers—those who act alone and those who work in partnership with others—Kelleher and Kelleher present a typology based on distinct motivation, selection of victim, and method of killing.[42] The categories include the *black widow*, who generally kills spouses and usually for economic

Serial killer Jeffrey Dahmer. Into which category of killers would Dahmer fit?

A still frame from the Showtime TV series *Dexter*, in which the main character plays a police blood spatter expert who is also a serial killer. For those familiar with the show: What makes Dexter "different" from other serial killers?

profit, and the *angel of death*, who generally kills "those in her care or who rely on her for some form of medical attention or similar support."[43] The typical career of a female serial killer is longer than that of her male counterpart. Other than women who commit their crimes with others, usually men, female serial killers tend to approach their crimes in a

systematic fashion—a characteristic that may explain their longer careers.[44]

Apprehending Serial Killers

It is extremely difficult to identify and apprehend serial killers because of the cautiousness and skill with which they operate. Ironically, it is these very factors that allow them to operate long enough to be labeled serial killers. Individuals who are less skillful or cautious are generally apprehended because of evidence at the crime scene or the selection of their victim.

Dorothea Puente, the landlady who buried elderly tenants in the backyard of her California rooming house in the 1980s.

Mass Murder

Mass murder is the illegal killing of more than three individuals at a single time.[45] Mass murder can follow the political motivations of the offenders, as was the case with the 1995 Oklahoma City bombing, in which 168 individuals, including children, were killed. Other mass murderers kill for more personal reasons. The mass killing of 32 people at the Virginia Polytechnic Institute and State University (Virginia Tech) campus in Blacksburg, Virginia, in 2007 by student gunman Seung-Hui Cho (described in Chapter 6) appears to have been at least partially motivated by a seething anger against those whom Cho perceived as more successful than himself. **Mass murderers tend to surprise their victims because they often attack in everyday locales that are considered safe and because they erupt spontaneously.** Although mass murders do not occur with great frequency, they cause great concern because they shatter the sense of safety that characterizes everyday life.

Fox and Levin offer a four-part typology of mass murder that differentiates these crimes by motive:[46]

- *Revenge* murderers represent the largest category of such killers. They are motivated by *revenge* against either particular individuals or groups of individuals. Other revenge-motivated murderers may be less specific in the selection of a target, as in the case of George Hennard, who hated "all of the residents of the county in which he lived." In 1991, Hennard drove his truck through the front window of Luby's Cafeteria in Killeen, Texas, and then "indiscriminately opened fire on customers as they ate their lunch, killing 23."[47]

- Mass murderers motivated by *love* have a sense of love that is distorted and obsessive. They often commit suicide after they murder, and, in the case of a spouse killing, the may also kill their children.

- Mass murders who kill for *profit* are usually trying to eliminate witnesses in an effort to cover up a major crime.

- Some mass murderers are motivated by *terror*, such as the individuals who participated in the Charles Manson killings. These people want to send a message to society.

Although most mass murders strike the public as senseless acts of a crazy person, Levin and Fox contend that "most massacres are not madmen."[48] Yet why would someone like James Huberty, a former security guard, walk calmly into a fast-food restaurant in 1984 and fatally shoot 21 victims at random, most of whom were children? Why

Columbine High School security video showing Dylan Kleold (right) and Eric Harris in the school's cafeteria during their murderous 1999 rampage. How does mass murder differ from serial killing?

Bullet holes and broken glass are obvious at the McDonald's restaurant in San Ysidro, California, after James Huberty gunned down 20 people inside. What four types of mass murderers have been identified?

Mass murderers often select targets that hold some special significance for them.

would Patrick Edward Purdy shoot and kill 5 children and wound 30 others at Cleveland Elementary School in Stockton, California, in 1989?[49] Levin and Fox argue that **factors like frustration, isolation, blame, loss, failure, and other external and internal motivations and situational elements contribute to the activities of mass murders.** They delineate three types of contributing factors: *predisposers*, long-term and stable preconditions that become incorporated into the personality of the killer, which are nearly always present in his or her biography; *precipitants*, short-term and acute triggers, that is, catalysts; and *facilitators*, conditions, usually situational, that increase the likelihood of a violent outburst but are not necessary to produce that response."[50] Using this typology to

explain why, for example, most mass murderers are middle-aged, Levin and Fox contend that it takes a long time to accumulate the kind of rage and frustration that sets off some mass murderers. Mass murderers often select targets that have some significance for them, such as workers at a site of former employment. As Fox and Levin state, "A majority of mass killers target victims who are specially chosen, not just in the wrong place at the wrong time. The indiscriminate slaughter of strangers by a 'crazed' killer is the exception to the rule."[51] Unlike serial murderers, mass murderers are easy to apprehend because they rarely leave the scene of their crime, either because they commit suicide after the killings or because they stay long enough to be detected.

Rape

In contrast to the NCVS, which uses a *gender-neutral* definition of rape, the FBI continues to employ a traditional definition for statistical counting purposes, saying that **rape** is the carnal knowledge of a female forcibly and against her will. UCR/NIBRS statistics on rape, as currently reported, include cases of both rape and attempted rape. Statutory rape (sexual relations between an underage female minor and an adult male) and other sex offenses are excluded from the count of rape crimes. **In 2008, 89,000 rapes were reported nationwide under the UCR Program, a slight increase over the previous year. The rate of reported forcible rape was officially put at 58.6 rapes per 100,000 women.** As Figure 8–4 shows, the risk of sexual assault victimization for both females and males varies greatly by age.

Theoretical Perspectives on Rape

Several theoretical perspectives have been offered to explain individual motivations for rape, why rape is more prevalent in particular contexts, and how certain cultural values may reinforce rape. These perspectives attempt to explain how rape is patterned according to the context, the victim–offender relationship, and the motivations of the rapist.

Feminist Perspectives Feminists view gender as a social construct rather than as a biological given, and they regard as problematic the way in which gender is used to structure social relations and institutions. Rape is viewed as an act of power or domination in which the "tool" used to subordinate is sexual. Rape is a crime of violence that is sexual in nature, but this aspect is considered to be secondary to the power dynamics that occur in rapes.[52]

Socialization patterns, cultural practices, structural arrangements, media images, norms surrounding sexuality, and women's status in society all combine to create a rape culture in which both men and women come to view male aggression as

Dr. Edward F. Jackson during his first trial on charges stemming from a seven-year spree of rapes that he committed in Franklin County, Ohio, during the 1970s. Jackson was eventually convicted of 98 felonies, including 21 rapes.

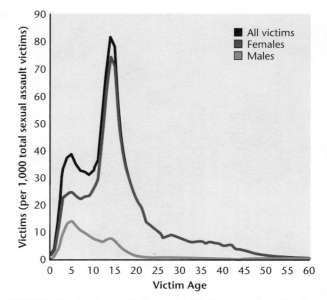

FIGURE 8–4 Sexual Assault Victimization Rates by Age and Sex

Source: Office of Juvenile Justice and Delinquency Prevention, *Juvenile Offenders and Victims: 2006 National Report* (Washington, DC: OJJDP, 2006). p. 31.

normal, even in sexual relations.[53] Within this culture, women are blamed for their own rape by virtue of the fact that males are naturally incapable of controlling their sexual desire.

The Psychopathological Perspective The psychopathological perspective on rape is based on two assumptions: (1) Rape is the "result of idiosyncratic mental disease," and (2) "it often includes an uncontrollable sexual impulse."[54] While acknowledging that rape is connected to issues like power and anger, **Nicholas Groth,**[55] based on an analysis of 348 imprisoned convicted rapists, found that 55% reported that rape was committed to exert control over the women—a type of crime Groth labeled *power rape.* Power rapists, unlike anger rapists, did not purposefully set out to harm the victim. Power rapes are generally planned, Groth said, "although the actual assault may be opportunistic in origin."[56] In the attacks that Groth labeled *anger rapes,* which totaled about 40% of the sample, the men attacked their victims in anger; usually the attack was impulsive and involved no prior planning on the part of the offender. These assaults were often quite brutal, and following the rape the offender felt relief because he was able to relieve his anger. The remaining 5% were considered *sadistic rapes* because they involved a combination of power and anger motives and often involved torture.[57]

Evolutionary/Biological Perspectives Within the evolutionary perspective, propagation is the key to survival of a trait, as a genetic predisposition

"Take Back the Night" demonstrators drawing attention to issues of sexual violence. How have rape shield laws helped in the prosecution of sex offenders?

can be passed on only through offspring."[58] Natural selection favors those traits that are most adaptive, and over several generations it is these traits that survive. An evolutionary perspective does not identify rape per se as an adaptation but, rather, focuses on certain motives and ends that are conducive to rape. According to Randy Thornhill and Craig T. Palmer, "[s]election favored different traits in females and males, especially when the traits were directly related to mating. Although some of these differences could have arisen from what Darwin called natural selection, most of them are now believed to have evolved through sexual selection."[59] *Sexual selection* **refers to the fact that some traits appear to survive not because they are related to survival, but because they increase the attraction of mates or the defense against competition over mates.** This is said to apply primarily to males because "male fitness is limited by access to the opposite sex much more directly than is female fitness, with the result that females compete for mates much less than do males."[60] The evolutionary perspectives have been severely criticized for justifying rape as "natural." Proponents of the usefulness of evolutionary perspectives argue that "biology provides understanding, not justification, of human behavior."[61]

Changing Understandings of Rape

The crime of rape has generated much controversy over the years. To understand why, it is important to examine the changing legal definitions of *rape*, as well as our societal understanding of rape.

Until the 1970s in the United States and the 1980s in Canada, most jurisdictions followed a **common law definition of rape**, which saw the crime as "carnal knowledge of a woman not one's wife, by force or against her will." **Rape was construed quite narrowly and specifically, and did not recognize men as victims. The law also did not recognize rape within marriage, did not allow for acts of sexual penetration other than vaginal penetration by a penis, and did not allow for various means by which force could occur.** Moreover, the rules of evidence required that the victim who claimed rape had to demonstrate physical resistance to the attack and must have some form of corroboration (like physical injuries) to show that the rape had actually occurred. The victim's previous sexual history could be admitted as relevant information. Furthermore, the understanding of rape relied on gender stereotypes in which only certain kinds of women were deemed to be credible victims and only certain kinds of men were regarded as possible offenders.

Rape Law Reform Rape law reform attempted to make statutory definitions of rape compatible with those of other violent crimes. Rape investigations, especially at the trial stage, too often forced the victim through further trauma rather than focusing on assessing the offender's guilt or innocence.[62] Feminist groups were joined by law enforcement officials and prosecutors who supported efforts "to remove obstacles to the apprehension and conviction of offenders."[63] In 1975, Michigan became the first state to dramatically redefine *rape* to encompass a broader range of sexually assaultive behaviors, circumstances, and victims. Other states followed Michigan's lead, and by 1992, all states had made significant statutory changes to the common law offense definition of *rape*.[64]

In one key way, individual rape law reform in states and at the federal level proceeded along a common route: **rape shield laws**. **Rape shield laws, first introduced in the 1970s, were intended to protect rape victims by ensuring that defendants did not introduce irrelevant facts about the victim's sexual past into evidence. Previously, no guidelines prevented the defense from bringing into evidence the victim's sexual history as a way to discredit her. Rape shield laws sent the message that the courts would no longer be a party to a "second assault" on the victim.**[65]

Rape: A Closer Look

Although rape can occur in almost any social context, certain social situations are characterized by a higher prevalence of rape and by a difference in the offender's motivation.

Acquaintance Rape

The vast majority of rapes occur when the victim and the offender have some prior relationship—though not necessarily an intimate or a familial one. Some researchers and

Kristen Stewart, star of the 2005 Showtime TV movie *Speak*. The movie dramatizes the experiences of a teenage girl traumatized by a date rape. What is date rape?

activists who work with rape victims have stated that **acquaintance rape** is the most common scenario for rapes. Among adults, acquaintance rape usually occurs within the context of a dating relationship, and is sometimes referred to as *date rape*.

Researchers have identified college campuses as places that typically have a high incidence of rape. Societal awareness and concern for rape on college campuses did not emerge until the 1980s. Helping to publicize the problem have been a number of high-profile rape cases on college campuses in which the victims not only went public with their experiences but also grabbed headlines and the covers of major publications like *Time*, *Newsweek*, and *People*.[66] Not only has media publicity emphasized the reality of the college setting as a site of rape, but also in 1992 the Campus Sexual Assault Victims' Bill of Rights Act became law.[67] It requires campus authorities to "conduct appropriate disciplinary hearings, treat sexual

assault victims and defendants with respect, making their rights and legal options clear, and cooperate with them in fully exercising those rights."[68]

A great deal of the research on rape in college settings has focused on identifying the unique factors of campus life that may be conducive to rape. Some researchers contend that college fraternities "create a sociocultural context in which the use of coercion in sexual relations with women is normative and in which the mechanisms to keep this pattern of behavior in check are minimal at best and absent at worst."[69] The increased awareness of campus rape has led to the development of services and programs that assist victims of sexual violence and that present information that challenges rape myths.

Spousal Rape

As previously mentioned, until the 1970s under common law a legally married husband could not be charged with raping his wife. **Rape, as research indicates, happens to many women within marriage, as part of a practice of spousal abuse that may involve beatings and other violence. Until 1976, spousal rape could not be prosecuted in any state. Today, it is illegal in every state in the United States.**

The first researcher to systematically examine spousal rape was **Diana E. H. Russell**. Based on an analysis of interview data, Russell developed a four-part typology of men who rape their wives:

- Husbands who prefer raping their wives to having consensual sex with them
- Husbands who are able to enjoy both rape and consensual sex with their wives or who are indifferent to which it is
- Husbands who would prefer consensual sex with their wives but are willing to rape them when their sexual advances are refused
- Husbands who might like to rape their wives but do not act out these desires

Thus, rather than being one-dimensional, rape within marriage has several forms that reflect the various nuances of motivation on the part of offenders.

Rape in Prison

Prison rape, which is generally considered to involve physical assault, represents a special category of sexual victimization behind bars. **In 2003, Congress mandated the collection of statistics on prison rape as part of the Prison Rape Elimination Act (PREA).**[70] The purposes of the PREA are to[71]

- establish a zero-tolerance standard for prison rape,

● Crime against Persons ● The Crime Picture

- make prison rape prevention a top priority in correctional facilities and systems,
- develop and implement national standards for the detection, prevention, reduction, and punishment of prison rape,
- increase the availability of information on the incidence and prevalence of prison rape, and
- increase the accountability of corrections officials with regard to the issue of sexual violence in U.S. prisons.

The PREA requires the BJS to collect data in federal and state prisons, county and city jails, and juvenile institutions, with the U.S. Census Bureau acting as the official repository for collected data. In 2007, the BJS completed its third annual national survey of administrative records and adult correctional facilities for PREA purposes.[72] The survey found that reports of sexual violence varied significantly between prisons and across states, with every state prison system except Alaska and New Mexico reporting at least one allegation of sexual violence. Among the 344 local jail jurisdictions participating in the survey, 47% reported at least one allegation of sexual violence. About 52% of privately operated prisons and jails similarly reported at least one such allegation. Overall, the survey found 5,605 allegations of sexual violence. Extrapolating from that data, BJS estimated that the total number of prison and jail sexual assaults throughout the nation for that year was around 6,500.

The PREA survey is only a first step in understanding and eliminating prison rape. As BJS notes, "Due to fear of reprisal from perpetrators, a code of silence among inmates, personal embarrassment, and lack of trust in staff, victims are often reluctant to report incidents to correctional authorities."[73]

Lee H. Bowker, a criminologist who specializes in studying life inside prisons, summarizes studies of sexual violence in prison with the following observations:[74]

- Most sexual aggressors do not consider themselves homosexuals.
- Sexual release is not the primary motivation for sexual attack.
- Many aggressors must continue to participate in gang rapes to avoid becoming victims themselves.
- The aggressors have themselves suffered much damage to their masculinity in the past.

As in cases of heterosexual rape, sexual assaults in prison are likely to leave psychological scars on the victim long after the physical event is over.[75] Victims of prison rape live in fear, may feel constantly threatened, and can turn to self-destructive activities.[76] Many victims question their masculinity and undergo a personal devaluation.

The collection of statistics on prison rape were mandated under the Prison Rape Elimination Act of 2003. What do the data tell us?

Child Sexual Abuse

Child sexual abuse (CSA) is a term encompassing a variety of criminal and civil offenses in which an adult engages in sexual activity with a minor, exploits a minor for purposes of sexual gratification, or exploits a minor sexually for purposes of profit. The term includes a variety of activities and motivations, including child molestation, child sexual exploitation (CSE), and the commercial sexual exploitation of children (CSEC).

The National Institute of Justice (NIJ) observes that "few criminal offenses are more despised than the sexual abuse of children, and few are so little understood in terms of incidence (the number of offenses committed), prevalence (the proportion of the population who commit offenses), and reoffense risk."[77]

NIJ also notes that sexual offenses are more likely than other types of criminal conduct to elude the attention of the criminal justice system. **Self-reports from both sex offenders and sexually abused children reveal far more abuse than officially reported.[78] The Child Molestation Research and Prevention Institute, based in Atlanta, Georgia, estimates that at least two out of every ten girls, and one out of every ten boys, are sexually abused by the time they turn 14.[79]**

One of the most informative offender self-report studies on the adult sexual victimization of children comes from research conducted slightly more than two decades ago.[80] In that study, investigators recruited 561 adult subjects who engaged in what the researchers described as "child-focused sexual behavior." The subjects, who were guaranteed anonymity, were recruited through health care workers, media advertising, presentations at meetings, and in other ways. All were free from confinement at the time of the interviews. The 561 adults interviewed reported a total of 291,737 "paraphiliac acts" over the course of their adult lives committed against 195,407 victims under the age of 18. The results of this study make it clear that, in cases of child sexual abuse, a relatively small number of offenders can commit a large number of crimes.

behaviors. Figure 8–5 shows the number of registered predatory child sex offenders by state.

In 1983 Nicholas Groth and his associates proposed a simple, two-part distinction among pedophiles whereby offenders were classified as either "regressed" or "fixated."[83] Regressed offenders, said Groth, are attracted sexually primarily to their own age groups but are passively aroused by minors. Generally speaking, the use of alcohol, drugs, or other inhibition-lowering substances, combined with social circumstances providing opportunity, can cause the regressed offender to act out his interest in having sexual encounters with children. Fixated offenders, said Groth, are adult pedophiles who engage in planned sexual acts with children, and whose behavior is not necessarily influenced by drugs or alcohol.

A U.S. Department of Justice publication, representing a compilation of studies produced by the NIJ, shows that most victims of childhood sexual abuse do not go on to become child molesters.[84] However, NIJ points out, **sexual victimization as a child, if accompanied by other factors—such as the co-occurrence of physical and verbal abuse—may contribute to the child-victim's development as a perpetrator of child sexual abuse later in life.** Similarly, says the NIJ, social competence deficits are significant in child molestation,

Types of Child Sex Abusers

Almost all pedophiles are male, with one study of more than 4,400 offenders finding fewer than 0.5% of convicted child sex offenses committed by females.[81] Other than that, little can be said about similarities among child sexual abusers. As individuals, they tend to be highly dissimilar from one another in terms of personal characteristics, life experiences, and criminal histories. No single "molester profile" exists.[82] Child molesters appear to arrive at deviancy via multiple pathways and engage in many different sexual and nonsexual "acting-out"

A still frame from the NBC Dateline series *To Catch a Predator*. What different types of pedophiles have been identified?

but an individual's inadequate social and interpersonal skills do not, by themselves, make his or her sexual abuse of children inevitable.

Some evidence exists to suggest that child molestation may be related to an offender's restaging of his or her own childhood sexual victimization.[85] Tests of the restaging theory on a sample of 131 rapists and child molesters revealed that child molesters who committed their first assault when they were 14 or younger were sexually victimized at a younger age than offenders who committed their first assault in adulthood; they also experienced more severe sexual abuse than offenders with adult onset of sexual aggression.[86]

Nonetheless, sexual victimization alone appears to be unable to fully explain child molestation. Studies show that most victims of childhood sexual abuse do not go on to become perpetrators.[87] As is true for other kinds of maltreatment, childhood sexual victimization may be one critical element in the presence or absence of a variety of other factors (for example, co-occurrence of other types of abuse, availability of supportive caregivers, ego strength of child-victim at the time of abuse, availability of treatment, and so forth), all of which appear to moderate the likelihood of becoming a child molester.

Not all adults involved in the sexual abuse of children pursue personal sexual gratification. Some have a profit motive, as is the case in instances of *commercial sexual exploitation of*
children, or CSEC. CSEC refers to all offenses in which an adult victimizes a child sexually for profit, including the prostituting of a child, and creating or trafficking in child pornography.

Awareness of **child pornography** exploded onto the American scene in the 1990s, as the advent of rapid transmission of high-quality images and video became possible through the growth of the Internet. Child pornography can be defined as a visual representation of any kind that depicts a minor engaging in sexually explicit conduct and is obscene, and which lacks serious literary, artistic, political, or scientific value.

The Internet created special problems in enforcement of the laws designed to control pedophiles and child pornographers. Because it is an international medium, the Internet is hard to police, and activities through which information on the Internet is transmitted may be illegal in one jurisdiction and not so in another. Similarly, the relative anonymity of both buyers and sellers of child pornography over the Internet provides both a sense of security and impersonality to those involved in such transactions.

According to the United Nations Children's Fund (UNICEF), tens of thousands of children in the United States and tens of millions of children worldwide are involved in CSEC.[88] UNICEF says the number of sexually exploited children worldwide may exceed 100 million, not all of whom are located in "poor" or "developing" countries.

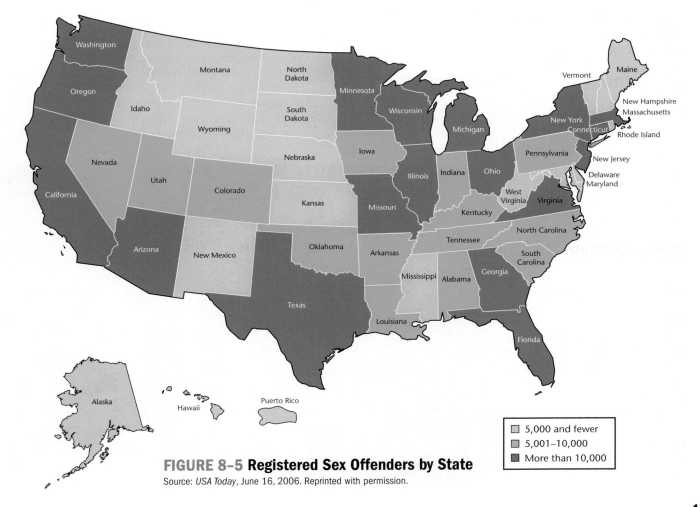

FIGURE 8–5 Registered Sex Offenders by State
Source: *USA Today*, June 16, 2006. Reprinted with permission.

Legend:
- 5,000 and fewer
- 5,001–10,000
- More than 10,000

Robbery

Robbery is classified as a violent crime because it involves the threat or use of force. It is, however, also a property crime in that the express purpose of robbery is to take the property of another.[89] UCR/NIBRS data for 2008 show that 441,855 robberies came to the attention of authorities across the nation that year, meaning that the rate of robbery was 145.3 per every 100,000 people in the United States. Large metropolitan areas recorded the highest rates of robbery, while rural areas had the lowest. In 2008, according to the FBI 40% of robberies were committed using strong-arm tactics (without a weapon), and firearms were the weapon of choice in 44% more. Knives were used in 11%, with a variety of other dangerous weapons used in the remainder.

Robberies can occur in different locations (Figure 8–6) and are often categorized according to location by both law enforcement agencies and social science researchers. Robberies that occur on the street are often referred to as **highway robberies** or "muggings." Muggings and robberies that happen in residences are types of personal robbery. Homes and persons appear as more or less attractive targets based on their perceived vulnerability and the social context of the surrounding neighborhood in which they are found.

Robberies that occur in commercial settings, such as convenience stores, gas stations, and banks, are known as **institutional robberies**.[90]

The Lethal Potential of Robbery

Robbery carries the threat of injury or death for the victim. Robbery provides the context for 7% of all homicides annually, and accounts for almost one-half (43%) of all felony murders (that is, murders that occur during the commission of another felony).[91] The weapon most often used in robbery homicides is a firearm, accounting for 44% of all cases; the type of firearm used in the vast majority of these cases (85%) is a handgun.[92]

The Motivation of Robbers

Research tends to support the idea that most robberies, of both people and places, involve very little planning on the part of the offender.

A man robs a store while his young daughter looks on. Why is robbery a potentially lethal crime?

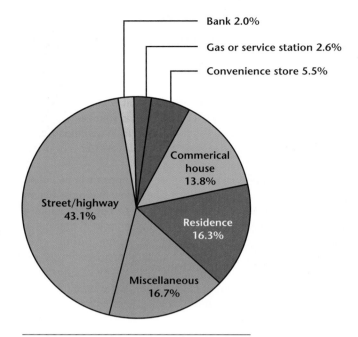

Bank 2.0%

Gas or service station 2.6%

Convenience store 5.5%

Commerical house 13.8%

Street/highway 43.1%

Residence 16.3%

Miscellaneous 16.7%

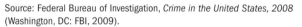

Note: Due to rounding, the percentages may not add to 100.0

FIGURE 8–6 Robbery Locations

Source: Federal Bureau of Investigation, *Crime in the United States, 2008* (Washington, DC: FBI, 2009).

Floyd Feeney's research in California during the early 1970s found little evidence that the majority of bank robbers had even been in the bank they robbed before the act of robbery.[93] Most of the robbers Feeney studied did very little planning, no matter what the target, and the planning that did occur was minor and "generally took place the same day as the robbery and frequently within a few hours of it."[94] The motivation and decision making of street robbers have been

The "Barbie bandits," Ashley Miller (L), and Heather Lyn Johnson, both 19. The pair, who worked as strippers in a local club, robbed a Georgia bank of $11,000 in 2007.

evaluated in a series of research studies conducted by Bruce A. Jacobs, Richard Wright, and others at the University of Missouri at St. Louis. To be considered an active robber for the purpose of the research study, "the individual had committed a robbery in the recent past, defined him- or herself as currently active, and was regarded as active by other offenders."[95] Researchers found that the decision to offend, like other decisions, occurs as part of ongoing social action that is "mediated by prevailing situations and subcultural conditions."[96] "Fast cash" is the direct need that robbery satisfied, but this need can be properly understood only against the backdrop of street culture. Jacobs and Wright hypothesized that street culture was the intervening force that connected background factors (such as low self-esteem, deviant peer relations, and weak social bonds) to the motivation to offend. They found that the majority of robbers gave little thought to planning

A home invasion robbery in progress. Why is robbery one of the most gender-differentiated serious crimes in America?

robberies until they found themselves needing money. For less than half of the robbers, the financial need was for basic necessities; mostly, it was connected to a fairly hedonistic lifestyle. The daily activity of most street robbers was characterized as a "quest for excitement and sensory stimulation" with a "general lack of social stability" in terms of residence or ties to conventional activities or institutions.[97]

Jacobs and Wright conclude that the economic motivation behind robbery should not be interpreted as "genuine financial hardship" but, rather, as a constant, ongoing crisis situation experienced as a result of the logic of the street context of robbers' daily lives.[98] For the individuals whom Jacobs and Wright interviewed, "being a street robber is a way of behaving, a way of thinking, an approach to life."[99]

The Gendered Nature of Robbery

According to Jody Miller, "[w]ith the exception of forcible rape, robbery is perhaps the most gender differentiated serious crime in the United States."[100] Women represent robbery offenders in only 11% of all incidents.[101] Miller's research goal was to assess the extent to which gender organizes robbery offending. To accomplish this, she analyzed a subset of the interviews with active robbers from the research data used by Jacobs and Wright. The sample that Miller used consisted of 37 robbers, 14 of whom were women and 23 of whom were men. Miller found that economic incentives were the primary motivation among both men and women. There were, however, significant differences in the way in which men and women carried out street robberies. Men exhibited a fairly uniform pattern. Their robberies were characterized by "using physical violence and/or a gun placed on or at close proximity to the victim in a confrontational manner."[102] The presence of a gun was almost a constant in robberies conducted by men. While perceiving women to be easier targets, male robbers tended to rob other men rather than women because of the perception that men tended to carry more money. The majority of the males targeted as victims were those involved in "street life."

Female robbers, on the other hand, did not exhibit one clear style but instead tended to fall into one of three patterns. The robbery of other women in a "physically confrontational manner" was the most prevalent way in which female robbers worked, but also present were the strategies of using their sexuality to attract male victims and acting as accomplices to male robbers in offenses against other men.[103] Except when robbing men, female robbers as a general rule did not use guns. Miller concludes that, rather than reflecting different motivations, the different strategies for robbery selected by men and women "reflect practical choices made in the context of a gender-stratified environment—one in which, on the whole, men are perceived as strong and women are perceived as weak."[104] While similar cultural and structural forces can drive the offending of men and women in the same way, gender continues to exert an influence on shaping the nature of these interactions in robbery incidents.

Aggravated Assault

There are two types of assault: simple and aggravated. **Aggravated assault**, which the FBI defines as "the unlawful attack by one person upon another wherein the offender uses a weapon or displays it in a threatening manner, or the victim suffers obvious or severe bodily injury,"[105] is the more serious type of assault, and the one that concerns us here. According to the FBI, 834,885 aggravated assaults were reported to police agencies across the nation in 2008, producing an aggravated assault rate of 274.6 for every 100,000 people in the country.

The profile of a typical offender in aggravated assault mirrors that of homicide, with disproportionate involvement of males, African-Americans, 15- to 34-year-olds, those of lower socioeconomic status, those with prior arrest records, and offenders demonstrating little evidence of offense specialization.[106] Also consistent with most homicides, aggravated assaults are "spontaneous, triggered by a trivial altercation or argument that quickly escalates in the heat of passion."[107]

Based on statistics from the NCVS, which tallies simple as well as aggravated assault, the majority of assaults reported by victims to NCVS interviewers are simple rather than aggravated assault. According to the NCVS, the overall decline in the nation's crime rate between 1993 and 2008 was mostly due to decreases in the rate of simple assault.

Aggravated assaults are distinguished according to those involving injury and those without injury. The victims and offenders in aggravated assault are for the most part equally likely to be strangers or nonstrangers to each other. When you look at the gender of the victim, a pattern emerges. A slight majority of male victims are assaulted by a stranger, whereas slightly more than one-third (39%) of female victims are assaulted by a stranger in aggravated assaults. Simple assaults, by contrast, are more likely in general to involve nonstrangers (58%). Almost one-half (47%) of male victims are assaulted by nonstrangers, whereas 71% of female victims are assaulted by nonstrangers in these cases. Whether it is an aggravated or a simple assault, the largest category of nonstranger offenders of female victims is represented by friends and acquaintances, followed by intimate partners. Weapons

are present in less than one-fourth (23%) of all assaults, and when a weapon is present, it is most likely to be something other than a gun or a knife.[108]

Stranger Assault

The possibility of stranger violence elicits a great deal of fear and concern among most members of the population. But, based on research using victimization data in both the United States and Great Britain, "the probability of suffering a serious personal crime by strangers is very low,"[109] with this likelihood varying by demographic characteristics like gender, age, marital status, and lifestyle. For example, individuals who have an active social life away from home and in the evening are far more likely to be victimized by strangers, but this effect depends very much on the community context in which the individuals engage in their leisure pursuits.

Assault within Families

The majority of assaults involve victims and offenders who are known to each other, quite often in a familial or an intimate relationship. Criminology as a discipline began to give more attention to violent behavior within the family just as society began viewing the wall of privacy that has long surrounded the family with a bit more scrutiny. The family as a social institution is intensely private and the discussion of physical, emotional, and sexual violence among family members invades this privacy. These types of abuse also represent extremely sensitive parts of a

Why do so many assaults occur in domestic settings? What's the difference between simple and aggravated assault?

person's experience, which individuals may be reluctant to discuss. Two of the most common reasons for not reporting crimes to the police are that it was a "private matter" and that there might be reprisal from the offender. Current research shows that such rationales supporting nonreporting continue to characterize incidents involving violence among family members.[110]

Initial research on violence within the family came from official records and small clinical studies that consistently revealed that women were more likely than men to become victims. Based on an examination of emergency room victims in the late 1970s, Evan Stark and colleagues found that approximately 25% of all women who had been injured had been the victim of a spousal attack.[111]

In the years since survey research was first used to estimate violence against family members, other surveys have emerged to assess this phenomenon, and existing data sources have been improved to better measure family violence. NIBRS data reveal that while assault is the most frequently occurring violent crime both among the general population and within the family, the percentage is even higher within the family.[112]

> The majority of assaults involve victims and offenders who are known to each other.

Compared with aggravated assaults generally, firearms are less likely to be used within the family; instead, fists, hands, and knives are more common. A slight majority of aggravated assault offenses involve some type of injury both in the general population (57.5%) and within the family (60.8%). Women are more likely to be the victims of both aggravated assaults and simple assaults within the family than in the general population (60% versus 41% and 72% versus 60%, respectively).[113]

Intimate-Partner Assault

Intimate-partner assault is one of several terms used to characterize assaultive behavior that takes place between individuals involved in an intimate relationship. Several researchers have noted that terms like *spouse assault* are inappropriate because they give the misleading impression that male and female spouses are equally likely to be victims.[114] The overwhelming majority of victims of marital violence within heterosexual relationships are women. This empirical reality does not deny that men can be the victims of violence at the hands of their wives; it merely acknowledges that based on official records, self-reports, hospital emergency room records, and small clinical samples, it is women who emerge as victims.

Trisha Meili, left, known as the "Central Park Jogger" after becoming the victim of a savage rape and beating that gained national attention in 1989. Meili, whose identity was long kept secret, is shown with New York governor David A. Paterson. Why is stranger assault the source of so much fear?

Assault between intimate partners that results in a break-up of the relationship is referred to as **separation assault**.[115] Separation assault illustrates what feminists like Liz Kelly mean when they say that "the use of explicit force/violence is in fact a response to the failure of, or resistance to, other forms of control."[116] A woman who attempts to leave a violent relationship might be seen as violating the right of her husband to control her, and even if she does manage to leave, many times the husband will follow her and attempt to take her back. Physical assaults often involve other tactics of abuse, such as emotional abuse and attacks or threats against children. This is especially salient in that most women who have reported abuse by intimate partners also had dependent children.[117]

One goal of the NVAW Survey was to estimate both the extent and the nature of physical abuse among intimate partners. The survey found that at some point during their lifetime, 22% of women and slightly more than 7% of men report having been physically assaulted by an intimate partner. During any given year, slightly more than 1% of women and less than 1% of men report physical assault by an intimate partner. On the extent of injury in intimate-partner assaults, the NVAW Survey reveals that women are more likely than men to report injuries and that most of the injuries received are minor in nature.

Other Forms of Interpersonal Violence

This chapter concludes with an overview of three special forms of interpersonal violence. They are (1) workplace violence, (2) hate crimes, and (3) stalking.

Workplace Violence

Workplace violence is a significant problem in the United States today, and is considered the third leading cause of occupational injury or death. Workplace violence includes murder, rape, robbery, and assault committed against persons who are at work or on duty. On average, 1.7 million nonfatal, violent workplace victimizations are committed every year. Assaults, both simple and aggravated, account for the largest number of workplace violence incidents, affecting approximately 11.7 out of every 1,000 persons in the workforce annually. Another 900 or so work-related homicides occur annually. Workplace violence accounts for approximately 18% of all violent crime that occurs in the United States. As might be expected, police officers experience workplace violence at rates higher than persons employed in any other occupation, while college or university professors are among persons least likely to be victimized (Figure 8–7).

All workplace violence falls into four broad categories, as follows:

Type 1: Violent acts by criminals who have no other connection with the workplace, but enter to commit robbery, acts of terrorism, or another crime.

Type 2: Violence directed at employees by customers, clients, patients, students, inmates, or any others for whom an organization provides services.

Type 3: Violence against coworkers, supervisors, or managers by a present or former employee.

Type 4: Violence committed in the workplace by someone who doesn't work there, but has a personal relationship with an employee, such as an abusive spouse or domestic partner.

Hate Crimes

An important recent change in the UCR Program involves the collection of **hate crime** information, and was mandated by

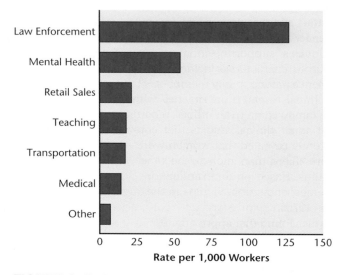

FIGURE 8–7 Annual Rate of Violent Workplace Victimization by Occupation

Source: Detis T. Duhart, *Violence in the Workplace, 1993-99* (Washington, DC: Bureau of Justice Statistics, 2001), p. 4.

the U.S. Congress with passage of the Hate Crime Statistics Act of 1990.[118] Under the law, the FBI is required to serve as a repository for data collected on crimes motivated by religious, ethnic, racial, or sexual orientation prejudice. The Violent Crime Control and Law Enforcement Act of 1994[119] mandated the addition to the hate crimes category of crimes motivated by biases against people with disabilities, and the UCR Program began reporting such crimes in 1997.

According to the BJS, hate crimes, also called "bias crimes," are crimes characterized by "manifest evidence of prejudice based on race, religion, sexual orientation, or ethnicity, including where appropriate the crimes of murder, non-negligent manslaughter, forcible rape, aggravated assault, simple assault, intimidation, arson, and destruction, damage, or vandalism of property."[120]

Stalking

While **stalking** behavior is not new, the labeling of such behavior as criminal is relatively recent.

Stalking can be defined as a course of conduct directed at a specific person that involves visual or physical proximity, nonconsensual verbal communication, or implied threats that would cause a reasonable person fear. All states and the federal government have antistalking laws. Rather than being an offense that occurs once, stalking is a repeated pattern of behavior that causes victims to fear for their personal safety.

Statutory definitions of *stalking* encompass a number of diverse but interrelated behaviors, such as making phone calls, following the victim, sending letters, making threats in some manner, vandalizing property, and watching the victim. Rather than

Weapons confiscated from students in Leon County, Florida. How are workplace violence and school violence related?

viewing these behaviors in isolation from one another, antistalking laws take into account the totality of the circumstances, so that seemingly benign behaviors are seen in light of how they are connected to other behaviors. This acknowledges that while sending unwanted letters might be seen as innocuous behavior, when this activity is combined with following the victim and standing outside his or her place of work or residence the behavior takes on a more threatening tone and may be the precursor for more serious offenses like assault, rape, and murder.[121]

The only national-level data on the nature and extent of stalking come from the National Violence Against Women Survey (NVAWS). For behavior to satisfy the definition of *stalking* used in the NVAW Survey, the respondents had to have reported victimization on more than one occasion and to have reported they were "very frightened or feared bodily harm."[122]

Employing these criteria, the survey asked individuals to report relevant experiences both over their lifetime and during the past 12 months. In the late 1990s, approximately 8% of women and 2% of men reported being stalked at some point during their life. Using the survey data to generate estimates for the general population, this means that about 1 in every 12 women (8.2 million) and 1 in every 45 men (2 million) are stalked at some point in their life. An overwhelming majority (90%) of individuals surveyed reported being stalked by only one individual during their life.[123] When a lower threshold of reported fear is used to measure stalking, the estimates are even higher: 12% of women and 4% of men reported being stalked at some point in their life, and 6% of women and 1.5% of men reported being stalked annually.[124]

Types of Stalkers A psychiatric study of 145 Canadian stalkers who had been referred to a forensic psychiatry center for treatment found that most were men (79%), and that many were unemployed (39%).[125] Perhaps not surprisingly, most (52%) had never had an intimate relationship. Five types of stalkers were identified as follows:

- **Rejected stalkers** who pursue their victims in order to reverse, correct, or avenge a felt rejection (for example, divorce, separation, termination)
- **Intimacy seeking stalkers** who want to establish an intimate, loving relationship with their victims, and

TV talkshow host Tyra Banks (L), and convicted stalker Brady Green (R). In 2009, Green was tried and found guilty of stalking Banks. What are the various kinds of activities in which stalkers engage?

may see the victim as a soul mate with whom they are fated to be

- **Incompetent suitors** who have a romantic or sexual interest in their victims despite having poor social or courting skills
- **Resentful, vendetta-motivated stalkers** who act out of a sense of wrong or a grievance against their victims, and whose intent is generally to frighten and distress the victim
- **Predatory stalkers** who spy on their victims in preparation for attacks, which are usually sexual in nature

Delusional disorders were found to be common among the stalkers treated, and 30% were determined to suffer consistently from delusions about those they stalked. Stalking behavior among those studied lasted anywhere from 4 weeks to 20 years, with an average of 12 months. Rejected and intimacy-seeking stalkers tended to persist the longest in stalking behavior. Sixty-three percent of the stalkers made threats toward their victims, and 36% were assaultive. The researchers concluded that "stalkers have a range of motivations, from reasserting power over a partner who rejected them to the quest for a loving relationship."[126]

Cyberstalking Another type of stalking, **cyberstalking**, has received attention as efforts progress to better understand the consequences of our increased reliance on electronic communication and the Internet.[127] While no standard definition of cyberstalking exists, this term refers to the use of electronic communication like e-mail or the Internet to harass individuals.

Washington, D.C.'s Holocaust Museum, which became the site of a hate crime killing in 2009. What are the characteristics of a hate crime?

In August 2005, Dennis Rader, the confessed Bind Torture and Kill (BTK) serial killer who terrorized Wichita, Kansas, for 30 years, was sentenced to ten consecutive life sentences behind bars. The sentence, imposed by Iowa judge Gregory Waller denied Rader any possibility of parole and meant that he would spend the rest of his life in prison.

Rader's murderous criminal career began on the morning of January 15, 1974, when he killed four members of the Otero family. They were the father, Joseph, mother Julie, 11-year-old Josephine, and 9-year-old Joseph II. Each victim was subjected to various acts of torture before ultimately being dispatched. The two males died from asphyxiation after Rader tied them up at gunpoint and placed plastic bags over their heads. The females were strangled, with Rader later reporting that the mother woke up after he thought she was dead, and had to be strangled again. In court testimony many years later he attributed the killings to sexual needs, and he apparently moltested at least one of the females. The four bodies were discovered when 15-year-old Charlie Otero returned from school later that afternoon.[i]

The Otero murders were the start of a long series of murders. Kathryn Bright, 20, was stabbed to death just three months later, on April 4, 1974. Amazingly, her 19-year-old brother, Kevin, survived the attack by Rader despite being shot twice in the head.

Almost three years elapsed before the BTK struck again on March 17, 1977, by strangling 26-year-old Shirley Vian. Uncharacteristically, the BTK locked the three young Vian children in the closet, permitting them to survive. Just nine months later, on December 8, 1977, police found Nancy Jo Fox, 25, dead in her bed-

room, strangled with a nylon stocking. BTK's final three killings occurred on April 27, 1985 (Marine Hedge), September 16, 1986 (Vicki Wegerle), and January 18, 1991 (Dolores Davis); all were strangled.[ii]

A strange component of the BTK murders was the way the killer periodically wrote taunting letters to the local police and newspapers. His goal seemed to be to receive some kind of credit for the murders. In some writings, he expressed his indignation that other suspects were being accused of crimes he had committed, or that the story of his murderous activities was not receiving adequate press coverage. "How many do I have to kill before I get my name in the paper or some national attention?" he complained in the letter in which he also coined his BTK nickname.[iii]

The frequency of the BTK letters decreased by the end of the 1980s, as he apparently became dormant. In 1991, Rader became a Park City Compliance Officer,[iv] where he developed a reputation as a by-the-book "bureaucratic bully."[v]

In March 2004, new BTK letters began surfacing. Over the course of the next year, a total of 11 communications were received. One, that had been mailed to police on a computer floppy disk, was forensically identified as having been created on Rader's church computer, and had electronic residue that included the name "Dennis." That disk directly led to Rader's arrest on February 25, 2005. At his arraignment on May 3, Rader stood mute, and a trial date of June 27 was set.

Rader subsequently surprised everyone when, on June 27, he confessed in open court to the murders of ten people. In response to direct questioning from the judge, Rader recounted in chillingly graphic and dispassionate detail exactly how he had killed each of his ten victims.

The Causes Behind the Crime
Dennis Rader (The BTK Killer)

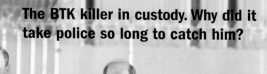

The BTK killer in custody. Why did it take police so long to catch him?

Can What We Know about Serial Killers Explain This Crime?

- Dennis Rader was born March 9, 1945, the eldest of four brothers. After high school, he did a four-year stint in the U.S. Air Force before returning to Park City, where he completed an undergraduate degree in administration of justice at Wichita State University in 1979. *Does Rader fit the profile of serial killers described in this chapter?*

- Beginning in 1974, Rader worked in a variety of positions at ADT Security Services over the next 14 years. Investigators believe that knowledge gained in this experience later enabled him to bypass home security systems so as to break into homes undetected.[vi] It was also in 1974 that Rader committed the first of what eventually became ten grisly murders. *Why did Rader kill? What other motivations might serial killers have?*

- Rader "hid for more than 30 years in plain sight."[vii] That's how a leading news service described Rader's evasion of capture for more than three decades. Rader lived a normal, rather mundane existence with his wife and two children. All the while, he concealed his second persona as a murderous predator. His "front" included his ordinance enforcement officer job in the Wichita suburb of Park City, service as a Cub Scout troop leader, and active participation in his Lutheran church.[viii] *How was Rader able to hide his crimes for so long? What can his behavior help us understand about serial killers?*

Author's Note: Graphic testimony from Dennis Rader's 2007 trial is available at http://www.kansas.com/214/story/16541.html.

NOTES:

[i]Marilyn Bardsley, Rachael Bell, and David Lohr, "BTK—Birth of a Serial Killer," CourtTV Crime Library, http://www.crimelibrary.com/serial_killers/unsolved/btk/index_1.html (accessed June 16, 2007).

[ii]Ibid.

[iii]"Neighbors Paint Mixed Picture of BTK Suspect," MSNBC, February 27, 2005, http://www.msnbc.msn.com/id/7036219 (accessed June 16, 2007).

[iv]"Report: Daughter of BTK Suspect Alerted Police," Cable News Network, April 19, 2005.

[v]Bardsley, "BTK—Birth of a Serial Killer."

[vi]"Neighbors Paint Mixed Picture of BTK Suspect," MSNBC.

[vii]Ibid.

[viii]Ibid.

Rader was once president of the church council at this Park City, Kansas, church. His use of a church computer to write a letter to police led to his arrest.

Go to mycrimekit.com to explore the following resources for Chapter 8:

- **MULTIMEDIA:** Videos about the types of violent crime, homicide, forcible rape, robbery, and aggravated assault
- **PRACTICE QUIZ:** Multiple-choice, true/false, short-answer, and essay questions
- **FLASHCARDS:** Thirty-three flashcards to test your knowledge of the chapter's key terms
- **WEB EXTRAS & LIBRARY EXTRAS:** Links to websites, online articles, and resources for violent crimes, homicide research, intimate partner violence, the FBI's Behavioral Analysis Unit, rape victims and rape law reform, sexual crimes against children, workplace violence, stalking and cyberstalking, robbery, and violence prevention
- **ENDNOTES:** Chapter 8 bibliography

Summary and Key Concepts

CRIMES AGAINST PERSONS

Crimes against persons is an offense category that includes violent personal crimes, such as murder, rape, robbery, and aggravated assault.

Crime Facts

To fully understand the nature of crime, it is necessary to gain an appreciation for crime statistics—including how they are gathered, how they affect our understanding of crime, and how they are accessed.

National Crime Victimization Survey (NCVS) A survey conducted annually by the Bureau of Justice Statistics that provides data on households that report they were affected by crime.

Uniform Crime Reporting (UCR) Program An FBI summation of crime statistics tallied annually and consisting primarily of data on crimes reported to the police and on arrests.

National Incident-Based Reporting System (NIBRS) A new and enhanced statistical reporting system that will collect data on each single incident and arrest within 22 crime categories. NIBRS expands the data collected under the UCR Program.

 Q: *What are the major differences between the Uniform Crime Reporting program and the National Crime Victimization Survey?*

The Uniform Crime Reporting Program

Part I offenses The crimes of murder, rape, robbery, aggravated assault, burglary, larceny, and motor vehicle theft, as defined under the FBI's Uniform Crime Reporting Program. Also called *major crimes*.

clearance rate The proportion of reported or discovered crimes within a given offense category that are solved.

 Q: *What are the major forms of violent crime?*

Changing Crime Patterns

Major shifts in crime rates occur because of demographics, economics, and other cultural factors. Three noteworthy shifts have occurred since the FBI began keeping national crime data.

dark figure of crime The large number of unreported crimes that never make it into official crime statistics.

self-report surveys A survey in which anonymous respondents, without fear of disclosure or arrest, are asked to report confidentially any violations of the criminal law they have committed.

National Youth Survey (NYS) A longitudinal panel study of a national sample of 1,725 individuals that measured self-reports of delinquency and other types of behavior.

Monitoring the Future A national self-report survey on drug use that has been conducted since 1975.

 Q: *What significant changes in crime rates have occurred since FBI record-keeping began?*

Murder

murder The willful (nonneligent) and unlawful killing of one human being by another.

criminal homicide The causing of the death of another person without legal justification or excuse.

first-degree murder Criminal homicide that is planned or involves premeditation.

second-degree murder Criminal homicide that is unplanned and that is often described as "a crime of passion."

negligent homicide The act of causing the death of another person by recklessness or gross negligence.

felony murder A special class of criminal homicide in which an offender may be charged with first-degree murder when that person's criminal activity results in another person's death.

Homicide: A Closer Look

sibling offense An offense or incident that culminates in homicide. The offense or incident may be a crime, such as robbery or an incident that meets a less stringent criminal definition, such as a lover's quarrel involving assault or battery.

victim precipitation Contributions made by the victim to the criminal event, especially those that led to its initiation.

Q: *What are the key issues to be considered in explaining patterns of homicide?*

Serial Murder

serial murder Criminal homicide that involves the killing of several victims in three or more separate events.

visionary serial killers Serial killers who hear voices and have visions that are the basis for a compulsion to murder.

comfort serial killers Serial killers who are motivated by financial or material gain.

hedonistic serial killers Serial killers who murder because they find it enjoyable and derive psychological pleasure from killing.

power seekers Serial killers who operate from some position of authority over others.

James Alan Fox and Jack Levin The vast majority of serial killers are not legally insane or medically psychotic.

Q: *What's the difference between serial murder and mass murder?*

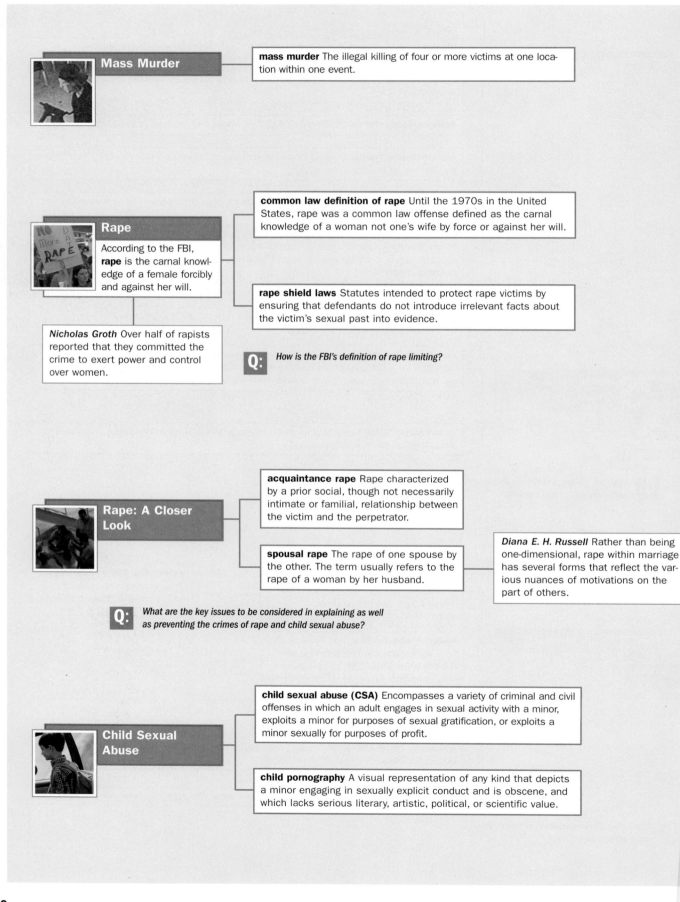

Mass Murder

mass murder The illegal killing of four or more victims at one location within one event.

Rape

According to the FBI, **rape** is the carnal knowledge of a female forcibly and against her will.

Nicholas Groth Over half of rapists reported that they committed the crime to exert power and control over women.

common law definition of rape Until the 1970s in the United States, rape was a common law offense defined as the carnal knowledge of a woman not one's wife by force or against her will.

rape shield laws Statutes intended to protect rape victims by ensuring that defendants do not introduce irrelevant facts about the victim's sexual past into evidence.

Q: *How is the FBI's definition of rape limiting?*

Rape: A Closer Look

acquaintance rape Rape characterized by a prior social, though not necessarily intimate or familial, relationship between the victim and the perpetrator.

spousal rape The rape of one spouse by the other. The term usually refers to the rape of a woman by her husband.

Diana E. H. Russell Rather than being one-dimensional, rape within marriage has several forms that reflect the various nuances of motivations on the part of others.

Q: *What are the key issues to be considered in explaining as well as preventing the crimes of rape and child sexual abuse?*

Child Sexual Abuse

child sexual abuse (CSA) Encompasses a variety of criminal and civil offenses in which an adult engages in sexual activity with a minor, exploits a minor for purposes of sexual gratification, or exploits a minor sexually for purposes of profit.

child pornography A visual representation of any kind that depicts a minor engaging in sexually explicit conduct and is obscene, and which lacks serious literary, artistic, political, or scientific value.

Robbery

robbery The taking of or attempting to take anything of value under confrontational circumstances from the control, custody, or care of another person by force or threat of force or violence and/or by putting the victim in fear of immediate harm.

highway robberies Robberies that occur on the highway or street or in a public place (and that are often referred to as a "mugging").

institutional robberies Robberies of commercial establishments, such as convenience stores, gas stations, and banks.

Q: *What are the different kinds of robbery?*

Q: *Is robbery primarily a rational activity? Why or why not?*

Aggravated Assault

aggravated assault The unlawful attack by one person upon another wherein the offender uses a weapon or displays it in a threatening manner, or the victim suffers obvious or severe bodily injury.

intimate-partner assault A gender-neutral term used to characterize assaultive behavior that takes place between individuals involved in an intimate relationship.

separation assault Violence inflicted by partners on significant others who attempt to leave an intimate relationship.

Q: *What's the difference between simple and aggravated assault?*

Other Forms of Interpersonal Violence

workplace violence The crimes of murder, rape, robbery, and assault committed against persons who are at work or on duty.

hate crime A criminal offense in which the motive is hatred, bias, or prejudice based on the actual or perceived race, color, religion, national origin, ethnicity, gender, or sexual orientation of another individual or group of individuals. Also called *bias crime*.

stalking A course of conduct directed at a specific person that involves repeated visual or physical proximity; nonconsensual communication; verbal, written, or implied threats; or a combination thereof that would cause a reasonable person fear.

cyberstalking The use of electronic communication like e-mail or the Internet to harass individuals.

Q: *How would you define workplace violence? What do we know about the offense?*

Crimes against Property
It's What We Lose

OHIO ORGA
CRIME TASK
EVIDEN
PROPER

The professional thief does not regard society in general as an enemy or perpetrate crimes against society because of hatred toward society. Rather than hate society, the professional thief rejoices in the welfare of the public. He would like to see society enjoy continuous prosperity, for then his own touches will naturally be greater.

–Edwin Sutherland

CRIMINOLOGY
INTERACTIVE

In the **Types of Crime** section of Criminology Interactive, click on **Property Crimes**.

Types of Property Crime

Both the Uniform Crime Reporting (UCR) Program and the National Crime Victimization Survey (NCVS) report data on property crimes. According to the FBI, the major property crimes are burglary, larceny, motor vehicle theft, and arson (Table 9–1).

TABLE 9–1

Property Crimes Known to the Police, 2008

Offense	Number	Rate Per 100,000	Clearance Rate (%)
Burglary	2,222,196	730.8	12.5
Larceny	6,588,873	2,176.0	19.9
Motor vehicle theft	956,846	314.7	12.0
Arson	62,807	24.1	17.8
U.S. total	9,830,722	3245.6	

Source: Federal Bureau of Investigation, *Crime in the United States, 2008.*

Detective Andy Bodzar stands in front of items seized from members of a theft-to-order burglary ring that operated in and around Youngstown, Ohio. What's the difference between larceny and burglary?

Larceny-Theft

Larceny-theft is defined by the UCR Program as "the unlawful taking, carrying, leading, or riding away of property from the possession, or constructive possession, of another."[1] Just about anything can be stolen. In California during November 2000, for example, thieves stole "more than 1,200 young orange trees during nightly raids at the San Joaquin Valley, heartland of the state's citrus crop."[2]

The FBI reports that during 2008 there were an estimated 6.6 million larceny-thefts nationwide, and larceny-thefts accounted for an estimated 66.7% of all property crimes. The rate of larceny-theft is 2,176 per every 100,000 people living in the United States. On average, larceny-theft offenses cost victims an estimated $6.1 billion dollars in lost property annually.

Larceny is the most frequently occurring property offense according to both official data compiled by the FBI and data from the NCVS. Within the offenses subsumed under the category of larceny in UCR/NIBRS data, the largest category is theft from motor vehicles, followed by shoplifting and theft from buildings (Figure 9–1).[3] Offenses like pocket picking and purse snatching constitute a small percentage of all larcenies, less than 1% each. Just as rates of different offenses within the category of larceny differ, so, too, do estimated losses to victims.

As a form of theft, larceny (as opposed to burglary) does not involve the use of force or other means of illegal entry. For this reason, among others, larceny is a crime "less frightening than burglary because to a large, perhaps even to a preponderant extent, it is a crime of opportunity, a matter of making off with whatever happens to be lying around loose: Christmas presents in an unlocked car, merchandise on a store counter, a bicycle in a front yard."[4]

Shoplifting and Employee Theft

Thefts cost U.S. retailers a staggering $33.6 billion in an average year.[5] Some retail theft is shoplifting, but other theft is committed by store employees. "The theft of merchandise by employees can range from the simple act of walking out the door with stolen goods to complex schemes requiring the manipulation of documents and/or involving several employees."[6] Most of the employees engaging in theft of either cash or merchandise are short-term workers. They are typically found in retail establishments with higher-than-average sales and a significant degree of turnover in management. **Many retailers**

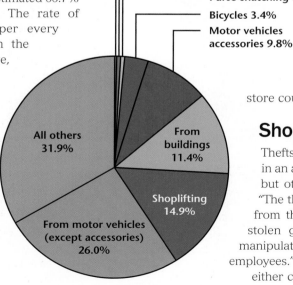

Pocket-picking 0.4%
From coin-operated machines 0.4%
Purse-snatching 0.5%
Bicycles 3.4%
Motor vehicles accessories 9.8%

All others 31.9%
From buildings 11.4%
Shoplifting 14.9%
From motor vehicles (except accessories) 26.0%

Due to rounding, the percentages may not total 100.

FIGURE 9–1 Larceny-theft distribution, 2008
Source: Federal Bureau of Investigation.

perceive the issue of internal theft to be much more serious than the economic loss caused by customer shoplifting.

Nonetheless, retailers must consider that efforts to combat shoplifting might impact sales. This concern was reflected by a marketing director who commented, "You don't want to hinder sales by intimidating the shopper. We used to think just about stopping shoplifting. We didn't think enough about selling more merchandise."[7]

Technology represents one of the best ways to address both shoplifting and employee theft. The use of computerized inventory counts to track merchandise is quite useful in quickly identifying thefts by employees. As will be discussed shortly, the widespread prevalence of shoplifting among youths who are fast and often operate together in small gangs means that increased security personnel in stores are less successful at detection than are electronic and other devices.

Shoplifting continues to be an offense that crosses class lines, although it is not an offense committed primarily by women. The dominant motivation used today to explain shoplifting does not rely on medical labels. Even though "respectable" people continue to be found among those who commit this offense, there is no evidence that these individuals constitute a significant segment of offenders.

Who Shoplifts?

On December 6, 2002, actress Winona Ryder was sentenced to three years of probation and required to perform 480 hours of community service for shoplifting more than $5,500 in merchandise from a Beverly Hills, Calfornia, Saks Fifth Avenue store a year earlier.

Ryder's case was not that of a typical shoplifter. In self-reports of offending, official arrest data, and store records,

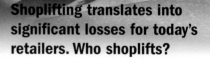

Shoplifting translates into significant losses for today's retailers. Who shoplifts?

juveniles are overrepresented as shoplifters. While variation exists in the frequency of offending among adolescents, most offending patterns are fairly sporadic and characterized by a greater prevalence among younger adolescents. The sporadic nature of shoplifting among adolescents is typical across all social classes, even though the most serious and chronic forms are found among the economically disadvantaged. While females represent the majority of offenders in some shoplifting data sources, this finding has been seriously challenged in research since the 1970s.[8]

Lloyd W. Klemke's research, which used self-report techniques to assess juvenile shoplifting, revealed that almost two-thirds of the sample had shoplifted at some point in their lifetime.[9] Although previous research by **Mary Owen Cameron** using department store records had revealed that females were more likely than males to be apprehended for shoplifting,[10] Klemke found the reverse to be true. The difference in these findings may be attributed to the fact that Klemke's research included only adolescents, whereas Cameron's research also included adults.

Youths from lower-income households are more likely to shoplift than their higher-income counterparts. However, this relationship is a moderate one at best, and the fact remains that shoplifting is reported by a solid majority of youths in several self-report studies. The relationship between social class and likelihood of shoplifting is stronger among adults.

Among Klemke's other findings was a "maturing out" pattern, whereby "shoplifting activity peaked in the under ten age category" and decreased considerably as the youths entered adolescence.[11] These findings are contrary to other research that supports escalation during late adolescence.

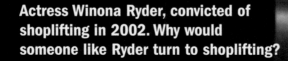

Actress Winona Ryder, convicted of shoplifting in 2002. Why would someone like Ryder turn to shoplifting?

Burglary

Burglary is a common crime. The FBI defines **burglary** as the unlawful entry into a structure for the purpose of felony commission, generally a theft. The structure may be a business, a residence, or some other type of building. Force is not a necessary ingredient of burglary, but the FBI distinguishes among burglaries involving forcible entry, unlawful entry, and attempted forcible entry.[12] Based on a recent examination of victimization data, 72% of households within the United States are burglarized at least once.[13] In contrast to lifetime risk, however, the risk of burglary occurring within any given year is much lower. Even so, burglary is feared because the offense invades the sanctity of the home and threatens the existence of businesses.

In 2008, according to the FBI, there were an estimated 2,222,196 burglaries throughout the country. In that year, burglary accounted for 22.7% of the total number of property crimes that were committed. In 2008, burglary offenses cost victims an estimated $4.6 billion in lost property, and the average dollar loss per burglary offense was $2,079. Burglary of residential properties accounted for 70.3% of all burglary offenses, and 36% of residential burglaries occurred during the daytime while 56.4% of nonresidential burglaries occurred during nighttime hours. Only 12.5% of burglaries were cleared by arrest or other means in 2008 (Figure 9–2).

In contrast to UCR/NIBRS reports, NCVS statistics on burglary paint quite a different picture. The NCVS reported 3,188,620 household burglaries and attempted burglaries in 2008—nearly 90% more than UCR/NIBRS estimates.[14] Rates of burglary were generally higher for African-American households than for white households, regardless of family income levels, although wealthy African-American families had far lower burglary rates than did low-income white families.

According to UCR/NIBRS data for 2008, the majority of burglaries involve forcible entry, followed in prevalence by unlawful entry and then by attempted forcible entry. Most residential burglaries are likely to occur during the daytime.[15] Most residential burglars commit their offenses at a time when residents are unlikely to be home. This is an important factor in their choice of target.

The consequences of both residential and commercial burglary can be profound for the victim. Residential

A burglar in action. Do all burglaries involve forcible entry?

burglaries, by definition, do not involve direct confrontation between the victims and the perpetrators, although the invasion of one's home produces a level of fear and apprehension beyond the dollar loss of the property taken. In cases of commercial burglary, because the targets are likely to be smaller, less stable businesses, the loss from burglaries can seriously affect the business's viability.[16]

The Social Ecology of Burglary

Burglary rates are higher in large metropolitan areas and in particular regions of the country, such as the South. Most research on variations in property crime at the aggregate level has examined how economics influences rates of crime. Lifestyle theory[17] and routine activities theory[18] have had a significant impact on explanations of how the nature and level of property crime offending have changed in response to alterations in the routine activities and structures of daily living. For a criminal act to occur, three ingredients are necessary: (1) someone who wants something (a *motivated offender*) coming into direct contact with (2) someone who has that thing (a *suitable target*) and (3) the lack of anything or anyone to inhibit the crime (a *capable guardian*).

Advances in technology have made televisions, radios, stereos, and other electronic devices lighter,

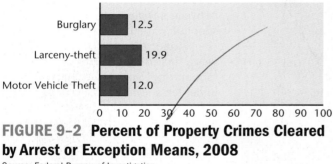

FIGURE 9–2 Percent of Property Crimes Cleared by Arrest or Exception Means, 2008

Source: Federal Bureau of Investigation.

smaller, and more portable. Hence, they've become more suitable targets because they are easier to steal.[19] Consequently, some of the observed changes in crime rates since the 1970s, when downsizing of electronics began in earnest, are not solely related to an increased supply of motivated offenders, but to changes in the patterns of routine activities. **The basic contention of both lifestyle theory and routine activities theory is that what people do, where they do it, how often they do it, and with whom they do it all influence the risk of criminal victimization.** The idea is to explore not why people commit crimes, but rather "how the structure of social life makes it easy or difficult for people to carry out these inclinations," which are taken as a given.[20] The structure of everyday life in one's city, neighborhood, home, workplace, and so forth not only constrains the opportunity for individuals to act on inclinations to commit crimes, but also limits the ability of people to avoid victimization.

Residential Burglary

In a study of residential burglary, Lawrence E. Cohen and David Cantor set out to resolve often contradictory findings of previous research on the relationship between the impact of income and race on burglary victimization.[21] Cohen and Cantor found that, independent of race, the highest income households and the lowest income households in areas both within and outside the central city had the highest victimization risk. Their findings appear to show that high income

and low income households are both targeted—one because it is thought to have items of special value, and the other because it provides ease of access.

The Costs of Burglary

According to the NCVS, well over three-fourths (86%) of all household burglaries involve some type of economic loss. Approximately 20% of household burglaries involve losses exceeding $1,000, with 21% involving loss amounts between $250 and $1,000, 24% involving loss amounts between $50 and $249, and slightly more than 14% involving losses under $50.[22] Remaining categories, not described here, total another 21%. Twenty-nine percent of items stolen from homes are personal in nature, with the largest category being jewelry or clothing. Household furnishings represent 11% of all stolen items, and tools and cash represent the items most likely to be stolen in about 12% (6% each) of incidents. Another type of crime cost can be gauged by looking at whether victims lose time from work as a result of their victimization. Among all victims of household burglaries, approximately 7% lose some time from work. Of this group, one-third lose less than one day, and slightly over one-half lose anywhere from one to five days, with the remaining 7% losing six days or more.[23]

Another cost can be found in stability of residence. Using NCVS data to test the relationship between criminal victimization and a household's decision to move, criminologist **Laura Dugan**'s research reveals that property crimes like burglary have a greater effect on the decision to move than do violent crimes.[24]

A burglarized home. What can the social ecology of burglary teach us?

Motor Vehicle Theft

The UCR Program defines **motor vehicle theft** as "the theft or attempted theft of a motor vehicle," where the term *motor vehicle* refers to various means of transportation, including automobiles, buses, motorcycles, and snowmobiles.[25] Automobiles are the type of vehicle most often stolen. Cars represent more than merely a possession; for many Americans they are an extension of their identity. The type of car one drives reflects social status and personal identity.

The theft of a car, then, violates the victim in a way that

percentage is higher (90%) for completed motor vehicle thefts than for attempted incidents (54%).[29] While the rate of motor vehicle victimization is the same for the lowest-income households (under $7,500) as for the highest-income households ($75,000 or more), the rate of reporting increases with the income level of the household.[30] Based on available data, approximately 62% of stolen cars are recovered.[31] Both law enforcement agencies and insurance companies keep records of recovered vehicles, but each uses its own definition of *recovery*, and some "recovered" cars may actually have been totally destroyed.

An auto thief hot wires a car. How do the motivations of car thieves differ?

goes beyond financial loss. Auto theft also makes it difficult for many people to get to work and sometimes requires them to take time away from work to take care of the incident.[26]

Approximately, 956,850 vehicles were reported stolen in 2008 (for an auto theft rate of 314.7 per every 100,000 people), with an estimated total value in excess of $6.4 billion (or $6,751 per vehicle stolen). The largest percentage of stolen vehicles was in a parking lot or garage at the time of the theft.[27] A significant percentage of motor vehicle thefts take place either at or quite near the victim's residence, with approximately 17% taking place on a street near the home.[28] Depending on the neighborhood in which the victim resides, *near home* can mean different things, and the same distance from the residence in urban communities may be more of a risk for motor vehicle theft than in other communities. Marcus Felson contends that the risks posed by where one parks are related to population density.

Based on data from NCVS, on average 81% of all motor vehicle thefts, both attempted and completed, are reported to the police. As is seen with other offenses, the reporting

Theft of Car Parts

Cars are stolen for a variety of reasons, including joyriding, temporary transportation needs, use in a crime, and stripping. Each of these rationales is representative of a fairly distinctive offender profile. Given the wide variety of rationales supporting automobile theft, almost any type of car is a target. However, thieves tend to prefer certain cars. According to Robert Bryant, chief executive officer of the National Insurance Crime Bureau, "Vehicle thieves follow market trends and target the most popular vehicles because they provide the best market for stolen vehicle parts and illegal export to other countries."[32]

Approximately one-third of stolen vehicles that are scored as "recovered" are completely stripped at "chop shops," and another third are stripped of easy-to-sell accessories like radios, air bags, and seats.[33] The theft of car parts is variously motivated. Some car parts are worth a significant sum on the illegal market and can be sold easily by even the most inexperienced thieves. Novice thieves usually do not have access to the type of network required to sell "hot cars." Also, stolen car parts are more difficult to identify than are entire cars.[34]

In the United States, the Motor Vehicle Theft Law Enforcement Act,[35] passed by Congress in 1984, "called for the marking of the major sheet metal parts of high-theft automobiles with Vehicle Identification Numbers (VINs). The point of the law was to enable detection of persons engaged in the presumably widespread sale of stolen parts to the auto body repair industry."[36] While data on how many car thefts are carried out for stripping are scarce, some research has been conducted in this regard both in the United States and elsewhere.

Joyriders: Car Theft for Fun

A certain percentage of car thefts are opportunistic in nature, committed by teenagers, usually in groups, for the purpose of fun or thrills. These offenses are referred to as **joyriding**. Because these thefts involve the temporary use of a vehicle primarily to satisfy needs ranging from excitement to personal autonomy, joyriding is often characterized as an "expressive act with little or no extrinsic value."[37] This motivation for auto theft is not characterized by planning and quite often involves an unlocked car left in a public place, frequently with the keys in the ignition.[38]

Most vehicles stolen for purposes of joyriding are recovered, usually found abandoned, often after they have been crashed. While adolescents may select a vehicle for joyriding that belongs to strangers, they are more likely to select the car of a known owner.[39]

Research offers no definite answer as to whether there is a distinctive social class profile of the joyriding offender. Some research indicates that higher social class can be associated with greater involvement in auto theft because of greater access to cars and an earlier association of cars as status symbols. On the other hand, the "disadvantaged-group hypothesis" contends that youths from lower socioeconomic classes are more likely to be involved in car thefts because conventional means of acquiring status symbols like cars are blocked, and they are left with only the avenue of illegitimate acquisition.[40] Although some support has been found for each of these perspectives, other research has failed to find a link between social class and involvement in auto theft among adolescents.[41]

While representing the most costly and most serious form of auto theft, professional thefts are not as common as thefts for other uses, such as joyriding. Like joyriders, professional auto thieves operate in groups, but their groups are characterized by a great deal more planning and calculation in target selection. The cars targeted by professional thieves are luxury cars that may be driven across national borders or shipped overseas. Professional thefts have the lowest recovery rates. Still, professionals are only a small part of the vehicle theft problem.

This car was stolen by joyriders. What tells you that professional thieves were not likely involved?

Arson

The FBI defines **arson** as "any willful or malicious burning or attempt to burn, with or without intent to defraud, a dwelling house, public building, motor vehicle or aircraft, personal property of another, etc."[42] It is only after a fire has been investigated and officially classified as arson by the proper investigative authorities that the FBI records the incident as an arson. Fires that are suspicious or of unknown origins are not included in the FBI's arson statistics.[43]

In 2008, the FBI received reports of 62,807 arsons the occurred throughout the country, for an arson rate of 24.1 offenses for every 100,000 inhabitants. Arsons involving structures (residential, storage, public, etc.) accounted for 43.4% of the total number of arson offenses. Mobile property was involved in 28.9% of arsons, and other types of property (such as crops, timber, fences, etc.) accounted for 27.7% of reported arsons. The average dollar loss due to arson was $16,015 per offense, while arsons of industrial/manufacturing structures resulted in the highest average dollar losses (an average of $212,388 per arson). In 2008, arson offenses decreased 2.6% when compared with arson data reported in 2007. Nationally, the clearance rate for arson was only 17.8% in 2008. Of all arson arrests, 37% involve juveniles—a higher percentage than for any other major crime. Additionally, 76% of arson arrestees are white, and 83% are male.

Several diverse motives may underlie arson, from profit to thrill seeking. On August 1, 2003, for example, a 206-unit San Diego condominium complex burned down while under construction. A 12-foot banner found at the scene declared, "If you build it, we will burn it." The banner was signed with the letters *ELF,* which stand for the Earth Liberation Front. Less than a month later, ELF arsonists attacked a number of car dealerships in Los Angeles, targeting those that sold gas-guzzling SUVs such as Hummers. Although one person was arrested, he was soon released.

The ELF, described as an ecoterrorist group by law enforcement officials, may have begun in California as the Environmental Life Force in 1977. The present-day ELF targets what it deems to be threats to the environment—including residential and commercial construction in environmentally sensitive areas, certain types of animal research facilities, and—sometimes—even Starbucks restaurants.

> Of all arson arrests, 37% involve juveniles—a higher percentage than for any other major crime.

This California fire was caused by arson. What were the arsonists' likely motives?

Three general groups of juvenile fire setters can be identified.[49] The first consists of children younger than 7 who generally start fires either accidentally or out of curiosity. The second group is children between the ages of 8 and 12 who may start fires out of curiosity, but "a greater proportion of their fire setting represents underlying psychosocial conflicts."[50] The final group, youths between the ages of 13 and 18, has had a history of fire setting, usually undetected. It is believed that many of the fires started by juveniles may go undetected by law enforcement officials because they are started on school property, perhaps even accidentally, and are discovered early by janitors or other school staff who do not report the incidents. In response to a growing awareness of the problem created by juvenile fire setters, several agencies and organizations, including the U.S. Fire Administration, have developed model programs to mobilize community agencies across the nation to deal more effectively with juvenile fire setters.

Between 1989 and 1996, a wave of arsons at predominantly African-American churches throughout the United States caused enormous concern that these arsons were hate crimes. The level of concern about church arsons resulted in President Clinton's signing of the Church Arson Prevention Act of 1996,[44] legislation designed to increase penalties for church arsons and to accomplish other objectives, such as the rebuilding of destroyed churches. The National Church Arson Task Force arrested 199 suspects in 150 of the 429 arsons under investigation and concluded that most of the arsons were the result of individuals acting alone rather than as part of an organized conspiracy.[45] While members of hate groups were certainly among the suspects arrested, so, too, were religious zealots, Satanists, and those motivated by revenge and greed. In November 1999, however, a minister and his accomplices were arrested for setting fire to their church; the suspected motive was a $270,000 insurance policy.[46]

Fire Setters

Whatever the motive, the vast majority of those involved in arson are juveniles. According to UCR/NIBRS data, juveniles represent the offenders in arson incidents at a much higher rate than is found in any other index offense; 49% of all arsons that are cleared are found to have involved a juvenile offender. Juveniles are a bit more likely to be involved in arsons in cities than in suburbs or rural areas. Overall, among the arson types, "juveniles account for 21 percent of the clearances for arsons of mobile property, 40 percent of structural arson clearances and 41 percent of clearances for arsons of all other property."[47] According to Jay K. Bradish, editor of *Firehouse* magazine, "Arson is the third leading cause of residential fires and the second-leading cause of residential fire deaths nationwide. Arson is the leading cause of deaths and injuries and accounts for the highest dollar loss in commercial fires."[48] In both residential and commercial arson, juveniles are involved more often than adults.

The remains of an African-American church in Alabama that was ravaged by an arson fire. Might such arson be classified as a hate crime?

Persistent and Professional Thieves

While legal distinctions separate the offenses of larceny and burglary, both are basically property crimes of theft and those who commit such offenses are thieves. While many thieves are persistent, this does not make them professionals. Willie Sutton, a famous bank robber, saw himself as a professional and defined a professional thief quite simply as "a man who wakes up every morning thinking about committing a crime, the same way another man gets up and goes to his job."[51] In a classic study of the professional thief, Edwin H. Sutherland defines this offender as one who "makes a regular business of stealing," plans carefully, possesses "technical skills and methods which are different from those of other professional criminals," and moves from locale to locale in offending pursuits.[52] The criminologist **Neil Shover** defines **professional criminals** as those "who commit crime with some degree of skill, earn reasonably well from their crimes, and despite stealing over long periods of time, spend rather little time incarcerated."[53] This is certainly not the profile of most offenders, who continue to commit crimes but never exhibit signs of a professional approach to crime. Rather than being viewed as professional, they are best understood as persistent.

Persistent thieves are those who continue in "common-law property crimes despite their, at best, ordinary level of success."[54] Rather than specializing, the vast majority of persistent thieves alternate between a variety of crimes like burglary, robbery, car theft, and confidence games. Even though they exhibit a generalist approach to offending, persistent thieves may have "crime preferences" that take the form of characteristics like "whether to avoid or to confront their victim(s)."[55]

Similarly, property offenders rarely have a preference for a particular kind of offense. A significant number of property offenders are fully immersed in a street culture and lifestyle characterized by a hedonistic approach to life and a disregard for conventional pursuits. Their everyday lives are usually filled with a wide array of petty crimes, including confidence games, gambling, and minor thefts.[56]

Shover, who has studied burglary and professional thieves, suggests that designations like "burglar" have little meaning if conceived of in a strict sense of exclusive offending. Many burglary offenders prefer this type of offending to other crimes like robbery because burglary does not involve direct contact with victims. Still, burglars may engage in other types of offenses, even occasional robbery, when the need for money arises.[57]

Because of the short-term and sporadic nature of their offending, property offenders are also known as **occasional offenders**.[58] The label "occasional" refers not to the frequency of offending but to the nature and character of offending. John R. Hepburn defines occasional property offenders as those whose crimes "occur on those occasions in which there is an opportunity or situational inducement to commit the crime."[59] This observation, which fits well with rational choice theory, has been confirmed in subsequent research, most recently in the work of Richard T. Wright and Scott H. Decker. Scott and Decker found that the burglars they interviewed are not a "continually motivated group of criminals; the motivation for them to offend is closely tied to their assessment of current circumstances and prospects."[60] This does not mean that offenders plan their crimes

The infamous bank robber Willie Sutton, under arrest in 1952. Sutton used many disguises and stole over $2 million before his career ended. Was Sutton a professional criminal?

carefully; it means only that they are seeking to achieve some personal benefit through criminal activity. Because an offender's assessment of the situation at hand may not even be accurate, some don't succeed in obtaining the benefits they desire. This is because they rarely have all the information they need, they do not devote enough time to planning their actions, they take unnecessary risks, and they make mistakes. This is how we all behave in everyday decision making and it is what theorists call *limited* or *bounded rationality*.[61] So, while some degree of rationality characterizes the criminal activity of most property offenders, it is limited.

The Criminal Careers of Property Offenders

Criminologists have long studied the criminal careers of offenders, both violent offenders and property offenders. The concept of a *career* reflects the same meaning as a traditional career to a limited extent. It implies a rational progression through defined stages, with some type of planning or formalized logic to the progression.

According to Alfred Blumstein and colleagues, a criminal career in property offending consists of three distinct phases.[62] The first phase is the "break-in" period, which characterizes the early years of an offender's career. It is a time when young offenders become increasingly committed to criminal careers and explore various kinds of criminality. During this period, residual career length (the expected time still remaining in a career) increases. The initial phase generally lasts for the first 10 to 12 years for a property offender's career. The second, or "stable" period, which begins around age 30 for those who first embark on criminal careers when they are around 18, is the time of highest commitment. It is the period in an offender's career when he or she identifies most closely with a criminal lifestyle; it is probably also the period when rehabilitation efforts are most likely to fail. The final, or "burnout," phase of a criminal career begins around age 40, says Blumstein. It is characterized by increasing dropout rates and by a lowered commitment to criminal lifestyles.

In a study of violent offending, however, D. S. Elliott and his colleagues examined data from the National Youth Survey and found that the careers of violent offenders were typically quite short—averaging just 1.58 years.[63] Only about 4% of subjects studied by Elliott had a violent criminal career of five years or more. Unlike other researchers, however, Elliott defined career length as the maximum number of consecutive years the individual was classified as a serious violent offender during the study period.

An assumption long attached to criminal careers was the idea that offending becomes more serious and more frequent over time, an assumption strongly challenged by Michael R. Gottfredson and Travis Hirschi.[64] While the idea of deviance and crime as an orderly process may be appealing for social policy purposes, evidence shows that crime is more a fragmented pursuit than a "career." Some researchers have found that while there exists certain logic to the lifestyle of most offenders, it is not one that easily complies with "a concept appropriate in a distinctly different culture (lawful society)."[65]

Property Offenders and Rational Choice

Research on property crimes is often scrutinized from the perspective of rational choice theories. One definition of *rationality* is "activities identified by their impersonal, methodical, efficient, and logical components."[66] While the decision making, motivation, and target selection of property offenders will be explored throughout this chapter, it is crucial to understand now that the rationality of the typical criminal offender is not the same as "the rationality used by the civil engineer."[67] In line with the research of Thomas Bennett and Richard Wright on the rationality surrounding decision making by burglars,[68] Walsh's research concludes that offenders employ a "limited, temporal rationality." Walsh says, "Not all these men are highly intelligent, and few are equipped to calculate Bentham-style, even supposing the information were available. Yet it is very common for rationality to be used. Of course it is partial and limited rather than total, but at the time, the actor feels he has planned enough and weighed enough data."[69] This is in many ways no different from the limited type of rationality that many conventional individuals employ in their daily activities. While some offenders, certainly those closer to the end of the continuum marked professional, will use a higher degree of rationality and still others will at times exhibit behavior that is totally senseless, most expressions of rationality are not as dramatically clear. The extent to which property crimes are rational pursuits for either expressive or instrumental gains is a question that will be addressed at places throughout this chapter.

A scene from the movie *The Italian Job*. How would rational choice theory explain a crime like the one depicted here?

Types of Burglars

While the image of the professional burglar is part of our popular culture, it does not accurately describe most burglars. **Mike Maguire offers three basic categories of burglars: low-level, middle-range, and high-level.**[70] *Low-level burglars*, primarily juveniles, often commit their crimes "on the spur of the moment," usually work with others, and are easily deterred from a target by secure locks, alarms, and/or other such security devices. The rewards gained from offending for this group are generally not significant, and many desist from burglary as they get older and as they feel "the pull of conventional relationships and fear of more severe adult sanctions."[71]

Middle-range burglars are generally a bit older, though they may have begun their offending in burglary as juveniles. These offenders quite often go back and forth between legitimate pursuits and involvement in crime. The use of alcohol and other drugs is more common among middle-range offenders than among the other two groups of burglars. These offenders select targets that take into account both the potential payoff and the risk involved; however, this group is not as easily discouraged by security devices as are the low-level burglars. While their take from their crimes may be substantial at times, they lack the connections for dealing in stolen goods on a large scale.

High-level burglars are professionals. Burglary is an offense characterized by a large prevalence of co-offending, and high-level burglars work in organized crews and "are connected with reliable sources of information about targets."[72] Members of this group earn a good living from the proceeds of their crimes, which are carefully planned, including target selection, generally with the assistance of outside sources. Professional burglars may be known to the police, but due to their "task-force approach to organization," their activities remain largely concealed from detection.[73] It is only high-level burglars who would attempt large-scale art thefts.

Burglary Locales

Burglars at any level may target both residences and commercial buildings. Police reports detail the time of the burglary; nighttime residential burglary and daytime commercial burglary are considered the most serious. Evening hours are the time that burglars are most likely to face homeowners, and daytime hours are the time considered to present the greatest risk of confrontation between offenders and customers or workers.[74] According to NCVS data, however, a larger percentage of residential burglaries take place during the daytime than during the evening hours.[75]

Burglary is known as a "cold" crime because there is usually very little physical evidence to link the offender to the offense, and by the time that the victims realize that they have been burglarized and have called the police, the burglar is usually long gone. This is truer of residential than commercial burglaries, as the latter are more likely to involve alarms or other security devices.[76]

Target Selection

Retail establishments are four times as likely to be burglarized as are other types of establishments, such as wholesale or service businesses. Based on a study of commercial

An open door may seem inviting to some burglars. How do different types of burglars select their targets?

burglaries in Philadelphia, researchers Simon Hakim and Yochanan Shachmurove offer three reasons for the dominance of retail stores as burglary targets: "The merchandise is exposed so that the burglar knows precisely what his expected loot is, the merchandise is new and enjoys a high resale value to a fence, and burglars do not need to spend intrusion time searching for the loot."[77] Because burglars can "survey the facility while legitimately shopping or browsing through the store," retail establishments, especially those located away from major thoroughfares in places where police response time will be slower, are prime targets.[78]

Burglars may select a target based on information from "tipsters," those who "regularly pass on intelligence about good burglary opportunities for a fee or a cut of the take."[79] Some offenders use tipsters who work in service capacities within households and businesses, while others act in collusion with insurance agents or other middle-class people who feed the offender information in exchange for money or for some of the stolen merchandise.

The ethnographic research that Wright and Decker conducted in St. Louis made clear that only very rarely is a burglary target chosen on the "spur of the moment," but the type of observation that went into the selection was often quite fragmented. Even so, fragmented observation may sometimes

> Some burglars select targets based on information provided by "tipsters."

be all that is required. Given the lackadaisical nature of much household security and the fact that approximately one-fourth of burglaries do not involve any type of forced entry, "the world affords abundant poorly protected opportunities for burglars."[80] This does not mean, however, that burglars are primarily opportunistic. An open door or window is viewed less as an opportunity to commit burglary and more as a sign that the residence is occupied and hence an undesirable target. More commonly, by chance alone, the offender happens to be in a place to observe the resident of a household departing.

Target selection is also influenced by other key elements. One of the most important is signs is occupancy because most offenders are reluctant to burglarize occupied dwellings. Burglars have reported that they avoid occupied homes because they want to avoid injury to their victims and to themselves. For some offenders, the fear of their own injury was greater than the fear of apprehension. Most residential burglars avoid residences with complex security devices because they generally lack the expertise to bypass the system. Even the offenders who engaged targets with alarms would only do so with certain alarms, again because of their lack of expertise. Dogs will deter an offender from a potential target as well. Many offenders will also choose a target that is in the same area and is in walking distance of their residence, because of a lack of access to cars. As one offender in Wright and Decker's research noted, "It's hard as hell getting on a bus carrying a big picture or a vase."[81]

Is a sign like this likely to deter what this chapter calls "high-level burglars"?

YOU ARE BEING VIDEOTAPED SMILE!

The Motivation of Burglars

Rational choice perspectives have guided a great deal of research on decision making among property offenders. Decision making is thought to be guided by the peculiar logic of the offender's perspective. The way in which offenders work out the logic of their decisions may not make sense objectively, but their decisions have their own internal logic from the standpoint of the offenders' social world.[82]

The most prevalent rationale behind the offense of residential burglary is the need for fast cash.[83] However, this need for cash is not necessarily characterized by the demand to satisfy the basic necessities of life or to maintain a conventional lifestyle. Based on ethnographic research conducted in Texas[84] and in St. Louis,[85] active burglars do not, as a whole, have a conventional lifestyle; most of their everyday concerns revolve around maintaining their street status and supporting a lifestyle of self-indulgence and often gratuitous consumption of drugs. Wright and Decker contend that the need to maintain a party lifestyle, to "keep up appearances," and to provide basic necessities for themselves and their families are all key factors that drive offenders' decisions to commit a burglary.[86]

As in the ethnographic research on the lifestyle of armed robbers, Wright and Decker found that the vast majority of the residential burglars they interviewed were committed to an "every night is a Saturday night" lifestyle. Thus, when offenders discussed their offending as a means of survival, it had to be interpreted against the backdrop of this lifestyle, for it was only within this context that an understanding of what they meant by "survival" emerged. The vast majority of offenders were committed to street culture, and almost three-fourths of the money they obtained from burglary went to support their lifestyle—a lifestyle that included illicit drugs, alcohol, and sexual pursuits. Keeping up appearances, another crucial part of street culture resulted in the "need" to buy things that helped them to maintain street status, such as the right clothes and the right car. While some of the offenders interviewed by Wright and Decker did use the proceeds from their burglaries to pay their bills, the researchers also note that "the bills were badly delinquent because the offenders avoided paying them for as long

as possible—even when they had the cash—in favor of buying, most typically, drugs."[87] Burglaries of commercial establishments are generally thought to be associated even more with instrumental ends, usually economic gain, than are residential burglaries. The same is true of professional burglars who invest more planning and strategy into their offenses. Far from operating from a standpoint of limited rationality, these offenders are calculating and carefully

The decision making of property offenders is thought to be guided by the logic inherent in the offender's perspective. What is the fundamental motivation of most home burglars?

Crimes against Property ● The Crime Picture

weigh risks and benefits. As Shover details in his work on burglars, professionals use quite sophisticated planning techniques because they are motivated to find targets with high payoffs.[88]

Because most of the offenders interviewed by Wright and Decker regarded themselves as hustlers, or "people who were always looking to get over by making some fast cash," they would commit offenses other than burglary if a chance opportunity presented itself.[89] Otherwise, they stayed with the familiar, which was burglary. For many, burglary was not as risky as selling drugs. Robbery was perceived as too risky because it involves direct confrontation with the victim and hence a higher likelihood of being injured. Some offenders stated that they did not own the necessary equipment for robberies—namely, guns. Because guns can be easily translated into cash in the street economy, "offenders who are in need of immediate cash often are tempted to sell their weapon instead of resorting to a difficult or risky crime."[90]

A small number of offenders in Wright and Decker's research in St. Louis indicated that "they did not typically commit burglaries as much for the money as for the psychic rewards."[91] This is consistent with Jack Katz's concept of sneaky thrills. As Katz contends, "If we looked more closely at how [offenders] define material needs, we might get a different image of these 'serious thieves.'"[92] Based on his ethnographic research with property offenders, Kenneth D. Tunnell concluded that "excitement was present but only as a latent benefit—a by-product of the criminal act."[93]

During the 1980s, an increased demand for crack cocaine changed the nature of criminal offending.

Drug offenders need fast money to pay for the substances they abuse. Which crime do they see as riskier: robbery or burglary?

The Burglary-Drug Connection

During the 1980s, the once parallel rates of robbery and burglary began to diverge, with robbery increasing and burglary decreasing. Using city-level data from 1984 to 1992, research by Eric Baumer and colleagues linked these changes to the effects that an increased demand for crack cocaine had in altering structures of offending.[94] As a stimulant, crack use is characterized by short highs that are then "followed by an intense desire for more crack."[95] If users are funding their drug habit through criminal pursuits, they need to rely on offenses that complement the demands of their drug of choice. This means that offenses like robbery, which can net cash quickly, directly, and at any time, are better suited to the habits and needs of crack users than is burglary, which is more likely to net stolen goods than cash.

Workers in Stolen Property

As previously discussed, a small number of thieves steal for their own consumption and steal mostly cash. In these cases, there is no need to translate the goods into cash. But in other cases, **it is necessary to turn stolen goods into cash.** In such cases, "there are many paths that stolen property may take from thieves to eventual customers."[96] Receiving stolen property allows for various levels of profit by individuals and groups with varying skill levels. Some burglars commit their offenses specifically to get something they know someone wants. In this case, the burglar may sell the merchandise directly to a waiting customer.[97] Burglars also may sell to people who are known to them or may take stolen goods to places like flea markets or auctions. Other paths to disposing of stolen goods include "dabbling middlemen" who buy and sell stolen property "under the cover of a bar, a luncheonette, or an auto service station with the encouragement, if not the active participation, of the proprietor."[98] Some burglars also sell their merchandise to legitimate retailers, representing it as legal goods.

The most complicated path from the thief to end users is through a **fence**. The use of a professional fence is the least common method of disposing of stolen goods for the majority of thieves, but it is the most common method used by professional thieves. **Carl Klockars**, a criminologist who studied the lives of thieves, detailed the career of a professional fence named Vincent Swaggi, who had worked as a fence for more than 20 years.[99] Building on Klockars's work, **Darrell Steffensmeier** defines a *fence* as one who "purchases stolen goods both on a regular basis, and for resale."[100] The most crucial defining characteristics of the professional fence, says Steffensmeier, are that he or she has "direct contact with thieves," "buys and resells stolen goods regularly and persistently," and thus is a "public dealer—recognized as a fence by thieves, the police, and others acquainted with the criminal community."[101]

The Role of Criminal Receivers

In their research on residential burglary, **Paul F. Cromwell** and his colleagues offer a three-part typology of criminal receivers: **professional receivers, avocational receivers,** and **amateur**

receivers.[102] *Professional receivers* are those who fit the definition provided by Steffensmeier. Use of a professional fence to dispose of stolen goods is uncommon among the majority of residential burglars, who lack "sophisticated underworld connections."[103] Such connections often distinguish "high-level burglars" from the more typical and prevalent residential burglars.[104] Burglars and other thieves who have relationships with fences have a number of advantages in disposing of stolen goods. The professional fence offers a safe and quick means of resale. This is especially the case with burglars who have committed a high-visibility crime, stealing goods that are easily recognizable. Fences are also the best outlet for a large volume of stolen goods, and this is one factor that distinguishes professional fences from other types. Some professional fences are "generalists" who deal in a wide variety of stolen goods, and others are "specialists" who deal only in certain types of goods. Goodman, the professional fence described in Steffensmeier's research, started as a specialist but evolved into a generalist as a "function of greater capital and a growing knowledge of varied merchandise."[105]

According to insights provided by Goodman, fences need several conditions in order to be successful. Since they deal in cash, they must have plenty of cash available. They must understand the trade by knowing acceptable prices and the right time to buy. They must have relationships with those who supply stolen goods and know those who will buy the goods, often with the knowledge that they are stolen. And, finally, they must have a relationship with law enforcement that may involve bribery or barter.

The majority of professional fences are involved in legitimate businesses that serve as cover for their criminal activity. A "partly covered fence," may, for example, operate a secondhand store whose inventory largely matches the stolen goods received. Fences who are "fully covered" do not deal in stolen goods that are outside of their inventory in their legitimate business. "Noncovered" fences are those whose "illicit lines of goods are distinct from the legitimate commerce."[106] **The more a fence is able to cover illicit activities by incorporating them into legitimate enterprises, the safer the fence is from criminal detection and prosecution.**

Fences use many types of businesses as fronts for criminal activity. They generally range from businesses seen by the "community-at-large as strictly clean," like restaurants, to businesses that "are perceived as clean but somewhat suspect," like auto parts shops and antique shops, to businesses that are viewed as "quasi-legitimate or marginal," like pawnshops.[107]

Some residential burglars avoid pawnshops when disposing of stolen goods because owners must often demand identification and take photos of those selling to them, and they have "hot sheets" of recently stolen goods. In addition, pawnshops generally do not provide the greatest return on stolen merchandise. Residential burglars who do regularly use pawnshops have probably established a relationship with the owner that enables them "to pawn stolen property 'off camera.'"[108]

A second type of fence is the *avocational receiver*. For this person, the buying of stolen property is a part-time endeavor "secondary to, but usually associated with, their primary business activity."[109] This is a fairly diverse group that can include individuals involved in respectable occupations, such as the lawyers or bail bondsmen who "provide legitimate professional services to property offenders who cannot pay for these services with anything but stolen property."[110] Others involved in illegitimate occupations, such as drug dealers, may also accept stolen goods in lieu of cash. As opposed to the professional fence, the avocational receiver is distinguished by the "frequency of purchase, volume of activity, and level of commitment to the criminal enterprise."[111]

Amateur receivers are those "otherwise honest citizens who buy stolen property on a relatively small scale, primarily, but not exclusively, for personal consumption. Crime is peripheral rather than central to their lives."[112] These individuals are sporadic in their involvement in activities that generate stolen goods. Cromwell and colleagues cite as an example a "public-school teacher who began her part-time fencing when she was approached by a student who offered her a 'really good deal' on certain items."[113] While these individuals do not engage in receiving stolen property at the same level as professional or avocational fences, "they represent a large market for stolen goods" because they "compensate for lack of volume with their sheer numbers."[114]

Professional fences provide a huge market for stolen goods. What kind of fence would provide a market for this work of art—a stolen Giuseppe Cesari masterpiece, recovered by Italian police in 2009?

Frank W. Abagnale, Jr., was a 16-year-old runaway when he made his first big score—$40,000—by printing up a bunch of bank deposit slips with his own account number (obtained, of course, under a false name) in magnetic ink. He then placed them at the service desk in the bank's lobby in place of the generic deposit slips provided by the bank for customer use. Other customers used the slips to make deposits, thinking that the deposit would be credited to their own accounts. In reality, the automated processing equipment read Abagnale's account number that he had magnetically encoded on the slip, and credited his account for the amount of the deposit. When the account balance reached $40,000, he simply withdrew the funds and closed the account.

A few years later, Abagnale impersonated a Pan American pilot for more than 24 months, but he wisely never attempted to fly a plane. He simply used the role as a means to obtain free air travel all over the world by invoking an employment perk that is common throughout the industry: being able to fly free in a "jump" or vacant seat.

It was this very scam that finally got the then-21-year-old arrested in 1969, when an Air France flight attendant recognized him from a wanted poster on the bulletin board in the employee's lounge. Abagnale subsequently served time in prisons in France (six months) and Sweden (six months) before he was finally extradited to the United States. Convicted of federal forgery charges, he received a 12-year sentence to federal prison.[i]

After Abagnale had served four years of his sentence, his tale significantly diverged from that of the ordinary felon. Because he had been so incredibly good at what he had done—he did, after all, confound the best investigators in the world for more than five years—Abagnale received an offer from the U. S. government that changed his life.

Seeking to learn how to prevent future Abagnale-like scams, the U.S. government asked Abagnale to teach them how he did the things he did and how to prevent them in the future. Specifically, they wanted to tap his innate ability to manipulate official documents in such a way as to virtually eliminate any chance of detection. In exchange, the government offered to immediately release him from prison.[ii]

And that is how Frank Abagnale, the most successful con man of the twentieth century, morphed into a world-renowned expert on forgery, embezzlement, and document security. Today, he heads Abagnale and Associates, a highly respected secure document consultancy. Abagnale has become an extraordinarily successful author and lecturer whose speeches, according to multiple-Oscar-winner Tom Hanks, "may be the best one-man show you will ever see."[iii] In 2002, Abagnale's exploits became the subject of Steven Spielberg's highly successful film *Catch Me If You Can*.

The Causes Behind the Crime
Frank W. Abagnale, Jr.

Can What We Know about Professional Thieves Help to Explain Abagnale's Behavior?

- Born April 17, 1948, Frank Abagnale started his life of crime by conning his father out of $2,500 just after the younger Abagnale's sixteenth birthday. Allowed to use his father's gas credit card, Abagnale schemed for spending money by using the card to buy tires from a gas station, then sell them back to the station owner at half price for cash.[iv] The scam was discovered at the same time that Abagnale's parents were divorcing, which gave him an excuse to run off to New York. *What might life course theory say about Abagnale's early deviance? How did his behavior differ from others who commit property crimes?*

- Abagnale simply assumed any role that needed a credential and let people assume that he had it—or helped people assume he had it by showing convincing forgeries of qualifying documents. Airline pilot? Not a problem for a guy wearing the right uniform and carrying a fake ID card.

Frank Abagnale impersonating a Pan American Airlines copilot in the 1960s.

Leonardo DiCaprio plays Abagnale in a scene from the movie *Catch Me If You Can*.

[ii]Ibid.

[iii]Keppler Speakers home page, http://www.kepplerspeakers.com/speakers/speakers.asp?1+EV+1175 (accessed May 21, 2007).

[iv]Bernie Alexander, "Frank Abagnale: From Fraud to FBI," AskMen.com, http://www.askmen.com/toys/special_feature/36_special_feature.html (accessed July 10, 2007).

[v]Norman Swan, "Frank Abagnale–New Life," *Life Matters*, March 17, 2000, http://www.abc.net.au/rn/talks/lm/stories/s111098.htm (accessed July 10, 2007).

Abagnale today. Would you trust him to secure your valuables?

Lawyer? Simply forge a Harvard Law diploma, pass the bar, and hire on as a staff attorney in a state attorney general's office. Pediatrician? College professor at Brigham Young University? Stockbroker? FBI Agent? (Yes, FBI Agent!) These are but a few of the personas this bright and charming phony assumed during a five-year con spree in the 1960s.[v] *Why did Abagnale persist in criminal behavior, even though he knew he'd probably get caught? Abagnale has developed a fraud prevention business. How do you think this criminal skill crime has aided his new professional career?*

NOTES:

[i]Rachael Bell, "Skywayman: The Story of Frank W. Abagnale Jr.," CourtTV Crime Library, http://www.crimelibrary.com/criminal_mind/scams/frank_abagnale/index.html (accessed July 10, 2007).

Go to mycrimekit.com to explore the following resources for Chapter 9:

- **MULTIMEDIA:** Videos about an introduction to property crime, burglary, larceny-theft, motor vehicle theft, and arson
- **PRACTICE QUIZ:** Multiple-choice, true/false, short-answer, and essay questions
- **FLASHCARDS:** Eleven flashcards to test your knowledge of the chapter's key terms
- **WEB EXTRAS & LIBRARY EXTRAS:** Links to websites, online articles, and resources for data and trends in property crime, juvenile arson, motor vehicle theft, shoplifting, art theft recovery, regulating markets for stolen goods, campus crime and security, and the Earth Liberation Front
- **ENDNOTES:** Chapter 9 bibliography

PEARSON **mycrimekit**

Summary and Key Concepts

CRIMES AGAINST PROPERTY

Property crimes are distinguished from violent personal crimes because they target things rather than people.

Types of Property Crime

According to the FBI, the major property crimes are burglary, larceny, motor vehicle theft, and arson.

 Q: *What are the major forms of property crime?*

Larceny-Theft

larceny-theft is the unlawful taking, carrying, leading, or riding away of property from the possession, or constructive possession, of another.

Q: *How does larceny-theft differ from burglary? From robbery?*

Lloyd W. Klemke Used self-report research to reveal that almost two-thirds of individuals had shoplifted at some time in their lives.

Mary Owen Cameron Used department store records to reveal that females are more likely to be apprehended for shoplifting than are males.

Burglary

The FBI defines **burglary** as the unlawful entry into a structure for the purpose of felony commission, generally a theft.

Laura Dugan Property crimes rather than violent crimes can cause a family to move from a neighborhood.

 Q: *How do the motivations of burglars vary? In what ways are they the same?*

Motor Vehicle Theft

Motor vehicle theft is "the theft or attempted theft of a motor vehicle," where the term *motor vehicle* refers to various means of transportation, including automobiles, buses, motorcycles, and snowmobiles.

joyriding An opportunistic car theft, often committed by a teenager seeking fun or thrills.

 Q: *What is a motor vehicle for statistical reporting purposes? What kinds of motorized vehicles are excluded?*

Arson

Arson is any willful or malicious burning or attempt to burn (with or without intent to defraud) a dwelling, house, public building, motor vehicle, aircraft, or personal property of another.

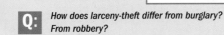

Persistent and Professional Thieves

professional criminal A criminal offender who makes a living from criminal pursuits, is recognized by other offenders as professional, and engages in offending that is planned and calculated.

persistent thief One who continues in property crimes despite no better than an ordinary level of success.

occasional offender A criminal offender whose offending patterns are guided primarily by opportunity.

Neil Shover Distinguished between persistent and professional thieves.

 Explain the difference between persistent and professional thieves.

Types of Burglars

Mike Maguire Offers three basic categories of burglars: low-level, middle-range, and high-level.

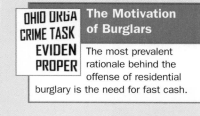

The Motivation of Burglars

The most prevalent rationale behind the offense of residential burglary is the need for fast cash.

Q: *To what extent are property offenders rational actors?*

Workers in Stolen Property

fence An individual or a group involved in the buying, selling, and distribution of stolen calls. Also called a *criminal receiver*.

Carl Klockars Used the case study method to detail the career of a professional fence.
Darrell Steffensmeier Studied the life of the professional fence.
Paul F. Cromwell Offered a three-part typology of criminal receivers: professional receivers, avocational receivers, and amateur receivers.

 What kinds of illegal activities are receivers of stolen property generally involved in? How do stolen goods get resold?

White-Collar and Organized Crime

Crime as a Job

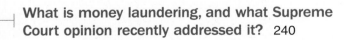

More money has been stolen at the point of a pen than at the point of a gun.
—*Woody Guthrie*

Two men can keep a secret, as long as one of them is dead.
—*Organized crime proverb*

CRIMINOLOGY INTERACTIVE

In the **Types of Crime** section of Criminology Interactive, click on **White-Collar and Organized Crime**.

White-Collar Crime

In 1939, **Edwin H. Sutherland** defined **white-collar crime** as violations of the criminal law "committed by a person of respectability and high social status in the course of his occupation."[1] Many criminologists do not properly understand crime, Sutherland claimed, because they fail to recognize that the secretive violations of public and corporate trust by those in positions of authority are just as criminal as predatory acts committed by people of lower social standing.

How has our understanding of white-collar crime changed over time?

Sutherland also noted that white-collar criminals are far less likely to be investigated, arrested, or prosecuted than are other types of offenders. In Sutherland's day, when they were convicted, white-collar offenders were much less likely to receive active prison terms than were "common criminals." The deference shown to white-collar criminals, said Sutherland, is due primarily to their social standing. Many white-collar criminals have been well respected in their communities, and many have taken part in national affairs.

Given these kinds of sentiments, criminologists felt compelled for years to address the question "Is white-collar crime really crime?" As recently as 1987, writers on the subject were still asking, "Do persons of high standing commit crimes?"[2] Although most criminologists today would answer the question with a resounding *yes*, members of the public were slower to accept the notion that violations of the criminal law by businesspeople share conceptual similarities with street crime. Attitudes, however, have quickly changed during the past few years as headline-making charges have been filed against a number of corporate scam artists and financial managers who duped investors out of billions of dollars.

Definitional Evolution of White-Collar Crime

The chief criterion for a crime to be "white-collar" is that "it occurs as a part of, or a deviation from, the violator's occupational role."[3] This focus on the violator, rather than on the offense, in deciding whether to classify a crime as white-collar was accepted by the 1967 Presidential Commission on Law Enforcement and Administration of Justice. In its classic report, *The Challenge of Crime in a Free Society*, members of the commission wrote, "The 'white-collar' criminal is the broker who distributes fraudulent securities, the builder who deliberately uses defective material, the corporation executive who conspires to fix prices, the legislator who peddles his influence and votes for private gain, or the banker who misappropriates funds in his keeping."[4]

Over the past few decades, the concept of white-collar crime has undergone considerable refinement.[5] The reason, according to the U.S. Department of Justice, is that "the focus has shifted to the nature of the crime instead of the persons or occupations involved."[6] The methods used to commit white-collar crime, such as the use of a computer and the Internet, and the special skills and knowledge necessary for attempted law violation have resulted in a contemporary understanding of white-collar crime that emphasizes the type of offense being committed, rather than the social standing or occupational role of the person committing it. Some reasons for this shift are changes in the work environment and in the business world itself. Others are pragmatic. In the words of the Justice Department, "The categorization of 'white-collar crime' as crime having a particular modus operandi [committed in a manner that utilizes

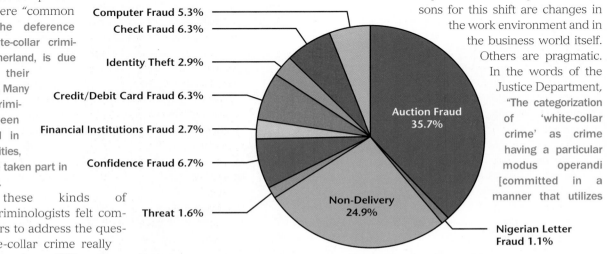

FIGURE 10–1 Top Ten Internet Crime Complaint Categories

- Computer Fraud 5.3%
- Check Fraud 6.3%
- Identity Theft 2.9%
- Credit/Debit Card Fraud 6.3%
- Financial Institutions Fraud 2.7%
- Confidence Fraud 6.7%
- Threat 1.6%
- Auction Fraud 35.7%
- Non-Delivery 24.9%
- Nigerian Letter Fraud 1.1%

Source: National White Collar Crime Center, *Annual Report, 2008*, p. 20; Web available at http://www.nw3c.org/research/site_files.cfm?fileid=4032feb1-9f5d-486a-8f76-10b29dc602ae&mode=p (accessed August 11, 2009).

White-Collar and Organized Crime ● The Crime Picture

deception and special knowledge of business practices and committed in a particular kind of economic environment] is of use in coordinating the resources of the appropriate agencies for purposes of investigation and prosecution."[7]

The National White Collar Crime Center (NW3C.org), for example, operates the Internet Crime Complaint Center (IC3.gov), and reports on white collar crimes committed via the Internet. Figure 10–1 shows the top ten Internet crime complaint categories recorded by the IC3 for 2008.

Occupational crime has recently emerged as a kind of new catchall category. **Occupational crime** can be defined as "any act punishable by law that is committed through opportunity created in the course of an occupation which is legal."[8] Occupational crimes include the job-related law violations of both white- and blue-collar workers.

What is occupational crime? How does it differ from white collar crime?

TABLE 10–1

The Terminology of White-Collar Crime

Antitrust violation: Any activity that illegally inhibits competition between companies and within an industry, such as price fixing and monopolies in restraint of trade. Antitrust violations are infractions of the Sherman Act (15 U.S.C. §§ 1–7) and the Clayton Act (15 U.S.C. §§ 12–27).

Bank fraud (also financial fraud or financial institution fraud): Fraud or embezzlement that occurs within or against financial institutions that are insured or regulated by the U.S. government. Financial institution fraud includes commercial loan fraud, check fraud, counterfeit negotiable instruments, mortgage fraud, and false credit applications.

Bankruptcy fraud: The misleading of creditors through the concealment and misstatement of assets. Bankruptcy fraud also involves illegal pressure on bankruptcy petitioners.

Economic espionage/trade secret theft: The theft or misappropriation of proprietary economic information (that is, trade secrets) from an individual, a business, or an industry.

Embezzlement: The unlawful misappropriation for personal use of money, property, or other thing of value entrusted to the offender's care, custody, or control.

Environmental law violation: Any business activity in violation of federal and state environmental laws, including the discharge of toxic substances into the air, water, or soil, especially when those substances pose a significant threat of harm to people, property, or the environment.

Government fraud: Fraud against the government, especially in connection with federal government contracting and fraud in connection with federal and/or federally funded programs. Such programs include public housing, agricultural programs, defense procurement, and government-funded educational programs. Fraudulent activities involving government contracting include bribery in contracts or procurement, collusion among contractors, false or double billing, false certification of the quality of parts or of test results, and substitution of bogus or otherwise inferior parts.

Health-care fraud: Fraudulent billing practices by health-care providers, including hospitals, home health care, ambulance services, doctors, chiropractors, psychiatric hospitals, laboratories, pharmacies, and nursing homes that affect health-care consumers, insurance providers, and government-funded payment providers, such as Medicare and Medicaid. Fraudulent activities include receiving kickbacks, billing for services not rendered, billing for unnecessary equipment, and billing for services performed by a lesser qualified person.

Insider trading: Equity trading based on confidential information about important events that may affect the price of the issue being traded. Because confidential information confers advantages on those who possess it, federal law prohibits them from using that knowledge to reap profits or to avoid losses in the stock market.

Insurance fraud: Fraudulent activity committed by insurance applicants, policy holders, third-party claimants, or professionals who provide insurance services to claimants. Such fraudulent activities include inflating, or "padding," actual claims and fraudulent inducements to issue policies and/or establish a lower premium rate.

Kickbacks: The return of a certain amount of money from seller to buyer as a result of a collusive agreement.

Mail fraud: The use of the U.S. mail in furtherance of criminal activity.

Money laundering: The process of converting illegally earned assets, originating as cash, to one or more alternative forms to conceal such incriminating factors as illegal origin and true ownership.

Securities fraud: The theft of money resulting from intentional manipulation of the value of equities, including stocks and bonds. Securities fraud also includes theft from securities accounts and wire fraud.

Tax evasion: Fraud committed by filing false tax returns or not filing tax returns at all.

Wire fraud: The use of an electric or electronic communications facility to intentionally transmit a false and/or deceptive message in furtherance of a fraudulent activity.

Sources: Cynthia Barnett, *The Measurement of White-Collar Crime Using Uniform Crime Reporting Data*, FBI, Criminal Justice Information Services Division, http://www.fbi.gov/ucr/whitecollarforweb.pdf (accessed June 18, 2009); Clifford Karchmer and Douglas Ruch, "State and Local Money Laundering Control Strategies," *NIJ Research in Brief* (Washington, DC: National Institute of Justice, 1992); and Legal Information Institute, *White-Collar Crime: An Overview*, http://www.law.cornell.edu/topics/white_collar.html (accessed July 1, 2009).

Corporate Crime

Corporate malfeasance, which is essentially another form of white-collar crime, has been dubbed "corporate crime." **Corporate crime** can be defined as "a violation of a criminal statute either by a corporate entity or by its executives, employees, or agents acting on behalf of and for the benefit of the corporation, partnership, or other form of business entity."[9] Corporate crimes come in many forms, ranging from prior knowledge about exploding gas tanks on Pinto automobiles and GM pickup trucks to price fixing and insider securities trading. Culpability, which often results in civil suits against the corporation along with possible criminal prosecutions, is greatest where company officials can be shown to have had advance knowledge about product defects, dangerous conditions, or illegal behavior on the part of employees.

In 2002, in an example of how corporations can be held criminally responsible for the acts of their officials, the accounting firm of Arthur Andersen was convicted of obstruction of justice after its employees destroyed documents related to Enron Corporation audits. Arthur Andersen, which had served as Enron's auditor, was forced to relinquish its U.S. licenses and closed its American offices. The company had also paid more than $130 million to settle issues relating to questionable accounting practices in its work with another company, Waste Management, in the late 1990s. The company had provided accounting services for WorldCom, Inc., prior to the arrest of that company's chief financial officer and other executives.[10] In 2005, however, the firm was at least partially vindicated when its conviction was overturned by the U.S. Supreme Court, which found that the instructions given to the jury in the 2002 trial had been flawed.[11]

In a somewhat similar but earlier case, aircraft maintenance company SabreTech was convicted in 1999 in federal court in Miami of eight counts of causing the air transportation of hazardous materials and of one count of failing to provide training in the handling of hazardous materials. The charges resulted from the actions of company employees in improperly packaging oxygen canisters, blamed for the 1996 crash of a ValuJet airplane in the Florida Everglades. In that disaster, 110 people died. The case marked the first time that a maintenance company faced criminal charges in connection with an

The financial debacle that grew out of the energy trading activities of Enron Corporation, and the infamous 1989 Exxon Valdez oil spill off the coast of Alaska are often cited by those who would hold corporations criminally responsible for the acts of their officials. Can a corporation be tried for criminal activity, just like an individual?

air disaster in the United States. The company, which went out of business, was also charged in state court with numerous counts of murder and manslaughter in the crash. "This is the first criminal homicide prosecution involving a passenger aircraft tragedy in the United States," said Florida state attorney Katherine Fernandez-Rundle.[12]

A relatively new area of corporate and white-collar criminality, which is defined solely in terms of violations of the criminal law, is that of crimes against the environment.[13] **Environmental crimes** are violations of the criminal law, which, although typically committed by businesses or by business officials, may also be committed by other individuals or organizational entities, and which damage some protected or otherwise significant aspect of the natural environment.

Whaling in violation of international conventions, for example, constitutes a form of environmental crime. So, too, does intentional pollution, especially when state or federal law contravenes the

> Crimes against the environment constitute a relatively new area of corporate and white-collar criminality.

practice. Sometimes negligence contributes to environmental criminality, as in the case of the 1,000-foot *Valdez* supertanker owned by Exxon Corporation, which ran aground off the coast of Alaska in 1989, spilling 11 million gallons of crude oil over 1,700 miles of pristine coastline. In September 1994, an Alaskan jury ordered Exxon to pay $5 billion in punitive damages to 14,000 people affected by the 1989 spill and another $287 million in actual damages to commercial fishermen in the region. Exxon also agreed to pay $100 million in criminal fines.

Other acts against the environment violate more conventional statutes, although their environmental impact may be obvious. The devastating fires set in oil fields throughout Kuwait by retreating Iraqi Army troops during the Gulf War in 1991 provide an example of arson that resulted in global pollution while negatively affecting fossil fuel reserves throughout much of the Middle East. These intentional fires, while properly classified as environmental criminality, also serve as an example of ecological terrorism because they were set for the purpose of political intimidation.

Causes of White-Collar Crime

When Edwin H. Sutherland first coined the term *white-collar crime*, he wrote, "A hypothesis is needed that will explain both white-collar criminality and lower-class criminality."[14] The answer Sutherland gave to his own challenge was that "white-collar criminality, just as other systematic criminality, is learned."[15] He went on to apply elements of his famous theory of differential association (discussed in Chapter 8) to white-collar crime, saying that "it is learned in direct or indirect association with those who already practice the behavior."[16]

Other authors have since offered similar integrative perspectives. Travis Hirschi and Michael Gottfredson, for example, in an issue of the journal *Criminology* published half a century after Sutherland's initial work, write, "In this paper we outline a general theory of crime capable of organizing the facts about white-collar crime at the same time it is capable of organizing the facts about all forms of crime."[17] Their analysis of white-collar crime focuses squarely on the development of the concept itself. Hirschi and Gottfredson suggest that if we were not aware of the fact that the concept of white-collar crime arose "as a reaction to the idea that crime is concentrated in the lower class, there would be nothing to distinguish it from other" forms of crime.[18] "It may be, then," they write, "that the discovery of white-collar criminals is important only in a context in which their existence is denied by theory or policy."[19] **In other words, nothing is unusual about the idea of white-collar crime other than the fact that many people are loath to admit that high-status individuals commit crimes just as do those of lower status.**

In fact, say Hirschi and Gottfredson, white-collar criminals are motivated by the same forces that drive other criminals: self-interest, the pursuit of pleasure, and the avoidance of pain. White-collar crimes certainly have special characteristics. They are not as dangerous as other "common" forms of crime, they provide relatively large rewards, the rewards they produce may follow quickly from their commission, sanctions associated with them may be vague or only rarely imposed, and they may require only minimal effort from those with the requisite skills to engage in them.

Hirschi and Gottfredson conclude, however, that criminologists err in assuming that white-collar criminality is common or that it is as common as the forms of criminality found among the lower classes. They reason that the personal characteristics of most white-collar workers are precisely those that we would expect to produce conformity in behavior. High educational levels, a commitment to the status quo, personal motivation to succeed, deference to others, attention to conventional appearance, and other inherent aspects of social conformity—all of which tend to characterize those who operate at the white-collar level—are not the kinds of personal characteristics associated with crime commission. "In other words," say Hirschi and Gottfredson, "selection processes inherent to the high end of the occupational structure tend to recruit people with relatively low propensity to crime."[20]

One other reason most criminologists are mistaken about the assumed high rate of white-collar criminality is because "white-collar researchers often take organizations as the unit of analysis" and confuse the crimes committed by organizational entities with those of individuals within those organizations.[21] Similarly, rates of white-collar offending tend to lump together the crimes of corporations with crimes committed by individual representatives of those organizations when making comparisons with the rate of criminal activity among blue-collar and other groups.

A complementary perspective by Australian criminologist **John Braithwaite** says that

> Edwin Sutherland said that white-collar criminality is learned, just like other forms of criminal activity.

What features might an integrated theory of organizational crime include?

When pressured to achieve goals that may be unattainable within the framework of laws and regulations surrounding their businesses, some business people may turn to crime. Why?

white-collar criminals are frequently motivated by a disparity between corporate goals and the limited opportunities available to businesspeople through conventional business practices.[22] When pressured to achieve goals that may be unattainable within the existing framework of laws and regulations surrounding their business's area of endeavor, innovative corporate officers may turn to crime to meet organizational demands.[23]

Braithwaite believes that a general theory covering both white-collar and other forms of crime can be developed by focusing on inequality as the central explanatory variable in all criminal activity.[24] Although alienation from legitimate paths to success may lead lower-class offenders to criminal activity in an effort to acquire the material possessions necessary for survival, greed can similarly motivate relatively successful individuals to violate the law in order to acquire even more power and more wealth.[25] New types of criminal opportunities and new paths to immunity from accountability arise from inequitable concentrations of wealth and power. Inequality thus worsens both crimes of poverty motivated by the need to survive and crimes of wealth motivated by greed.

Braithwaite also suggests that corporate culture socializes budding executives into clandestine and frequently illegal behavioral modalities, making it easier for them to violate the law when pressures to perform mount. The hostile relationship that frequently exists between businesses and the government agencies that regulate them may further spur corporate officers to evade the law. Braithwaite emphasizes his belief that the potential for shame associated with discovery—whether by enforcement agencies, the public, or internal corporate regulators—can have a powerful deterrent effect on most corporate executives because they are fundamentally conservative individuals who are otherwise seeking success through legitimate means.[26]

Braithwaite also recommends implementation of an "accountability model," which would hold all those responsible for corporate crimes accountable.[27] Rather than merely punishing corporations through fines, personal punishment meted out to corporate lawbreakers, says Braithwaite, should have the potential to substantially reduce white-collar offending.[28]

In sum, Braithwaite contends that an integrated theory of organizational crime would include insights garnered from (1) strain theories, as to the distribution of legitimate and illegitimate opportunities; (2) subcultural theory, as applied to business subcultures; (3) labeling theory, or the way stigmatization can foster criminal subculture formation; and (4) control theory, as to how potential white-collar offenders can be made accountable.[29]

Curtailing White-Collar and Corporate Crime

It is generally agreed that it is far easier to convict street criminals than white-collar criminals. It may even be difficult for prosecutors to show that a white-collar crime has occurred. "When someone breaks into a house and takes the TV and VCR," says Harvard University criminal law professor William Stuntz, "it's a matter of proving who did it. With white-collar crime it's usually not even clear what happened."[30]

White-collar crimes are often difficult to investigate and prosecute for a number of other reasons. For one thing, white-collar criminals are generally better educated than other offenders and are therefore better able to conceal their activities.[31] Similarly, cases against white-collar offenders must often be built on evidence of a continuing series of offenses, not a single crime, such as a bank robbery. Often, the evidence involved is only understandable to financial or legal experts and can be difficult to explain to jurors. Finally, business executives, because they often have the financial resources of an entire corporation at their disposal, and because they sometimes earn salaries and bonuses in the millions of dollars, are able to hire excellent defense attorneys and can tie up the courts with motions and appeals that might not be as readily available to defendants with lesser resources.

Events such as the 2001 collapse of Enron Corporation left investors around the world leery of American stock markets and forced federal legislators to enact sweeping financial reform. At the same time, the Securities and Exchange Commission (SEC) renewed efforts to enforce existing regulations and mandated new rules for investment bankers. By the start of 2001, the atmosphere of distrust that had been created by corporate criminals had become so severe that President George W. Bush felt it necessary to make significant efforts to help restore investor confidence and to bring order to American financial markets. Consequently, the president created a federal **Corporate Fraud Task Force** within the U.S. Department of Justice and on July 30, 2002, signed the **Sarbanes-Oxley Act** (officially known as the Public Company Accounting Reform and Investor Protection Act), which set stiff penalties for corporate wrongdoers.[32]

In 2007 the U.S. Department of Justice announced that activities of the task force had resulted in 1,236 fraud convictions, including those of 214 chief executive officers and 53 chief financial officers since 2002.[33] In announcing the convictions, then-attorney general Alberto Gonzales noted that "perhaps the most important accomplishment is the criminal conduct that never occurred because of the widespread deterrent effect" of the task force.[34]

The Sarbanes-Oxley Act has been called the most far-reaching reform of U.S. business practices since the time of Franklin Delano Roosevelt. The law authorizes funding for investigators and for the development of new technologies at the SEC targeted at uncovering corporate wrongdoing. Under the

President George W. Bush signing the Sarbanes-Oxley Act into law. What does the law require?

CORPORATE RESPONSIBILITY

The Securities and Exchange Commission grew out of the Great Depression of the 1930s. Is it still relevant today?

selling stock during periods when employees are prevented from making stock transactions in their retirement or 401(k) accounts.

The Sarbanes-Oxley Act was the latest in a long line of federal legislation relating to the conduct of U.S. business that extends back more than 100 years. Some of the earliest such legislation can be found in the federal Sherman Act,[35] which became law in 1890. The Sherman Act was passed to eliminate restraints on trade and competition and, specifically, to prevent the development of trusts and monopolies in restraint of trade. The Clayton Act,[36] passed in 1914, prohibits mergers and acquisitions in which the effect "may be substantially to lessen competition, or to tend to create a monopoly."

The Securities Act of 1933[37] and the Securities Exchange Act of 1934[38] were enacted by federal legislators reeling from the effects of the Great Depression, which began with the stock market crash of 1929. Often referred to as the "truth in securities" law, the Securities Act of 1933 has two basic objectives: (1) to require that investors receive financial and other significant information concerning securities being offered for public sale and (2) to prohibit deceit, misrepresentations, and other fraud in the sale of securities.

The Securities Exchange Act of 1934 gave birth to the SEC and conferred upon the SEC broad authority over all aspects of the securities industry. This includes the power to register, regulate, and oversee brokerage firms, transfer agents, and clearing agencies as well as the nation's stock exchanges. The act also identified and prohibited certain types of conduct in the markets and provides the SEC with disciplinary powers over regulated entities and persons associated with them. Finally, the act empowered the SEC to require periodic reporting of information by companies with publicly traded securities.

Sarbanes-Oxley Act, the SEC has the authority to bar dishonest corporate directors and officers from ever again serving in positions of corporate responsibility. Similarly, penalties for obstructing justice and for shredding documents are greatly increased, corporate officers who profit illegally can be forced to return their gains to investors, and the maximum federal prison term for common types of corporate fraud is increased from 5 to 20 years.

The Sarbanes-Oxley Act also requires chief executive officers and chief financial officers to personally vouch for the truth and fairness of their companies' financial disclosures and establishes an independent oversight board to regulate the accounting profession. The board is required to set clear standards to uphold the integrity of public audits and has the authority to investigate abuses and to discipline offenders. Similarly, the Sarbanes-Oxley Act prohibits auditing firms from providing consulting services that create conflicts of interest. Finally, under the law, officials in public corporations are barred from buying or

Certain forms of occupational crime may be easier to address than others. Individual occupational crimes especially may be reduced by concerted enforcement and protective efforts, including enhanced Internal Revenue Service (IRS) auditing programs, theft-deterrent systems, and good internal financial procedures. Consumer information services can help eliminate fraudulent business practices, and increases in both victim awareness and reporting can help target both businesses and individuals responsible for various forms of white-collar or occupational crime.

Organized Crime

Organized crime specifically refers to unlawful activities of the members of a highly organized, disciplined association engaged in supplying illegal goods and services, include prostitution, gambling, loan-sharking, narcotics, and labor racketeering. In 1967, the President's Commission on Law Enforcement and Administration of Justice investigated organized crime in the United States and found that—at the time—many organized crime families were of Italian descent. The Commission depicted the structure of a typical Italian-American organized crime family as shown in Figure 10–2.

Much of what most Americans traditionally think of today as organized crime—sometimes called the **Mafia** or **La Cosa Nostra**—has roots that predate the establishment of the United States. For hundreds of years, secret societies have flourished in Italy.[39] Italian criminal organizations that came to the United States with the wave of European immigrants during the late nineteenth and early twentieth centuries included the Mafia and the Black Hand. The Black

A New York City neighborhood around 1890. American organized crime got its start in the late 1800s and early 1900s. How did it begin?

Hand (in Italian, *La Mano Negro*) "specialized in the intimidation of Italian immigrants,"[40] typically extorting protection money and valuables.

The Mafia worked to become a quasi-police organization in the Italian ghetto areas of the burgeoning American cities of the industrial era—often enforcing its own set of laws or codes. Secret societies in Italy were all but expunged during the 1930s and early 1940s under Fascist dictator Benito Mussolini. Surviving Mafia members became vehemently anti-Fascist, sentiments that endeared them to American and allied intelligence services during World War II. Following the war, mafioso leaders resumed their traditional positions of power within Italian society, and links grew between American criminal organizations and those in Italy.

Other organized criminal groups, including Jewish and Irish gangs, flourished in New York City prior to the arrival of large numbers of Italian immigrants in the late 1800s. Ethnic succession has been as much a reality in organized crime as in most other aspects of American life. **Ethnic succession** refers to the continuing process whereby one immigrant or ethnic group succeeds another through assumption of a particular position in society.

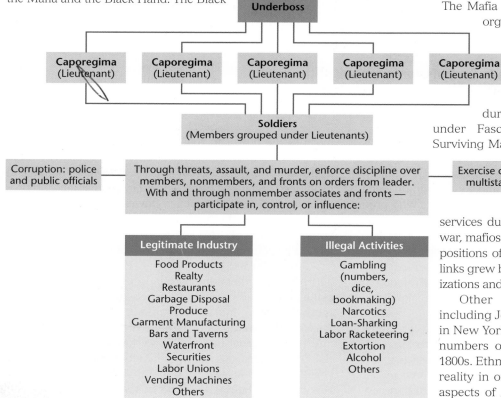

FIGURE 10–2 A Typical Italian-American Organized Crime Family

Source: President's Commission on Law Enforcement and Administration of Justice. *The Challenge of Crime in a Free Society* (Washington, DC: U.S. Government Printing Office, 1967), p. 47.

Throughout the late nineteenth and early twentieth centuries, for example, Jewish gangsters like Meyer Lansky, Benjamin "Bugsy" Siegel, "Dutch" Schultz, and Lepke Buchalter ran many of the "rackets" in New York City, only to have their places taken by Italian immigrants who arrived a few years later.

Around the middle of the twentieth century, organized criminal activity in the United States became the domain of Italian American immigrants and their descendants, especially those of Sicilian descent. Keep in mind that most Sicilians who immigrated to this country did not have ties or experience with Mafia organizations in the old country. Many Sicilian Americans immigrated to the United States to escape Mafia despotism at home, and most became productive members of their adopted society. The few who did involve themselves in organized crime created an organization known variously as the Mafia, the Outfit, the Mob, La Cosa Nostra ("our thing"), the syndicate, or simply the organization. Because Mafia is in the most widespread use, we will use it to describe Sicilian American organized criminal groups.

Prohibition and Official Corruption

In many ways, the advent of Prohibition was a godsend for Mafia leaders. Prior to Prohibition, Mafia operations in American cities were concerned mostly with gambling, protection rackets, and loan-sharking. Many mafiosi, however, were well versed in the manufacture of low-cost, high-proof, untaxed alcohol,[41] an expertise that had been brought from their native country. In addition, the existing infrastructure of organized crime permitted easy and efficient entry into the running and sale of contraband liquor. The huge profits to be had from bootlegging led to the wholesale bribery of government officials and to the quick corruption of many law enforcement officers throughout the country. Nowhere was corruption more complete than in Chicago, where runners working for organized crime distributed illegal alcohol under police protection[42] and corrupt city government officials received regular payoffs from criminal cartels.

American gangster Meyer Lansky descends the steps of a Manhattan court in 1958. What is ethnic succession?

Activities of Organized Crime

The 1976 federal Task Force on Organized Crime identified five types of activity that may qualify as organized crime: racketeering, vice operations, theft/fence rings, gangs, and terrorism. Throughout the past half century, Sicilian American criminal cartels have continued to be involved in (1) the establishment and control of both legalized and illicit forms of gambling, including lotteries, bookmaking, horse-race wagering, and bets on athletic contests; (2) loan-sharking, which involves the lending of money at rates far higher than legally prescribed limits; (3) large-scale drug trafficking; (4) the fencing of stolen goods, including securities; (5) infiltration of legitimate businesses, including labor unions and corporations that can be used as quasi-legitimate fronts for money laundering and other activities; and (6) labor union racketeering via which legitimate businesses are intimidated through threats of strikes, walkouts, and sabotage.

Organized crime is involved in many kinds of rackets, including gambling and the illegal copying and distribution of copyrighted software, music, and other forms of recorded media, including videotapes, compact discs, and cassette tapes. The provision of elaborately staged videotaped pornographic productions, including "snuff movies" (in which a sex "star" is actually killed in front of the camera), and elements of child pornography can also be traced to organized criminal activity.

A meeting of organized crime bosses in Chicago in 1978. How does official corruption contribute to the success of organized crime?

Other Organized Criminal Groups

According to **Howard Abadinsky**, a hallmark of true criminal organizations is that they function independently of any of their members, including their leaders, and have a continuity over time as personnel within them change.[43] Abadinsky describes the James Gang, which dissolved with the death of its leader, Jesse James. In contrast, says Abadinsky, "when Al Capone was imprisoned fifty years later, the 'Capone Organization' continued, and in its more modern form (the 'Outfit') it continues to operate in Chicago."[44]

There are other organized criminal groups in the United States. Among such criminal associations are groups that have been diversely referred to as the Black Mafia, the Cuban Mafia, the Haitian Mafia, the Colombian cartels, the Russian Mafia, Asian criminals (Chinese Tongs and street gangs, Japanese Yakuza, Vietnamese gangs, and Taiwan's Triads), and others. Included here, as well, might be inner-city gangs (the most well known of which are probably the Los Angeles Crips and Bloods and the Chicago Vice Lords), international drug rings, outlaw motorcycle gangs (such as the Hell's Angels and the Pagans), and other looser associations of small-time thugs, prison gangs, and drug dealers.

Noteworthy among these groups are the Latino organized bands, including Dominican, Colombian, Mexican, and Cuban importers of cocaine and other drugs. Although it is not known precisely how much cocaine has entered this country illegally, much of it has been handled by the Medellín and Cali Cartels, headquartered in Colombia, South America.

> Russian organized crime has grown quickly and has taken root in the United States and in other countries.

Transnational Organized Crime

While the focus of most organized crime scholars in this country has been on big-city crime families, transnational organized crime is emerging as one of the most pressing challenges of the early twenty-first century. **Transnational organized crime** refers to unlawful activity undertaken and supported by organized criminal groups operating across national boundaries.

Russian organized crime is of special interest, both because it has grown quickly following the collapse of the Soviet Union and because it has taken root in the United States and in other countries outside of the former Soviet sphere of influence.

With the dissolution of Soviet-style controls between 1992 and 1994, the Russian mafia quickly seized control of the country's banking system through the investment of ill-gotten gains, money laundering, intimidation, fraud, murder, and the outright purchase of financial institutions. Ninety-five Russian bankers were murdered by *Mafiya* operatives between 1995 and 2000, and hundreds of reform-minded business leaders and investigative journalists have been assassinated or kidnapped.[45] In September 2006, Russian Central Bank deputy chairman Andrei Kozlov was fatally shot as he left a soccer stadium in Moscow. Kozlov had been a crusader against money laundering and had suspended or withdrawn the licenses of dozens of banks. After Kozlov's death, President Vladimir Putin created a task force to combat financial crime.

The FBI says that there are 15 separate organized crime groups and 4,000 hard-core criminals from the former Soviet Union at work in the U.S. What kind of "work" do they do?

Florencia Molina, a victim of human trafficking, became virtually enslaved at a dressmaking shop on the outskirts of Los Angeles—forced to work 7 days a week without breaks. What is transnational organized crime?

The Analytical Center for Social and Economic Policies, a Russian think tank, estimates that four out of every five Russian businesses pay protection money to the mob.[46] In response to the wave of organized crime that Russia is currently experiencing, more than 25,000 private security firms have sprung up throughout the country. Analysts say, however, that few of these firms are legitimate, with many being fronts for Russian gangsters.[47]

Russian organized criminals differ from their counterparts in the United States because their ranks consist largely of ex-KGB officers, veterans of the 1979–1989 war in Afghanistan, underpaid military officers, and former Communist Party operatives who formed powerful economic alliances with traditional gangsters and black marketers years ago. As some observers note, Russian organized crime seems to be a natural outgrowth of the corrupt practices of officials who operated in the days of strict Soviet control, combined with a huge underground criminal black market that had already developed a complex organizational structure long before the Soviet Union fell apart.[48]

While Russian organized crime profits from American-style activities like narcotics, prostitution, racketeering, and illicit gambling, it is also heavily involved in human trafficking, product

Andrei Kozlov, 41, Russia's Central Bank first deputy chairman, became the victim of assassins' bullets in 2006. The attack was likely prompted by Kozlov's campaign to clean up the country's corrupt banking system. How might corruption in one country impact economic activity in others?

diversion and counterfeiting of popular Western goods (including software, video, and music duplication), and illicit arms sales and smuggling on a massive scale.

Over the past decade or two, hundreds of thousands of Russian citizens have immigrated to the United States. As U.S. officials have now discovered, many of these people were former black market profiteers and hard-core offenders who had been released by the KGB from the Soviet gulag.[49]

Russian organized criminal groups today operate out of 17 American cities in 14 states. According to one source, "The FBI believes there are 15 separate organized crime groups and 4,000 hard-core Mafia criminals from the former Soviet Union at work in the U.S. They are engaged in money laundering, automobile theft, smuggling, contract murder, loan-sharking, medical insurance fraud, narcotics, and credit card and telecommunications fraud. The theft of electronic serial numbers from cellular phones and the duplication (cloning) of these PIN numbers have grown into a multimillion-dollar industry."[50]

The globalization of crime has necessitated the enhanced coordination of law enforcement efforts in different parts of the world and the expansion of American law enforcement activities beyond national borders. U.S. police agencies routinely send agents to assist law enforcement officers in other countries who are involved in transnational investigations.

Organized Crime and the Law

For many years, American law enforcement agencies had few special weapons in the fight against organized crime. Instead, they prosecuted organized criminal operatives under statutes directed at solitary offenders, using laws like those against theft, robbery, assault, gambling, prostitution, drug abuse, and murder. Innovative prosecutors at times drew upon other statutory resources in the drive to indict leaders of organized crime. On October 17, 1931, for example, Al Capone was convicted on various charges of income tax evasion after federal investigators were able to show that he had paid no taxes on an income in excess of $1 million. Laws regulating the sale of alcohol and drugs and statutes circumscribing acts of prostitution have also been used against organized criminals, although with varying degrees of success.

The first federal legislation aimed specifically at curtailing the activities of organized crime is known as the Hobbs Act, a term that encompasses a series of statutes that were passed beginning in 1946. In essence, the Hobbs Act made it a violation of federal law to engage in any form of criminal behavior that interferes with interstate commerce. It also criminalized interstate or foreign travel in furtherance of criminal activity and made it a crime to use the highways, telephone, or mail in support of activities like gambling, drug trafficking, loan-sharking, and other forms of racketeering.

The single most important piece of federal legislation ever passed that specifically targets the activities of organized crime is the **Racketeer Influenced and Corrupt Organizations (RICO) Act**, which was part of the federal Organized Crime Control Act of 1970. The Organized Crime Control Act defines *organized crime* as "the unlawful activities of the members of a highly organized, disciplined association engaged in supplying illegal goods and services, including but not limited to gambling, prostitution, loansharking, narcotics, labor racketeering, and other unlawful activities of members of such organizations."[51]

The RICO portion of the act brought together under one single piece of legislation the many and diverse activities of American organized crime and made each punishable in a variety of new ways. RICO did not make racketeering itself illegal but, rather, focused on the ill-gotten gains derived from such activity, specifying that it shall be unlawful for anyone involved in a pattern of racketeering to derive any income or proceeds from that activity.

RICO's definition of *racketeering activity* includes

a. any act or threat involving murder, kidnapping, gambling, arson, robbery, bribery, extortion, dealing in obscene matter, or dealing in narcotic or other dangerous drugs, which is chargeable under state law and punishable by imprisonment for more than one year,

b. any act that relates to bribery, including sports bribery; counterfeiting; embezzlement from pension and welfare funds; extortionate credit transactions; fraud and related activity in connection with access devices; transmission of gambling information; mail or wire fraud; financial institution fraud; obscene matter; obstruction of justice; obstruction of criminal investigations; obstruction of state or local law enforcement; tampering with a witness, victim, or an informant; retaliating against a witness, victim, or an informant; interference with commerce; robbery; extortion; racketeering; interstate transportation of wagering paraphernalia; unlawful welfare fund payments; the prohibition of illegal gambling businesses; relating to the laundering of monetary instruments; engaging in monetary transactions in property derived from specified unlawful activity; use of interstate commerce facilities in the commission of murder-for-hire; sexual exploitation of children; interstate transportation of stolen motor vehicles; interstate transportation of stolen property; trafficking in certain motor vehicles or motor vehicle parts; trafficking in contraband cigarettes); and white slave traffic,

Alphonsus "Scarface" Capone, aka Al Capone.

At this Florida racetrack, gambling on horses is legal. Why is illicit gambling such a lucrative area of activity for organized crime?

c. any act that deals with restrictions on payments and loans to labor organizations, embezzlement from union funds,

d. any offense involving fraud in the sale of securities, or the felonious manufacture, importation, receiving, concealment, buying, selling, or otherwise dealing in narcotics or other dangerous drugs, punishable under any law of the United States, or

e. any act that is indictable under the Currency and Foreign Transactions Reporting Act.

Punishments provided for under RICO include **asset forfeiture**, which makes it possible for federal officials to seize the proceeds of those involved in racketeering. In the words of the statute, "Whoever violates any provision of this chapter shall be fined or imprisoned not more than 20 years (or for life if the violation is based on a racketeering activity for which the maximum penalty includes life imprisonment), or both, and shall forfeit to the United States, irrespective of any provision of State law any property derived from any proceeds that the person obtained, directly or indirectly, from racketeering activity or unlawful debt collection."[52] Hence, as a result of RICO federal agents are empowered to seize the financial and other tangible fruits of organized criminal activity, including businesses, real estate, money, equities, gold and other commodities, vehicles (including airplanes and boats), and just about anything else that can be shown to have been acquired through a pattern of racketeering activity.

Martha Stewart leaving federal court in Manhattan. Stewart was convicted of securities fraud and served five months in prison. What characteristics does Stewart share with other white collar criminals?

Money Laundering

Money laundering refers to the process by which illegal gains are disguised as legal income. A more formal definition is offered by the National Institute of Justice, which says that money laundering is "the process of converting illegally earned assets, originating as cash, to one or more alternative forms to conceal such incriminating factors as illegal origin and true ownership."[53]

Title 18, Section 1956 of the U.S. Criminal Code specifically prohibits what it calls the "laundering of monetary instruments" and defines *money laundering* as efforts "to conceal or disguise the nature, the location, the source, the ownership, or the control of the proceeds of specified unlawful activity." To assist in the identification of money launderers, a provision of the 1986 federal Money Laundering Control Act requires that banks report to the government all currency transactions in excess of $10,000. Similarly, the Bank Secrecy Act (BSA), formally known as the Currency and Foreign Transactions Reporting Act, requires financial institutions in the United States to assist government agencies in detecting and preventing activities related to money laundering. The law requires that financial institutions report cash transactions exceeding an aggregate amount of $10,000 daily per account, and to report suspicious financial activity to authorities. These requirements are well known to high-end money launderers, who routinely evade them by dealing in commodities like gold, by using foreign banks, or by making a series of smaller deposits and transfers, often involving numerous financial institutions.

Reliable official estimates of the amount of money laundered in the United States are hard to establish. In 1984, however, the President's Commission on Organized Crime estimated that approximately $15 billion of illicit U.S. drug proceeds move illegally every year into international financial channels.[54] Of that amount, $5 billion was thought to be taken out of the country as currency. In 2007, the Drug Enforcement Administration reported that estimates provided to it by the International Monetary Fund pegged worldwide money laundering activities at between 2% and 5% of the world's gross domestic product, or about $600 billion annually.[55]

A few years ago, the most notorious of foreign banks set up to serve the needs of money launderers, drug dealers, terrorists, and other assorted ne'er-do-wells was closed when banking regulators in the United States, England, and several other countries seized branch assets and arrested many of the bank's officers. The Bank of Credit and Commerce International (BCCI) was chartered in Luxembourg and opened branches throughout the world, including at least one in the Bahamas—islands already known for their role in providing infamous "offshore" banking services, which, while trading in currencies internationally, offer customers considerable secrecy and very limited reporting requirements.

BCCI soon grew into one of the largest banks in the world and opened offices in 72 countries. Its friends in the United States included former president Jimmy Carter, Washington lawyer Clifford Clark, and Orrin Hatch, a powerful senator.[56] Although evidence suggests that BCCI may have provided assistance to U.S. Central Intelligence Agency (CIA) operatives, it also "served to smuggle arms to Syria, Iran, and Libya, and to launder money for the Medellín cartel and Golden Triangle drug warlord Khun Sa."[57] After repeated indictments of top officials, BCCI closed its doors in 1991. During the decade or so that it was in existence, however, it is estimated that many billions of dollars flowed through its numerous branch offices, the majority of it from drug cartels and terrorist organizations seeking to hide the source of their revenues.

A portion of the $206 million seized by Mexican authorities from a methamphetamine ring in 2007. Most of the money is in U.S. dollars. What is money laundering?

In a now-famous case, Waldemar and Loretta Ratzlaf, two high-stakes Oregon gamblers, were acquitted of charges brought against them under the 1986 federal Money Laundering Control Act. What are the act's requirements?

If anything, the money laundering problem appears to be getting worse. A report by the Senate Permanent Subcommittee on Investigations found, for example, that "billions of dollars are now leaving our country every year to be put into the flow of commerce and returned to this country as laundered capital."[58]

In 1994, however, in what many experts saw as contrary to the trend in enforcement activities needed to curb organized crime and drug trafficking, the U.S. Supreme Court made money laundering convictions harder to obtain. The case involved Waldemar and Loretta Ratzlaf, high-stakes gamblers from Oregon with lines of credit at 15 casinos in New Jersey and Nevada.[59] In 1988, in an apparent attempt to hide $160,000 in gambling losses from the IRS, the Ratzlafs went to several banks in Nevada and California and bought cashier's checks of less than $10,000 each to pay the debt. Their check purchases came under IRS scrutiny as a result of an investigation into the couple's 1986 tax return. In that year, casino records showed that the couple had engaged in large cash transactions with a number of casinos, but they had reported no gambling income on their tax return.

> In 1994, the U.S. Supreme Court made money laundering convictions harder to obtain.

Authorities accused the Ratzlafs of "organizing financial transactions" to evade the currency-reporting requirement of the 1986 federal Money Laundering Control Act. Both Ratzlafs were convicted in federal court in Nevada on charges of conspiracy and interstate travel in aid of racketeering. Waldemar Ratzlaf was sentenced to 15 years in prison and fined $26,300, while Loretta Ratzlaf was sentenced to 10 months of home detention and fined $7,900.

The couple's lawyers appealed through the Ninth U.S. Circuit Court of Appeals and finally to the U.S. Supreme Court. The Court, in a 5-to-4 decision, found in favor of the Ratzlafs, saying that federal authorities had failed to prove that the couple knew they were violating the law.[60] The words of Justice Ruth Bader Ginsburg summarize the opinion of the majority: "Not all currency structuring serves an illegal goal. Under the government's construction an individual would commit a felony against the United States by making cash deposits in small doses, fearful that the bank's reports would increase the likelihood of burglary, or in an endeavor to keep a former spouse unaware of his wealth."[61]

In a separate dissenting opinion, however, Justice Harry A. Blackmun criticized the Court's majority, writing, "Waldemar Ratzlaf—to use an old phrase—will be laughing all the way to the bank."[62] Ratzlaf, said Blackmun, "was anything but uncomprehending as he traveled from bank to bank converting his bag of cash to cashier's checks in $9,500 bundles" to pay the debt.

Policy Issues: The Control of Organized Crime

In a cogent analysis of organized crime, **Gary W. Potter** tells us that "the question of what we [should] do about organized crime is largely predicated on how we conceptualize [of] organized crime."[63] To understand organized crime and to deal effectively with it, according to Potter, we must study the social context within which it occurs. Such study reveals "that organized crime is simply an integral part of the social, political, and economic system,"[64] says Potter. Any effective attack on organized crime, therefore, would involve meeting the demands of the consumers of organized crime's products and services. Potter suggests this can be accomplished either by punishing the consumers more effectively or by educating them about the perils of their own behavior.

Fighting corruption in politics and among law enforcement personnel and administrators is another track Potter suggests in the battle against organized crime. If organized crime has been successful at least partially because it has been able to corrupt local politicians and enforcement agents, then, Potter asks, why not work to reduce corruption at the local level?

Howard Abadinsky recommends four approaches to the control of organized crime, each involving changes at the policy-making level:[65]

- Increasing the risk of involvement in organized crime by increasing the resources available to law enforcement agencies that are useful in fighting organized crime.

- Increasing law enforcement authority so as to increase the risks of involvement in organized crime. Money laundering statutes that expand the scope of law enforcement authority, racketeering laws, and forfeiture statutes all may be helpful in this regard.[66]

- Reducing the economic lure of involvement in organized crime by making legitimate opportunities more readily available. Educational programs, scholarships, job-training initiatives, and so on might all play a role in such a strategy.

- Decreasing organized criminal opportunity through decriminalization or legalization. This last strategy is perhaps the most controversial. It would decriminalize or legalize many of the activities from which organized crime now draws income, including state-run gambling and the ready and legitimate availability of narcotics.

Strict enforcement of existing laws is another option. It is a strategy that has been used with considerable success by a number of federal and state law enforcement operations that have targeted organized crime. In 1987, for example,

Mob boss John Gotti, right, confers with his lawyers in U.S. District Court prior to his 1992 conviction of multiple felonies. Gotti died in prison in 2002. What can be done to better control the activities of organized crime?

Victoria Gotti, center, daughter of the late mob boss John Gotti and her sons John, left, Frank, and Carmine Gotti Agnello pose for photographers in 2004 in New York City after attending a viewing of the TV reality show, *Growing Up Gotti*. Why is the American public so interested in organized crime?

Nicholas "The Crow" Caramandi agreed to testify in 11 criminal trials against organized crime figures, resulting in more than 52 convictions, mostly in the Pennsylvania and New Jersey areas. Caramandi had bargained for lessened sentences in his own convictions on murder, racketeering, and extortion charges. A few years ago, Caramandi was released from prison and now lives far from Philadelphia under the federal witness relocation program with a new identity and a mob-ordered sentence of death hanging over him.

Some say that in the face of increased law enforcement pressure, the Mafia is doomed. According to the FBI, most major crime families have now been decimated by enhanced investigation efforts, often supplemented by wiretaps and informant testimony. The FBI claims that a total of 1,173 Cosa Nostra bosses, soldiers, and associates throughout the country have been convicted during the last six years alone. Imprisoned bosses now include not only New York's John Gotti, Jr., but also Los Angeles's Peter Milano and the leaders of Kansas City's Civella family. Also, a few years ago, 13 members of New England's Patriarca family were convicted of murdering Billy Grasso, one of their underbosses, and were sent to

prison. In 1999, federal authorities issued indictments charging 39 reputed members of five different New York City–area Mafia families with racketeering, murder, extortion, robbery, mail fraud, loan-sharking, illegal gambling, and trafficking in stolen property and counterfeit goods. Among those targeted was 54-year-old Vincent "Vinny Ocean" Palermo, reputed to be the acting head of the New Jersey–based DeCavalcante family.

Can the Mafia survive such pressure? Nicholas Caramandi says yes. "It's such a bureaucracy this thing of ours," says Caramandi. "You can't kill it. It's the second government. We serve needs. People come to us when they can't get justice, or to borrow money that they can't get from the bank. It never dies. It's as powerful today as it ever was. It's just more glorified and more out in the open."[67] The Mob, says Caramandi, reaches all the way to the highest levels of political power. Survival is ensured through well-placed friends in America's highest elected offices. Just before going to prison, John Gotti, Sr., told his underbosses, "This is gonna be Cosa Nostra till I die. Be it an hour from now or be it tonight or a hundred years from now, it's gonna be Cosa Nostra."[68]

> Some say that in the face of increased law enforcement pressure, the Mafia is doomed.

On July 24, 2009, convicted Ponzi schemer and formerly wealthy investment counselor Bernard (Bernie) Madoff arrived by prison bus at the federal correctional institution in Butner, North Carolina, to begin serving a 150-year sentence.[i] The 71-year-old Madoff had been convicted only days earlier of multiple fraud and securities violations stemming from a scheme in which he exploited thousands of clients who had entrusted him with their money for over 20 years. Among his victims were some very wealthy people from places as diverse as New York City and Palm Beach, Florida.[ii]

Some estimates put losses to investors as high as $65 billion dollars—money that seemed to evaporate into thin air, and which investigators struggled to recover. By the time Madoff went to prison, only about $1.2 billion had been found, and insurance payments of around $500,000 had been made to investors.[iii] Madoff's scheme has been called "the largest investor fraud ever committed by a single person."[iv]

In fact, Madoff may not have actually invested any of his client's money, instead paying off redemptions from his fund with money taken in from new clients. The false account statements that Madoff issued to "investors" showed their accounts rapidly growing in value—outpacing the investment results of even the most savvy investment managers. The stock market downturn of 2008, however, led to a record number of redemption requests—and when Madoff was unable to meet them, the game was up.

The Causes Behind the Crime

Bernie Madoff

Can We Understand Madoff's Crimes?

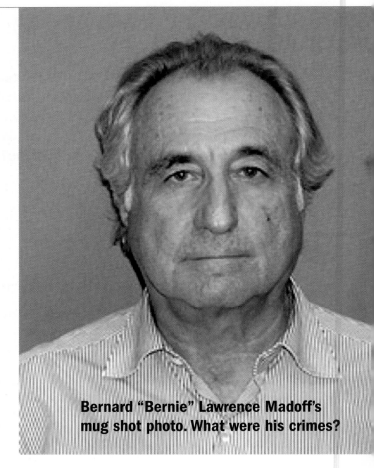

Bernard "Bernie" Lawrence Madoff's mug shot photo. What were his crimes?

- Born Bernard Lawrence Madoff on April 29, 1938, in Queens, New York, Madoff began his adult life as a plumber, and also worked as a lifeguard and landscaper. He soon went to college, graduating from New York's Hofstra University in 1960 with a degree in political science. A year later he dropped out of Brooklyn Law School to become a stockbroker, eventually rising through the financial ranks to serve as a chairman of the NASDAQ stock exchange. In 1960 Madoff founded his own firm, Bernard L. Madoff Investment Securities, LLC. He served as chairman of that company until his arrest on December 11, 2008. *Do you think that Madoff originally set out to build a Ponzi scheme? If not, how might the scheme have evolved?*

- Doubts about Madoff preceded his arrest by at least ten years, as his firm had faced a number of investigations by the SEC, some of which had apparently been dropped by the SEC for lack of money. *What can be done to ensure better enforcement in the future?*

- At the time of this writing, only one other person— Madoff's longtime accountant, David Friehling—has been charged in connection with the fraud, although authorities suspect that others must have been involved. Madoff refused to cooperate in the investigation, claiming that he was the only person with knowledge of the scam. Federal prosecutors reached a settlement with Madoff's wife under which she abandoned claims to $85 million in assets that the couple had owned, leaving her with $2.5 million in cash. The couple's sons, Mark and Andrew, both of whom had worked with their father, continue to deny claims of any wrongdoing. *Why haven't more people been arrested?*

- Some estimates put the actual amount of money lost in the fraud at around $10 billion, and say that

Madoff in better times, and after his arrest (below). Why wasn't he caught earlier?

additional moneys were merely paper losses shown on investment documents generated by Madoff, and were listed as gains on investments. *How would you compare Madoff to other white collar criminals? What do they have in common?*

- During the sentencing stage of the proceedings against him, Madoff apologized to his victims, saying, "I have left a legacy of shame . . . to my family and my grandchildren. This is something I will live in for the rest of my life. I'm sorry."[v] *Do you think that Madoff is truly sorry for his crimes, or merely for the fact that he got caught? How can we know?*

NOTES:

[i]Zachery Kouwe, "Madoff Arrives at Federal Prison in North Carolina," *New York Times*, July 14, 2009, Web available at http://www.nytimes .com/2009/07/15/business/15madoff.html (accessed July 21, 2009).

[ii]Michael Moore, "Bernie Madoff," The 2009 Time 100, Web available at http://www.time.com/time/specials/packages/article/0,28804, 1894410_1893837_1894189,00.html (accessed July 20, 2009)

[iii]The Ticker, *Washington Post*, July 14, 2009; Elizabeth Dwoskin, "Bernie Madoff's Accountant Charged, Pleads Not Guilty," *The Village Voice*, July 17, 2009, Web available at http://blogs.villagevoice.com/runninscared/archives/ 2009/07/bernie_madoffs.php (accessed July 21, 2009);

[iv]"Topic: Bernard Madoff," *New York Post* (various dates), http://www.nypost .com/topics/topic.php?t=Bernard_Madoff (accessed August 12, 2009).

[v]"Transcript of Madoff's Sentencing Statement," The New York Post, June 29, 2009, http://www.nypost.com/seven/06292009/news/regionalnews/ partial_transcript_of_madoffs_sentencing_176718.htm (accessed August 12, 2009).

Go to mycrimekit.com to explore the following resources for Chapter 10:

- **MULTIMEDIA:** Videos about the definition and extent of white-collar crime, corporate crime, definition of organized crime, and organized crime today
- **PRACTICE QUIZ:** Multiple-choice, true/false, short-answer, and essay questions
- **FLASHCARDS:** Seventeen flashcards to test your knowledge of the chapter's key terms
- **WEB EXTRAS & LIBRARY EXTRAS:** Links to websites, online articles, and resources about white-collar crime, check fraud, Enron, environmental crime, corporate crime and ethics, organized crime, and transnational organized crime
- **ENDNOTES:** Chapter 10 bibliography

PEARSON mycrimekit

Summary and Key Terms

WHITE-COLLAR AND ORGANIZED CRIME

This chapter distinguishes between white-collar, occupational, corporate, and organized crime.

White Collar Crime

The classic definition of **white collar crime** is "violations of the criminal law committed by persons of respectability and high social status in the course of their occupation."

occupational crime Any act punishable by law that is committed through opportunity created in the course of an occupation that is legal.

Edwin H. Sutherland White-collar crime is little understood by some criminologists because they fail to recognize that the secretive violations of public and corporate trust by those in positions of authority are just as criminal as predatory acts committed by people of lower social standing.

Q: *How does white-collar crime differ from most of the other kinds of criminal offenses discussed in this book?*

Corporate Crime

Corporate crime is a violation of a criminal statute either by a corporate entity or by its executives, employees, or agents acting on behalf of and for the benefit of the corporation, partnership, or other form of business entity.

environmental crime A violation of the criminal law that, although typically committed by businesses or by business officials, may also be committed by other people or by organizational entities and that damages some protected or otherwise significant aspect of the natural environment.

Q: *Is corporate crime a form of white-collar crime?*

Causes of White-Collar Crime

John Braithwaite White-collar criminals are frequently motivated by a disparity between corporate goals and the limited opportunities available to businesspeople through conventional business practices.

Q: *What leads people to commit white-collar crime?*

Curtailing White-Collar and Corporate Crime

White-collar crimes are often difficult to investigate and prosecute.

The U.S. Department of Justice's **Corporate Fraud Task Force**

The 2002 **Sarbanes-Oxley Act** (officially known as the Public Company Accounting Reform and Investor Protection Act) set stiff penalties for corporate wrongdoers.

Organized Crime

Organized crime refers to the unlawful activities of the members of a highly organized, disciplined association engaged in supplying illegal goods and services, including gambling, prostitution, loan-sharking, narcotics, and labor racketeering.

Mafia Another name for Sicilian organized crime, or *La Cosa Nostra*.

La Cosa Nostra Literally, "our thing." A criminal organization of Sicilian origin. Also called *the Mafia, the Outfit, the Mob, the syndicate,* or simply *the organization*.

ethnic succession The continuing process whereby one immigrant or ethnic group succeeds another by assuming its position in society.

Q: *What linkages, if any, might exist between white-collar and organized crime?*

Other Organized Criminal Groups

Other organized criminal groups include the Black Mafia, the Cuban Mafia, the Haitian Mafia, the Colombian cartels, the Russian Mafia, Asian criminals (Chinese Tongs and street gangs, Japanese Yakuza, Vietnamese gangs, and Taiwan's Triads), and so on.

transnational organized crime Unlawful activity undertaken and supported by organized criminal groups operating across national boundaries.

Howard Abadinsky A hallmark of true criminal organizations is that they function independently of any of their members, including their leaders, and have a continuity over time as personnel within them change.

 Explain the concept of ethnic succession.

Organized Crime and the Law

The first federal legislation aimed specifically at curtailing the activities of organized crime is known as the Hobbs Act, a term that encompasses a series of statutes that were passed beginning in 1946.

Racketeer Influenced and Corrupt Organizations (RICO) Act A statute that was part of the federal Organized Crime Control Act of 1970 and that is intended to combat criminal conspiracies.

asset forfeiture The authorized seizure of money, negotiable instruments, securities, or other things of value. In federal antidrug laws, the authorization of judicial representatives to seize all monies, negotiable instruments, securities, or other things of value furnished or intended to be furnished by any person in exchange for a controlled substance, and all proceeds traceable to such an exchange.

Money Laundering

Money laundering refers to the process of converting illegally earned assets, originating as cash, to one or more alternative forms to conceal such incriminating factors as illegal origin and true ownership.

 What is money laundering? How might it be reduced or prevented?

Policy Issues: The Control of Organized Crime

Organized crime is an integral part of the social, political, and economic systems in our society.

Gary W. Potter Any effective attack on organized crime would involve meeting the demands of the consumers of organized crime's products and services.

Q: *What strategies seem best to combat the activities of organized crime? Why?*

Public Order and Drug Crimes
Recreational Offenses

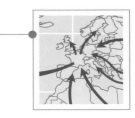

As the Republican governor of New Mexico, I'm neither soft on crime nor pro-drugs in any sense. I believe a person who harms another person should be punished. But as a successful businessman, I also believe that locking up more and more people who are nonviolent drug offenders, people whose real problem is that they are addicted to drugs, is simply a waste of money and human resources.
—*Former Governor Gary E. Johnson*

The Nature of Public Order Offenses

According to the criminal law, a **public order offense** is an act that is willfully committed and that disturbs the public peace or tranquility. Public order offenses include such things as fighting, disorderly conduct, vagrancy, loitering, public intoxication, obstructing public passage, and illegally carrying weapons. A **drug offense** is any violation of the laws prohibiting or regulating the possession, use, distribution, sale, or manufacture of illegal drugs. While public order and drug offenses are seen somewhat differently by the law, they share in common the fact that they are generally disapproved of, while not being as directly threatening to life or property as the more traditional violent and property crimes discussed in Chapters 8 (Crimes Against Persons) and 9 (Crimes Against Property). In a sense, we can think of both public order and drug crimes as *recreational crimes* because many of them are the kinds of offenses in which people tend to get involved when they have too much time on their hands.

History of Drug Abuse in the United States

The rampant and widespread use and abuse of mind- and mood-altering drugs is of relatively recent origin. Throughout the 1800s and early 1900s, the use of illegal drugs in the United States was mostly confined to a small group of artists seeking to enhance their creativity. Although it is true that medicinal elixirs of the period contained a variety of potent substances, including cocaine, alcohol, and opium, relatively few Americans were seriously affected at the time by any drug other than alcohol. One significant exception was opium, which was brought to the United States by Chinese immigrants and used in dens in West Coast cities. Opium eventually made its way across the country as a result of increased Asian immigration.

Psychoactive substances gained widespread acceptance during the hippie movement, a period of newfound freedoms embraced by a large number of American youths during the late 1960s and early 1970s.

Costs of Drug Abuse

The **Office of National Drug Control Policy (ONDCP)** estimates that Americans annually spend around $63 billion to purchase illegal drugs (see Figure 11–1). The true costs of drug abuse, however, are difficult to measure, but Table 11–1 and Table 11–2 quantify them in a way that makes sense.

Similarly, acquired immunodeficiency syndrome (AIDS), many cases of which can be traced to intravenous drug use, has proved to be a costly disease in social terms. Researchers at the Centers for Disease Control and Prevention (CDC) say that AIDS is already the leading cause of death of black and Hispanic men aged 25 to 44. AIDS, says the CDC, has become the second leading cause of death among black women aged 25 to 44. Homicide is the second leading cause of death for black and Hispanic men in that age group. The CDC finds 73 AIDS cases for every 100,000 black women, but only 5 per 100,000 white women. Of AIDS cases among minority women, 47% are traceable to intravenous drug use, while 37% appear to be due to heterosexual intercourse.

Other costs, such as lost productivity due to drug abuse, are estimated to total $77.6 billion annually. More than half of the total, or $43.8 billion, is estimated lost earnings due to drug-related crime victimization, while the remainder of the total is estimated to be suffered by drug abusers themselves.

Table 11–2 shows the estimated financial and social costs of illegal drug use in the United States per year. While Table 11–1 includes dollar amounts spent on system-wide efforts at drug control, Table 11–2 lists types of costs that are much more difficult to quantify.

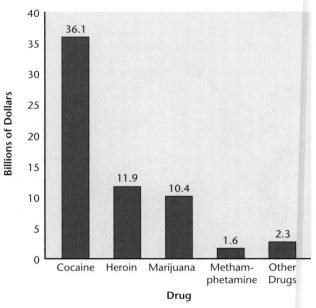

FIGURE 11–1 Annual Amount Spent on Illegal Drugs in the United States

Source: Office of National Drug Control Policy, *Drug Data Summary* (Washington, DC: ONDCP, 2003).

TABLE 11–1

Direct Costs of Illegal Drug Use

Type of Cost	Millions
Federal drug expenditures	$12,630
Law enforcement	3,200
Interdiction	2,600
International	1,150
Drug prevention	1,960
Drug treatment	3,720
State and local drug-crime expenditures	5,239
Enforcement of drug laws	2,007
Adjudication of drug-law violators	123
Correction of drug-law violators	3,071
State prisons	1,158
Local jails	890
Juveniles	224
Probation, pardon, and parole	677
Other corrections	122
Other criminal justice–related expenditures	38
Health care costs for illegal drug users	2,272
Short-stay hospitals	1,242
Specialty institutions	570
Office-based physicians	52
Support services	201
Other professional services	17
Medical care for drug-related AIDS cases	126
Support services for drug-related AIDS cases	64
Total	$20,141

Sources: Figures are the author's estimates from a variety of sources, including Office of National Drug Control Policy, *The National Drug Control Strategy* 2007 (Washington, DC: ONDCP, 2007); and Office of National Drug Control Policy, *National Drug Control Strategy: FY 2008 Budget Summary* (Washington, DC: ONDCP, 2007).

TABLE 11–2

Indirect Costs of Illegal Drug Use

Criminal Justice Expenditures on Drug-Related Crime
- Costs to prosecute drug offenders
- Investigating robberies, burglaries, and thefts for drug money and adjudicating and punishing the offenders
- Investigating assaults and homicides in the drug business (or by a drug user who has lost control) and adjudicating and punishing the offenders

Health Care Costs
- Injuries resulting from drug-related child abuse or neglect
- Injuries from drug-related accidents
- Injuries from drug-related crime
- Premature death
- Other medical care for illegal drug users, including volunteer services and outpatient services, such as emergency room visits
- Resources used in nonhospital settings

Lost Productivity Costs
- Lost time at work due to drug-related accidents
- Lost work time due to drug-related crimes
- Time away from work and home-making to care for drug users and their dependents
- Drug-related educational problems and school dropouts
- Offenders incarcerated for drug-related or drug-defined crimes

Other Costs to Society
- Loss of property values due to drug-related neighborhood crime
- Property damaged or destroyed in fires and in workplace and vehicular accidents
- Agricultural resources devoted to illegal drug cultivation or production
- Toxins introduced into public air and water supplies by drug production
- Workplace prevention programs, such as drug-testing and employee-assistance programs
- Protective efforts undertaken by potential victims of drug-related crime
- Pain and suffering costs to illegal drug users and their families and friends
- Private legal costs

Sources: National Institute on Drug Abuse and National Institute on Alcohol Abuse and Alcoholism, *The Economic Costs of Alcohol and Drug Abuse in the United States, 1992* (Washington, DC: U.S. Government Printing Office, 1998); Bureau of Justice Statistics, *Drugs, Crime and the Justice System: A National Report from the Bureau of Justice Statistics* (Washington, DC: U.S. Government Printing Office, December 1992); and *The Real Cost of the Drug War*, http://briancbennet.com (accessed, October 1, 2009).

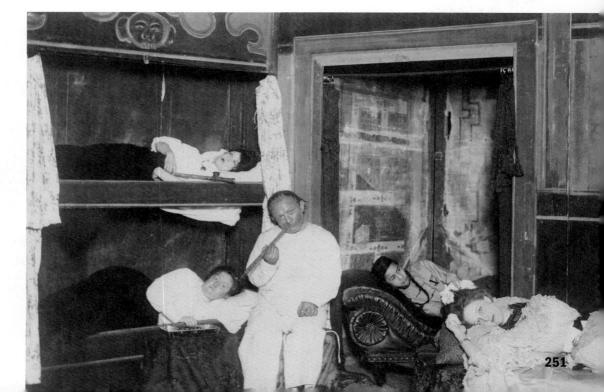

An opium den in New York City's Chinatown around 1900. Is drug use truly a "victimless" crime?

Types of Illegal Drugs

Controlled substances are grouped into the following seven categories: narcotics, depressants, stimulants, hallucinogens, cannabis, anabolic steroids, and inhalants. An eighth category, **dangerous drugs**, is used by the Drug Enforcement Administration (DEA) to refer to "broad categories or classes of controlled substances other than cocaine, opiates, and cannabis products."[1]

Stimulants

Stimulants include cocaine and crack cocaine, amphetamines like Dexedrine and Benzedrine, and methamphetamine. Stimulants stimulate the central nervous system and result in higher heart rate, elevated blood pressure, and increased mental activity. Legitimate uses of stimulants include increasing alertness, reducing fatigue, weight control, and topical analgesic (pain-killing) action. Such drugs are used illegally, however, by those seeking to produce states of excitability and feelings of competence and power.

Cocaine is available in powdered form or as small "rocks" of crack and is smoked. Crack cocaine, which is much less expensive than powdered cocaine, is made by mixing cocaine powder with water and baking soda or ammonia. It is usually smoked in a "crack pipe" and is named for the fact that it makes crackling sounds when burned.

Powdered cocaine is inhaled or snorted, but it may also be mixed with volatile chemicals and "freebased" or smoked or injected. Cocaine produces effects similar to other stimulants—euphoria, a sense of intense stimulation, a sense of psychic and physical well-being, and what may seem like boundless energy.

Other stimulants include amphetamines, which produce mental alertness and increase the ability to concentrate. They are used medically to treat narcolepsy, obesity, and some forms of brain dysfunction. Abuse produces irritability, overexhaustion, and—in cases of prolonged abuse—psychosis and death from cardiac arrest.

One drug that deserves special mention is methamphetamine, a stimulant related to other amphetamines but with stronger effects on the central nervous system. Street names for the drug include "speed," "meth," and "crank." Methamphetamine is used in pill form or in powdered form for snorting or injecting.[2] Crystallized methamphetamine, known as "ice," "crystal," or "glass," is a smokable and still more powerful form of the drug. The effects of methamphetamine use include increased heart rate and blood pressure, increased wakefulness, insomnia, increased physical activity, decreased appetite, and anxiety, paranoia, or violent behavior.

Depressants

The depressant family includes barbiturates, sedatives, and tranquilizers like Nembutal, Seconal, Phenobarbital, Quaalude, Sopor, Valium, Librium, Thorazine, and Equanil. Depressants are used legitimately to obtain release from anxiety, for the treatment of psychological problems, and as mood elevators. Illegitimate users employ these substances to produce intoxication, to counter the effects of other drugs, or as treatment for drug withdrawal.

Cannabis

The cannabis category includes marijuana, hashish, cannabis plants, sinsemilla, and hashish oil—all of which are collectively referred to as "marijuana." Marijuana is a relatively mild, non-addictive drug with limited hallucinogenic properties. Although legitimate uses for cannabis have not been fully recognized, some research suggests that the substance can be used in the treatment of pain and glaucoma and as a supplement to cancer treatments (cannabis appears to control the nausea associated with chemotherapy). Marijuana is used illegitimately to induce states of euphoria, gaiety, detachment, relaxation, intoxication, and focused

From left: Two forms of cocaine, crack and powdered; marijuana; and heroin. What are the physical and psychological effects of various types of illegal drugs?

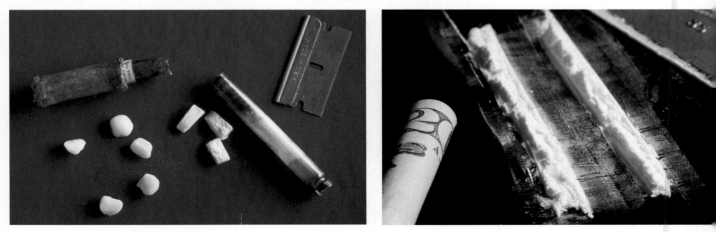

awareness. Time distortion, increased sex drive, enhanced appetite, uncontrollable giddiness, and short-term memory loss tend to accompany its use.

Most marijuana is smoked in the form of dried leaves, stems, and flowers of the marijuana plant (or, more accurately, the Indian hemp plant), although processed marijuana "oil" and the cake form of hashish are also widely available. Hashish is made from resins found on the surface of the female marijuana plant and is considerably more potent than other forms of cannabis.

Narcotics

Narcotics, including such drugs as opium, morphine, heroin, methadone, codeine, and Dilaudid, have a number of legitimate uses, including pain relief, antidiarrheal action, and cough suppression. Street use of these drugs is intended to induce euphoria, a lack of concern, and a general feeling of well-being. The use of narcotics produces drowsiness and relaxation, accompanied by a dreamlike state.

Heroin and morphine, which are generally sold as a white powder, are derived from opium and are injected into the body, although they may also be smoked or eaten. Sometimes users inject these drugs under the skin, a practice called "skin-popping," but most addicts prefer direct intravenous injection for the strong and immediate effects it produces.

Although narcotics, including heroin, tend to be highly toxic when taken in large doses, frequent users build up tolerances and require ever larger doses for the desired effects to be induced. Physical addiction may result and withdrawal may appear if the drug is not available. Withdrawal symptoms include nervousness, restlessness, severe abdominal cramps, watery eyes, nasal discharge, and—in later stages—vomiting,

St. Louis Cardinals slugger Mark McGwire (left) and Chicago Cubs slugger Sammy Sosa. Both men retired after a Congressional investigation into steroid use among professional baseball players.

diarrhea, weight loss, and pain in the large muscles of the body.

Hallucinogens

Hallucinogens, which include drugs like LSD (lysergic acid diethylamide), PCP, peyote, mescaline, psilocybin, MDA, MDMA, belladonna, and mandrake, have no official legitimate use. Street use of these drugs is intended to produce "mind expansion," hallucinations, creative mental states, and perceptual distortions—all of which have been popularly called "psychedelic experiences" or "trips."

Anabolic Steroids

Anabolic steroids include the substances nandrolene, oxandrolene, oxymetholone, and stanozolol. Steroids are used legitimately for weight gain; for the treatment of arthritis, anemia, and connective tissue disorder; and in the battle against certain forms of cancer. Some bodybuilders, professional athletes, and others seeking to build body bulk and to increase strength have created a secondary illegal market for steroids. Such well-known athletes as baseball players Sammy Sosa and Mark McGwire have tested positively for steroids.

Inhalants

Nitrous oxide, carbon tetrachloride, amyl nitrite, butyl nitrite, chloroform, Freon, acetate, and toluene, as well as other volatile solvents, are all in the inhalant category. Inhalants are found in fast-drying glues, nail polish remover, room and car deodorizers, lighter fluid, paint thinner, kerosene, cleaning fluids, household sealants, and gasoline. Although some of these substances, such as ether, nitrous oxide, amyl nitrate, and chloroform, have legitimate medical uses, others are employed only to produce a sense of light-headedness often described in colloquial terms as a "rush." Inhalants are generally sniffed, inhaled, huffed, or snorted. It has been estimated that there are over 1,000 substances that are abused. The use of inhalants "can disturb vision, impair judgment, and reduce muscle and reflex control."[3]

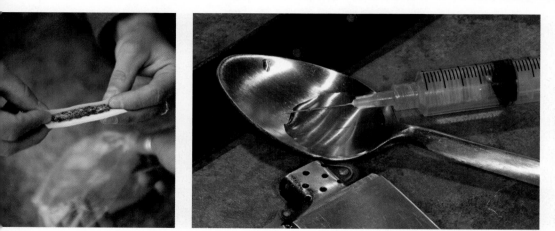

Drug Trafficking

The phrase *drug trafficking* can have a variety of meanings. On one hand, it can refer to the illegal shipment of controlled substances across state and national boundaries. On the other hand, it can mean the sale of controlled substances. Hence, in colloquial usage, a person who "traffics" in drugs may simply sell them. Technically speaking, **drug trafficking** includes manufacturing, distributing, dispensing, importing, and exporting (or possessing with intent to do the same) a controlled or counterfeit substance.[4] Federal law enforcement agencies, in their effort to reduce trafficking, focus largely on the prevention of smuggling and on the apprehension of smugglers.

Drugs like cocaine, heroin, and LSD are especially easy to smuggle because relatively small quantities of these drugs can be adulterated with other substances to provide large amounts of illicit commodities for sale on the street. Figures 11–2 and 11–3 provide maps of major cocaine and heroin trafficking routes (sometimes called "pipelines") worldwide. Most cocaine that enters the United States originates in the Western Hemisphere, especially in the South American nations of Colombia, Peru, and Bolivia. Transportation routes into the United States include (1) shipment overland from South America through Central America, (2) direct shipments to U.S. ports while concealed in containers or packed with legitimate products, (3) flights into the United States via commercial airplanes or in private aircraft, and (4) airdrops to vessels waiting offshore for smuggling into the United States.

The DEA follows heroin trafficking through its **heroin signature program (HSP)**, which identifies the geographic source area of a heroin sample through the laboratory detection of specific chemical characteristics in the sample that are peculiar to that area. The signature program employs special chemical analyses to identify and measure chemical constituents of a sample of seized heroin. Results of the HSP show that 62% of heroin in the United States originates in South America, 17% in Southeast Asia, 16% in Southwest Asia, and 5% in Mexico. According to the DEA, most heroin originating in Southeast Asia is produced in the Golden Triangle area, which encompasses Burma, Laos, and Thailand. Shipments are "controlled by ethnic Chinese criminal groups. . . while U.S.-based ethnic Chinese traffickers with links to these international criminal groups [are] the most prolific importers and distributors of Southeast Asian heroin" within the United

> Drug trafficking involves manufacturing, distributing, dispensing, importing, or exporting a controlled substance.

A scene from the movie *Maria Full of Grace* shows a female drug mule preparing to swallow prophylactics filled with cocaine. What other techniques do smugglers use?

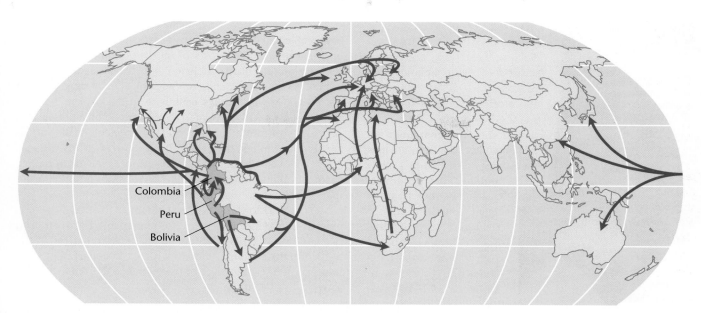

FIGURE 11–2 Global Cocaine Trafficking: Source Countries and Pipelines

Source: Adapted from the Office of National Drug Control Policy, *The National Drug Control Strategy: 2000 Annual Report* (Washington, DC: U.S. Government Printing Office, 2000), p. 78.

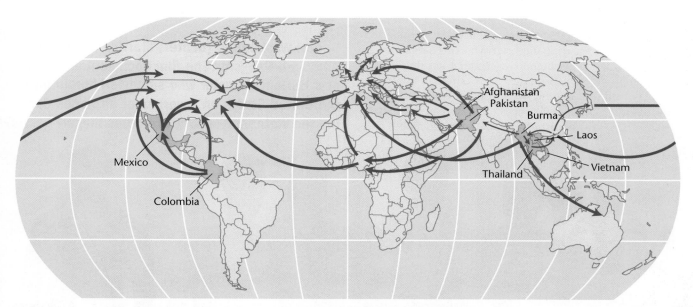

FIGURE 11–3 Global Heroin Trafficking: Source Countries and Pipelines

Source: Adapted from Office of National Drug Control Policy, *The National Drug Control Strategy: 2000 Annual Report* (Washington, DC: U.S. Government Printing Office, 2000), p. 81.

States.[5] HSP data were based on examination of over 800 random samples, including some obtained through undercover purchases, domestic seizures, and seizures made at U.S. ports of entry.

Pharmaceutical Diversion and Designer Drugs

The pharmaceutical diversion and subsequent abuse of legitimately manufactured controlled substances are a major source of drug-related addiction or dependence,

medical emergencies, and death. **Pharmaceutical diversion** occurs through illegal prescribing by physicians and illegal dispensing by pharmacists. "Doctor shopping," the process of finding a physician who is liberal in prescribing types and amounts of certain drugs, and visits to numerous physicians for the purpose of collecting large quantities of prescribed medicines exacerbate the problem. Depressants, including sedatives, tranquilizers, and antianxiety drugs (especially Xanax and Valium), along with stimulants and anabolic steroids, constitute the types of drugs most often diverted.

A number of drugs, especially those that fall into the "designer" category, are manufactured in drug facilities that are sometimes called "basement laboratories" because they are operated by individuals out of their homes. **Designer drugs are so named because "they are new substances designed by slightly altering the chemical makeup of other illegal or tightly controlled drugs."**[6] Designer drugs like Nexus, a new reputed aphrodisiac, usually fall under the rubric "synthetic narcotic" or "synthetic hallucinogen."

Drugs and Crime

While the manufacture, sale, transportation, and use of controlled substances are themselves criminal, drugs and crime are also linked in other ways. The addict who is so habituated to the use of illegal drugs that he or she steals to support a "habit," the drug importer who kills a rival dealer and the offender who commits a criminal act due to the stimulation provided by drugs are all examples of how drug abuse may be linked to other forms of criminal activity.

Recognizing these differences, the Bureau of Justice Statistics (BJS) distinguishes between drug-defined and drug-related crimes. **Drug-defined crimes** are "violations of laws prohibiting or regulating the possession, use, or distribution of illegal drugs."[7] The costs of all drug-defined crime, says BJS, are directly attributable to illegal drug use. **Drug-related crimes**, on the other hand, "are not violations of drug laws but are crimes in which drugs contribute to the offense."[8] Illegal drug use, says BJS, "is related to offenses against people and property in three major ways: (1) pharmacologically drugs can induce violent behavior, (2) the cost of drugs induces some users to commit crimes to support their drug habits, [and] (3) violence often characterizes relations among participants in the drug distribution system."[9]

According to the U.S. Department of Justice, "There is extensive evidence of the strong relationship between drug use and crime." This relationship can be summarized in the following three points, each of which, the department says, is supported "by a review of the evidence":[10]

- Drug users report greater involvement in crime and are more likely than nonusers to have criminal records.
- People with criminal records are much more likely than others to report being drug users.
- Crimes rise in number as drug use increases.

Denzel Washington (center) starring in the movie *American Gangster.* **The film documented the life of a Harlem gangster who smuggled heroin into the United States on government airplanes during the Vietnam War. Why are drugs illegal?**

Social Policy and Drug Abuse

Prior to 1907, any and all drugs could be bought and sold in the United States without restriction. Manufacturers were not required to disclose the contents of their products. Patent medicines of the time were trade secrets. This came to an end with the federal Pure Food and Drug Act of 1906, which required manufacturers to list their ingredients and specifically targeted mood-changing chemicals.

was enacted. Objections to Prohibition included the claims that it gave the government too much power over people's personal lives, that it was impossible to enforce, that it corrupted agents of enforcement, and that it made many bootleggers wealthy. The coming of the Great Depression, which began in 1929, magnified the effect of lost alcohol tax revenues on the federal government and in 1933 Congress proposed and the states ratified the Twenty-first Amendment, which repealed Prohibition.

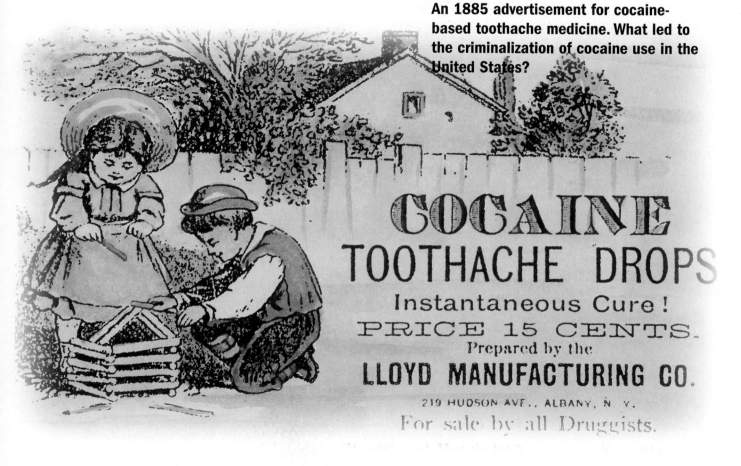

An 1885 advertisement for cocaine-based toothache medicine. What led to the criminalization of cocaine use in the United States?

COCAINE TOOTHACHE DROPS

Instantaneous Cure!

PRICE 15 CENTS.

Prepared by the

LLOYD MANUFACTURING CO.

219 HUDSON AVE., ALBANY, N. Y.

For sale by all Druggists.

The Harrison Act, passed by Congress in 1914, was the first major piece of federal antidrug legislation. It required anyone dealing in opium, morphine, heroin, cocaine, or their derivatives to register with the federal government and to pay a tax of $1.00 per year. The act, however, only authorized the registration of physicians, pharmacists, and other medical professionals, effectively outlawing street use of these drugs. However, by 1920, court rulings severely curtailed the use of heroin for medical purposes, claiming that it only caused addiction.

In 1919, the Eighteenth Amendment to the U.S. Constitution, which prohibited the manufacture, sale, and transportation of alcoholic beverages, was ratified. Support for Prohibition began to wane not long after the amendment

In 1937, passage of the Marijuana Tax Act effectively outlawed marijuana, a federal stance that was reinforced by the Boggs Act of 1951. The Boggs Act also mandated deletion of heroin from the list of medically useful substances and required its complete removal from all medicines.

In 1991, steroids were added to the list of Schedule III controlled substances by congressional action, and in 1996, the Drug-Induced Rape Prevention Act[11] increased penalties for trafficking in the drug Rohypnol, which is known as the "date rape drug" because of its use by "young men [who] put doses of the drug in women's drinks without their consent in order to lower their inhibitions."[12] The drug is variously known as "ropies," "roche," "ruffles," "roofies," and "rophies" on the street.

penalties for the manufacture and possession of equipment used to make controlled substances.

The far-reaching Violent Crime Control and Law Enforcement Act of 1994 included a number of drug-related provisions. Specifically, the act allocated other drug-treatment monies for the creation of state and federal programs to treat drug-addicted prisoners and provided $1 billion for drug court programs for nonviolent offenders with substance-abuse problems. The law also expanded the federal death penalty to include large-scale drug trafficking and mandated life imprisonment for criminals convicted of three drug-related felonies.

Drug-Control Strategies

Major policy initiatives in the battle against illicit drugs have included antidrug legislation and strict enforcement, interdiction, crop control, forfeiture, and antidrug education and drug treatment.[13] Much legislative emphasis in recent years has shifted from targeting users to the arrest, prosecution, and incarceration of the distributors of controlled substances. Similar shifts have occurred among employers requiring routine drug testing as a condition of employment and retention.

Interdiction is an international drug-control policy designed to stop drugs from entering the country illegally. Another antidrug strategy, crop control, has both international and domestic aspects. During 2005, for example, the Domestic Cannabis Eradication and Suppression Program was responsible for the eradication of 3,938,151 cultivated outdoor marijuana plants and 270,935 indoor marijuana plants in the United States. In addition, the same program was responsible for 11,922 arrests, and agents seized 3,707 weapons and $26,911,262 in assets.[14]

Forfeiture, or asset forfeiture, is another strategy in the battle against illegal drugs. **Forfeiture** is a legal procedure that authorizes judicial representatives to seize "all moneys, negotiable instruments, securities, or other things of value furnished or intended to be furnished by any person in exchange for a controlled substance . . . [and] all proceeds traceable to such an exchange."[15]

Another date rape drug, gammahydroxybutyrate (GHB), has effects similar to those of Rohypnol, but was once sold in health food stories to enhance body building. In 1990, the FDA banned the use of GHB except under the supervision of a physician.

Recent Legislation

Recent drug-control legislation includes the Comprehensive Methamphetamine Control Act (CMCA) of 1996 and relevant portions of the Violent Crime Control and Law Enforcement Act of 1994. The CMCA, which contains provisions for the seizure of chemicals used in the manufacture of methamphetamine, regulated the use of iodine (used in meth labs); created new reporting requirements for distributors of combination products containing ephedrine, pseudoephedrine (a common decongestant), and phenylpropanolamine; and increased

Another strategy, antidrug education and drug treatment, has gained significant popularity over the past decade. Those favoring educational attacks on the problem of drug abuse are quick to claim that other measures have not been effective in reducing the incidence of abuse. Antidrug education programs often reach targeted individuals through schools, corporations, and media campaigns.

Those who favor educational attacks on the problem of drug abuse claim that other techniques have not been effective.

An indoor marijuana-growing area seized by Hayward, California, police in 2008. If you were in charge of the nation's anti-drug efforts, how would you lead the fight against drugs?

Prostitution

Prostitution can be defined as the offering of one's self for hire for the purpose of engaging in sexual relations, or the act or practice of engaging in sexual activity for money or its equivalent. As the second part of this definition indicates, in heterosexual prostitution involving men as clients (or "johns"), and women as sexual "service providers," the man can also be charged with and found guilty of the offense of prostitution. Except for parts of Nevada, prostitution is a criminal act throughout the United States and is generally classified as a misdemeanor.

In the United States, over 92,000 men, women, and juveniles are arrested yearly for the crime of prostitution.[16] The number of juveniles engaging in prostitution is estimated to be between 100,000 and 300,000 annually.

A Typology of Prostitutes

Sexual services are sold[17] in red-light districts, commercial houses of prostitution, massage parlors, nude photography studios, strip clubs, erotic dance theaters, and at stag parties. Using location as the basis for a typology of prostitutes results in the following categories: streetwalkers, bar/hotel prostitutes, call girls, hotel/brothel prostitutes, and others who don't clearly fit any of these categories.

Streetwalkers are generally seen as the lowest class of prostitute because they solicit customers in public. Their dress is revealing, which advertises their services and entices customers. Streetwalkers service customers in cars, alleyways, hotels, darkened doorways, and so on. Streetwalkers command the lowest prices and have little

A prostitute and a "John" discuss services. What different kinds of prostitutes have been identified?

bargaining power over things like condom use and choice of sexual practices. They also face the highest risk of harm from customers and others and the highest risk of arrest.

Bar/hotel prostitutes work in bars, clubs, and hotels. They may have a standing relationship with hotel professionals, with whom they share their profits. They tend to "work" conventions, sporting events, and business meetings. Services are typically provided in the establishment itself. The prices charged by bar/hotel prostitutes vary considerably according to the prestige of the establishment. The woman's risk of harm and arrest are low to moderate as long as the collaborative relation with the establishment is maintained.

Call girls work for escort services. Escort services frequently advertise with flyers, in newspapers, or even in the yellow pages, on TV, and via the Internet (where it is sometimes referred to as "cyberprostitution"). Consequently, call girls are not restricted to specific locales. Most see well-to-do clients who prefer the anonymity of a referral service. Many of the service's customers are regulars who maintain a standing relationship with the service. Fees are often charged to credit cards by the customer before the girl is dispatched. Once on site, however, prostitutes may negotiate with the customer for specific services. This arrangement tends to insulate itself from legal action—claiming that it simply arranged for companionship. Call girls depend on the agency to screen customers. Prices in this market segment reach the

A prostitute waits for clients behind a window in the red light district of Amsterdam in 2008. Prostitution was legalized in Holland in 2000. What are the social policy advantages of legalization?

United States, brothel prostitution is an option available to the governments of rural counties in Nevada. Nevada's house prostitutes operate with posted fees, and generally earn 40% to 60% of the revenue they generate. State law requires that they be fingerprinted, undergo regular health examinations, and keep financial records for tax purposes. Rhode Island is the only other state in the United States in which the selling of sexual services is not specifically outlawed, although operating a brothel and engaging in solicitation for the purpose of prostitution is.

Feminist Perspectives on Prostitution

Prostitution is a significant issue in today's feminist thought. Some feminist thinkers argue that prostitution exploits and demeans women, while also subjecting them to the dangers of violence and disease.

Others take quite a different approach, saying that selling sex need not be exploitative and might actually be liberating because it fulfills a woman's rights to control her body and her sexuality. They are likely to see prostitution as legitimate and to argue for the legalization of prostitution with added protections for those who choose sex work as a trade. The recent redefinition of prostitution as sex work has been accompanied by the development of a sex worker activism movement, comprising organizations such Call Off Your Old Tired Ethics (COYOTE) in the United States, and the Australian Prostitutes Collective in that country.

highest levels, and escorts have considerable bargaining power over such things as the use of condoms and the kinds of sexual services provided. Call girls face the lowest risk of harm or arrest.

House or brothel prostitutes ply their trade in legal environments—but are limited to only a few venues in the United States. Legalized prostitution, however, is common in a number of other countries, including Australia (where laws vary by state), New Zealand, the Netherlands, and Germany. In countries where prostitution is legal, it is subject to health and locality controls, as well as age and other restrictions. Prostitutes are generally licensed sex workers who pay taxes, belong to unions, and are eligible for government benefits such as unemployment wages, medical services, and so on. In the

Dennis Hof's World Famous

Bunny Ranch

"America's Cathouse"-Larry Flynt   "The West's Best Whorehouse"-PENTHOUSE
WWW.BUNNYRANCH.NET • 1-888-BUNNYRANCH

RING BUZZER
PUSH GATE
Have Fun!!

XXX ADULT
FANTASY CAMP
STARS NOW APPEARING
SUNSET THOMAS
PENTHOUSE PET

RAYVENESS
DAISY
ANNA-LISA
DIANE DIAMONDS

BAD BOYS
ONLY

The Moonlight Bunny Ranch brothel outside Carson City, Nevada. Why does prostitution remain a crime in most of the United States?

261

Policy Consequences

The war on drugs has been costly. Domestic law enforcement activities (including all federal law enforcement programs within the nation's borders) account for the lion's share of federal antidrug expenditures, while demand-reduction programs (that is, educational activities) absorb the smallest part of the antidrug budget. Figure 11–4 depicts actual and projected federal drug-control spending by functional area for fiscal year 2008. When state monies are added in the total cost of the war on drugs has been enormous.

The drug war has been costly in other ways as well. Court resources must be diverted to deal with the enormous influx of drug prosecutions. **In some jurisdictions, drug cases account for as much as two-thirds of the criminal case filings. America's major cities have been especially affected.[18]** Strict enforcement has combined with a lock-'em-up philosophy to produce astonishingly high rates of imprisonment for drug offenders. The proportion of federal prisoners who are sentenced drug offenders rose from 38% in 1986 to 53% in 1990 and is 55% today.[19] Part of the increase is due to congressional action that has required high mandatory minimum sentences in drug cases, so that even first-time offenders were sentenced to long prison terms instead of probation. Approximately 70% of all first-time offenders in federal prisons are serving drug sentences. This is also true of 85% of illegal immigrants who are federal prisoners and 66% of female federal prisoners.[20]

Alternative Drug Policies

Decriminalization and legalization have both been suggested drug control policies at the state and local levels. Both strategies are "based on the assumption that drug abuse will never be eliminated."[21] Whereas **decriminalization** typically reduces criminal penalties associated with the personal possession of a controlled substance, **legalization** eliminates "the laws and associated criminal penalties that prohibit its production, sale, distribution, and possession."[22] Decriminalization enhances personal freedoms in the face of state control, whereas legalization "is aimed," in part, "at reducing the control that criminals

have over the drug trade."[23] Other arguments in favor of legalization include the following notions:

- In a free society, people should be permitted to do what they want, as long as they don't harm others.

- Keeping drugs illegal means that they will continue to be high-priced. Legalizing them could greatly lower the price and make them taxable—providing the states with much needed revenue.

- The expense of illicit drugs, kept artificially high by their illegal status, encourages the commission of many drug-related crimes, including prostitution, robbery, and burglary, by users seeking to feed their habits.

- Legalizing drugs would reduce the influence of criminal cartels.

- The illegal status and associated high cost of drugs indirectly victimize others, such as property owners in drug-infested areas and taxpayers who foot the enforcement bill.

- Drug legalization would dramatically reduce the opportunity for official corruption, which is now frequently associated with the illicit drug trade.

- The legalization of drugs would allow for better control over public health issues related to drug use. The spread of AIDS, for example, caused in large part by the use of dirty needles in heroin injection, could be better controlled if sterilized needles were made legally available. Similarly, drug quality and potency could be monitored and ensured.

Opponents of drug legalization argue the following:

- Reducing official control over psychoactive substances is immoral, socially irresponsible, and would result in heightened costs to society from drug abuse.

- Drug legalization would simply increase the types of problems now associated with alcohol abuse, such as lost time from work, drug-induced criminality, the loss of personal self-control, and the severing of important social relationships.

- The fact that laws are not *easily* enforceable is no reason to eliminate them.

In 1996, California and Arizona voters passed resolutions legalizing the medical use of marijuana under certain circumstances. Arizona law requires prescribing physicians to write a scientific opinion explaining why the drug is appropriate for a specific patient, and a second opinion is required before the drug can be legally used. California's law, called the Compassionate Use Act,[24] was further modified by action of the state senate in 2003,[25] limiting the amount of marijuana a patient and his or her primary caregivers may possess.

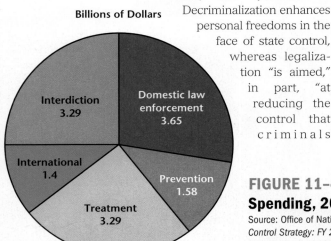

Billions of Dollars

- Interdiction 3.29
- Domestic law enforcement 3.65
- International 1.4
- Treatment 3.29
- Prevention 1.58

FIGURE 11–4 Federal Drug-Control Spending, 2008

Source: Office of National Drug Control Policy, *National Drug Control Strategy: FY 2008 Budget Summary* (Washington, DC: ONDCP, March 2000), p. 9.

In 1999, Maine voters passed a referendum permitting some sick people to use small amounts of marijuana, and 26 other states and the District of Columbia have passed various laws and resolutions allowing therapeutic research programs involving the use of marijuana or asking the federal government to lift its ban on medical use of the drug.[26] In May 2001, the U.S. Supreme Court prohibited California marijuana-growing clubs from distributing the drug to those who are ill or in pain.[27] The ruling technically prohibits the use of medical marijuana in virtually all situations.

In 2009, however, in a policy change initiated by the Obama administration, Attorney General Eric H. Holder, Jr., announced a shift in federal enforcement policy regarding medical marijuana. Holder said that federal agents would restrict their enforcement of marijuana law in states that have legalized the use of medical marijuana by focusing primarily on traffickers who falsely masquerade as medical dispensaries and who "use medical marijuana laws as a shield" for their illegal activities.[28]

Prostitution

A number of arguments have been made in favor of legalizing or decriminalizing prostitution. Under outright legalization, women beyond a specified age would be able to offer paid sexual services with few restrictions, as is currently the case in parts of Nevada. Decriminalization, on the other hand, would significantly reduce the criminal penalties associated with prostitution, but would still regulate the practice and might require counseling and alternative employment programs for women in that line of work in an effort to curtail the practice.

Those who argue in favor of legalization say that current practices by the justice system tend to force prostitution out of areas where it might naturally be found (that is, certain hotels, massage parlors, etc.), and onto the streets and into other parts of the community. Similarly, they say, keeping prostitution illegal means that prostitutes will continue to be viewed as easy targets for pimps, sex offenders, and violent predators. Finally,

legalization frees law enforcement resources to be used in the prevention and investigation of more serious types of crime.

Those who argue for keeping prostitution illegal point out that it is regarded as morally and ethically wrong, that it is often not a line of work that is freely chosen, and that it is dangerous for sex workers as well as for their clients because of the disease and violence that are often associated with it.

A Canadian pro-pot demonstrator greets Vancouver police. What's the difference between legalization and decriminalization?

At the height of her fame, Heidi Fleiss, the so-called Hollywood Madame, told reporters, "Alexander the Great conquered the world at 32. I conquered it at 22."[i] What more could the media have asked for? Hollywood; young, good-looking women selling sex; a mysterious list of rich celebrity clients that kept threatening to crop up; and a young, attractive, articulate, and outspoken advocate of a woman's right to sell her body for sex sensationally touted as the "Madam to the Stars."[ii]

Fleiss's cachet in the sex trade was the stable of exceptionally beautiful young women she kept available for clients willing to pay top dollar. And top dollar it was, with some of the prostitutes making from $1,500 to as much as $1 million per customer. Their services even included travel to Paris, London, and other overseas locations to meet the demands of the rich and desiring.[iii]

But Fleiss did not recruit members for her workforce—they found her. Some were drawn by the potential for high earnings, as Fleiss paid her girls 40% of the profit from each "booking," including tips. For others, the lure was the chance to frolic in the environment of the rich and famous. The lifestyle Fleiss's women enjoyed was beyond the dreams of most, and included the opportunity to party with some of the richest and most powerful men in the world. Through mid-1993, Fleiss pocketed several million dollars per year from her role in the enterprise.

Heidi Fleiss's notorious high-priced prostitution ring was the stuff of Hollywood lore, but no more so than her arrest, trial, incarceration, and post-release emergence as an unrepentant sex entrepreneur. Fleiss was initially arrested in June 1993 on state charges that included five counts of pandering and one count of narcotics possession. On July 28, 1994, during her state trial, she was indicted by a federal grand jury on charges of income tax evasion, money laundering, and 14 counts of conspiracy.

Fleiss was convicted in federal court of income tax evasion, money laundering, and eight counts of conspiracy in August 1995. She also pled guilty in state court to the pandering charges. The combined sentences resulted in her serving three years in prison.

The Causes Behind the Crime
Heidi Lynne Fleiss

Can We Understand Fleiss's Crimes?

- Born in Los Angeles on December 30, 1965, Heidi Fleiss showed a precocious flair for business as early as age 12. A popular and responsible babysitter, she soon found herself with more job offers than she could handle herself, so she established a babysitting service by hiring her friends from school to handle some of the jobs. She, of course, got a cut of all the fees. *Fleiss developed business acumen during her childhood. Why do you think she chose prostitution in her early adult life to apply her business sense?*

- Fleiss's school performance did not keep pace with her business enterprise. Low grades in junior high and high school ultimately led to her dropping out of school in the tenth grade. For the next few years, she held a variety of low-wage jobs from which she took little pleasure. Fleiss's aspirations never wavered, however, and she was constantly on the lookout for the right opportunity. That opportunity came about when she and a friend attended a party at 61-year-old millionaire financier Bernie Cornfeld's estate. Impressed with Fleiss, Cornfeld hired her as his personal secretary, an arrangement that, in short order, evolved into a personal relationship. Fleiss sought to deepen the relationship to a live-in level, which she hoped would result in her enjoying a financially secure life of privilege and hedonistic pursuits. Cornfeld,

Heidi Fleiss (center) poses with some of her high-priced call girls. Who were her clients?

however, had a well-known appetite for classical beauties, which he enthusiastically indulged, and the couple eventually broke up. *Was this a turning point in Fleiss's life? What might the implication of this incident have been for her future life?*

- Fleiss acquired business skills from associating with Cornfeld and his friends. A chance meeting with the reigning queen madam of the Los Angeles area, Madam Alex, gave Fleiss entrée to the sex industry. Madam Alex was, at that time, looking for a replacement to take over her business operations so that she could live a privileged retirement. Fleiss's business acumen fit the bill so well that she increased Madam Alex's profits by more than 400%. But when Madam Alex proved to be less than generous in sharing her largess, Fleiss went off on her own. *In your opinion, was Fleiss a smart businesswoman or a madam committing a series of crimes? Was she both?*

- Since her release from prison, Fleiss has parlayed her notoriety into a series of successful business ventures, including a men's apparel store in Los Angeles called "Heidi's Wear." A book (*Pandering*), a DVD (*Sex Tips*), a website, and repeated appearances on late-night talk shows have kept her in the public eye. Ever the sensationalist, Fleiss's current project, which she describes as a "stud farm,"[iv] involves converting a brothel in southern Nevada into a resort staffed by male prostitutes to service Fleiss's hoped-for female customers.[v] *Fleiss parlayed her illegal activities into a sex industry generating large amounts of money. Does that mean that high-level prostitution pays? If prostitution were legal in the states, what kind of impact would it have?*

NOTES:

[i]"Then & Now: Heidi Fleiss," CNN, June 19, 2005, http://www.cnn.com/2005/US/02/28/cnn25.tan.fleiss (accessed June 1, 2007).

[ii]Rachael Bell, "Heidi Fleiss: The Million Dollar Madam," Court TV Crime Library, http://www.crimelibrary.com/notorious_murders/celebrity/heidi_fleiss/index.html (accessed June 1, 2007).

[iii]Ibid.

[iv]"Fleiss Plans Makeover for Nevada Brothel," *USA Today*, November 16, 2005, http://www.usatoday.com/life/people/2005-11-16-fleiss_x.htm (accessed June 1, 2007).

[v]Steve Friess, "Betting on the Studs," *Newsweek*, December 12, 2005, http://www.msnbc.msn.com/id/10313009/site/newsweek (accessed June 1, 2007).

Heidi Fleiss on trial. Was she a criminal or a smart businesswoman?

Heidi Fleiss stands in her boutique, called "Hollywood Madam," in Hollywood, California. Is she likely to stay out of prison?

Summary and Key Concepts

Public order offenses include such things as fighting, disorderly conduct, vagrancy, loitering, public intoxication, obstructing public passage, and illegally carrying weapons. Drug crimes involve offenses such as drug cultivation or manufacture, drug sales or distribution, and drug use.

The Nature of Public Order Offenses

public order offense An act that is willfully committed and that disturbs the public peace or tranquility.

drug offense Any violation of the laws prohibiting or regulating the possession, use, distribution, sale, or manufacture of illegal drugs.

psychoactive substance A substance that affects the mind, mental processes, or emotions.

Office of National Drug Control Policy (ONDCP) A national office charged by Congress with establishing policies, priorities, and objectives for the nation's drug-control program. ONDCP is responsible for annually developing and disseminating the *National Drug-Control Strategy.*

Types of Illegal Drugs

controlled substances Defined by federal law as consisting of seven categories: narcotics, depressants, stimulants, hallucinogens, cannabis, anabolic steroids, and inhalants.

dangerous drug A term used by the DEA to refer to broad categories or classes of controlled substances other than cocaine, opiates, hallucinogens, inhalants, and cannabis products.

Q: *How did drug control laws come into being, and why?*

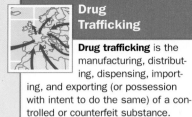

Drug Trafficking

Drug trafficking is the manufacturing, distributing, dispensing, importing, and exporting (or possession with intent to do the same) of a controlled or counterfeit substance.

heroin signature program (HSP) A DEA program that identifies the geographic source of a heroin sample through the detection of specific chemical characteristics in the sample peculiar to the source area.

pharmaceutical diversion The process by which legitimately manufactured controlled substances are diverted for illicit use.

designer drugs New substances designed by slightly altering the chemical makeup of other illegal or tightly controlled drugs.

drug-defined crime A violation of the laws prohibiting or regulating the possession, use, or distribution of illegal drugs.

drug-related crime A crime in which drugs contribute to the offense (excluding violations of drug laws).

 Q: *What is the relationship between drug trafficking, drug abuse, and other forms of crime?*

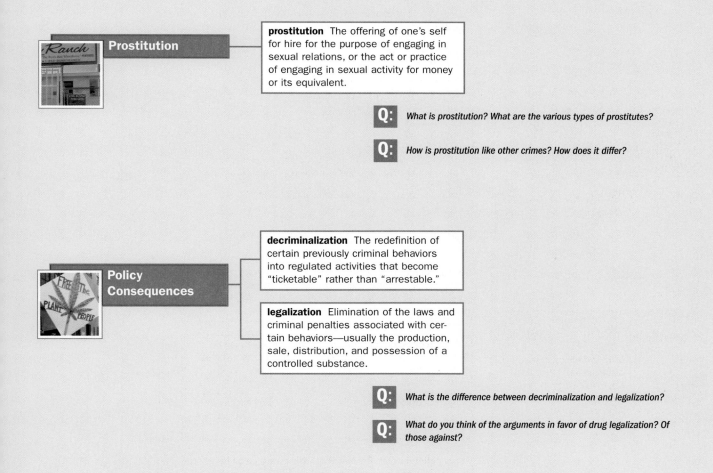

Social Policy and Drug Abuse

interdiction An international drug-control policy designed to stop drugs from entering the country illegally.

forfeiture A legal procedure that authorizes judicial representatives to seize "all moneys, negotiable instruments, securities, or other things of value furnished or intended to be furnished by any person in exchange for a controlled substance and all proceeds traceable to such an exchange.

Q: *What are some of the costs of illicit drug use in the United States today? How would you reduce those costs?*

Prostitution

prostitution The offering of one's self for hire for the purpose of engaging in sexual relations, or the act or practice of engaging in sexual activity for money or its equivalent.

Q: *What is prostitution? What are the various types of prostitutes?*

Q: *How is prostitution like other crimes? How does it differ?*

Policy Consequences

decriminalization The redefinition of certain previously criminal behaviors into regulated activities that become "ticketable" rather than "arrestable."

legalization Elimination of the laws and criminal penalties associated with certain behaviors—usually the production, sale, distribution, and possession of a controlled substance.

Q: *What is the difference between decriminalization and legalization?*

Q: *What do you think of the arguments in favor of drug legalization? Of those against?*

Crime in the Modern World
—Today's Headlines

"You bring me a select group of hackers, and within 90 days I'll bring this country to its knees."

—Jim Settle, retired director of the
FBI's Computer Crime Squad

Technology and Crime
It's a Double-Edged Sword

The world isn't run by weapons anymore, or energy, or money. It's run by ones and zeros—little bits of data—it's all electrons…There's a war out there, a world war. It's not about who has the most bullets. It's about who controls the information—what we see and hear, how we work, what we think. It's all about information.

—Sneakers (*The Movie*)

High Technology and Criminal Opportunity

The twenty-first century has been termed the postindustrial information age. Information is vital to the success of any endeavor, and certain forms of information hold nearly incalculable value for those who possess it. Patents, pharmaceutical formulations, corporate strategies, and the financial resources of corporations all represent competitive and corporate trade secrets. Government databases, if infiltrated, can offer terrorists easy paths to destruction and mayhem.

Some criminal perpetrators intend simply to destroy or to alter data without otherwise accessing or copying the information. Disgruntled employees, mischievous computer **hackers**, business competitors, and others may all have varied degrees of interest in destroying the records or computer capabilities of others.

High-tech criminals seeking illegitimate access to computerized information take a number of routes. **One is the path of direct access, wherein office workers or corporate spies, planted as seemingly innocuous employees, use otherwise legitimate work-related entry to a company's computer resources to acquire wanted information.**

Another path of illegal access is called *computer trespass*, and involves remote access to targeted machines. Anyone equipped with a computer and Internet access has potential access to numerous computer systems. Many such systems have few, if any, security procedures in place. Similarly, electromagnetic field (EMF) decoders can scan radio frequency emanations generated by all types of computers. Keystroke activity, internal chip-processed computations, disk reads, and the like can all be detected and interpreted at a distance by such sophisticated devices. Computers secured against such passively invasive practices are rarely found in the commercial marketplace, although the

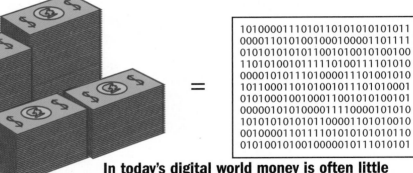

In today's digital world money is often little other than bits and bytes of computerized data.

military had adopted them for many applications. Within the last decade wireless networking has heightened fears of data theft, and cell phone use, handheld devices, and other forms of

President Obama with his prized Blackberry. Do you think the information it contains could compromise national security were it to be lost or stolen? Are there other ways of accessing digital information, such as that on the president's Blackberry?

radio communication offer opportunities for data interception.

The realities of today's digital world have led to a new form of crime, called cybercrime, and to new laws intended to combat it. Simply put, **cybercrime**, or *computer crime*, is **any violation of a federal or state computer crime statute.** Many argue that only those crimes that use computer technology as central to their commission may properly be called "cybercrimes." However, there are a number of other kinds of offenses that can also be described as cybercrimes.[1] An FBI typology distinguishes among five types of cybercrimes: (1) internal cybercrimes, such as viruses; (2) Internet and telecommunications crimes, including illegal hacking; (3) support of criminal enterprises, such as databases supporting drug distribution; (4) computer-manipulation crimes, such as embezzlement; and (5) hardware, software, and information theft.[2] Table 12–1 lists these five categories, with additional examples of each.

When discussing cybercrime, it is important to realize that a huge number of today's financial transactions are computerized. Although most people probably think of money as dollar bills, **money today is really only information**—information stored in a computer network, possibly located within the physical confines of a bank, but more likely existing as bits and bytes of data on service providers' machines. Typical financial customers give little thought to the fact that very little "real" money is held by their bank, brokerage house, mutual fund, or commodities dealer. Nor do they often consider the threats to their financial well-being by activities like electronic theft or the sabotage of existing accounts. Unfortunately, however, the threat is very real. Computer criminals equipped with enough information, or able to find the data they need, can quickly and easily locate, steal, and send vast amounts of money anywhere in the world.

No reliable estimates exist as to the losses suffered in such transactions due to the activities of technologically adept criminal perpetrators. Accurate estimates are lacking largely because sophisticated high-tech thieves are so effective at eluding apprehension.

TABLE 12–1
Categories of Cybercrime
Internal Cybercrimes (Malware)
Trojan horses
Logic bombs
Trapdoors
Viruses
Internet and Telecommunications Crimes
Phone phreaking
Hacking
Denial of service attacks
Illegal websites
Dissemination of illegal material (for example, child pornography)
Misuse of telecommunications systems
Theft of telecommunications services
Illegal eavesdropping
Illegal Internet-based gambling
Support of Criminal Enterprises
Databases to support drug distribution
Databases to support loan-sharking
Databases to support illegal gambling
Databases to keep records of illegal client transactions
Electronic money laundering
Communications in furtherance of criminal conspiracies
Computer-Manipulation Crimes
Embezzlement
Electronic fund transfer fraud
Other fraud/phishing
Extortion threats/electronic terrorism
Hardware, Software, and Information Theft
Software piracy (warez)
Thefts of computers
Thefts of microprocessor chips
Thefts of trade secrets and proprietary information
Identity theft

Dozens of rack-mounted computer servers. What is cybercrime? What categories of cybercrime can you identify?

The Extent of Cybercrime

A recent estimate by the U.S. Secret Service in conjunction with the CERT Cybersecurity Center puts the annual cost of cybercrime in the United States at around $666 million.[3] Another industry group, the Computer Security Institute (CSI), surveyed 313 business organizations and found that computer crime had identified more than 15,700 different phishing websites by January 1, 2009.[7] Figure 12–1 shows a map of the threat from phishing attacks on a global basis in 2009.

Phishing sites often attempt to hijack brand names, and some phishers are capable of sending out e-mails that are difficult to distinguish from legitimate ones. When that happens, and customers respond to those e-mails in significant numbers, a brand (such as the name of a bank or credit card company) is said to have been hijacked. Figure 12–2 shows the number of hijacked brands by month during the second half of 2008. Some observers have noted that in addition to losses suffered by individuals and institutions, phishing has the potential to threaten the viability of e-commerce and to call into question the safety of all Web-based financial transactions.[8]

FIGURE 12–1 Global Cyberthreat Map

Attack Percentages
- 3.32–32.38
- 0.31–3.04
- 0.03–0.29
- 0–0.02

Source: Websense Security Labs, Attack Information Center, Websence Global Threat Intelligence, web available at http://securitylabs.websense.com/content/CrimewarePhishing.aspx (accessed July 27, 2009).

cost companies an average of $168,000 each in 2006.[4] **Software piracy, or the unauthorized and illegal copying of software programs, is rampant.** According to the Business Software Alliance, global losses from pirated software (known as *warez* in the computer underground) totaled nearly $53 billion in 2008.[5] The Alliance found that 41% of all PC software installed in 2008 was pirated. The problem is worse in some countries than in others. In China, for example, it is estimated that 80% of all software used there has been illegally copied.

Phishing (pronounced "fishing") is a relatively new scam that uses official-looking e-mail messages to steal valuable information such as credit card numbers, social security numbers, user IDs, and passwords from victims. The e-mail messages appear to come from a user's bank, credit card company, retail store, or ISP and generally inform the recipients that some vital information in their account urgently needs to be updated. Those who respond are provided with an official-looking Web form on which they can enter their private financial information. Once the information is submitted, it enters the phisher's database.

Gartner and Associates, a research and business consulting firm, estimates that 3.6 million victims lost $3.2 billion in the U.S. in 2007 due to phishing attacks.[6] The Anti-Phishing Working Group, a coalition of banks and Internet service providers, says that a typical phishing scheme reaches up to 1 million e-mail inboxes. The watchdog group

Not all cybercrime is committed for financial gain. Some types of computer crime, including the creation and transmission of destructive computer viruses, "worms," spyware, and other malicious forms of programming code (often called *malware*), might better be classified as "criminal mischief." Perhaps not surprisingly, these types of activities are typically associated with young, technologically sophisticated male miscreants seeking a kind of clandestine recognition from their computer-savvy peers. Computer crimes committed by youthful and idealistic offenders may represent a novel form of juvenile delinquency—one aimed at expressing dissatisfaction with the status quo.

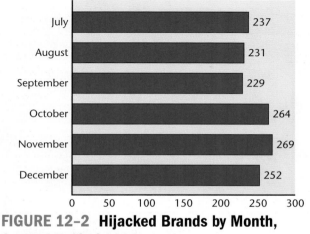

FIGURE 12–2 Hijacked Brands by Month, Second Half of 2008

Source: The Anti-Phishing Working Group, "Phishing Activity Trends Report: 2nd Half 2008," http://www.antiphishing.org/reports/apwg_report_H2_2008.pdf (accessed August 2, 2009), p. 6.

Viruses have shown signs of becoming effective terrorist-like tools in the hands of young, disaffected "technonerds" intent on attacking or destroying existing social institutions. A **computer virus** is simply a computer program that is designed to secretly invade computer systems and to either modify the way in which they operate or alter the information they store.[9] Other types of destructive programs are logic bombs, worms, and Trojan horse routines. Distinctions among these programs are based on either the way in which they infect targeted machines or on the way in which they behave once they have managed to find their way into a computer. Figure 12–3 provides an overview of some of the most damaging computer viruses of all time.

In a 2009 report on cybersecurity, the U.S. Department of Homeland Security provided the following recent examples of damage caused by malware:[10]

- In November of 2008, the Conficker botnet affected as many as 12 million computers worldwide, and is still attacking individual computers and networks.

- Symantec corporation, makers of computer security software, reports that there are more than 15,000 new types of malware entering networks worldwide every day.

- Consumer Reports estimates that U.S. consumers lost $8.5 billion and replaced 2.1 million computers because of viruses, spyware, and other forms of malware between 2006 and 2008.

Major government reports on cybersecurity (all of which can be accessed at http://www.cyber.st.hds.gov) are show in Figure 12–4.

1	Mydoom (2004) *Estimated damage: $38.5 billion*
2	Sobig.F (2003) *Estimated damage: $30 billion*
3	Klez (2001) *Estimated damage: $18.9 billion*
4	Sasser (2004) *Estimated damage: $14.8 billion*
5	ILOVEYOU, AKA Loveletter and The Love Bug (2000) *Estimated damage: $8.75–$15 billion*
6	Backdoor.Zagaban (2005) *Estimated damage: unknown, but thought to be in the billions of dollars*
7	Blaster (2003) *Estimated damage: $5 to $10 billion*
8	Code Red (2001) *Estimated damage: $2.6 billion*
9	Slammer (2003) *Estimated damage: unknown, but thought to total in the billions of dollars*
10	Storm (2007) *Estimated damage: $1 billion in lost productivity*

FIGURE 12–3 The Ten Most Damaging Computer Viruses and Worms of All Time

Sources: Buzzle.com, "The Most Damage Causing Computer Viruses Revealed," http://www.buzzle.com/articles/the-most-damage-causing-computer-viruses-revealed.html (accessed October 22, 2009); Christopher Null, "The Worst Computer Viruses of All Time," Yahoo! Tech, http://tech.yahoo.com/blogs/null (accessed October 22, 2009); and George Jones, "The 10 Most Destructive PC Viruses Of All Time," Tech Web, July 05, 2006, http://www.techweb.com/tech/160200005 (accessed June 26, 2008).

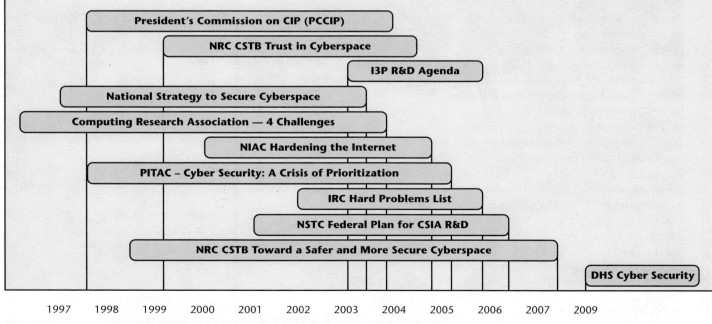

FIGURE 12–4 Timeline of Federal Research Reports on Cybercrime

Source: Adapted from, Kevin Thompson, *Cyber Security* (Washington, D.C.: U.S. Department of Homeland Security - Command, Control and Interoperability Division, June 24, 2009), p. 23.

Computer Crime and the Law

In late 2000, the Justice Department of the Philippines dismissed criminal charges against Onel de Guzman.[11] De Guzman, a former student at the Philippines AMA Computer College, admitted that he had unleashed the ILOVEYOU (or Love Bug) virus on the Internet on May 4, 2000, but refused to say whether he had authored it. The virus replicated rapidly throughout the world, gathering passwords from infected computers and sending them to several e-mail accounts in the Philippines. By the time the virus had run its course, official estimates were that it had caused over $10 billion in damages.[12] Because the Philippines had no law against computer crime, however, de Guzman was originally charged with theft and violation of an access device. Those laws, prosecutors finally decided, were not applicable to de Guzman's activities, and the charges were dropped. Although President Joseph Estrada signed a new law covering electronic commerce and computer hacking in June 2000, it could not be applied retroactively to the Love Bug case.

In the early years of computer-based information systems, most U.S. jurisdictions tried to prosecute unauthorized computer access under preexisting property crime statutes, including burglary and larceny laws. Unfortunately, because the actual carrying off of a computer is quite different than copying or altering some of the information it contains, juries were confused by how such laws apply to high-tech crimes, and computer criminals were often let free. As a result, all states and the federal government developed computer-crime statutes specifically applicable to invasive activities that illegally access stored information.

In 1996, President Bill Clinton signed into law the **Communications Decency Act (CDA)**,[13] which sought to protect minors from harmful material on the Internet. A portion of the CDA criminalized the knowing transmission of obscene or indecent messages to any recipient under 18 years of age. Another section prohibited the knowing sending or displaying to a person under 18 any message "that, in context, depicts or describes, in terms patently offensive as measured by contemporary community standards, sexual or excretory activities or organs." Shortly after the law was passed, however, the American Civil Liberties Union (ACLU) and a number of other plaintiffs filed suit against the federal government, challenging the constitutionality of the law's two provisions relating to the transmission of obscene materials to minors.

In 1996, a three-judge federal district court entered a preliminary injunction against enforcement of both challenged provisions, ruling that they contravened First Amendment guarantees of free speech. The government then appealed to the U.S. Supreme Court. The Court's 1997 decision **Reno v. ACLU**[14] upheld the lower court's ruling and found that the CDA's "indecent transmission" and "patently offensive display" provisions abridge "the freedom of speech" protected by the First Amendment. Most other federal legislation aimed at keeping online pornography

Philippine security officials display seized computer equipment. How did cybercrime laws in the Philippines fall short in prosecuting the creator of the Love Bug virus?

The U.S. Supreme Court has permitted very little regulation of Internet content. How can children be kept safe on the Web?

away from the eyes of children has not fared any better when reviewed by the Court. Although the Children's Internet Protection Act (CIPA), which requires public and school libraries receiving certain kinds of federal funding to install pornography filters on their Internet-linked computers, was approved by the justices, most observers acknowledge that the Court has placed the Internet in the same category as newspapers and other print media, where almost no regulation is permitted.

Enacted in 1997, the **No Electronic Theft Act** (NETA, or NET Act) criminalizes the willful infringement of copyrighted works, including by electronic means, even when the infringing party derives no direct financial benefit from the infringement (such as when pirated software is freely distributed online). In keeping with requirements of the NETA, the U.S. Sentencing Commission enacted amendments to its guidelines to increase penalties associated with electronic theft. The **Digital Theft Deterrence and Copyright Damages Improvement Act** of 1999 increased the amount of damages that could be awarded in cases of copyright infringement—a crime that is intimately associated with software piracy. The **Cyber Security Enhancement Act (CSEA)** of 2002,[15] which is part of the Homeland Security Act of 2002, directed the U.S. Sentencing Commission to take several factors into account in creating new sentencing guidelines for computer criminals. The law told the commission to consider not only the financial loss caused by computer crime, but also the level of planning involved in the offense, whether the crime was committed for commercial or private advantage, and whether malicious intent existed on the part of the perpetrator. Under the law, computer criminals can face life in prison if they put human lives in jeopardy. Certain future illegitimate activities using computer equipment may not be adequately covered by existing law. On the other hand, some crimes committed with the use of a computer may be more appropriately prosecuted under "traditional" laws. For that reason, some experts distinguish among computer crime, computer-related crime, and computer abuse. **Computer-related crime**

is "any illegal act for which knowledge of computer technology is involved for its investigation, perpetration, or prosecution," whereas **computer abuse** is said to be "any incident without color of right associated with computer technology in which a victim suffered or could have suffered loss and/or a perpetrator by intention made or could have made gain."[16]

COMPUTER ACCESS RELEASE FORM 2009-2010

There are multiple computers in this High School's library, computer lab and classrooms available for student use in both instructional and less supervised settings. Some of these computers have access to a wide range of educational materials by means of computer networks or online services. As the parent/guardian(s) of the student listed below, I understand and accept that the school staff cannot individually monitor all of the information that my student is able to access, download or transmit at these computers. I also accept that it is impossible for the school staff to completely prevent access to inappropriate or controversial materials.

My daughter and I have discussed this topic, read the acceptable use policies in the *Student/Parent Handbook*, and understand that the accessing, saving or distribution of any inappropriate or controversial materials will not be tolerated. The accessing, saving or distribution of such material may result in my daughter's loss of computer use at school and may also result in other disciplinary action by the school in accord with the policies and procedures contained in the *Student/Parent Handbook*.

Please complete and sign this form and return it to the front office by picture day at the beginning of the year.

____ I give permission for my daughter's computer access to network or online services.

____ I do not give permission for my daughter to use the computer to access network or online services. Since the school cannot always prevent student access to such services, I have directed my daughter not to access network or online services.

____ For identified medical/health reasons, I have instructed my daughter not to use a computer for more than __ hours per school day.

I release and hold the teachers, staff members, Board of Trustees, the High School and the immediate community harmless and not legally liable for the use of computers or for materials distributed to or acquired from the school's computers.

Parent/Guardian Printed Name	Parent/Guardian Signature	Date
Student Printed Name	Student Signature	Date

PUBLICITY/VIDEO RELEASE FORM

Nothing works better for getting the word out about the school than photos and quotes from students. These are positive, empowering images and words which work to continue our school's reputation as a great high school, and which may appear in school publications, newspapers, magazines, or on the school Website.

I give my permission for photos or videos taken of my daughter and her academic, artistic, athletic and literary accomplishments to be used in school promotions without compensation. I understand that some photos or videos of my daughter may be used following her graduation.

Parent/Guardian Printed Name	Parent/Guardian Signature	Date
Student Printed Name	Student Signature	Date

A Profile of Computer Criminals

In 1997, FBI agents arrested Adam Quinn Pletcher, 21, and charged him with trying to extort $5.25 million from Microsoft founder and chairman Bill Gates.[17] Pletcher, who spent hours in front of his computer, allegedly sent several letters to Gates, demanding the money and threatening to kill him or his wife, Melinda, if Gates did not respond to an America Online service known as "NetGirl." The service, an online dating forum, was to serve as a secure medium for the exchange of messages between Gates and the extortionist. FBI agents nabbed Pletcher after he sent a disk to Gates that held erased files containing the names of Pletcher's parents. Some months earlier, Pletcher had made headlines in Chicago when he was accused of running scams on his Internet Web page, including offering fake driver's licenses for sale, telling people he could get them cars at bargain prices and then pocketing their money, running an illegal raffle that offered $10 chances to win an expensive automobile, and offering "free" pagers that cost more than $50 in service charges. By all accounts, Pletcher was a hacker—a technologically sophisticated loner.

Hackers and hacker identities are a product of **cyberspace**, that etheric realm where computer technology and human psychology meet. Cyberspace exists only within electronic networks and is the place where computers and human beings interact with one another. For many hackers, cyberspace provides the opportunity for impersonal interpersonal contact, technological challenges, and game playing. Fantasy role-playing games are popular among hackers and may engross many "wave riders," who appear to prefer what in technological parlance is called "virtual reality" to the external physical and social worlds that surround them.

Computer-security experts have come up with a rough profile of the average hacker.[18] He is a male between the ages of 16 and 25 and lives in the United States. He is a computer user, but not a programmer, who hacks with software written by others. His primary motivation is to gain access to websites and computer networks, not to profit financially.

The History and Nature of Hacking

One of the earliest forms of cybercrime was phone phreaking, and some authors suggest that computer hacking began with the creation of the interstate phone system and direct distance dialing implemented by AT&T in the late 1950s.[19] Early switching devices used audible tones that were easily duplicated by electronics hobbyists, and "blue boxes" capable of emulating such tones quickly entered the illicit marketplace. **Phone phreaks used special telecommunications access codes and other restricted technical information to avoid paying long-distance charges. Some were able to place calls from pay phones, while others fooled telephone equipment into billing other callers.**

A modern form of phone phreaking involves the electronic theft of cellular telephone numbers and access codes. Thieves armed with simple mail-order scanners and low-end computers can "literally grab a caller's phone number and identification number out of the air."[20] Say experts, "Those numbers are [then] used to program computer chips, which are placed inside other cellular phones—or 'clones'—so the long-distance calls appear on the victim's bill."[21] Such high-profile figures as former New York mayor Rudolph Giuliani and his police commissioner have been among the victims of cellular phone piracy.

Adam Quinn Pletcher, 21, of Long Grove, Ill., leaves the federal courthouse in Seattle, Washington, on May 22, 1997. Pletcher pleaded innocent to charges of trying to extort millions from Microsoft Corp. founder Bill Gates. How can the Internet be used as a medium for criminal activities?

A scene from the virtual world *Second Life*. Are some of the activities undertaken in cyberspace the equivalent of those in the real world for purposes of the criminal law?

Another form of illegal telephone access that has recently become popular is voice-mail hacking. Private voice-mail boxes have become the targets of corporate raiders and young vandals alike. In a recent case, two teenage New York City brothers caused an estimated $2.4 million in lost business by gaining illegal access to the New Hampshire-based International Data Group's voice-mail system. Security experts at the company, who first thought that the mailboxes were malfunctioning, were alerted to the intentional disruptions by obscene outgoing messages planted by the brothers that greeted unsuspecting callers.[22]

Voice-mail fraud, another form of telephone crime, involves schemes in which mailbox access codes are shared in such a way that callers to toll-free numbers can leave messages for one another in voice-mail boxes, thereby avoiding personal long-distance charges.[23] Companies that provide access to voice-mail systems through toll-free numbers often learn of the need for access code security only after they have been victimized by such schemes.

Because most hackers are adolescent males, it is important to realize that, as one expert on hackers says, "their other favorite risky business is the time-honored adolescent sport of trespassing. They insist on going where they don't belong. . . . The only innovation is in the new form of the forbidden zone and the means of getting in it."[24]

David Kernell, 20, who was charged in 2008 with hacking into the personal Yahoo! e-mail account of former Republican vice presidential nominee Sarah Palin. What might a hacker learn from *your e-mail*?

Identity Theft

Identify theft—the misuse of another individual's personal information to commit fraud[25]— **appears to be rapidly growing.** Identity theft, which involves obtaining credit, merchandise, or services by fraudulent personal representation, is a special kind of larceny. Usually individuals learn that they have become identity theft victims only after being denied credit or employment, or when a debt collector seeks payment for a debt the victim did not incur. The most threatening aspects of identity theft are its potential relationship to international terrorism. Even where terrorism is not involved, identity theft could be used broadly by transnational crime rings.

The misuse of stolen personal information can be classified into two broad categories. *Existing account fraud* occurs when thieves obtain account information involving credit, brokerage, banking, or utility accounts that are already open. Existing account fraud is typically less costly, but more prevalent. A stolen credit card may lead to thousands of dollars in fraudulent charges, for example, but the card generally will not provide a thief with enough information to establish a false identity. Moreover, most credit card

An advertisement for Lifelock identity theft security services on a retaining wall at a NASCAR event. What is identity theft?

companies do not hold consumers liable for fraudulent charges, and federal law caps liability of victims of credit card theft at $50.

The second, and more serious, category is *new account fraud.* In new account fraud, identity thieves use personal information, such as Social Security numbers, birth dates, and home addresses, to open new accounts in the victim's name, make charges indiscriminately, and then disappear. While this type of identity theft is less likely to occur, it imposes much greater costs and hardships on victims. In addition, identity thieves sometimes use stolen personal information to obtain government, medical, or other benefits to which the criminal is not legally entitled.

A recent Federal Trade Commission (FTC) survey conducted estimated the annual number of victims of some form of identity theft at 9.91 million adults or about 4.6% of the United States population.[26] Approximately 27.3 million adults were estimated to have become victims

A Mississippi Department of Public Safety driver's license examiner compares previous photographs of a renewal applicant. The state's new facial recognition system uses software to identify suspicious profile changes in an effort to help deter identity thefts. What else might the state do?

during the previous five years. Actual dollar losses for businesses and victims in the United States are estimated roughly at $53 billion for 2004.[27] Losses can reach thousands of dollars for individual victims of new account identity theft, and the cost to repair one's identity can be enormous in terms of both time and money. Victims of new account identity theft often must correct fraudulent information in their credit reports and monitor their reports for future inaccuracies, close existing bank accounts and open new ones, and dispute charges with individual creditors.

In addition to the losses that result when identity thieves fraudulently open accounts or misuse existing accounts, monetary costs of identity theft include indirect costs to businesses for fraud prevention and mitigation of the harm once it has occurred (for example, for mailing notices to consumers and upgrading systems). Similarly, individual victims often suffer indirect financial costs, including the costs incurred in both civil litigation initiated by creditors and in overcoming the many obstacles they face in obtaining or retaining credit. Victims of nonfinancial identity theft, for example, health-related or criminal record fraud, face other types of harm and frustration.

Consumers' fears of becoming identity theft victims can also harm the digital economy. In a 2006 online survey conducted by the Business Software Alliance and Harris Interactive, nearly 30% of adults interviewed said that security fears caused them to shop online less or not at all during the 2005–2006 holiday season.[28] Identity theft became a federal crime in 1998 with the passage of the **Identity Theft and Assumption Deterrence Act**.[29] The law makes it a crime whenever anyone "knowingly transfers or uses, without lawful authority, a means of identification of another person with the intent to commit, or to aid or abet, any unlawful activity that constitutes a violation of federal law, or that constitutes a felony under any applicable state or local law."

The 2004 **Identity Theft Penalty Enhancement Act**[30] added two years to federal prison sentences for criminals convicted of using stolen credit card numbers and other personal data to commit crimes. It also prescribed prison sentences for those who use identity theft to commit other crimes, including terrorism, and it increased penalties for defendants who exceed or abuse the authority of their position in unlawfully obtaining or misusing means of personal identification.

Identity Thieves: Who They Are

Unlike some groups of criminals, identity thieves cannot be readily classified.[31] According to the FTC's survey of identity theft, about 14% of victims claim to know the perpetrator, who may be a family member, friend, or in-home employee. Identity thieves can act alone or as part of a criminal enterprise. Each poses unique threats to the public.

Identity thieves often have no prior criminal background and sometimes have preexisting relationships with the victims. They have been known to prey on people they know, including coworkers, senior citizens for whom they may be serving as caretakers, and even family members. Some identity thieves use minimal sophistication, such as stealing mail from homeowners' mailboxes or trash containing financial documents. In some jurisdictions, identity theft by illegal immigrants has resulted in passport, employment, and Social Security fraud. Occasionally, loosely-knit groups of individuals with no significant criminal records work together to obtain personal information and even to create false or fraudulent documents.[32]

Law enforcement agencies also have seen increased involvement of foreign organized criminal groups in computer- or Internet-related identity theft schemes. In Asia and Eastern Europe, for example, organized groups are increasingly sophisticated both in the techniques they use and in the complexity of their tools. According to law enforcement agencies, such groups also are demonstrating increasing levels of sophistication and specialization in their online crime, even selling goods and services—such as software templates for making counterfeit identification cards and payment card magnetic strip encoders—that make the stolen data even more valuable to those who have it.

Accused identity thieves Jocelyn Kirsch, 22, and Edward Anderton, 25. The two allegedly used stolen identities to spend more than $100,000 on trips to Paris, London, and Hawaii. Is there such a thing as a "typical" identity thief?

Technology in the Fight against Crime

Technology is a double-edged sword. On one hand, it arms potential criminals with potent new weapons of crime commission, and on the other, it provides criminal justice personnel with powerful tools useful in the battle against crime. Law enforcement capabilities commonly leapfrog one another. Consider, for example, the relatively simple case of traffic radar, which has gone through an elaborate technological evolution from early "always-on" units through trigger-operated radar devices to today's sophisticated laser speed-measuring apparatus. On the other hand, radar-jamming devices are now increasingly used by people who are apparently intent on breaking speed limit laws. Not to be outdone, suppliers to law enforcement agencies have created radar-detector detectors, which are used by authorities in states where radar detectors have been outlawed.[33]

DNA Technology

On January 16, 2001, Christopher Ochoa, 34, was released from a Texas prison after serving 13 years for a murder he did not commit.[34] Ochoa had confessed to the rape and murder of 20-year-old Nancy DePriest at a Pizza Hut in Austin in 1988. Although Ochoa later said he had been coerced by homicide detectives into confessing, no one believed him. A decade after he began serving a life sentence, however, law students at the Wisconsin Innocence Project at the University of Wisconsin–Madison took an interest in his case. They concluded that DNA evidence conclusively proved that someone else had killed DePriest. The students, led by their law professor, took the evidence to State District Judge Bob Perkins, who called the case "a fundamental miscarriage of justice" and ordered Ochoa set free. According to authorities, evidence of DePriest's murder now points to Texas inmate Achim Joseph Marino, who confessed to her murder in 1996 following a religious conversion. The law students involved in the case matched DNA samples taken from mouth swabs of Marino with the DNA found in semen taken from the victim's body. Without the technology known as **DNA profiling**, Ochoa would still be in prison—and DePriest's real killer would be unknown.

It appears to be only a matter of time until DNA evidence will be accepted throughout jurisdictions nationwide (and, probably, worldwide). Once that occurs, it is likely that DNA databases, similar in purpose to today's widely used fingerprint archives, will be established in individual states and at the national level. Today, a number of states and the federal government (through the FBI laboratory) have established digitized forensic DNA databases. At the federal level, the National DNA Index System (NDIS) enables public forensic laboratories throughout the United States to exchange and compare DNA profiles electronically, thereby linking unsolved serial violent crimes to each other and to known offenders.

Computers as Crime-Fighting Tools

Computers are now used to keep records of every imaginable sort, from point-of-sale contacts to inventory maintenance and production schedules. Computers assist in the design of new technologies and aid in the assignment of resources to problem areas.

Computers also connect people. The Internet contains a large number of law- and law enforcement–oriented newsgroups and provides access to United Nations and worldwide crime data through its link to the United Nations Criminal Justice Information Network. Other computer services provide access to security information and to

Christopher Ochoa stands outside the University of Wisconsin Law School building after being freed from prison where he was serving a life sentence for a murder that he didn't commit. What role did DNA technology play in his release?

Larry Fuller (center) celebrates with attorneys from the Innocence Project as he leaves a Dallas courthouse. Fuller was exonerated by DNA evidence and released from prison after being convicted of aggravated rape charges 25 years earlier. Should people like Fuller be compensated for mistakes made by the justice system?

software useful in law enforcement administration. Innovative computer technologies facilitate the work of enforcement agents. Among them are automated fingerprint identification systems, or AFISs (often with interstate and even international links); computerized crime scene simulations and reenactments; expert systems; and online clearinghouses containing data on criminal activity and on offenders. AFISs allow investigators to complete in a matter of minutes what would otherwise consume weeks or months of work manually matching a suspect's fingerprints against stored records. AFIS computers are able to compare and eliminate from consideration many thousands of fingerprints per second, sometimes leading to the identification of a suspect in a short time. Once crime-related information or profiles of criminal offenders have been generated, they are typically stored in a database and often made accessible to law enforcement agencies at other sites. Other specialized database programs now track inner-city gang activity and gang membership, contain information on known sexual predators, and describe missing children.

Forensic expert systems deploy machine-based artificial intelligence to draw conclusions and to make recommendations to investigators and others interested in solving problems related to crime and its

Forensics analyst Skip Burnham sits at his workstation in a new FBI computer crime lab in Centerville, Ohio, in 2009. What are "expert systems"?

commission. **Expert systems**, developed by professional "knowledge engineers" who work with "knowledge bases" and computer software called "inference engines," attempt to duplicate the decision-making processes used by skilled investigators in the analysis of evidence and in the recognition of patterns that such evidence might represent. One such system is currently being perfected by the FBI's National Center for the Analysis of Violent Crime (NCAVC). The NCAVC expert system attempts to profile serial killers by matching clues left at a crime scene with individual personality characteristics.

Finally, a number of specialized computer software programs, such as ImAger, which is produced by Face Software, Inc., and Compu-Sketch, a product of Visatex Corporation, assist police artists in rendering composite images of suspects and missing victims.

Combatting Computer Crime

In 1982, sales of information security software products to private companies and government agencies totaled only $51 million. By 1997, expenditures exceeded $425 million, and by 2003, they had grown astronomically to $1.17 billion.[35] Worldwide network security appliance and software sales reached more than $4.5 billion in 2006, and they surpassed $5 billion in 2007.[36] Among the products in use are **data encryption**, key log detectors, and Web servers supporting major security protocols. Data encryption is the process by which information is encoded, making it unreadable to all but its intended recipients.

Software alone, however, is not enough. Any effective program intended to secure a company or business operation against the threat of high-tech crime must be built on a realistic threat analysis. **Threat analysis, sometimes called "risk analysis," involves a complete and thorough assessment of the potential disasters facing an organization.** Some risks, such as floods, tornadoes, hurricanes, and earthquakes, arise from natural events and are often unpredictable. Others, including fire, electrical outages, and disruptions in public services, may be of human origin—but equally difficult to predict. Theft, employee sabotage, and terrorist attacks constitute yet another category of risk. Responses to unpredictable threats can nonetheless be planned, and strategies for dealing with almost any kind of risk can be implemented.

Once specific threats are identified, strategies tailored to dealing with them can be introduced. For example, one powerful tool useful in identifying instances of computer crime when they occur is the audit trail. Formally defined, an **audit trail** is "a sequential record of system activities that enables auditors to reconstruct, review, and examine the sequence of states and activities surrounding each event in one or more related transactions from inception to output of final results back to inception."[37] In other words, audit trails, which (once implemented) are recorded in some form of computer memory, trace and record the

Rhode Island State police officers remove computer equipment from a home in North Providence while executing a search warrant. What crime-fighting tools are available to combat computer crime?

> Any program intended to secure a company against high-tech crime must be built on a realistic threat analysis.

activities of computer operators and facilitate the apprehension of computer criminals.

Police Investigation of Computer Crime

Many state and local police departments do not have personnel skilled in the investigation of computer crimes. Most officers know little about tracing the activities of computer criminals, and some police investigators find it difficult to understand how a crime can actually have occurred when nothing at the scene appears to be missing or damaged. **Horror stories of botched police investigations are plentiful. They include tales of officers standing by** while high-tech offenders perform seemingly innocuous activities that destroy evidence, of seized magnetic or optical media allowed to bake in the sun on the dashboards of police vehicles, and of the loss of evidence stored on magnetic media due to exposure to police clipboards and evidence lockers containing magnets.

Police departments also sometimes intentionally avoid computer-crime investigations because they may be complex and demanding. The amount of time and money spent on computer-crime investigations, it is often felt, could better be spent elsewhere. Additionally, investigators who spend a lot of time on crimes involving computers tend to not be promoted as readily as their more glamorous counterparts in the homicide and property crime divisions, and personnel who are truly skilled in computer applications are apt to take jobs with private industries where pay scales are far higher than in police work. As a consequence of these considerations and others, many police departments and their investigators make cybercrime a low priority.

The situation is changing, however, thanks to federal intervention. In 1992, the FBI formed a National Computer Crime Squad (NCCS)[38] to investigate violations of the federal Computer Fraud and Abuse Act of 1984[39] and other federal computer-crime laws. Prior to the creation of the Department of Homeland Security, the FBI's Washington Field Office housed the agency's Infrastructure Protection and Computer Intrusion Squad (IPCIS). The

squad, whose duties have been transferred to DHS, investigated the illegal interception of signals (especially cable and satellite signal theft) and the infringement of copyright laws related to software.

Automated monitoring of network traffic is an area of considerable interest to law enforcement officials. One network "sniffer" created by the FBI called **DCS–1000** (previously known as "Carnivore") was a diagnostic tool intended to assist in criminal investigations by monitoring and capturing large amounts of Internet traffic. DCS–1000 was to be installed by FBI agents in ISP data centers as the need arose to monitor the electronic communications of individuals suspected of federal crimes like terrorism. The Carnivore/DCS–1000 initiative was later retitled DCS-3000, and changed its focus to intercepting suspect personal communications delivered via wireless services.[40]

Although goods and materials will always need to be created, transported, and distributed, it is information that forms the lifeblood of the new cyberworld. Nations that are able to effectively manage valuable information and that can make it accessible to their citizens will receive enhanced productivity and greater wealth as a reward. Moving information safely and securely is also important, and today a large part of that responsibility falls to the Internet. The **Internet**, the world's largest computer network, provides some amazing and constantly growing capabilities. Unfortunately, as the Internet has grown, it has been targeted by hackers and computer criminals, some of whom have introduced rogue computer programs into the network's machines.

Auditors at work. What is an "audit trail"?

Policy Issues: Personal Freedoms in the Information Age

The continued development of telecommunications resources has led not only to concerns about security and data integrity, but also to an expanding interest in privacy, free speech, and personal freedoms. While the **First and Fourth Amendments to the U.S. Constitution** guarantee each of us freedom of speech and security in our "persons, houses, papers, and effects, against unreasonable searches and seizures," it is understandably silent on the subject of electronic documents and advanced forms of communication facilitated by technologies that did not exist at the time of the Constitutional Convention.

In this new age, then, what is speech? What are papers? Do electronic communications qualify for protection under the First Amendment, as does the spoken word? In an era when most houses are wired for telephones and many support data links that extend well beyond voice capabilities, it becomes necessary to ask what constitutes one's "speech" or one's "home." Does e-mail qualify as speech? Where does the concept of a home begin and end for purposes of constitutional guarantees? Do activities within the home that can be accessed from without (as when a computer website is run out of a home) fall under the same constitutional guarantees as a private conversation held within the physical confines of a house?

Complicating matters still further are today's "supersnoop" technologies, which provide investigators with the ability to literally hear through walls (using vibration detectors), listen to conversations over tremendous distances (with parabolic audio receivers), record voices in distant rooms (via laser readings of windowpane vibrations), and even look through walls using forward-looking infrared (FLIR) devices, which can detect temperature differences of as little as two-tenths of one degree.

In 1990, concerned individuals banded together to form the **Electronic Frontier Foundation**, a citizens' group funded by private contributions that set for itself the task of actively

A police helicopter equipped with Forward Looking Infrared (FLIR) cameras. The cameras allow the pilots to "see" at night, and to detect the body heat given off by suspects. Do such technologies, when used by the police, exceed Constitutional limits?

Electronic Frontier Foundation executive director, Shari Steele (right), and Kevin Bankston, staff attorney, at their San Francisco office. What does the Electronic Frontier Foundation do?

The EFF works to ensure that the principles embodied in the Constitution and Bill of Rights are protected as new communications technologies emerge.

assisting in refining notions of privacy and legality as they relate to telecommunications and other computer-based media. In the foundation's own words, "The Electronic Frontier Foundation (EFF) was founded in July of 1990 to ensure that the principles embodied in the Constitution and the Bill of Rights are protected as new communications technologies emerge. From the beginning, EFF has worked to shape our nation's communications infrastructure and the policies that govern it in order to maintain and enhance First Amendment, privacy and other democratic values.

We believe that our overriding public goal must be the creation of Electronic Democracy."[41]

EFF, which also supports litigation in the public interest, has been an active supporter of the public advocacy group Computer Professionals for Social Responsibility (CPSR). CPSR maintains a Computing and Civil Liberties Project much in keeping with EFF's purpose. EFF also supported challenges to the Communications Decency Act that resulted in the 1997 Supreme Court ruling in *Reno* v. *ACLU,* which found key provisions of the act unconstitutional.

At the time of his arrest in February 1995, Kevin Mitnick was the most wanted computer criminal in United States history. There's little wonder as to why: His crimes included wire fraud, computer fraud, and wire communication interception, and the cost to his victims included millions of dollars in lost licensing fees, marketing delays, lost research and development, and the costs of repairing compromised computer systems.[i]

Cloned cellular telephones, hacker software programs, "sniffer" devices, and so-called "social engineering" were the tools Mitnick used to conduct the computer crime spree that launched a lengthy investigation beginning in 1992. The evidence amassed by the FBI during its three-year probe was sufficient to force Mitnick to accept a plea bargain rather than risk more severe penalties by going to trial.[ii] His corporate victims included Motorola, Novell, Fujitsu, Sun Microsystems, and Nokia Mobile Phones, Ltd., among others, and he used University of Southern California computer systems to hide software code and obscure his identity.

An intriguing element of Mitnick's case was the manner in which he was finally caught.[iii] Computer expert Tsutomu Shimomura, infuriated after Mitnick hacked into and stole information from his home computer, employed a dramatic cybersleuthing effort to track down Mitnick, resulting in Mitnick's arrest by the FBI in a Raleigh, North Carolina, apartment complex. Shimomura and *New York Times* reporter John Markoff subsequently published *Takedown*, an account of Shimomura's experience in chasing down the elusive Mitnick.[iv]

Mitnick was made unhappy by what he believed was excessive media hype that led to his being unfairly characterized as "Osama bin Mitnick."[v] His actual transgressions, he contends, were far less serious than those depicted in sensationalistic press reports.

As a result of his 1995 arrest, Mitnick spent more than five years in prison, with more than eight months of it in solitary confinement. Now in his forties, a significantly matured Mitnick has done a 180-degree turnaround in his approach to computer security. On March 1, 2000, he testified before the U.S. Senate's Governmental Affairs Committee, during which he suggested that the millions of dollars corporations spend on firewalls and secure access devices are negated by the "the weakest link in the security chain: the people who use, administer and operate computer systems."[vi] Mitnick regaled the committee with tales of his use of "social engineering" (what he defines as "using manipulation, influence and deception to get a trusted insider to release information and to perform some sort of action item"[vii]) that enables a hacker to successfully attack the insider's own computer system.

Mitnick now heads up a highly successful computer consulting firm that specializes—not too surprisingly—in advising on computer security issues. Disturbingly, he suggests that it is easier to hack today than it was years ago, citing social engineering as still an extraordinarily effective technique for computer exploit. Mitnick's message is clear: Notwithstanding tremendous advances in both hardware and software security measures, the weak link is still the human element.[viii]

The Cause Behind the Crime
Kevin Mitnick

Can We Understand Mitnick's Crimes?

- Kevin Mitnick was born in Southern California and had three arrests in his late teens and early twenties for computer-related crimes. *Why do you think these early arrests didn't curtail Mitnik's later illegal hacking?*

- The FBI attempted to chase down Mitnick. *Had ordinary citizen and computer expert Tsutomu Shimomura not gotten involved in his cybersleuthing effort to track Mitnick down, would he have been caught?*

- Mitnick felt that his transgressions were not as serious as those depicted in press reports. *Why did he feel that way?*

Kevin Mitnick, preparing to testify before Congress in 2000 on network security.

- After his 1995 arrest, Mitnick spent more than five years in prison and then testified before the Senate's Governmental Affairs Committee regarding cybersecurity. *Why do you think he made the decision to testify?*

Mitnick supporters (above), and Tsutomu Shimomura (left), the cybersleuth who helped track Mitnick down. What does Mitnick do today?

- Mitnick now heads up a successful computer firm that advises on security issues. *How do you feel about the way he parlayed a career in crime into a successful business?*

NOTES

[i] Kevin Mitnick Sentenced to Nearly Four Years in Prison, U.S. Department of Justice Press Release, August 9, 1999; and "Computer Hacker Ordered to Pay Restitution to Victim Companies Whose Systems were Compromised," United States Attorney's Office, Central District of California, August 9, 1999, http://www.cybercrime.gov/mitnick.htm (accessed June 2, 2007).

[ii] Ibid.

[ii] John Christensen, "The Trials of Kevin Mitnick" CNN, March 18, 1999, http://www.cnn.com/SPECIALS/1999/mitnick.background (accessed June 2, 2007).

[iv] Ibid.

[v] "A Convicted Hacker Debunks Some Myths," CNN, October 13, 2005, http://www.cnn.com/2005/TECH/internet/10/07/kevin.mitnick.cnna (accessed June 2, 2007).

[vi] Elizabeth Wasserman, "Mitnick Schools Feds on Hacking 101," CNN, March 3, 2000, http://archives.cnn.com/2000/TECH/computing/03/03/mitnick.the.prof/mitnick.the.prof.html (accessed June 2, 2007).

[vii] Kevin D. Mitnick, *The Art of Deception: Controlling the Human Element of Security* (Hoboken, NJ: Wiley, 2003).

[viii] "A Convicted Hacker Debunks Some Myths."

Go to mycrimekit.com to explore the following resources for Chapter 12:

- **PRACTICE QUIZ:** Multiple-choice, true/false, short-answer, and essay questions
- **FLASHCARDS:** Twenty-three flashcards to test your knowledge of the chapter's key terms
- **WEB EXTRAS & LIBRARY EXTRAS:** Links to websites, online articles, and resources about software piracy, fraud, theft of identity and intellectual property, computer viruses, and preventing and fighting computer crime
- **ENDNOTES:** Chapter 12 bibliography

Summary and Key Concepts

TECHNOLOGY AND CRIME

Much of today's crime is committed through the use of high technology and consists of efforts to obtain or manipulate data stored on computers or available through the Internet.

High Technology and Criminal Opportunity

Technologically skilled criminals seeking illegitimate access to computerized information take a number of routes to obtain the data they desire.

hacker A person who uses computers for exploration and exploitation.

cybercrime Any violation of a federal or state computer crime statute.

 How do changes in technology produce new forms of crime?

The Extent of Cybercrime

A huge number of today's financial transactions are computerized, but the sophistication of cybercriminals makes it difficult to quantify losses due to computer crime.

software piracy The unauthorized and illegal copying of software programs.

phishing Pronounced "fishing." An Internet-based scam to steal valuable information such as credit card numbers, social security numbers, user IDs, and passwords.

computer virus A set of computer instructions that propagates copies or versions of itself into computer programs or data when it is executed.

Computer Crime and the Law

In the early years of computer-based information systems, many U.S. jurisdictions tried to prosecute unauthorized computer access under preexisting statutes, including burglary and larceny laws. Since that time new laws have been developed at both the state and federal levels.

 Why do advancing technologies sometimes necessitate new criminal laws?

Communications Decency Act (CDA) A federal statute signed into law in 1996, the CDA is Title 5 of the federal Telecommunications Act of 1996 (Public Law 104–104, 110 Stat. 56). The law sought to protect minors from harmful material on the Internet, and a portion of the CDA criminalized the knowing transmission of obscene or indecent messages to any recipient under 18 years of age.

Reno v. ACLU The 1997 U.S. Supreme Court case that found the bulk of the CDA to be unconstitutional, ruling that it contravenes First Amendment free speech guarantees.

No Electronic Theft Act (NETA) A 1997 federal law that criminalizes the willful infringement of copyrighted works, including by electronic means, even when the infringing party derives no direct financial benefit from the infringement.

Digital Theft Deterrence and Copyright Damages Improvement Act A 1999 federal law that attempted to combat software piracy and other forms of digital theft by amending Section 504(c) of the Copyright Act, thereby increasing the amount of damages that could potentially be awarded in cases of copyright infringement.

Cyber Security Enhancement Act (CSEA) Part of the Homeland Security Act of 2002, this federal law directs the U.S. Sentencing Commission to take several specific factors into account in creating new sentencing guidelines for computer criminals.

computer-related crime Any illegal act for which knowledge of computer technology is involved in its perpetration, investigation, or prosecution.

computer abuse Any unlawful incident associated with computer technology in which a victim suffered or could have suffered loss, or in which a perpetrator by intention made or could have made gain.

A Profile of Computer Criminals

The typical computer hacker is a male between the ages of 16 and 25 and lives in the United States; is a computer user, but not a programmer; and is primarily motivated to gain access to websites and computer networks, not to profit financially.

cyberspace The computer-created matrix of virtual possibilities, including online services, wherein human beings interact with one another and with technology itself.

phone phreak A person who uses switched, dialed-access telephone services for exploration and exploitation.

 Q: *Is there a typical kind of computer criminal?*

Identity Theft

Identity theft is a new and a special kind of larceny that involves obtaining credit, merchandise, or services by fraudulent personal representation.

identity theft The unauthorized use of another individual's personal identity to fraudulently obtain money, goods, or services; to avoid the payment of debt; or to avoid criminal prosecution.

Identity Theft and Assumption Deterrence Act The first federal law to make identity theft a crime. The 1998 statute makes it a crime whenever anyone "knowingly transfers or uses, without lawful authority, a means of identification of another person with the intent to commit, or to aid or abet, any unlawful activity that constitutes a violation of federal law, or that constitutes a felony under any applicable state or local law."

Identity Theft Penalty Enhancement Act A 2004 federal law that added two years to federal prison sentences for criminals convicted of using stolen credit card numbers and other personal data to commit crimes.

 Q: *What is identity theft? How can identities be stolen?*

Technology in the Fight against Crime

Technology is a double-edged sword. On one hand, it arms potential criminals with potent new weapons of crime commission, and on the other, it provides criminal justice personnel with powerful tools useful in the battle against crime.

DNA profiling The use of biological residue found at the scene of a crime for genetic comparisons in aiding the identification of criminal suspects.

expert systems Computer hardware and software that attempt to duplicate the decision-making processes used by skilled investigators in the analysis of evidence and in the recognition of patterns that such evidence might represent.

 Q: *What is the difference between high-technology crime and traditional forms of criminal activity?*

Combatting Computer Crime

Moving information safely and securely is vitally important today, and security responsibilities are shared by law enforcement agencies, the public, corporations, businesses, and Internet service providers.

data encryption The process by which information is encoded, making it unreadable to all but its intended recipients.

threat analysis A complete and thorough assessment of the kinds of perils facing an organization.

audit trail A sequential record of computer system activities that enables auditors to reconstruct, review, and examine the sequence of states and activities surrounding each event in one or more related transactions from inception to output of final results back to inception.

DCS–1000 An FBI-developed network diagnostic tool that is capable of assisting in criminal investigations by monitoring and capturing large amounts of Internet traffic. Previously called *Carnivore*.

Internet The world's largest computer network.

Policy Issues: Personal Freedoms in the Information Age

The continued development of telecommunications resources has led not only to concerns about security and data integrity, but also to an expanding interest in privacy, free speech, and personal freedoms.

First and Fourth Amendments to the U.S. Constitution Guarantee each of us freedom of speech and security in our "persons, houses, papers, and effects, against unreasonable searches and seizures."

Electronic Frontier Foundation (EFF) A nonprofit organization formed in July of 1990 to help ensure that the principles embodied in the Constitution and the Bill of Rights are protected as new communications technologies emerge.

Q: *What are some of the personal freedoms that are threatened by today's need for enhanced security?*

Globalization and Terrorism
Our Small World

[I]nternational implications for America's criminal justice system have never been greater. As the country's social, economic, and technological climate continue to undergo major changes, globalization is also producing new challenges for criminal justice practitioners and researchers. Among the more significant aspects of this change…are the international dimensions of crime, the impact of legal and illegal immigration, transnational organized crime, technological influences on global criminality, and the influence of a more diversified American culture.

—*Richard Ward,* The Internationalization of Criminal Justice

Globalization

Globalization can be defined as a process of social homogenization by which the experiences of everyday life, marked by the diffusion of commodities and ideas, can foster a standardization of cultural expressions around the world.[1] The increasing integration of previously isolated events and their impact is an important aspect of globalization.

Transnational Crimes

Globalization is making it impossible to ignore criminal activity in other parts of the world, especially where that crime is perpetrated by transnational criminal and terrorist organizations. *Transnational crime*, or **transnational organized crime**, is unlawful activity undertaken and supported by organized criminal groups across national boundaries. Transnational crime has emerged as one of the most pressing challenges of the early twenty-first century. The growing globalization of crime has required the coordination of law enforcement efforts in different parts of the world and the expansion of U.S. law enforcement activities internationally. Transnational crimes range from relatively simple fraudulent e-mail and phishing schemes to the much more dangerous and threatening illegal trafficking in human beings, human organs, and illicit drugs. It includes the activities of multinational drug cartels, the support of terrorist groups by criminal organizations seeking armed protection, and well-funded and sophisticated efforts by organized criminal groups looking to overthrow the ruling regime in regions with others sympathetic to their operations.

Human Smuggling and Trafficking

According to the United Nations,[2] trafficking in persons and human smuggling are some of the fastest growing areas of international criminal activity today. There are important distinctions between the two. The U.S. State Department defines **human smuggling** as "the facilitation, transportation, attempted transportation or illegal entry of a person(s) across an international border, in violation of one or more country's laws, either clandestinely or through deception, such as the use of fraudulent documents."[3] In other words, human smuggling refers to illegal immigration in which an agent is involved for payment to help a person cross a border clandestinely.[4] Human smuggling may be conducted to obtain financial or other benefits for the smuggler, although sometimes people smuggle others to reunite their families. Human smuggling generally occurs with the

U.S. Customs and Border Protection agents take illegal aliens into custody near Brownsville, Texas. What's the difference between human smuggling and human trafficking?

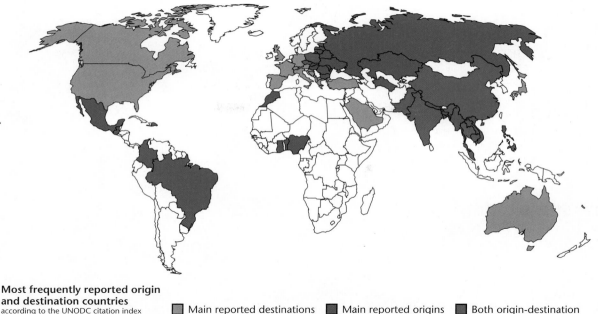

Most frequently reported origin
and destination countries
according to the UNODC citation index

■ Main reported destinations ■ Main reported origins ■ Both origin-destination

FIGURE 13-1 Human Trafficking—Countries of Origin and Destination

Source: United Nations Office on Drugs and Crime (UNODC), *Trafficking in Persons: Global Patterns* (April 2006), p. 17. Web available at
http://www.unodc.org/documents/human-trafficking/HT-globalpatterns-en.pdf.

consent of the persons being smuggled, and those people often pay for the services. Once in the country they've paid to enter, they will usually no longer be in contact with the smuggler. The State Department notes that the vast majority of people who are assisted in illegally entering the United States annually are smuggled, rather than trafficked.

Although smuggling might not involve active coercion, it can be deadly. In January 2007, for example, truck driver Tyrone Williams, 36, a Jamaican citizen living in Schenectady, New York, was sentenced to life in prison for causing the deaths of 19 illegal immigrants in the nation's deadliest known human smuggling attempt.[5]

The Intelligence Reform and Terrorism Prevention Act of 2004[6] established the Human Smuggling and Trafficking Center (HSTC), within the Department of Homeland Security (DHS). U.S. Immigration and Customs Enforcement (ICE), the largest investigative agency within DHS, has primary responsibility for enforcing laws related to human smuggling and trafficking. As a result, ICE plays a leading role in the fight against human smuggling and trafficking.

In contrast to smuggling, **trafficking in persons (TIP)** can be compared to a modern-day form of slavery. Trafficking involves the exploitation of unwilling people through force, coercion, threat, or deception, and includes human rights abuses such as debt bondage, deprivation of liberty, or lack of control over freedom and labor. Trafficking is often undertaken for purposes of sexual exploitation or labor exploitation. The Global Fast Fund, a nonprofit international charity that tracks TIP incidents, says that "the primary countries of destination for victims of trafficking are the United States, Italy, Japan, Canada, Australia, and other 'advanced nations.'"[7] A map from Global Fast is shown in Figure 13–1, showing both countries of origin and destination for victims of trafficking. Figure 13–2 shows where victims of trafficking into the United States end up.

It is sometimes difficult to distinguish between a smuggling and a trafficking case because trafficking often includes an element of smuggling (that is, the illegal crossing of a national border.) Some trafficking victims may believe they are being smuggled when they are really being trafficked, but are unaware of their eventual fate. This happens, for example, where women trafficked for

295

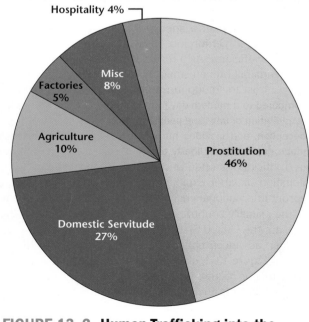

THE NEW YORK STATE
ANTI-TRAFFICKING COALITION

Social activist Gloria Steinem, along with other New Yorkers, calls for a strong law against human trafficking in a press conference on the steps of the state's supreme court. Why are such laws needed?

sexual exploitation may have thought they were agreeing to work in legitimate industries for decent wages—part of which they may have agreed to pay to the trafficker who smuggled them. They didn't know that upon arrival the traffickers would keep them in bondage, subject them to physical force or sexual violence, force them to work in the sex trade, and take most or all of their income. Table 13–1 draws some important distinctions between human trafficking and smuggling.

Human Trafficking—The Numbers

U.S. government officials estimate that 800,000 to 900,000 victims are trafficked globally each year and that 17,500 to 18,500 are trafficked into the United States. Women and children comprise the largest group of victims, and they are often physically and emotionally abused. Although TIP is often an international crime that involves

Pie Chart

- Hospitality 4%
- Misc 8%
- Factories 5%
- Agriculture 10%
- Prostitution 46%
- Domestic Servitude 27%

FIGURE 13–2 Human Trafficking into the United States—Endpoint Sectors

Source: Based on Free the Slaves and the Human Rights Center, University of California, Berkeley, *Hidden Slaves, Forced Labor in the United States* (September, 2004), p. 1. Web available at http://web.archive.org/web/20070830033751/ http://freetheslaves.net/files/Hidden_Slaves.pdf (accessed August 1, 2009).

TABLE 13–1

Distinguishing between Human Trafficking and Smuggling

Trafficking	Smuggling
Must contain an element of force, fraud, or coercion (actual, perceived, or implied), unless the victim is under 18 years of age and is involved in commercial sex acts.	The person being smuggled is generally cooperating.
Forced labor and/or exploitation.	No forced labor or other exploitation.
Persons trafficked are victims.	Persons smuggled are violating the law. They are not victims.
Enslaved, subjected to limited movement or isolation, or had documents confiscated.	Persons are free to leave, change jobs, etc.
Need not involve the actual movement of the victim.	Facilitates the illegal entry of person(s) from one country into another.
No requirement to cross an international border.	Smuggling always crosses an international border.
Person must be involved in labor/services or commercial sex acts (that is, must be "working").	Person must only be in the country or attempting entry illegally.

Source: Adapted from U.S. Department of State, Bureau for International Narcotics and Law Enforcement Affairs, Human Smuggling and Trafficking Center, *Distinctions Between Human Smuggling and Human Trafficking* (Washington, DC: January 1, 2005).
Note: This table is meant to be conceptual and is not intended to provide precise legal distinctions between smuggling and trafficking.

TABLE 13–2

Number of Alleged Human Trafficking Incidents in the U.S., 2007–2008

Type of Human Trafficking Incident	Total Incidents	
	Number	Percent
All incidents*	1,229	100.0%
Sex trafficking	**1,018**	**82.8%**
Forced prostitution	596	48.5
Child sex trafficking	391	31.8
Other sex trafficking	31	2.5
Labor trafficking	**146**	**11.9%**
Other	65	5.3

*One trafficking incident may involve many victims.
Source: Tracey Kyckelhahn, Allen J. Beck, and Thomas H. Cohen, *Characteristics of Suspected Human Trafficking Incidents, 2007–2008* (Washington, DC: Bureau of Justice Statistics, 2009), p. 1.

the crossing of borders, it is important to note that TIP victims can be trafficked within their own countries and communities. Traffickers can move victims between locations within the same country and often sell them to other trafficking organizations.

A few years ago, the Department of Justice funded the creation of the Human Trafficking Reporting System (HTRS) to report on human trafficking within the United States. The most recent HTRS report provides data on human trafficking incidents that were investigated between January 1, 2007, and September 30, 2008. Those data are shown in Table 13–2.

Seen globally, the International Labor Organization (ILO), the United Nations agency charged with addressing labor standards, employment, and social protection issues, estimates that there are 12.3 million people in forced labor, bonded labor, forced child labor, and sexual servitude throughout the world today.[8] Other estimates range as high as 27 million.

Comparative Criminology

Comparative criminology is the study of crime on a cross-national level. By comparing crime patterns in one country with those in another, theories and policies that have been taken for granted in one place can be reevaluated in the light of world experience. As some noted **comparative criminologists** have observed, "The challenge for comparative criminologists is to develop theories with increased specificity while managing to construct them in such a way that they can be applied across more than one culture or nation-state. This eventually must demand that theories be developed to conceptualize societies as totalities and that theories that manage to provide a world context in which total societies behave be further constructed."[9]

Some have used the term *globalization of knowledge* to describe the increase in understanding that results from a sharing of information between cultures. The globalization of knowledge is beginning to play a significant role in both the process of theory formation within criminology and the development of American crime control policies. According to some, "Globalization will make it increasingly difficult for nation-states to ignore the criminal justice information of other countries." Two years ago, as recipient of the prestigious Vollmer Award in Criminology, Franklin E. Zimring, of the University of California, Berkeley, addressed the American Society of Criminology, complaining about the fact that American criminology had been self-obsessed and "particularly inattentive to the value and necessity of transnational comparisons." Zimring sees comparative efforts as providing a context for evaluating knowledge and reviewing observations. Using this perspective, Zimring demonstrated that the crime decline in the United States during the 1990s was not unique to America—and that the same decline occurred in Canada at exactly the same time.

Ethnocentrism

One important issue facing comparative criminologists is **ethnocentrism**. Ethnocentrism, or culture-centeredness, can interfere with the work of comparative criminologists in a number of ways, including the ways in which crime statistics are gathered, analyzed, and presented.

Only in recent years have American specialists in criminology begun to closely examine crime in other cultures. Not all societies are equally open, and it is not always easy to explore them. In some societies, even the *study* of crime is taboo. As a result, data-gathering strategies taken for granted in Western culture may not be well received elsewhere. One author, for example, has observed that in China, "the seeking of criminal justice information through face-to-face questioning takes on a different meaning than it does generally in the Western world. While we accept this method of inquiry because we prize thinking on our feet and quick answers, it is offensive in China because it shows lack of

Commuters in Delhi, India (left), a crowded street in Beijing, China (center), and New York City's Times Square. How do differences in culture lead to differences in crime? In crime reporting?

**An Islamic fundamentalist, backed by
militant extremists, waives the Koran.
What is ethnocentrism?**

respect and appreciation for the information given through the preferred means of prepared questions and formal briefings."[10] Most of the information available about Chinese crime rates comes by way of officialdom, and routine Western social science practices like door-to-door interviews, participant observation, and random surveys might not produce results in China.

Similar difficulties arise in the comparison of crime rates from one country to another. The crime rates of different nations are difficult to compare because of (1) differences in the way a given crime is defined, (2) diverse crime-reporting practices, and (3) political, social, economic, and other influences on the reporting of statistics to international agencies.[11]

Issues in Reporting

Definitional differences create what may be the biggest problem. For cross-national comparisons of crime data to be meaningful, they must share conceptual similarities. Unfortunately, that is often not the case. Nations report offenses according to the legal criteria by which arrests are made and under which prosecution can occur. Switzerland, for example, includes bicycle thefts in its reported data on what we call "auto theft." The Netherlands has no crime category for robberies, counting them as thefts. Japan classifies an assault that results in death as an assault or an aggravated assault, not as a homicide. Greek rape statistics include crimes of sodomy, "lewdness," seduction of a child, incest, and prostitution. Communist China reports only robberies and thefts that involve the property of citizens; crimes against state-owned property fall into a separate category.

Crime statistics also reflect social and political contexts. Some nations do not accurately report certain kinds of culturally reprehensible crimes. Communist countries, for example, often do not report crimes like theft, burglary, and robbery because the very existence of such offenses might appear to create inadequacies in the communist system. Likewise, the social norms in some societies may make it almost impossible for women to report cases of rape or sexual abuse, while in others, women are encouraged to come forward.

Terrorism

The U.S. Department of State defines **terrorism** as "premeditated, politically motivated violence perpetrated against noncombatant targets by subnational groups or clandestine agents, usually intended to influence an audience."[12] Europol says that "Terrorism is not an ideology or movement, but a tactic or a method for attaining political goals."[13] Paul Pillar, former deputy chief of the CIA's Counterterrorist Center, has identified four key features of terrorism that distinguish it from other forms of violence.[14] Those features are shown in Table 13–3.

Terrorist acts are criminal because they violate the criminal law, because they involve criminal activity, and because they produce criminal results. The primary distinction between violent criminal acts and acts of terrorism, however, has to do with the political motivation or social ideology of the offender.[15]

Terrorist groups vary in their goals, and can be categorized as follows:

1. **Nationalist terrorists** seek to change the entire political, social, and economic system to an extreme right or ultraconservative model.

2. **Religious terrorists** use violence to bring about social and cultural changes that are in keeping with their religious views.

3. **State-sponsored terrorists** are deliberately employed by radical nations as foreign policy tools.

4. **Left-wing terrorists** seek to replace economies based on free enterprise with socialist or communist economic systems.

5. **Right-wing terrorists** are motivated by fascist ideals and work toward the dissolution of democratic governments.

6. **Anarchist terrorists** are revolutionary, anticapitalist, and antiauthoritarian. While these groups are often motivated by domestic politics they are usually also part of wider international campaigns and may fight against free trade agreements, what they see as ecologically-damaging practices, etc.

Table 13–4 lists examples of contemporary terrorist groups according to the categories listed here.

TABLE 13–3

Characteristics of Terrorism

Terrorism Usually Is	Terrorism Usually Is Not
Premeditated or planned	Impulsive, or an act of rage
Politically motivated (that is, intended to change the existing political order)	Perpetrated for criminal gain (that is, illicit personal or, financial benefit)
Aimed at civilians	Aimed at military targets or combat-ready troops
Carried out by subnational groups	Perpetrated by the army of a country

---

TABLE 13–4

Types of Terrorist Groups

Nationalist	Religious	State-Sponsored	Left-Wing	Right-Wing	Anarchist
Irish Republican Army, Basque Fatherland and Liberty, Kurdistan Workers' Party	Al-Qaeda, HAMAS, Hezbollah, Aum Shinrikyo (Japan)	Hezbollah (backed by Iran), Abu Nidal Organization (Syria, Libya), Japanese Red Army (Libya)	Red Brigades (Italy), Baader-Meinhof Gang (Germany), Japanese Red Army	Neo-Nazis, skinheads, white supremacists	Some contemporary antiglobalization groups

Source: Derived from information provided by the Council on Foreign Relations and the Markle Foundation, *Types of Terrorism,* http://www.terrorismanswers.com/terrorism/types.html, and http://www.cfr.org/issue/135/terrorism.html (accessed January 10, 2009, and July 10, 2009).

Palestinian youths train with wooden guns during a Hamas-run summer camp in the Gaza Strip, on August 11, 2009. What different types of terrorist groups can be identified?

terrorist attacks. The nine-story building was devastated by a homemade bomb. The fertilizer and diesel fuel device used in the attack was left in a parked rental truck beside the building, and the blast left a crater 30 feet wide and 8 feet deep and spread debris over a ten-block area.

In June 1997, a federal jury found 29-year-old Timothy McVeigh guilty of 11 counts ranging from conspiracy to

Part of the Oklahoma City memorial commemorating the 1995 attack on the Murrah federal building. What's the difference between domestic and international terrorism?

The United States is faced today with two major types of terrorism: domestic and international. **Domestic terrorism** uses unlawful force or violence by a group or an individual who is based and operates entirely within the United States and its territories without foreign direction and whose acts are directed at elements of the U.S. government or population.[16] **International terrorism** uses unlawful force or violence by a group or an individual who has a connection to a foreign power or whose activities transcend national boundaries against persons or property to intimidate or coerce a government, the civilian population, or any segment thereof, in furtherance of political or social objectives.[17] International terrorism is sometimes incorrectly called *foreign terrorism*, a term that, strictly speaking, refers only to acts of terrorism that occur outside of the United States.

Domestic Terrorism

The 1995 terrorist bombing of the Alfred P. Murrah federal building in downtown Oklahoma City, Oklahoma, which killed 168 people and wounded hundreds more, showed just how vulnerable the United States is to domestic

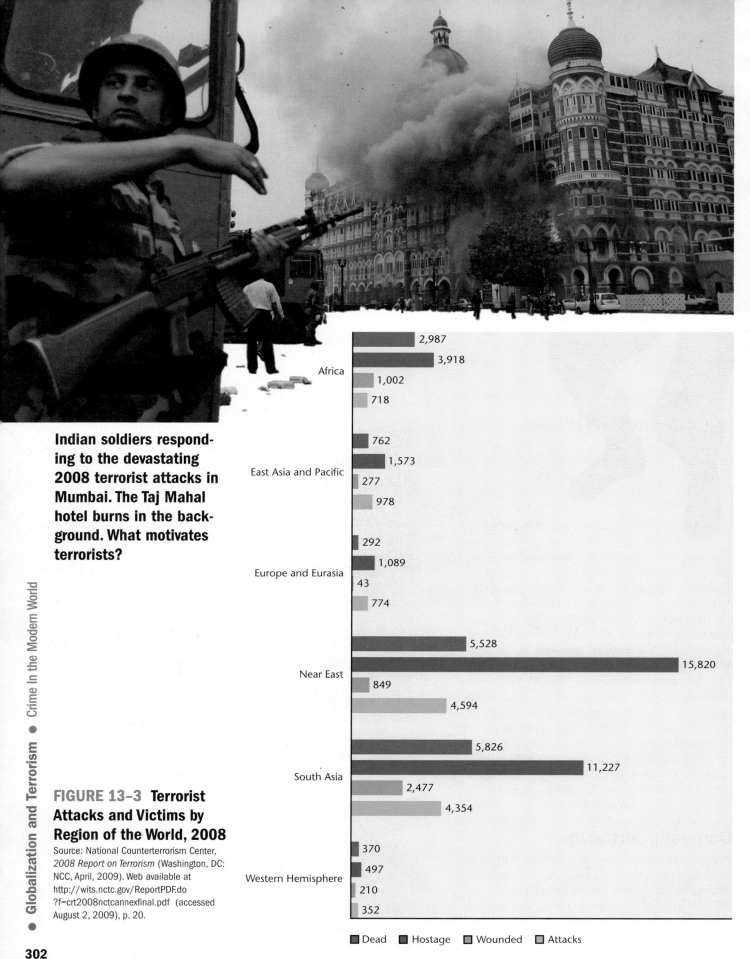

Indian soldiers responding to the devastating 2008 terrorist attacks in Mumbai. The Taj Mahal hotel burns in the background. What motivates terrorists?

FIGURE 13–3 **Terrorist Attacks and Victims by Region of the World, 2008**

Source: National Counterterrorism Center, *2008 Report on Terrorism* (Washington, DC: NCC, April, 2009). Web available at http://wits.nctc.gov/ReportPDF.do ?f=crt2008nctcannexfinal.pdf (accessed August 2, 2009), p. 20.

Africa
- 2,987
- 3,918
- 1,002
- 718

East Asia and Pacific
- 762
- 1,573
- 277
- 978

Europe and Eurasia
- 292
- 1,089
- 43
- 774

Near East
- 5,528
- 15,820
- 849
- 4,594

South Asia
- 5,826
- 11,227
- 2,477
- 4,354

Western Hemisphere
- 370
- 497
- 210
- 352

■ Dead   ■ Hostage   ■ Wounded   ■ Attacks

FIGURE 13-4 **Worldwide Terrorism Attacks, by Method, 2008**

Source: National Counterterrorism Center, *2008 Report on Terrorism* (Washington, DC: NCC, April, 2009). Web available at http://wits.nctc.gov/ReportPDF.do?f=crt2008nctcannexfinal.pdf (accessed August 2, 2009), p. 28.

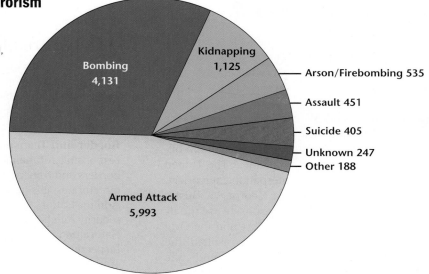

first-degree murder in the bombing. Jurors concluded that McVeigh had conspired with Terry Nichols, a friend he had met while both were in the army, and with unknown others to use a truck bomb to destroy the Murrah building.

International Terrorism

According to the National Counterterrorism Center (NCTC), 11,770 terrorist attacks against noncombatants occurred in various countries during 2008, resulting in over 54,000 deaths, injuries, and kidnappings.[18] In that year, the largest number of terrorist attacks took place in the Middle East, but South Asia had the greatest number of fatalities. These two regions were also the locations for 75% of the 235 high-casualty attacks (those that killed 10 or more people) that took place in 2008 (Figure 13–3). The NCTC reports the following for 2008:

- About 4,600, or nearly 40% of the 11,770 total number of attacks, occurred in the Middle East, where approximately 5,500 fatalities (35% of the worldwide total) were reported.

- Another 35% of the attacks occurred in South Asia.

- Afghanistan and Pakistan registered increased attacks, with attacks in Pakistan more than doubling in 2008 from the previous year.

- Violence against noncombatants in Africa, particularly in Somalia and the Democratic Republic of the Congo, rose 140% in 2008, totaling about 2,200 fatalities.

- The number of reported attacks in 2008 fell in the Western Hemisphere by about 25%, and in East Asia and the Pacific by 30%.

Most attacks in 2008 were perpetrated by terrorist organizations using conventional methods of terrorism, such as armed attacks, bombings, and kidnappings (Figures 13–4 and 13–5). Terrorists continued the practice of coordinated attacks that included secondary attacks on first responders at attack sites, and they continued to reconfigure weapons and other materials to create improvised explosive devices.

As has been the case since 2005, substantial numbers of victims of terrorist attacks in 2008 were Muslim. In fact, well over 50% of victims worldwide were Muslims, and most of those were victims of attacks in Iraq, Pakistan, and Afghanistan.

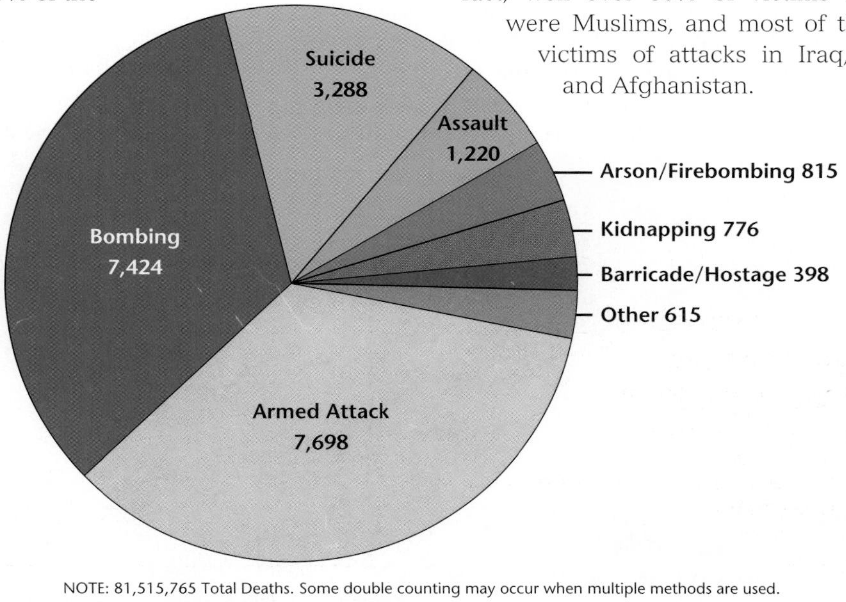

FIGURE 13-5 Worldwide Deaths from Terrorist Attacks by Method of Attack, 2008

Source: National Counterterrorism Center, *2008 Report on Terrorism* (Washington, DC: NCC, April, 2009). Web available at http://wits.nctc.gov/ReportPDF.do?f=crt2008nctcannexfinal.pdf (accessed August 2, 2009), p. 21.

NOTE: 81,515,765 Total Deaths. Some double counting may occur when multiple methods are used.

The War on Terrorism

 The most infamous attack of international terrorism to date took place on September 11, 2001, when members of Osama Bin Laden's al-Qaeda Islamic terrorist organization attacked New York City's World Trade Center and the Pentagon. The attacks left more than 3,000 people dead[19] and resulted in billions of dollars' worth of property damage. The United States declared a worldwide war on international terrorism.

During the first years of President George W. Bush's presidency, terrorist attacks and corporate scandals demanded the attention of federal legislators and the Oval Office. Three important legislative initiatives resulted: the USA PATRIOT Act,[20] the Sarbanes-Oxley Act, and the Homeland Security Act of 2002. In establishing the new Department of Homeland Security, the act restructured the executive branch of the federal government.

The USA PATRIOT Act

USA PATRIOT Act, which stands for Uniting and Strengthening America by Providing Appropriate Tools Required to Intercept and Obstruct Terrorism, was designed primarily to fight terrorism, but it contains provisions that apply to other forms of criminal activity as well. The act permits longer jail terms for certain suspects arrested without a warrant, broadens searches conducted without notice, and enhances the power of prosecutors. The law also increases the ability of federal authorities to tap phones (including wireless devices), share intelligence information, track Internet usage, crack down on money laundering, and protect the country's borders.

The USA PATRIOT Act led some to questions about whether the government threatened powers at the expense of individual rights and civil liberties. Prior to passage, the legislation had been questioned by the American Civil Liberties Union (ACLU), which feared that it would substantially reduce the constitutional rights of individuals facing justice system processing. After the bill became law, the ACLU pledged to work with the president and law enforcement agencies across the country "to ensure that civil liberties in America are not eroded."[21]

The Department of Homeland Security

The Homeland Security Act of 2002,[22] enacted to protect America against terrorism, established the federal **Department of Homeland Security (DHS)**, which coordinates the activities of 22 domestic agencies. The administration of those agencies falls under five divisions, or directorates, as follows:

1. **Border and Transportation Security (BTS).** BTS is responsible for maintaining security of the nation's borders and transportation systems. The largest of the directorates, it is home to the Transportation Security Administration, the U.S. Customs Service, the border security functions of the former Immigration and Naturalization Service, the Animal and Plant Health Inspection Service, and the Federal Law Enforcement Training Center.

2. **Emergency Preparedness and Response (EPR).** EPR works to ensure that the nation is prepared for, and able to recover from, terrorist attacks and natural disasters.

3. **Science and Technology (S&T).** This directorate coordinates the department's efforts in research and development, including preparing for and responding to the full range of terrorist threats involving weapons of mass destruction.

4. **Information Analysis and Infrastructure Protection (IAIP).** IAIP merges under one roof the functions of identifying and assessing a broad range of intelligence information concerning threats to the homeland, issuing timely warnings, and taking appropriate preventive and protective action. IAIP is especially focused on threats to our country's **infrastructure**.

5. **Management.** The Management Directorate is responsible for budgetary, managerial, and personnel issues within DHS.

Several other critical agencies were also folded into the new department or were created,[23] including the U.S. Coast Guard, United States Secret Service, Bureau of Citizenship and Immigration Services, Office of State and Local Government Coordination, Office of Private Sector Liaison, and Office of Inspector General. A brief description of each follows:

United States Coast Guard (USCG). The commandant of the Coast Guard reports

New Yorkers struggling through debris on September 11, 2001. What major federal anti-terrorism legislation was passed in the wake of the terrorist attacks?

directly to the secretary of DHS. However, the USCG also works closely with the undersecretary of BTS and maintains its existing identity as an independent military service. Upon declaration of war or when the president so directs, the Coast Guard will operate as an element of the Department of Defense, consistent with existing law.

United States Secret Service. The primary mission of the Secret Service is the protection of the president and other government leaders, as well as security for designated national events. The Secret Service is also the primary agency responsible for protecting U.S. currency from counterfeiters and safeguarding Americans from credit card fraud.

Bureau of Citizenship and Immigration Services. While BTS is responsible for enforcing our nation's immigration laws, the Bureau of Citizenship and Immigration Services, a new agency, dedicates its energies to providing efficient immigration services and easing the transition to American citizenship.

Office of State and Local Government Coordination. This office ensures close coordination between local, state, and federal governments to ensure an effective terrorism-prevention effort and to provide quick responses to terrorist incidents.

Office of Private Sector Liaison. The Office of Private Sector Liaison provides the business community with a direct line of communication to DHS. The office works directly with individual businesses and through trade associations and other nongovernmental organizations

A U.S. Coast Guard cutter patrolling near San Francisco. What agencies come under the Department of Homeland Security's administrative umbrella?

to foster dialogue between the private sector and DHS on the full range of issues and challenges that America's businesses face today.

Office of Inspector General. The Office of Inspector General serves as an independent and objective inspection, audit, and investigative body to promote effectiveness, efficiency, and economy in DHS's programs and operations, and to prevent and detect fraud, abuse, mismanagement, and waste.

Figure 13–6 shows the organizational chart of the DHS.

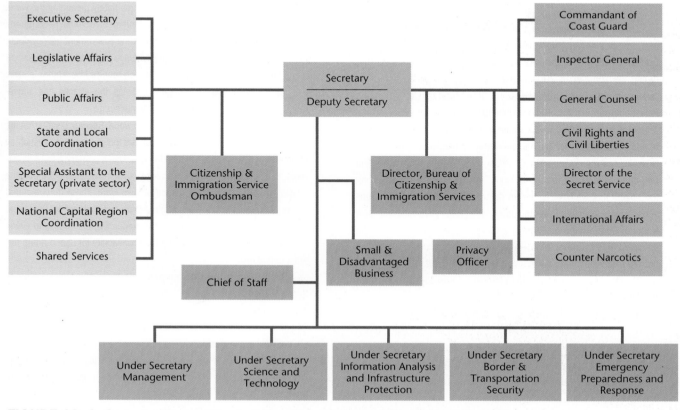

FIGURE 13–6 Organizational Chart of the Department of Homeland Security
Source: Department of Homeland Security.

The "Causes Behind the Crime" boxes found in preceding chapters have been presented in a way that seeks to describe the influences that led the subjects of the profiles to commit what many regard as sensational crimes. The intent of those profiles is to provide some insight into the evolution of markedly antisocial behavior. We were able to develop those profiles by researching the wealth of reliable and detailed information that is available on the personal backgrounds and offenses of each of the people profiled.

This profile box is somewhat different. Background information regarding Mohammed Atta, the subject of this box, is sparse, unreliable, and rife with conflicting claims. Given that Atta trained as a terrorist, came from the Middle East, and likely made efforts to live a life "under the radar," it is unsurprising that extensive research into Atta's pre-9/11 life yields little information about which one can feel confident. Although some facts about Atta's life are verifiable, many of the available sources appear to be speculative or outright rumor.

We know, for example, that Atta was born in Kafr El Sheikh in Egypt's Nile Delta, grew up in Cairo, and received an undergraduate degree in architecture from Cairo University. He is known to have resided in Germany from 1993 to 1999, where he pursued an urban planning degree at the University of Harburg-Hamburg, in Germany.[i] Reliable records also show that he was a licensed pilot who moved to Venice, Florida, in 2000 to pursue additional flight training at Huffman Aviation International. Records and witness information also show that he was a committed fundamentalist Muslim. We can conclude that he was intensely motivated by personal ideals and spiritual beliefs, most of which were acquired through his life experiences.

Other claims, however, cannot be as readily confirmed. For example, England's *Telegraph* online daily newspaper reported on December 13, 2003, that documents it had obtained showed that during the summer of 2001 Atta underwent an intensive three-day "work program" in Baghdad under the tutelage of notorious Palestinian terrorist Abu Nidal. The handwritten, top secret memo the *Telegraph* had acquired was, ostensibly, prepared by the former head of Iraq's intelligence service and submitted to then-president Saddam Hussein. The memo purportedly lauds Atta's "extraordinary effort" in preparing to lead the team that would be "responsible for attacking the targets that we have agreed to destroy."[ii] Unfortunately, numerous subsequent investigations—including the U.S. government's own National Commission on Terrorist Attacks on the United States (the so-called 9/11 Commission)—have failed to confirm a direct link between Hussein's Iraqi government and the al-Qaeda terrorist group of which Atta was a member and which later claimed responsibility for the World Trade Center attacks.[iii]

Likewise, there are persistent reports that Atta had been in Israeli custody following his arrest for blowing up a bus in Israel in 1986. Urban legend contends that Atta was subsequently released at the insistence of President Bill Clinton and Secretary of State Warren Christopher, to prevent Palestinian withdrawal from the Oslo peace accords unless the Israelis released Atta and others. (Other reports claim that the U.S. interventionists were actually President Ronald Reagan and Secretary of State George Schultz, which is absurd in view of the fact that the Oslo Agreement occurred during Clinton's presidency.) This tale has been debunked by reports from the *Jewish News Weekly*[iv] and the Anti-Defamation League.[v] Both agencies deny that Atta was ever held by the Israelis, and claim that the man the Israelis imprisoned for the 1986 attack was, in fact, Mahmoud Abed Atta, a Palestinian (the Anti-Defamation League identifies him as a Jordanian and a naturalized U.S. citizen) associate of Abu Nidal's terror organization.[vi]

These and many other examples illustrate the difficulty of pinning down reliable information on Atta. The more one digs, the more one encounters conflicting information that reduces effective research to the perusal of countless "did not, did too" reports. It appears to be an intentionally contrived morass designed by the terrorists themselves to aid in their evasion of detection and apprehension.

Thus, the predictable outcome of all but the most tenacious, obstinate, and creative investigative efforts focused on the secretive members of known terrorist organizations is exponentially increasing confusion. The more one comes to know, the less one is able to understand. Researchers inquiring into the intentionally obscured background of a man whose life was dedicated to the perpetration of illegal acts in the misguided pursuit of religious dogma—as defined by zealous adherence to radical Islamic fundamentalism—can hardly expect to find open records and free access to information. This is the predictable outcome of any investigative effort focused on a secretive member of a known terrorist organization.

In Atta's case, extensive scrutiny of existing information sources reveals a confusing and often conflicting profile of a man whose movements and activities during the period immediately preceding the World Trade Center attacks cannot be reliably confirmed. Available news reports starkly conflict with official documents. Some government agency documents conflict with the documentary evidence provided by other government agencies. "Highly reliable" information reported by reputable news sources in the period immediately following the attacks has subsequently proven to be almost completely inaccurate.

It is the nature of the terrorists' nether world. Secrecy, disinformation, obfuscation, and orchestrated confusion are tools of the trade in such an environment. The creation of uncertainty serves a primary goal of all terrorist agents: to delay official responses to terrorist activity by bogging official agencies down in the pursuit of false leads. These manufactured delays are tactical measures that serve to protect such agents from rapid official responses to their attacks, thus, enhancing their ability to evade capture and sometimes facilitating their availability for use in future terrorist operations.

The life experiences and complex motivations of terrorists do not fit the motivational patterns of the (for lack of a better word) *ordinary* criminals described in previous chapters. Those seeking to understand terrorist behavior would probably be best served by examining the cultural, educational, ideological, and religious influences that shape the terrorists' world views, as those same views also serve to justify in the terrorists' minds even the most horrendous behavior in their pursuit of "correcting" perceived wrongs.

The Causes Behind the Crime
Mohammed Atta

What Kind of Motivations Can Explain This Crime?

- Mohammed Atta has been described as motivated by personal ideals and zealous spiritual beliefs that he developed through his life experiences. *How could this have led him to a hideous episode of terrorism?*

- Atta apparently had some sort of charismatic leadership to inspire him to commit this crime. *What characteristics of his personality would have made him follow this leadership?*

- Information about the world of terrorists and their motivations is conflicting and sketchy. *How might we develop better profiles of terrorists so that we can predict future events?*

- Secrecy, disinformation, and intentional confusion are the tools terrorists use to confound government officials and the general public. *How might Atta have used these tools?*

A 1999 photo from Hamburg, Germany, showing various 9/11 plotters. Atta is the first from the right in the middle row.

A young Atta (second from right), poses with his two sisters (left), mother (center), and father at an Egyptian amusement park in 1981.

NOTES:

[i] John Hooper, "The Shy, Caring, Deadly Fanatic," *Observer* (Hamburg), September 23, 2001, http://observer.guardian.co.uk/waronterrorism/story/0,,556630,00.html (accessed June 3, 2007).

[ii] Con Cougher, "Terrorist Behind September 11 Strike Was Trained by Saddam," *Telegraph* (United Kingdom), December 13, 2003, http://www.telegraph.co.uk/news/worldnews/middleeast/iraq/1449442/Terrorist-behind-September-11-strike-was-trained-by-Saddam.html (accessed June 3, 2007).

[iii] Walter Pincus and Dana Mil bank, "Al-Qaddafi-Hussein Link Is Dismissed," *Washington Post*, June 17, 2004, http://www.washingtonpost.com/wp-dyn/articles/A47812-2004Jun16.html (accessed June 3, 2007).

[iv] "Internet Rumors Aside, Etta Held by Israel not Hijacker," *Jewish News Weekly*, November 16, 2001, http://www.jewishsf.com/content/2-0-/module/displaystory/story_id/17214/edition_id/340/format/html/displaystory.html (accessed June 3, 2007).

[v] "A Case of Mistaken Identity: Mohammad Etta Not Linked to Bus Bombing," Anti-Defamation League, 2001, http://urbanlegends.about.com/gi/dynamic/offsite.htm?site=http://www.adl.org/rumors/atta%5Frumors.asp (accessed June 3, 2007).

[vi] Netlore Archive, "Muhammad Atta," About.com: Urban Legends and Folklore, http://urbanlegends.about.com/library/blatta.htm (accessed June 3, 2007).

Summary and Key Concepts

Many of today's criminologists strive to develop theories that can be successfully applied across more than one culture or nation-state.

Globalization

Globalization is a process of social homogenization by which the experiences of everyday life, marked by the diffusion of commodities and ideas, fosters a standardization of cultural expressions around the world.

transnational organized crime Unlawful activity undertaken and supported by organized criminal groups operating across national boundaries.

human smuggling Illegal immigration in which an agent is involved for payment to help a person cross a border clandestinely.

trafficking in persons (TIP) The exploitation of unwilling or unwitting people through force, coercion, threat, or deception.

 Q: *How does globalization impact criminal activity in today's world? In the United States? How does it affect terrorism?*

Comparative Criminology

Comparative criminology refers to the cross-national study of crime.

comparative criminologist A criminologist involved in the cross-national study of crime.

ethnocentrism The phenomenon of "culture-centeredness" by which one uses one's own culture as a benchmark against which to judge all other patterns of behavior.

 Q: *What are the advantages of a comparative perspective in criminology? Are there any disadvantages?*

Terrorism

Terrorism is premeditated, politically motivated violence perpetrated against noncombatant targets by subnational groups or clandestine agents, usually intended to influence an audience.

domestic terrorism The unlawful use of force or violence by a group or an individual who is based and operates entirely within the United States and its territories without foreign direction and whose acts are directed at elements of the U.S. government or population.

international terrorism The unlawful use of force or violence by a group or an individual who has a connection to a foreign power, or whose activities transcend national boundaries, against people or property to intimidate or coerce a government, the civilian population, or any segment thereof in furtherance of political or social objectives.

Some people say that the only way to secure freedom is to curtail it during times of national crisis. Can this be true?

The War on Terrorism

The United States declared a worldwide war on international terrorism following the attacks of September 1, 2001, that destroyed the World Trade Center in New York, and resulted in other loss of life in Pennsylvania and at the Pentagon.

USA PATRIOT Act A post-9/11 federal law designed to fight terrorism. The name of the statute is an acronym that stands for Uniting and Strengthening America by Providing Appropriate Tools Required to Intercept and Obstruct Terrorism.

Department of Homeland Security (DHS) A federal agency established by the Homeland Security Act of 2002 whose responsibility it is to protect America against acts of terrorism.

infrastructure The basic facilities, services, and installations needed for the functioning of a community or society, such as transportation and communications systems, water and power lines, and public institutions, including schools, post offices, and prisons.

Has the "war against terrorism" affected you personally? If so, how?

Glossary

acquaintance rape Rape characterized by a prior social, though not necessarily intimate or familial, relationship between the victim and the perpetrator.

aggravated assault The unlawful attack by one person upon another wherein the offender uses a weapon or displays it in a threatening manner, or the victim suffers obvious or severe bodily injury.

alloplastic adaptation A form of adjustment that results from change in the environment surrounding an individual.

androcentric A single-sex perspective, as in the case of criminologists who study only the criminality of males.

anomie A social condition in which norms are uncertain or lacking.

antisocial (asocial) personality A term used to describe individuals who are basically unsocialized and whose behavior patterns bring them repeatedly into conflict with society.

arson Any willful or malicious burning or attempt to burn (with or without intent to defraud) a dwelling, house, public building, motor vehicle, aircraft, or personal property of another.

asset forfeiture The authorized seizure of money, negotiable instruments, securities, or other things of value. In federal antidrug laws, the authorization of judicial representatives to seize all monies, negotiable instruments, securities, or other things of value furnished or intended to be furnished by any person in exchange for a controlled substance, and all proceeds traceable to such an exchange.

atavism A term used by Cesare Lombroso to suggest that criminals are physiological throwbacks to early stages of human evolution.

audit trail A sequential record of computer system activities that enables auditors to reconstruct, review, and examine the sequence of states and activities surrounding each event in one or more related transactions from inception to output of final results back to inception.

autoplastic adaptation A form of adjustment that results from changes with an individual.

Balanced and Restorative Justice Model (BARJ) A model of restorative justice in which the community, victim, and offender should all receive balanced attention.

behavior theory Posits that individual behavior that is rewarded will increase in frequency, while that which is punished will decrease.

behavioral genetics The study of genetics and environmental contributions to individual variations in human behavior.

born criminal An individual who is born with a genetic predilection toward criminality.

bourgeoisie The class of people who own the means of production.

broken windows thesis A perspective on crime causation that holds that physical deterioration in an area leads to increased concerns for personal safety among area residents and to higher crime rates in that area.

Buck **v.** *Bell* A Supreme Court case that upheld the practice of sterilization as a way to rid society of those with criminal tendencies.

burglary The unlawful entry into a structure for the purpose of felony commission, generally a theft.

Cambridge Study in Delinquent Development A longitudinal (life-course) study of crime and delinquency tracking a cohort of 411 boys in London.

capable guardian One who effectively discourages crime.

capital punishment The legal imposition of a sentence of death upon a convicted offender.

Chicago Area Project A program focusing on urban ecology and originating at the University of Chicago during the 1930s, which attempted to reduce delinquency, crime, and social disorganization in transitional neighborhoods.

Chicago School of criminology An ecological approach to explaining crime that examined how social disorganization contributes to social pathology.

child pornography A visual representation of any kind that depicts a minor engaging in sexually explicit conduct and is obscene, and which lacks serious literary, artistic, political, or scientific value.

child sexual abuse (CSA) Encompasses a variety of criminal and civil offenses in which an adult engages in sexual activity with a minor, exploits a minor for purposes of sexual gratification, or exploits a minor sexually for purposes of profit.

Chronic Strategy for Serious, Violent, and Chronic Juvenile Offenders Program A program that works to strengthen families and core institutions in their efforts to reduce risk factors and develop their full potential.

class conflict Crime is a result of conflict, often between those with power and those without.

Classical School A criminological perspective developed in the late 1700s and early 1800s. It had its roots in the Enlightenment and held that men and women are rational beings and that crime is the result of the exercise of free will and personal choices based on calculations of perceived costs and benefits. Therefore, punishment can be effective in reducing the incidence of crime when it negates the rewards to be derived from crime commission.

clearance rate The proportion of reported or discovered crimes within a given offense category that are solved.

cohort analysis A social scientific technique that studies over time a population with common characteristics. Cohort analysis usually begins at birth and traces the development of cohort members until they reach a certain age.

comfort serial killers Serial killers who are motivated by financial or material gain.

common law definition of rape Until the 1970s in the United States, rape was a common law offense defined as the carnal knowledge of a woman not one's wife by force or against her will.

Communications Decency Act (CDA) A federal statute signed into law in 1996, the CDA is Title 5 of the federal Telecommunications Act of 1996 (Public Law 104–104, 110 Stat. 56). The law sought to protect minors from harmful material on the Internet, and a portion of the CDA criminalized the knowing transmission of obscene or indecent messages to any recipient under 18 years of age.

comparative criminologist A criminologist involved in the cross-national study of crime.

comparative criminology Refers to the cross-national study of crime.

computer abuse Any unlawful incident associated with computer technology in which a victim suffered or could have suffered loss, or in which a perpetrator by intention made or could have made gain.

computer virus A set of computer instructions that propagates copies or versions of itself into computer programs or data when it is executed.

computer-related crime Any illegal act for which knowledge of computer technology is involved in its perpetration, investigation, or prosecution.

conditioning A psychological principle that holds that the frequency of any behavior can be increased or decreased through reward, punishment, or association with other stimuli.

conduct norms Shared expectations of a social group relative to personal conduct.

conflict theory Applies the principles and concepts developed by Karl Marx to the study of crime, and holds that the causes of crime are rooted in social conditions that empower the wealthy and the politically well-organized but disenfranchise those who are less fortunate. Also sometimes referred to as *Marxist criminology*.

consensus perspective A viewpoint that holds that laws should be enacted to criminalize given forms of behavior when members of society agree that such laws are necessary.

constitutional theories Biological theories that explain criminality by reference to offenders' body types, inheritance, genetics, or external observable physical characteristics.

constitutive criminology The assertion that individuals shape their world, while also being shaped by it.

containment theory A form of control theory that suggests that a series of both internal and external factors contributes to law-abiding behavior.

containment The stabilizing force that, if effective, blocks pushes and pulls from leading an individual toward crime.

control ratio The amount of control to which a person is subject versus the amount of control that person exerts over others.

controlled substances Defined by federal law as consisting of seven categories: narcotics, depressants, stimulants, hallucinogens, cannabis, anabolic steroids, and inhalants.

corporate crime A violation of a criminal statute either by a corporate entity or by its executives, employees, or agents acting on behalf of and for the benefit of the corporation, partnership, or other form of business entity.

correctional psychology The branch of forensic psychology concerned with the diagnosis and classification of offenders, the treatment of correctional populations, and the rehabilitation of inmates and other law violators.

crime Human conduct that violates the criminal laws of a state, the federal government, or a local jurisdiction that has the power to make and enforce the laws.

criminal anthropology The scientific study of the relationship between human physical characteristics and criminality.

criminal career The longitudinal sequence of events committed by an individual offender.

criminal homicide The causing of the death of another person without legal justification or excuse.

criminal justice The scientific study of crime, criminal law, the criminal justice system, police, courts, and correctional systems.

criminal psychology See *forensic psychology*.

criminalist A specialist in the collection and examination of the physical evidence of crime.

criminalize To make an act illegal.

criminaloids A term used by Cesare Lombroso to describe occasional criminals who were pulled into criminality by environmental influences.

criminologist A person trained in the field of criminology who studies crime, criminals, and criminal behavior.

criminology The scientific study of crime and criminal behavior, including their manifestations, causes, legal aspects, and control.

criminology of place A perspective that emphasizes the importance of geographic location and architectural features as they are associated with the prevalence of criminal victimization.

cultural transmission The transmission of delinquency through successive generations of people living in the same area through a process of social communication.

culture conflict theory A sociological perspective on crime that suggests that the root cause of criminality can be found in a clash of values between variously socialized groups over what is acceptable or proper behavior.

Cyber Security Enhancement Act (CSEA) Part of the Homeland Security Act of 2002, this federal law directs the U.S. Sentencing Commission to take several specific factors into account in creating new sentencing guidelines for computer criminals.

cybercrime Any violation of a federal or state computer crime statute.

cyberspace The computer-created matrix of virtual possibilities, including online services, wherein human beings interact with one another and with technology itself.

cyberstalking The use of electronic communication like e-mail or the Internet to harass individuals.

cycloid A term developed by Ernst Kretschmer to describe a particular relationship between body build and personality type. The cycloid personality, which was associated with a heavyset, soft type of body, was said to vacillate between normal and abnormality.

dangerous drug A term used by the DEA to refer to broad categories or classes of controlled substances other than cocaine, opiates, hallucinogens, inhalants, and cannabis products.

dangerousness The degree of criminal threat that an offender represents.

dark figure of crime The large number of unreported crimes that never make it into official crime statistics.

data encryption The process by which information is encoded, making it unreadable to all but its intended recipients.

DCS–1000 An FBI-developed network diagnostic tool that is capable of assisting in criminal investigations by monitoring and capturing large amounts of Internet traffic. Previously called Carnivore.

deconstructionist theories A postmodern perspective that challenges existing criminological theories in order to debunk them and that works toward replacing traditional ideas with concepts seen as more appropriate to the postmodern era.

decriminalization The redefinition of certain previously criminal behaviors into regulated activities that become "ticketable" rather than "arrestable."

Department of Homeland Security (DHS) A federal agency established by the Homeland Security Act of 2002 whose responsibility it is to protect America against acts of terrorism.

designer drugs New substances designed by slightly altering the chemical makeup of other illegal or tightly controlled drugs.

desistance The cessation of criminal activity or the termination of a period of involvement in offending behavior (that is, abandoning a criminal career).

deviant behavior Human activity that violates social norms.

differential association An explanation for crime and deviance that holds that people pursue criminal or deviant behavior to the extent that they identify themselves with real or imaginary people from whose perspective their criminal or deviant behavior seems acceptable.

Digital Theft Deterrence and Copyright Damages Improvement Act A 1999 federal law that attempted to combat software piracy and other forms of digital theft by amending Section 504(c) of the Copyright Act, thereby increasing the amount of damages that could potentially be awarded in cases of copyright infringement.

diplastic A mixed group of offenders described by constitutional theorist Ernst Kretschmer as highly emotional and often unable to control themselves. They were thought to commit mostly sexual offenses and other crimes of passion.

disengagement The process of devaluing aggression by those who may still engage in it.

distributive justice The rightful, equitable, and just distribution of rewards within a society.

DNA profiling The use of biological residue found at the scene of a crime for genetic comparisons in aiding the identification of criminal suspects.

domestic terrorism The unlawful use of force or violence by a group or an individual who is based and operates entirely within the United States and its territories without foreign direction and whose acts are directed at elements of the U.S. government or population.

drug offense Any violation of the laws prohibiting or regulating the possession, use, distribution, sale, or manufacture of illegal drugs.

drug trafficking The manufacturing, distributing, dispensing, importing, and exporting (or possession with intent to do the same) of a controlled or counterfeit substance.

drug-defined crime A violation of the laws prohibiting or regulating the possession, use, or distribution of illegal drugs.

drug-related crime A crime in which drugs contribute to the offense (excluding violations of drug laws).

ecological theory A type of sociological approach that emphasizes demographics (the characteristics of population groups) and geographics (the mapped location of such groups relative to one another) and that sees the social disorganization that characterizes delinquency areas as a major cause of criminality and victimization.

ectomorph A body type originally described as thin and fragile, with long, slender, poorly muscled extremities and delicate bones.

ego The reality-testing part of the personality. Also called the reality principle. More formally, the personality component that is conscious, most immediately controls behavior, and is most in touch with external reality.

Electronic Frontier Foundation (EFF) A nonprofit organization formed in July of 1990 to help ensure that the principles embodied in the Constitution and the Bill of Rights are protected as new communications technologies emerge.

endomorph A body type originally described as soft and round or overweight.

environmental crime A violation of the criminal law that, although typically committed by businesses or by business officials, may also be committed by other people or by organizational entities and that damages some protected or otherwise significant aspect of the natural environment.

environmental criminology An emerging perspective that emphasizes the importance of geographic location and architectural features as they are associated with the prevalence of criminal victimization.

ethnic succession The continuing process whereby one immigrant or ethnic group succeeds another by assuming its position in society.

ethnocentrism The phenomenon of "culture-centeredness" by which one uses one's own culture as a benchmark against which to judge all other patterns of behavior.

eugenic criminology A perspective that holds that the root causes of criminality are passed from generation to generation in the form of "bad genes."

eugenics The study of hereditary improved by genetic control.

evolutionary ecology Blends elements of previous perspectives—building upon social ecology while emphasizing developmental pathways.

expert systems Computer hardware and software that attempt to duplicate the decision-making processes used by skilled investigators in the analysis of evidence and in the recognition of patterns that such evidence might represent.

Farrington's Delinquent Development Theory Persistence describes continuity in crime. Desistance refers to cessation of criminal activity or to a termination in a period of involvement in offending behavior.

felony murder A special class of criminal homicide in which an offender may be charged with first-degree murder when that person's criminal activity results in another person's death.

fence An individual or a group involved in the buying, selling, and distribution of stolen calls. Also called a *criminal receiver*.

First and Fourth Amendments to the U.S. Constitution Guarantee each of us freedom of speech and security in our "persons, houses, papers, and effects, against unreasonable searches and seizures."

first-degree murder Criminal homicide that is planned or involves premeditation.

focal concerns The key values of any culture, especially the key values of a delinquent subculture.

forensic psychiatry A branch of psychiatry having to do with the study of crime and criminality.

forensic psychology (also called *criminal psychology*) The application of the science and profession of psychology to questions and issues relating to law and the legal system.

forfeiture A legal procedure that authorizes judicial representatives to seize "all moneys, negotiable instruments, securities, or other things of value furnished or intended to be furnished by any person in exchange for a controlled substance and all proceeds traceable to such an exchange."

GBMI Guilty But Mentally Ill A GBMI verdict means that a person can be held responsible for a specific criminal act, even though a degree of mental incompetence may be present.

gender gap The observed differences between male and female rates of criminal offending in a given society, such as the United States.

general deterrence A goal of criminal sentencing that seeks to prevent others from committing crimes similar to the one for which a particular offender is being sentenced.

general strain theory (GST) A perspective that suggests that lawbreaking behavior is a coping mechanism that enables those who engage in it to deal with the socioemotional problems generated by negative social relations.

general theory of crime A theory that attempts to explain all (or at least most) forms of criminal conduct through a single, overarching approach, and which holds that low self-control accounts for all crime at all times.

general theory A theory that attempts to explain most forms of criminal conduct through a single, overarching approach.

globalization A process of social homogenization by which the experiences of everyday life, marked by the diffusion of commodities and ideas, fosters a standardization of cultural expressions around the world.

hacker A person who uses computers for exploration and exploitation.

hate crime A criminal offense in which the motive is hatred, bias, or prejudice based on the actual or perceived race, color, religion, national origin, ethnicity, gender, or sexual orientation of another individual or group of individuals. Also called bias crime.

hedonistic calculus The belief, first proposed by Jeremy Bentham, that behavior holds value to any individual undertaking it according to the amount of pleasure or pain that it can be expected to produce for that person.

hedonistic serial killers Serial killers who murder because they find it enjoyable and derive psychological pleasure from killing.

heroin signature program (HSP) A DEA program that identifies the geographic source of a heroin sample through the detection of specific chemical characteristics in the sample peculiar to the source area.

highway robberies Robberies that occur on the highway or street or in a public place (and that are often referred to as a "mugging").

human agency Individuals construct their own life course through the choices they make and the actions they take within the opportunities and constraints of history and social circumstances.

human development The relationship between the maturing individual and his or her changing environment, as well as the social processes that the relationship entails.

human smuggling Illegal immigration in which an agent is involved for payment to help a person cross a border clandestinely.

hypoglycemia A medical condition characterized by low blood sugar.

id The aspect of the personality from which drives, wishes, urges, and desires emanate. More formally, the division of the psyche associated with instinctual impulses and demands for immediate satisfaction of primitive needs.

Identity Theft and Assumption Deterrence Act The first federal law to make identity theft a crime. The 1998 statute makes it a crime whenever anyone "knowingly transfers or uses, without lawful authority, a means of identification of another person with the intent to commit, or to aid or abet, any unlawful activity that constitutes a violation of federal law, or that constitutes a felony under any applicable state or local law."

Identity Theft Penalty Enhancement Act A 2004 federal law that added two years to federal prison sentences for criminals convicted of using stolen credit card numbers and other personal data to commit crimes.

identity theft The unauthorized use of another individual's personal identity to fraudulently obtain money, goods, or services; to avoid the payment of debt; or to avoid criminal prosecution.

illegitimate opportunity structure Subcultural pathways to success of which the wider society disapproves.

infrastructure The basic facilities, services, and installations needed for the functioning of a community or society, such as transportation and communications systems, water and power lines, and public institutions, including schools, post offices, and prisons.

insanity A type of defense allowed in criminal courts.

institutional robberies Robberies of commercial establishments, such as convenience stores, gas stations, and banks.

integrated theory An explanatory perspective that merges concepts drawn from different sources.

interactional theory A theoretical approach to exploring crime and delinquency that blends social control and social learning perspectives.

interdiction An international drug-control policy designed to stop drugs from entering the country illegally.

international terrorism The unlawful use of force or violence by a group or an individual who has a connection to a foreign power, or whose activities transcend national boundaries, against people or property to intimidate or coerce a government, the civilian population, or any segment thereof in furtherance of political or social objectives.

Internet The world's largest computer network.

intimate-partner assault A gender-neutral term used to characterize assaultive behavior that takes place between individuals involved in an intimate relationship.

irresistible-impulse test A standard for judging legal insanity that holds that a defendant is not guilty of a criminal offense if the person, by virtue of his or her mental state or psychological condition, was not able to resist committing the crime.

joyriding An opportunistic car theft, often committed by a teenager seeking fun or thrills.

Juke family A well-known "criminal family" studied by Richard Dugdale.

just deserts model The notion that criminal offenders deserve the punishment they receive at the hands of the law and that punishments should be appropriate to the type and severity of crime committed.

justice model A contemporary model of imprisonment in which the principle of just deserts forms the underlying social philosophy.

Juvenile Mentoring Program (JUMP) A program that places at-risk youth in a one-on-one relationship with favorable adult role models.

Kallikak family A well-known "criminal family" studied by Henry H. Goddard.

La Cosa Nostra Literally, "our thing." A criminal organization of Sicilian origin. Also called the Mafia, the Outfit, the Mob, the syndicate, or simply the organization.

larceny-theft The unlawful taking, carrying, leading, or riding away of property from the possession, or constructive possession, of another.

learning theory A perspective that places primary emphasis upon the role of communication and socialization in the acquisition of learned patterns of criminal behavior and the values that support that behavior.

legalization Elimination of the laws and criminal penalties associated with certain behaviors—usually the production, sale, distribution, and possession of a controlled substance.

legitimate opportunities Opportunities generally available to individuals born into middle-class culture; participants in lower-class subcultures are often denied access to them.

liberal feminism A perspective that holds that the concerns of women can be incorporated within existing social institutions through conventional means and without the need to drastically restructure society.

life course criminology A developmental perspective that draws attention to the fact that criminal behavior tends to follow a distinct pattern across the life cycle.

life course Pathways through the life span involving a sequence of culturally defined, age-graded roles and social transitions enacted over time.

lifestyle theory Another term for the routine activities approach of Lawrence Cohen and Marcus Felson.

low self-esteem Low self-esteem is linked to delinquency.

M'Naughten rule A standard for judging legal insanity that requires that offenders did not know what they were doing, or if they did, that they did not know it was wrong.

Mafia Another name for Sicilian organized crime, or *La Cosa Nostra*.

Marxist feminism A perspective that sees capitalism as the root cause of women's oppression because it perpetuates economic inequality, dependence, and political powerlessness, ultimately leading to unhealthy social relations between men and women.

masculinity hypothesis The belief that criminal women exhibit masculine features and mannerisms.

mass murder The illegal killing of four or more victims at one location within one event.

mesomorph A body type described as athletic and muscular.

modeling The process of learning how to behave by observing others.

modeling theory A psychological perspective that contends that people learn how to behave by modeling themselves after others whom they have the opportunity to observe.

money laundering Refers to the process of converting illegally earned assets, originating as cash, to one or more alternative forms to conceal such incriminating factors as illegal origin and true ownership.

Monitoring the Future A national self-report survey on drug use that has been conducted since 1975.

monozygotic (MZ) twins Twins that develop from the same egg and have virtually the same genetic material.

Montreal Prevention Treatment Program A program designed to address early childhood risk factors for gang involvement by targeting boys in kindergarten who exhibit disruptive behavior.

moral enterprise The efforts made by an interest group to have its sense of moral ethical propriety enacted into law.

motor vehicle theft "The theft or attempted theft of a motor vehicle," where the term motor vehicle refers to various means of transportation, including automobiles, buses, motorcycles, and snowmobiles.

murder The willful (nonnegligent) and unlawful killing of one human being by another.

National Crime Victimization Survey (NCVS) A survey conducted annually by the Bureau of Justice Statistics that provides data on households that report they were affected by crime.

National Incident-Based Reporting System (NIBRS) A new and enhanced statistical reporting system that will collect data on each single incident and arrest within 22 crime categories. NIBRS expands the data collected under the UCR Program.

National Youth Survey (NYS) A longitudinal panel study of a national sample of 1,725 individuals that measured self-reports of delinquency and other types of behavior.

negative affective states Adverse emotions that derive from the experience of strain, such as anger, fear, depression, and disappointment.

negligent homicide The act of causing the death of another person by recklessness or gross negligence.

neoclassical criminology Focuses on the importance of character, the dynamics of character development, and the rational choices that people make as they are faced with opportunities for crime.

neurosis A functional disorder of the mind or of the emotions involving anxiety, phobia, or other abnormal behavior.

No Electronic Theft Act (NETA) A 1997 federal law that criminalizes the willful infringement of copyrighted works, including by electronic means, even when the infringing party derives no direct financial benefit from the infringement.

nothing-works doctrine The belief popularized by Robert Martinson in the 1970s that correctional treatment programs have little success in rehabilitating offenders.

occasional offender A criminal offender whose offending patterns are guided primarily by opportunity.

occupational crime Any act punishable by law that is committed through opportunity created in the course of an occupation that is legal.

Office of National Drug Control Policy (ONDCP) A national office charged by Congress with establishing policies, priorities, and objectives for the nation's drug-control program. ONDCP is responsible for annually developing and disseminating the National Drug-Control Strategy.

operant behavior Behavior that affects the environment in such a way as to produce responses or further behavioral clues.

organized crime The unlawful activities of the members of a highly organized, disciplined association engaged in supplying illegal goods and services, including gambling, prostitution, loan-sharking, narcotics, and labor racketeering.

Panopticon A prison designed by Jeremy Bentham that was to be a circular building with cells along the circumference, each clearly visible from a central location staffed by guards.

Part I offenses The crimes of murder, rape, robbery, aggravated assault, burglary, larceny, and motor vehicle theft, as defined under the FBI's Uniform Crime Reporting Program. Also called major crimes.

participatory justice A relatively informal type of criminal justice case processing that makes use of local community resources rather than requiring traditional forms of official intervention.

patriarchy The tradition of male dominance.

peace model An approach to crime control that focuses on effective ways for developing a shared consensus on critical issues that could seriously affect the quality of life.

persistence Continuity in crime, or continual involvement in offending.

peacemaking criminology Holds that crime control agencies and the citizens they serve should work together to alleviate social problems and human suffering and thus reduce crime.

persistent thief One who continues in property crimes despite no better than an ordinary level of success.

pharmaceutical diversion The process by which legitimately manufactured controlled substances are diverted for illicit use.

phishing Pronounced "fishing." An Internet-based scam to steal valuable information such as credit card numbers, social security numbers, user IDs, and passwords.

phone phreak A person who uses switched, dialed-access telephone services for exploration and exploitation.

phrenology The study of the shape of the head to determine anatomical correlates of human behavior.

pluralist perspective A viewpoint that recognizes the importance of diversity in our society and says that behaviors are typically criminalized through a political process.

positivism A scientific approach to the study of crime and its causation. Early positivism was built upon evolutionary principles and saw criminals as throwbacks to earlier evolutionary epochs.

power seekers Serial killers who operate from some position of authority over others.

power-control theory A perspective that holds that the distribution of crime and delinquency within society is to some degree founded upon the consequences that power relationships within the wider society hold for domestic settings and for the everyday relationships among men, women, and children within the context of family life.

Preparing for the Drug-Free Years (PDFY) A program designed to increase effective parenting for children in grades four to eight in an effort to reduce drug abuse and behavioral problems.

primary deviance Initial deviance often undertaken to deal with transient problems in living.

professional criminal A criminal offender who makes a living from criminal pursuits, is recognized by other offenders as professional, and engages in offending that is planned and calculated.

Project on Human Development in Chicago Neighborhoods (PHDCN) A longitudinal analysis of how individuals, families, institutions, and communities evolve together.

proletariat The working class.

prosocial bonds Bonds between the individual and the social group that strengthen the likelihood of conformity. Prosocial bonds are characterized by attachment to conventional social institutions, values, and beliefs.

prostitution The offering of one's self for hire for the purpose of engaging in sexual relations, or the act or practice of engaging in sexual activity for money or its equivalent.

psychoactive substance A substance that affects the mind, mental processes, or emotions.

psychoanalysis A technique for examining the contents of human consciousness developed by Freud. From the point of view of psychoanalysis, criminal behavior is the product of inadequacies in the offender's personality.

psychopath An individual who has a personality disorder, especially one manifested in aggressively antisocial behavior, and who is lacking in empathy.

psychosis A form of mental illness in which sufferers are said to be out of touch with reality.

psychotherapy A form of psychiatric treatment based on psychoanalytical principles and techniques.

public order offense An act that is willfully committed and that disturbs the public peace or tranquility.

punishment An undesirable behavioral consequence likely to decrease the frequency of occurrence of that behavior.

Racketeer Influenced and Corrupt Organizations (RICO) Act A statute that was part of the federal Organized Crime Control Act of 1970 and that is intended to combat criminal conspiracies.

radical-critical criminology A conflict perspective that sees crime as engendered by the unequal distribution of wealth, power, and other resources that its adherents believe is especially characteristic of capitalist societies.

radical feminism A perspective that holds that any significant change in the social status of women can be accomplished only through substantial changes in social institutions such as the family, law, and medicine.

rape The carnal knowledge of a female forcibly and against her will.

rape shield laws Statutes intended to protect rape victims by ensuring that defendants do not introduce irrelevant facts about the victim's sexual past into evidence.

rational choice theory A perspective that holds that criminality is the result of conscious choice and that predicts that individuals choose to commit crime when the benefits outweigh the costs of disobeying the law.

reaction formation The process by which a person openly rejects that which he or she wants or aspires to but cannot obtain or achieve.

recidivism The repetition of criminal behavior.

relative deprivation A sense of social or economic inequality experienced by those who are unable, for whatever reason, to achieve legitimate success within the surrounding society.

Reno v. ACLU The 1997 U.S. Supreme Court case that found the bulk of the CDA to be unconstitutional, ruling that it contravenes First Amendment free speech guarantees.

restorative justice A postmodern perspective that stresses "remedies and restoration rather than prison, punishment and victim neglect."

reward A desirable behavioral consequence likely to increase the frequency of occurrence of that behavior.

robbery The taking of or attempting to take anything of value under confrontational circumstances from the control, custody, or care of another person by force or threat of force or violence and/or by putting the victim in fear of immediate harm.

routine activities theory (RAT) A brand of rational choice theory that suggests that lifestyles contribute significantly to both the volume and the type of crime found in any society.

schizoid A person characterized by schizoid personality disorder. Such disordered personalities appear to be aloof, withdrawn, unresponsive, humorless, dull, and solitary to an abnormal degree.

schizophrenia A form of mental illness in which the sufferer is out of touch with reality and suffers from disjointed thinking.

second-degree murder Criminal homicide that is unplanned and that is often described as "a crime of passion."

secondary deviance Deviant behavior that results from official labeling and from association with others who have been so labeled.

Seductions of Crime Crime is often pleasurable for those committing it, and pleasure of one sort or another is the major motivation behind crime.

selective incapacitation An imprisonment policy based on the notion of career criminality; that is, on the long-term confinement of career criminals.

self-control A person's ability to alter his or her own states and responses.

self-report surveys A survey in which anonymous respondents, without fear of disclosure or arrest, are asked to report confidentially any violations of the criminal law they have committed.

semiotics Everything we know, say, do, think, and feel is mediated through signs. Semiotic criminology identifies how language systems communicate uniquely encoded values.

separation assault Violence inflicted by partners on significant others who attempt to leave an intimate relationship.

serial murder Criminal homicide that involves the killing of several victims in three or more separate events.

sibling offense An offense or incident that culminates in homicide. The offense or incident may be a crime, such as robbery or an incident that meets a less stringent criminal definition, such as a lover's quarrel involving assault or battery.

situational choice theory A brand of rational choice theory that views criminal behavior "as a function of choices and decisions made within a context of situational constraints and opportunities."

situational crime prevention An approach that looks to develop greater understanding of crime and more effective crime prevention strategies through concern with the physical, organizational, and social environments that make crime possible.

social bond The link created through individuals and the society of which they are a part.

social capital The degree of positive relationships with others and with social institutions that individuals build up over the course of their lives.

social class Distinctions made between individuals on the basis of important defining social characteristics.

social control theories A perspective that predicts that when social constraints on antisocial behavior are weakened or absent, delinquent behavior emerges.

social development perspective An integrated view of human development that examines multiple levels of maturity simultaneously, including the psychological, biological, familial, interpersonal, cultural, societal, and ecological levels.

social development theories An integrated view of human development that examines multiple levels of maturation simultaneously, including the psychological, biological, familial, interpersonal, cultural, societal, and ecological levels.

social disorganization theory A perspective on crime and deviance that highlights the role that the breakdown of social institutions, such as the family, the economy, education, and religion, play in crime causation.

social ecology (also called *ecological school of criminology*) An approach to criminological theorizing that attempts to link the structure and organization of a human community to interactions with its localized environment.

social life The ongoing and (typically) structured interaction that occurs between persons in a society, including socialization and social behavior in general.

social pathology A concept that compares society to a physical organism and that sees criminality as an illness or disease.

social policy A government initiative, person, or plan intended to address problems in society.

social process The interaction between and among social institutions, individuals, and groups.

social process theories Suggest that criminal behavior is learned in interaction with others and that socialization and learning processes occur as the result of group membership and relationships.

social relativity The notion that social events are interpreted differently according to the cultural experiences and personal

interests of the initiator, the observer, or recipient of that behavior.

social structure The stable pattern of social relationships that exists within a society.

social structure theories Theories that explain crime by reference to some aspect of the social fabric. These theories emphasize relationships among social institutions and describe the types of behavior that tend to characterize groups of people rather than individuals.

socialist feminism A perspective that examines social roles and the gender-based division of labor within the family, seeing both as a significant source of women's subordination within society.

sociobiology A theoretical perspective developed by Edward O. Wilson that includes "the systematic study of the biological basis of all social behavior." It is a branch of evolutionary biology and particularly of modern population biology.

sociological theories A group of perspectives that focus on the nature of the power relationships that exist between social groups and on the influences that various social phenomena bring to bear on the types of behaviors that tend to characterize groups of people.

sociopath A term used interchangeably with psychopath.

software piracy The unauthorized and illegal copying of software programs.

specific deterrence A goal of criminal sentencing that seeks to prevent a particular offender from engaging in repeat criminality.

spousal rape The rape of one spouse by the other. The term usually refers to the rape of a woman by her husband.

stalking A course of conduct directed at a specific person that involves repeated visual or physical proximity; nonconsensual communication; verbal, written, or implied threats; or a combination thereof that would cause a reasonable person fear.

statute A formal written enactment of a legislative body.

stimulus-response Alternate name of behavior theory.

strain theory Points to a lack of fit between socially approved success goals and the availability of socially approved means to achieve those goals. As a consequence, according to the perspective of strain theory, individuals who are unable to succeed through legitimate means turn to other avenues that promise economic and social recognition.

subcultural theory A sociological perspective that emphasizes the contribution made by variously socialized cultural groups to the phenomenon of crime.

subculture A collection of values and preferences that is communicated to subcultural participants through a process called socialization.

sublimation The psychological process whereby one aspect of consciousness comes to be symbolically substituted for another.

superego The moral aspect of personality, much like the conscience. More formally, the division of the psyche that develops by the incorporation of the perceived moral standards of the community, is mainly unconscious, and includes the conscience.

supermale A male individual displaying the XYY chromosome structure.

tagging A term that explains what happens to offenders following arrest, conviction, and sentencing.

target hardening The reduction in criminal opportunity for a particular location, generally through the use of physical barriers, architectural design, and enhanced security measures.

techniques of neutralization Culturally available justifications that can provide criminal offenders with the means to disavow responsibility for their behavior.

terrorism Premeditated, politically motivated violence perpetrated against noncombatant targets by subnational groups or clandestine agents, usually intended to influence an audience.

testosterone The primary male hormone. Produced in the testes, its function is to control secondary sex characteristics and sexual drive.

threat analysis A complete and thorough assessment of the kinds of perils facing an organization.

trafficking in persons (TIP) The exploitation of unwilling or unwitting people through force, coercion, threat, or deception.

transnational organized crime Unlawful activity undertaken and supported by organized criminal groups operating across national boundaries.

transnational organized crime Unlawful activity undertaken and supported by organized criminal groups operating across national boundaries.

unicausal Of or having one cause. Theories posing one source for all that they attempt to explain.

Uniform Crime Reporting (UCR) Program An FBI summation of crime statistics tallied annually and consisting primarily of data on crimes reported to the police and on arrests.

USA PATRIOT Act A post-9/11 federal law designed to fight terrorism. The name of the statute is an acronym that stands for Uniting and Strengthening America by Providing Appropriate Tools Required to Intercept and Obstruct Terrorism.

victim precipitation Contributions made by the victim to the criminal event, especially those that led to its initiation.

visionary serial killers Serial killers who hear voices and have visions that are the basis for a compulsion to murder.

white collar crime "Violations of the criminal law committed by persons of respectability and high social status in the course of their occupation."

workplace violence The crimes of murder, rape, robbery, and assault committed against persons who are at work or on duty.

Photo Credits

Subject Index

NOTE: Page ranges in **bold** indicate chapter-level discussions.

Name Index